D0845158

DAVID MAMET

CASEBOOKS ON MODERN DRAMATISTS
(VOL. 12)

GARLAND REFERENCE LIBRARY
OF THE HUMANITIES
(VOL. 1211)

CASEBOOKS ON MODERN DRAMATISTS
(*General Editor*, Kimball King)

1. *Tom Stoppard: A Casebook*, edited by John Harty, III
2. *Sam Shepard: A Casebook*, edited by Kimball King
3. *Caryl Churchill: A Casebook*, edited by Phyllis R. Randall
4. *Christopher Hampton: A Casebook*, edited by Robert Gross
5. *Harold Pinter: A Casebook*, edited by Lois Gordon
6. *David Rabe: A Casebook*, edited by Toby Silverman Zinman
7. *Lanford Wilson: A Casebook*, edited by Jackson R. Bryer
8. *Howard Brenton: A Casebook*, edited by Ann Wilson
9. *David Storey: A Casebook*, edited by William Hutchings
10. *Peter Shaffer: A Casebook*, edited by C.J. Gianakaras
11. *Alan Ayckbourn: A Casebook*, edited by Bernard F. Dukore
12. *David Mamet: A Casebook*, edited by Leslie Kane

DAVID MAMET
A Casebook

Leslie Kane

GARLAND PUBLISHING, INC. • NEW YORK & LONDON
1992

© 1992 Leslie Kane
All rights reserved

Library of Congress Cataloging-in-Publication Data

David Mamet : a casebook / [edited by] Leslie Kane.
    p. cm. — (Garland reference library of the humanities ; vol.
1211. Casebooks on modern dramatists ; vol. 12)
    Includes bibliographical references (p.   ) and index.
    ISBN 0–8240–8196–X
    1. Mamet, David—Criticism and interpretation. I. Kane, Leslie,
1945– . II. Series. Garland reference library of the humanities ;
vol. 1211. III. Series: Garland reference library of the
humanities. Casebooks on modern dramatists ; vol. 12.
PS3563.A4345Z65 1992
812'.54—dc20   91–18448
                                                                      CIP

Printed on acid-free, 250-year-life paper
Manufactured in the United States of America

47.00

mw.

pbscd

To Stu,
with all my love

CONTENTS

GENERAL EDITOR'S NOTE

David Mamet: A Casebook is the twelfth in a series of collected essays on recent British and American playwrights published by Garland Publishing, Inc. All essays, with the exception of Pascale Hubert-Leibler's (reprised) and Henry Schvey's (reprised and expanded), which were recently published in *Modern Drama* and *New Theatre Quarterly*, respectively, have been commissioned for this volume from scholars identified with critical appraisals of the author's work and scholars who have published widely on contemporary British and American drama. *David Mamet: A Casebook* also includes interviews with Gregory Mosher and Joe Mantegna conducted by the editor specifically for this collection. Both have collaborated with David Mamet for more than fifteen years, and their interviews complement the critical essays with personal insights and professional perspectives.

Because David Mamet is widely considered to be one of the most prolific and powerful voices in contemporary American theatre, Kane has selected essays that reflect his range and complexity. A brief glimpse at the table of contents reveals essays of diverse critical approaches and subjects that cover the entirety of Mamet's career, ranging from stage and radio plays to filmscripts, from text to audience response, from thematic explications to examinations of individual plays. Several focus on better known achievements such as *American Buffalo* and *Glengarry Glen Ross,* and all illuminate the immense appeal and power of Mamet's canon.

The editor, Leslie Kane, is Professor of English at Westfield State College in Massachusetts. She has previously written articles on David Mamet, Harold Pinter, Marsha Norman, and Lanford Wilson. Recently she was commissioned to write an essay to honor Pinter's sixtieth birthday for a special issue of *The Pinter Review.* She published *The Language of Silence: On the Unspoken and the Unspeakable in Modern Drama* in 1984 and is currently writing *Weasels and Wisemen: Jewish Identity in Pinter and Mamet* as well as editing a collection of essays on dramatist Israel Horovitz.

Kimball King

ACKNOWLEDGMENTS

For their many suggestions and their encouragement, I would like to thank Kimball King, general editor of the Casebooks on Modern Dramatists series, and Paula Ladenburg, my Editor at Garland Publishing. I would like to thank all of the contributors, who enthusiastically tailored their research to my proposals, who sent their manuscripts in a timely fashion, and who responded to my suggestions receptively and immediately. Among the contributors I would especially like to single out Matthew Roudané and Steven Gale, whose advice in the early stages of this project was invaluable. And for their suggestions of scholars who were interested in Mamet's work, I thank Enoch Brater, Al Wertheim and Kathy Burkman.

I would like to acknowledge my debt to my research assistant, Gay Brewer for his contribution to and preparation of the secondary bibliography, to Robyn Milano for her transcription of the personal interviews, and to Pamela Kane for her preparation of the chronology and her assistance at every stage of this book. Special mention should also be made of David Mamet's secretary, Catherine Shaddix, and his agent, Howard Rosenstone and his staff, for their prompt response to my endless queries and requests for unpublished manuscripts, of Alison and Scott and the Bison staff for facilitating my visit to the set of *Homicide*, and of Becky, Gregory Mosher's administrative assistant, for her continuing cooperation.

I would like to express my gratitude to Gregory Mosher, Joe Mantegna, and Lynn Mamet Weisberg who generously contributed their time, insights and candor. And, I am indebted to David Mamet for the inspiration of his work, for his warm welcome to the set of *Homicide*, and for his gift of the unpublished screenplay, *Homicide*.

I am grateful to my children, Pamela and David, for their unqualified support, continuing patience, and technological expertise. Finally, I especially want to thank my husband, Stu, for contributing his wisdom and wit, for sharing problems as well as progress, and for sustaining me with a love that encourages me to grow.

The editor and the publisher would like to thank the following publishers and journals for permission to reprint from published works:

Professors Clive Barker and Simon Trussler, editors, *New Theatre Quarterly* for permission to reprint "The Plays of David Mamet: Games of Manipulation and Power" by Henry Schvey, *New Theatre Quarterly* 4 (1988): 77–86.

Professor Hersh Zeifman, co-editor, *Modern Drama* for permission to reprint "Dominance and Anguish: The Teacher-Student Relationship in the Plays of David Mamet" by Pascale Hubert-Leibler, *Modern Drama* 31, no. 4 (December 1988): 557–570.

INTRODUCTION

"I have always felt like an outsider;" writes David Mamet in "On Paul Ickovic's Photographs," and "I am sure that the suspicion that I perceive is the suspicion that I provoke by my great longing to *belong.*"[1] Indicative of that which is missing in the lives that he dramatizes, the bonds of friendship, trust, and memory are absolutely central to his aesthetic vision. This essential need and desire to belong, to forge communal relationships, to participate in communal endeavors, to stand alone and act together, to establish a relationship to God and an ethical relationship with one another is a remarkably consistent theme in a body of work distinguished by its diversity. Mamet unifies the secular with the spiritual, the past with present, the individual with the community, the teacher with the student, the taleteller and the listener, the actor and the audience. But, he is aware that despite our need for communication and connection, unions are tenuous, transitory, even exploitive, a point he reiterates in recurring images of disappointing reunions, dissolving marriages, and disintegrating values. Although Mamet encourages us in essay "to change the habit of coercive and frightened action and substitute it for the habit of trust, self-reliance and cooperation,"[2] he dramatizes characters who want to be good men, but faced with impossible choices abandon "a sense of community and collective social goals" in their "obsessive search for success and individuality."[3] Artistically, Mamet bridges European and American traditions, combines social satire with metaphysics, unites scatological language with lyricism, and connects the frenzied pace of urban life with scrupulous attention to form.[4] For Mamet even the presentation of the play "from its inception in the unconscious of the playwright to its presentation before the public as a whole" must be viewed as a "*community endeavor*" by the artistic community.[5]

While at Goddard College Mamet co-founded and directed just such an artistic community called the St. Nicholas Company, which performed Mamet's *Duck Variations* at Goddard in 1972. Shortly thereafter, the playwright returned to Chicago from Goddard, where he had been teaching. "Chicago," observes Todd London, "has been rightly called one of the most racist and divided cities in America," but its "arts community has a unique history of cooperation."[6] Mamet became an integral and influential part of Chicago's artistic community, bringing to it his example of professionalism and perfection. Mamet's theatre group, renamed the St. Nicholas Theatre Company, joined Mamet in Chicago, but his plays would be staged at the Organic Theatre, the St. Nicholas Theatre, and the Goodman Theatre. By the time that Mamet left the St. Nicholas Theatre Company in 1976, he had established a close personal and professional relationship with Gregory Mosher, Artistic Director of the Goodman, who directed the premiere of *American Buffalo* and has continued to direct most of the premieres of Mamet's plays. Although Mamet's *Sexual Perversity in Chicago* and *American Buffalo* were well received in Chicago, it would not be until 1975 that *Sexual Perversity* opened at the St. Clement's Theatre in New York and until 1977 that the Broadway production of *American Buffalo* established Mamet's national reputation.

Since then, Mamet has written more than twenty-five plays, numerous sketches, three children's plays, poetry, two collections of essays, reminiscences, a book on film directing, and twelve screenplays. Mamet's most recent film, *Homicide*, premiered at the 1991 Cannes Film Festival and will be released in the fall. Additionally, he has adapted Chekhov's *Three Sisters, Uncle Vanya, The Cherry Orchard,* and "Vint," and translated and adapted Pierre Laville's play, *Le Fleuve rouge,* as well as founding the Atlantic Theatre Company.

Winner of two Obies, a New York Drama Critics Award for *American Buffalo,* and the Pulitzer Prize for *Glengarry Glen Ross,* Mamet is widely considered to be one of the most prolific and powerful voices in contemporary American theater. His sensitivity to language, precision of social observation, concern for metaphor and its dramatic force, theatrical imagination and inventiveness, images of alienation, striking tone poems of betrayal and loss, brilliant use of comedy, and continuing productivity account in large part for his staying power and critical respect.

The richness and complexity of Mamet's work affords the critic wide opportunity to explore such recurring paradigms as the gambling ritual, reunion, and implied community of teacher and student and storyteller and listener. Additionally, the centrality of the city—whether Chicago or New York—the exploitation of the individual by the institution, the use of theatrical metaphors, the function and presence of women, the impact of autobiography, analogues to Chekhov, Beckett, and Pinter, whom Mamet has acknowledged as influential, the focus on rootlessness and estrangement, a preoccupation with recollected national and cultural history, and innovative linguistic strategies invite critical examination. Moreover, specific plays and Mamet's substantial body of work invite thematic, structural, and comparative consideration. But neither this volume nor any individual essay attempts to reduce Mamet's work to a central theme. Rather, reflecting the breadth, imagination, and diversity of Mamet's canon, I have attempted to provide a range of critical approaches that would offer retrospectives and perspectives on Mamet's drama and screenplays from *Lakeboat* to *Homicide*.

This collection presents nine original and two reprised essays on a range of subjects covering the entirety of the playwright's career. Each essay makes a sound argument independent of other essays. When taken together, the essays provide a comprehensive and cohesive overview of Mamet's texts and provide a context for furthering our understanding of them. This is especially true when an individual work, such as *American Buffalo* or *Glengarry Glen Ross*, is considered in more than one article. While I do not concur with some interpretations presented in this volume, the arguments have been carefully delineated and articulated. That critics hold opposing viewpoints is a reflection of both the critic's philosophy and the complexity of Mamet's writing.

The essays in *David Mamet: A Casebook* have been arranged mostly on the basis of chronological order, but this has been impossible in articles that consider both early and late work. Matthew Roudané's overview, taking its cue from Mamet's "First Principles," sets the tone for ethical and aesthetic consideration, while Christopher Hudgins's concluding essay invites further introspection. Interviews with Gregory Mosher and Joe Mantegna conducted by the editor specifically for this collection, complement the critical essays with personal insights and professional perspectives. A chronology is offered at the beginning of the casebook to refresh the memories of readers about the sequence of performances; a selected annotated bibliography of seminal works and scholarship from 1988 to 1990 appears at the conclusion to assist both the scholar and the student.

Matthew Roudané, Associate Professor of English at Georgia State University, is the author of *Understanding Edward Albee* (1987), and *Who's Afraid of Virginia Woolf?: Necessary Fictions, Terrifying Realities* (1990) and *American Drama Since 1960: A Critical History* (forthcoming) as well as the editor of numerous books on modern drama, including *Conversations with Arthur Miller* (1987) and *Public Issues, Private Tensions: Contemporary American Drama* (1988; revised and expanded 1991). Roudané, who conducted the first scholarly interview with David Mamet in 1984, has previously examined Mamet's ethical principles and cultural poetics in "Public Issues, Private Tensions: David Mamet's *Glengarry Glen Ross.*" In "Mamet's Mimetics," Roudané expands his theoretical and aesthetic considerations of Mamet's theater, drawing upon his vast knowledge of American literary tradition that he views integral to Mamet's ethical vision.

"At the center of Mamet's moral view," suggests Roudané, "lies an amoral universe, a postmodern American view of Nature spotlighting our organic disconnection from the historical, cultural and mythic resonances from the past." Reading theater space culturally, Roudané postulates that if American drama from O'Neill to Shepard has traditionally employed the home as primary setting—even if "embittered and embattled"—the "not-home play space" that characterizes Mamet's drama situates cultural and spiritual relationships in the workplace, where they are devalued, exchanged, and compromised. Crucial to Roudané's argument is his fascinating study of the classic American View of Nature and the distance Mamet has traveled from historical and aesthetic traditions of his American literary past. Although Mamet tempers his mimetics with "mythic *traces* of an authentic past," concludes Roudané, his characters and sets "map out a predatory world" in which only "the fittest (and surely the greediest) might survive." No longer benevolent, Nature in Mamet's world is shattered and reinvented to reflect a discordant American cultural landscape.

Best known for his extensive O'Neill scholarship, specifically his recent *Long Day's Journey Into Night: Native Eloquence*, Michael Hinden, professor of English at the University of Wisconsin, Madison, presents a very different perspective of Mamet's workplaces and aesthetic vision. Drawing upon the playwright's recent collections of essays to illuminate his earliest play, *Lakeboat,* Hinden convincingly argues that Mamet's quest for community informs his drama, as evidenced by the fact that Mamet's characters—and the playwright—

repeatedly care more about loneliness and intimacy than sexual conquest and business.

Mamet's "nostalgia for family ties, the importance of the father-son relationship, the brooding loneliness of the midwestern landscape, a fascination with men whose lives are dedicated to dollars, suspense, and dark journeys, and the mysterious intimacy of the human voice" collectively combine, in Hinden's view, to form Mamet's "continuing quest to establish a vision of community that could create the closeness of family life." Hinden suggests that for Mamet the community is an "idealized nexus of human relationships," an emotional locale not to be confused with specific geographic locations—Chicago, for example—or cultural places. *Lakeboat*, Mamet's first and still one of his best plays, argues Hinden, provides the playwright's fully articulated attitude toward community conveyed through a substitute family sharing comradeship in close quarters at "the *margins* of the city." Whether through mythmaking or intimate confessions, Mamet not only glamorizes their shared fate, he "illustrates the crew's potential to cohere through the shared medium of language."

Deborah Geis, too, is concerned with margins, but her focus is not the boundaries of community. Rather, Geis maintains that Mamet's plays, which "reveal a passionate concern with the boundaries of the theatrical situation and with the awareness that they are performed before an audience," encourage us to consider the extent of the playwright's indebtedness to the metadramatic tradition evident in such metadramatic "tricks," or strategies, as choral figures, soliloquy, storytelling, stock characters, and manipulation of the audience. But argues Geis, "like other postmodern dramatists such as John Guare, David Rabe and Maria Irene Fornes, Mamet problematizes and even stigmatizes the devices of the metadramatic tradition" while challenging us to rethink these strategies. In other words, Mamet plays with and against metadramatic tradition, often employing an entire work to "con" or persuade the audience.

An assistant professor at Queens College, CUNY, specializing in modern and contemporary drama, on which she has published a number of essays, Geis is currently at work on a book on monologue in contemporary drama. Her fresh reading of Mamet's canon is supported by her obvious understanding and breadth of knowledge of both classical tragedy and comedy and Renaissance drama and by her pointed examination of a variety of strategies employed in such Mamet plays as *Duck Variations, A Life in the Theatre, Sexual Perversity in Chicago, American Buffalo*, and *The Water Engine*. Of special interest is Geis's treatment of the evolution of soliloquy and storytelling in Mamet's plays. Geis's concern is not merely to define and to elucidate metadrama but to direct attention to Mamet's innovative postmodern use, or "tricking," of metadramatic tradition that results in theater as a "house of games."

Pascale Hubert-Leibler's approach to Mamet's drama is thematic rather than structural. Exploring what she terms the "master-disciple paradigm" in Mamet's drama, Hubert-Leibler emphasizes the centrality of this relationship as well as its crucial ethical and moral function—as a forum for "revising questions of competence and pretense, fairness and injustice" and as a format for the imposition of the teacher's "prerogatives of questioning, testing and punishing." In other words, asserts Hubert-Leibler, the teacher-student relationship is first and foremost a power relationship characterized by "dominance and anguish."

In order to underscore a hierarchy of power crucial to the teacher-student paradigm, Mamet accentuates the age difference between teacher and student integral to the establishment, evolution and finality of that relationship. Drawing her models from *Lakeboat, A Life in the Theatre, Squirrels, Sexual Perversity in Chicago*, and *American Buffalo*, Hubert-Leibler suggests that older characters are typically attracted to the pedagogical role for the real or imagined "empowerment" they achieve, while other "teachers" view the exercise of authority as a variant of the father-son relationship "mitigated" and/or driven "by feelings of solicitude and love." Such relationships cut both ways, because the student both derives knowledge from and gives sanction to the teacher. In Hubert-Leibler's view, however, Mamet's treatment of the teacher-student paradigm is essentially ironic, because in a world in which knowledge, satisfying human relationships, and values are conspicuously absent, " the very notion of teaching becomes obsolete." "Dominance and Anguish: The Teacher-Student Relationship in the Plays of David Mamet," written and published by Hubert-Leibler when she was a Fulbright Scholar at Cornell University in 1988, is reprised in this collection. Currently Maître de Conférence (associate professor) in the English Department of the University of Reims, France, Professor Hubert-Leibler teaches Renaissance and contemporary drama;

her scholarship includes translations of two books by Anthony Burgess into French.

Expanding upon the concept of manipulative relationships, Professor Henry Schvey's contribution to this collection is a revision of an essay on David's Mamet's theatre previously published in 1988. Professor of Drama and chairman of the Performing Arts Department at Washington University, Schvey has published extensively on modern European and contemporary British and American drama. The author of *Oskar Kokoschka: The Painter as Playwright* and co-editor of *American Drama: New Essays*, Dr. Schvey is currently completing a critical history of American drama. In "Power Plays: David Mamet's Theatre of Manipulation," Schvey argues that Mamet's work from *Duck Variations* to *Glengarry Glen Ross* and *The Shawl* is a "highly unified articulate expression of an attack on the materialistic values of American society." Using *The Shawl* as "an instructive example of Mamet's theatrical mind," Schvey examines exploitation, betrayal, and man's capacity for self-knowledge in a corrupt world that is repeated in his complex plays, such as *American Buffalo, Edmond*, and *Glengarry Glen Ross*.

While acknowledging that *American Buffalo,* and *Glengarry Glen Ross* are brilliant plays about corruption in American business, the focus of his essay is Mamet's *Edmond*, "a remarkable work of manifest darkness and depravity." A morality play that explicitly reveals Mamet's "apocalyptic vision of a society bent upon self-destruction," *Edmond* is a dark and ugly portrayal of the "filthy underbelly of New York City" that is counterpointed by the protagonist's unconscious spiritual quest. In naming his protagonist Edmond, argues Schvey, Mamet is not indulging in deliberate mystification; rather, he is drawing direct parallels between the individual and the social order professed by his namesake, Edmund Burke. Observing that Mamet merges the grifters of *American Buffalo* with the hustlers of *Edmond* in *Glengarry Glen Ross*, his "purest examination of a society built on merciless exploitation," Schvey maintains that Mamet's morality plays are unique because they retain the power to move us without moralizing.

Best known for her three superb books on Samuel Beckett (*Samuel Beckett: The Comic Gamut*; *Back to Beckett*; and *From Desire to Godot*) Ruby Cohn has contributed innumerable essays to journals and collections on modern British and American drama. Professor of

Dramatic Literature at the University of California, Davis, she is currently an associate editor of the *Journal of American Drama and Theater, Modern Drama,* and *Theater Journal.* Forthcoming are her *New American Dramatists: 1960–1990* and *Retreats from Realism in Recent English Drama.* In "How Are Things Made Round?" Professor Cohn applies her brilliant mind and sensitive ear to the nuances and rhythms of Mamet's language in what she terms his "Business Trilogy": *American Buffalo, Glengarry Glen Ross,* and *Speed-the-Plow.* Critics have noted and admired Mamet's rhythmic use of speech for twenty years, but Cohn elucidates the innumerable linguistic devices by which Mamet "quickens and energizes speech," employs sound "strategically," controls rhythms "pungently," and "conveys the frenzied pace of contemporary life." Nowhere, asserts Cohn, is this rapid rhythm more obvious or effective than in the "Business Trilogy." "At first glance, or rather on first hearing of a Mamet play," suggests Cohn, "grammatical chaos reinforces lexical poverty to convey a general impression of illiteracy." Indeed, "Mamet bases his grammatical chaos on the solecisms, digressions and tautologies of everyday speech," but argues Cohn, they are brilliant comic inventions. Her detailed analysis of Mamet's idiosyncratic use of rhetorical questions, recurrent queries, rising interrogative rhythms, monosyllabic words—the most striking of which are obscenities—elisions, inverted syntax, contradictions, and repetitions convincingly provides testimony of what Cohn terms Mamet's "fecund creativity." Essentially, Mamet has, to quote Don in *American Buffalo,* the "skill and talent and the balls"[7] to craft dramatic language by "whittling words," and Cohn, who spares no words, is as critical, comic and compelling as the playwright.

Rather than address the metaphoric and linguistic structure in *American Buffalo* and *Glengarry Glen Ross,* Hersh Zeifman's wickedly funny and searingly accurate examination of dramaturgic strategy is the subject of his "Phallus in Wonderland: Machismo and Business in *American Buffalo* and *Glengarry Glen Ross.*" Zeifman, an associate professor at York University, Toronto, Canada, president of the Samuel Beckett Society, and coeditor of *Modern Drama,* has published widely on the plays of Beckett, Stoppard and Pinter. He is the editor of *David Hare: A Casebook* (forthcoming, from Garland) and coeditor of *Contemporary British Drama* (forthcoming, from Macmillan).

In this essay Zeifman observes that Mamet's "closed moral universe" in *American Buffalo* and *Glengarry Glen Ross* is "closed even more tightly by being portrayed as exclusively male." Zeifman suggests that "the exclusion of women from these plays" implicitly conveys that "the values males traditionally associate with the feminine" are viewed as "threatening to their business ethos." Indeed, Zeifman cogently persuades us to view "the homosocial world of American business" that is critiqued by Mamet in these two plays as a "topsy-turvy world" of "debased values" in which all characters "think with their crotch."

Zeifman is especially perceptive on homosocial institutions, such as the military and police, epithets hurled at those who fail "the test of manhood," and the boundaries of women in a male world. Zeifman argues that both *American Buffalo* and *Glengarry Glen Ross* might have been more appropriately entitled *Sexual Perversity*, not only because the denial of an entire gender is perverse but because characterizing "women *as a gender*" is its own form of misogyny. While Zeifman's observations of homosocial business ethics specifically concern *American Buffalo* and *Glengarry Glen Ross*, they are, of course, applicable to the entire Mamet canon.

Co-author and producer of an original play entitled *Women Who Kill*, Ann Hall brings a unique perspective to this collection. Hall, an assistant professor at Marquette University who has published numerous articles and reviews on modern drama and fiction, is currently at work on a book entitled *A Kind of Alaska: The Representation of Women in the Plays of Eugene O'Neill, Harold Pinter, and Sam Shepard*. The central premise of "Playing to Win: Sexual Politics in David Mamet's *House of Games* and *Speed-the-Plow*" is that *House of Games* and *Speed-the-Plow* are to some extent complementary works: the former illustrates "the effects of men upon a woman," whereas the latter presents "the effects of a woman upon the company of men." Despite the fact that the women characters in both screenplay and play resist codification and remain enigmatic, male characters in both works "view women dualistically" as either "Madonnas or whores."

Drawing upon psychoanalytic and feminist theory—specifically that of Lacan and Irigaray—Hall suggests that Mamet's female characters "falling between two stools," constantly elude labels and "expose the male system of oppression as a house of cards." Female portraits in *House of Games* and *Speed-the-Plow* differ from most twentieth-century plays and early Mamet plays such as *Sexual Perversity* and *The Woods*, asserts Hall, in that the "battle of the sexes . . . occurs in the context of business, power and wealth." Furthermore, by challenging the power structure established in the screenplay and the play, the expectation of other characters, and their audiences, Dr. Ford and Karen, respectively, embody revolutionary femininity. However, neither screenplay nor play dramatizes feminist triumph. In both works, asserts Hall, "phallic power" is overturned "by subtle, subversive strategies" so that patriarchial, social, and cultural disturbances are implicitly conveyed by Mamet through enigmatic women who violate stereotypical models.

Steven Gale's perceptive explication of David Mamet's work may be traced to his 1981 essay on scenic analysis in David Mamet's *The Duck Variations, Reunion, A Life in the Theatre, The Woods*, and *The Water Engine*. Endowed professor of Humanities at Kentucky State University, Gale is best known for his extensive publications on the drama of Harold Pinter. Coeditor of *The Pinter Review* and president of the Pinter Society, Gale has recently developed an interest in film. His book on Mamet's screenplays and another on Pinter's filmscripts are forthcoming.

In "David Mamet's *The Verdict*: The Opening Cons," Gale argues that *The Verdict*, "generally considered to be Mamet's best screenplay," reflects characteristics of the author's writing since 1972 when *The Duck Variations* was first staged. Acknowledging that Mamet has developed an interest in "professions as professions" (used both universally and metaphorically) in his later work, Gale contends that *The Verdict* is "about lawyers," because lawyers in general are "related to the second characteristic of Mamet's more recent work in drama and films": the confidence game as "topic" and "structural device." The law profession and the opening con fuse meaningfully, "particularly in the opening segment."

Thus, it is the artistry of the opening segment, "the nine-minute, fifteen-second long, thirty-six shot segment" constituting approximately seven per cent of the film (typically considered "the set-up" after which plot hooks are introduced) that is the focus of Gale's critical eye. Gale walks us through the composition of each shot of the opening segment while analyzing Mamet's effective and efficient use of "camera eye, sound, and lighting." Gale observes that Mamet pares unnecessary words and actions, so that each shot collectively and cumulatively creates a "successful montage of 'uninflected' shots" that reveal information visually rather than narratively, establish the protagonist's character, and introduce the premise upon which the conflict/confirmation of the movie is based. Especially interesting is Gale's analysis of Mamet's use of windows, interior and exterior space, and transitional devices.

Dennis Carroll is perhaps best known for *David Mamet*, his excellent critical analysis of David Mamet's theatre and early screenplays. A professor of Theatre at the University of Hawaii at Manoa, Carroll has published extensively on modern American and Australian playwrights in essay collections and such journals as *Modern Drama* and *Theatre Journal*. His exhaustive study, *Australian Contemporary Drama: 1909–1982*, was published in 1985.

In "Recent Mamet Films: 'Business' versus Communion" Carroll relates major thematic concerns discussed more fully in his book on David Mamet to Mamet's recent screenplays: *The Untouchables, House of Games, Things Change, We're No Angels*, and *Homicide*. Asserting that the tensions between the spirit of "business" (read self-interest) and communion (read sexual or familial friendship) present in the plays and earlier films similarly operate in screenplays written and sometimes directed by Mamet since 1985. Carroll illustrates this premise by a detailed thematic explication of the recent screenplays in light of previous work.

Although *The Water Engine* and *The Untouchables* may be compared in period and locale, suggests Carroll, of greater interest to this scholar are the parallels between Capone's business founded on "coercion," "fear," and "teamwork" for business profit and the essentially "altruistic" law enforcement group of "untouchables" working to destroy Capone's machine. Carroll's discussion traces the education of Ness and his critical bonding scenes with Malone. In Carroll's view *House of Games* is a much darker work comparable to early plays in which "'business' is triumphant over communion" and especially to *Edmond* in which "self-knowledge is achieved only in the most ironic context." Indeed, suggests Carroll, business "wins out" in *House of Games* because of moral, ethical and emotional betrayal. *Things Change*, however, presents a more positive outcome of the "'business' versus communion dialectic" similar to Mamet's children's plays in which moral education and communion are vindicated. Similarly, in *We're No Angels*, sexual attraction "triumphs over negativeness and self-interest." Noting Mamet's extensive use of "oppositional images," Carroll maintains that in this screenplay Mamet showcases the values of "compromise, belief and instinct." *Homicide*,

Mamet's most recent screenplay, is mentioned briefly as reflective of a continuity of Mamet's themes and moral vision.

Appropriately, the function and power of comedy in communal and moral vision are addressed in the concluding essay of this collection. "Comedy and Humor in the Plays of David Mamet" by Christopher Hudgins, chairmen of the Department of English at the University of Nevada, Las Vegas, wonderfully captures the essense of Mamet's comedic philosophy and structure. Hudgins, whose fine scholarship on the drama of Harold Pinter (especially on *The Homecoming, Old Times,* and *The Basement*), the ironic mode, and audience response is deservedly respected, was a founding member of the Pinter Society and serves on the editorial board of *The Pinter Review.* In this essay, based on a detailed consideration of *American Buffalo, Glengarry Glen Ross, Speed-the-Plow,* and Mamet's essays, Hudgins provides a very compelling argument that Mamet's complex use of irony and comedy is essentially celebratory: that is, it celebrates one's capacity and "tenacity" to survive even if that survival is "venal."

"The sources and mechanism's of Mamet's humor are broad," suggests Hudgins, subtly balancing moralism and pleasure. That we laugh at truth in Mamet's world, in Hudgins' view, "is deeply ironic." Thus, argues Hudgins, Mamet encourages us "to laugh at and identify with his central characters, to know ourselves, forgive ourselves and to change," with the expectation that ironic identification with these characters should lead to criticism of the system, of the culture, and a recognition of how to act morally. Hudgins's fresh readings of *American Buffalo, Glengarry Glen Ross,* and *Speed-the-Plow* are based in good part on what he terms "our enjoyment in response to a Mamet play." Indeed, concludes Hudgins, laughter with Mamet, "at his characters, and at ourselves," points to "celebration" at "the core of all of Mamet's work" and is an essential component of our aesthetic communion and "ethical pleasure."

Leslie Kane

Notes

1. David Mamet, "On Paul Ickovic's Photographs," *Writing in Restaurants* (New York: Viking, 1986), p. 73.

2. Mamet, "First Principles," *Writing in Restaurants*, p. 27.

3. Interview with Don Ranvaud, *Sight and Sound* 57, No. 4 (Autumn 1988): 232.

4. C. W. E. Bigsby, *David Mamet* (London: Methuen, 1985), p. 20.

5. Mamet, "A National Dream-Life," *Writing in Restaurants*, p. 10.

6. Todd London, "Chicago Impromptu," *American Theatre* 7, No. 4 (July–August 1990): 21;62.

7. David Mamet, *American Buffalo* (New York: Grove, 1976), p. 4.

CHRONOLOGY

1947   David Mamet is born in Chicago on November 30 to Bernard and Lenore Mamet.

1947–1965   Mamet grows up on Chicago's South Side and attends Rich Central and Francis Parker High School. While he is a teenager, Mamet begins working backstage at Hull House Theatre.

1965–1969   Mamet attends Goddard College in Plainfield, Vermont, graduating with a B.A. in Literature. During his junior year (1968–1969), Mamet studies acting at New York's Neighborhood Playhouse under Sanford Meisner.

While at Goddard, Mamet completes the first drafts of *Sexual Perversity in Chicago*, *The Duck Variations*, and *Reunion*.

1968   *Camel* is presented at Goddard College.

1970–1971   Mamet teaches drama for a year at Marlboro College in Vermont.

Lakeboat is produced by Marlboro Theatre Workshop.

1971–1973   Mamet returns to Goddard College as Artist-in-Residence. While at Goddard, Mamet forms a nucleus of actors who will become the St. Nicholas Theatre Company.

The St. Nicholas Theatre Company presents the first productions of *The Duck Variations* and *Reunion*.

Litko: A Dramatic Monologue is staged at Body Politic in Chicago.

Mamet is founder, together with Steven Schacter, William H. Macy and Patricia Cox, and Artistic Director of the St. Nicholas Theatre Company. (Mamet is a member 1973–1976.)

1974   The St. Nicholas Theatre Company, now in Chicago, presents the premieres of *Squirrels* and *The Poet and the Rent*, directed by Mamet.

Sexual Perversity in Chicago opens at the Organic Theatre, Chicago, directed by Stuart Gordon.

Mamet is appointed a faculty member on the Illinois Arts Council.

1975   *American Buffalo* premieres October 23 at the Goodman Theatre, Stage Two, Chicago, directed by Gregory Mosher and featuring J. J. Johnston, Bernard Erhard, and William H. Macy.

In December, this production moves to open the new St. Nicholas Theatre space on North Halsted Street, with Mike Nussbaum replacing Erhard. *American Buffalo* wins a Joseph Jefferson Award for Outstanding Production.

Sexual Perversity in Chicago wins a Joseph Jefferson Award.

Sexual Perversity in Chicago and *The Duck Variations* are produced as a double-bill at St. Clement's Theatre, New York, directed by Albert Takazauckas.

Mackinac and *Marranos* premiere at Center Youth Theater at the Bernard Horwich Jewish Community Center, Chicago.

Under the Auspices of Younger Audiences Grant from the New York State Council on the Arts, Mamet writes *Revenge of the Space Pandas* for St. Clement's Theatre.

Mamet is a visiting lecturer at the University of Chicago (1975–1976). Mamet is also a contributing editor for *Oui* magazine.

1976   *Sexual Perversity in Chicago* and *Duck Variations* moves to Cherry Lane Theatre, New York, on January 6.

Reunion is staged at the St. Nicholas Theatre on January 9.

American Buffalo opens at St. Clement's Theatre, directed by Gregory Mosher. This production stars Michael Egan, Mike Kellin, and J. T. Walsh.

Mamet wins an Obie for Distinguished Playwriting for *Sexual Perversity in Chicago* and *American Buffalo*.

Mamet is a recipient of a New York State Council on the Arts grant and of a Rockefeller grant.

1976–1977   Mamet is appointed Teaching Fellow at the Yale School of Drama.

1977   *All Men Are Whores: An Inquiry* is staged at the Yale Cabaret Theatre, New Haven, in February, directed by David Mamet.

A Life in the Theatre premieres February 3, at the Goodman Theatre, Stage Two, directed by Gregory Mosher. This production features Mike Nussbaum and Joe Mantegna.

American Buffalo is staged on Broadway. Directed by Ulu Grosbard, and featuring Robert Duvall, John Savage, and Kenneth MacMillan, production opens February 28.

The Water Engine premieres at the St. Nicholas Theatre under the direction of Steven Schacter on May 11.

Dark Pony and *Reunion* are staged at the Yale Repertory Theatre, New Haven, under auspices of C.B.S. Creative Writing Fellowship on October 14.

A Life in the Theatre is produced in October at New York's Theatre de Lys, directed by Gerald Guiterrez and starring Ellis Rabb and Peter Evans.

The Woods premieres at the St. Nicholas Theatre on November 11. This production, directed by David Mamet, stars Peter Weller and Patti Lupone.

The Revenge of the Space Pandas or Binky Rudich and The Two-Speed Clock is staged at the St. Nicholas Theatre, Children's Theatre. The play is also staged at Flushing Town Hall, Queens, New York.

Sexual Perversity in Chicago and *Duck Variations* open at the Regent Theatre, London, on December 1. This is Mamet's first production abroad.

Mamet receives the New York Drama Critics Award for *American Buffalo*.

1978   *The Water Engine*, directed by Steven Schacter, with music by Alaric Jans, opens in January at the New York Shakespeare Festival, Cabaret Theatre. This production features Dwight Schultz, Penelope Allen, Bill Moor, and Colin Stinton.

Mr. Happiness premieres in March at the Plymouth Theater, New York, as a curtain raiser for Schacter's production of *The Water Engine*.

American Buffalo becomes the first American play to be produced in England's new National Theatre space, Cottesloe Theatre.

Mamet wins Outer Critics Circle John Gassner Award for Distinguished Playwriting.

Mamet is named Associate Artistic Director and Playwright-in-Residence at Goodman Theatre.

Prairie du Chien is broadcast on the British Broadcasting Corporation and Public Radio. *The Water Engine* is broadcast on "Earplay" on National Public Radio.

1979   *The Blue Hour: City Sketches* is staged at the New York Shakespeare Festival, Public Theatre, in February.

The Woods is staged at the New York Shakespeare Festival, Public Theatre, on April 25. This production is directed by Ulu Grosbard and stars Christine Lahti and Chris Sarandon.

Lone Canoe, Or The Explorer premieres at the Goodman Theatre under the direction of Gregory Mosher on May 18. Music is by Alaric Jans.

A revival of *A Life in the Theatre* is staged by Gregory Mosher in May to open the Goodman Theatre's new Studio Theatre. This production stars Mike Nussbaum and Cosmo White.

WNET New York's production of *A Life in the Theatre* is telecast by Public Broadcasting on June 27. It is the first of Mamet's plays to be filmed.

A Life in the Theatre is staged in the Open Space Theatre, London.

A Sermon is staged at the Apollo Theatre Center, Chicago.

The Sanctity of Marriage premieres at the New Circle Repertory Theatre, New York, on October 18, in a triple-bill with *Reunion* and *Dark Pony*. Directed by David Mamet, this production features Lindsay Crouse and Michael Higgins.

Shoeshine is staged at the Ensemble Studio Theatre in New York on December 14.

Mamet is named to the faculty of The University of Chicago as a Special Lecturer.

1980   *Lakeboat* (revised) opens at the Milwaukee Repertory Theatre, directed by John Dillon.

Mamet directs Shakespeare's *Twelfth Night* for New York's Circle Repertory Company, where he serves as its Playwright-in-Residence.

The revival of *American Buffalo*, directed by Arvin Brown, is staged at the Long Wharf Theatre in New Haven. This production stars Al Pacino, Bruce MacVittie and J. J. Johnston.

1981   Mamet's first film project, *The Postman Always Rings Twice*, directed by Bob Rafaelson, premieres starring Jack Nicholson and Jessica Lange.

American Buffalo revival opens at Circle in the Square, New York.

Mamet begins work on a second screenplay, *The Verdict*, with director Sidney Lumet.

Mamet directs *A Sermon* at Circle in the Square, New York.

Mamet is a Visiting Lecturer at New York University.

Dark Pony and *Reunion* are staged in London.

1982   *Lakeboat* is staged at the Long Wharf Theatre, New Haven, directed by John Dillon.

Lakeboat is also produced at the Goodman Theatre, directed by Gregory Mosher.

Edmond premieres, on June 4, at the Goodman Theatre Studio, directed by Gregory Mosher and featuring Colin Stinton, Rich Cluchey, and Jack Wallace.

Edmond opens in New York on October 27, directed by Gregory Mosher. Both Mamet and Mosher win Obies for *Edmond* in 1983.

A revival of *The Woods* is staged at Second Stage in New York, featuring Patti Lupone and Peter Weller.

Mamet is nominated for an Academy Award for Best Adapted Screenplay for *The Verdict*.

1983   *American Buffalo* revival opens on Broadway.

The Red River, translated and adapted by Mamet from Pierre Laville's *Le Fleuve rouge*, is staged at the Goodman Theatre on May 2.

In May, *Two Conversations, Two Scenes* and *Yes But So What* are produced by the Ensemble Studio Theatre, New York, as part of their 1983 One-Act Marathon.

The Disappearance of the Jews premieres at the Goodman Theatre on June 3 on a bill with two other one-acts by Shel Silverstein and Elaine May. Gregory Mosher directs.

The Dog, The Film Crew, Four A.M. are staged in Jason's Park Royal, New York, on July 14.

Glengarry Glen Ross premieres at the National Theatre in London, directed by Bill Bryden, on September 21. This production stars Jack Shepard, Derek Newark and Karl Johnson.

Glengarry Glen Ross wins the Society of West End Theatres' Award in London for Best Play.

1984   *Glengarry Glen Ross*, directed by Gregory Mosher, opens in Chicago at the Goodman Theatre on January 27, starring Joe Mantegna, Robert Prosky, J. T. Walsh, and Mike Nussbaum.

Glengarry Glen Ross opens at the Golden Theatre, New York, in March.

Glengarry Glen Ross wins Mamet the Pulitzer Prize, the Drama Critics' Award for Best American Play 1984, a Joseph Dintenfass Award, and four Tony Award nominations, including Best Play and Best Director (Gregory Mosher).

The Frog Prince opens at the Milwaukee Repertory Theatre on April 19.

Ensemble Studio Theatre mounts *Vermont Sketches* (*Conversations with the Spirit World, Pint's A Pound the World Around, Downing, Deer Dogs*) on May 24 in their 1984 Marathon. Gregory Mosher directs.

Mamet directs *Litko: A Dramatic Monologue* and *Shoehorn* (double-bill) at the Hartley House Theatre, New York.

Edmond is given its West Coast premiere at the Odyssey Theatre under Ron Sossi's direction as part of the Olympic Arts Festival.

The Woods and *The Water Engine* open in London.

1985   Mamet is founding member and Associate Director of the New Theatre Company in Chicago.

Mamet adapts Chekhov's *The Cherry Orchard* as their first production. *The Cherry Orchard*, directed by Gregory Mosher and featuring Peter Riegert and Lindsay Crouse, opens on March 1.

Goldberg Street, is broadcast on WNUR Radio, Northwestern University, Evanston, Illinois on March 4. *Cross Patch* is broadcast on WNUR Radio, Northwestern University, Evanston, Illinois, on March 4.

Premieres of two one-act plays, *The Shawl* and *The Spanish Prisoner* are staged at the Goodman Theatre on April 19 by the New Theatre Company.

The Frog Prince opens at the Ensemble Studio Theatre, New York, in their 1985 Marathon.

Mamet wins the Dramatists Guild's Annual Hull-Warriner Award for Best Play for *Glengarry Glen Ross*.

Prairie du Chien premieres with *The Shawl*, on December 23, at the Mitzi Newhouse Theatre, Lincoln Center, under the direction of Gregory Mosher.

Edmond runs successfully in London as a co-production by the Newcastle Playhouse and the Royal Court Theatre.

Mamet begins work on the screen adaptation of *The Untouchables* for Paramount Pictures.

1986   Mamet wins the Academy Institute Award in Literature.

Vint, adapted by Mamet from Anton Chekhov's story, is mounted at the Ensemble Theatre on April 22.

Prairie du Chien and *The Shawl* open in London.

1987   Paramount Pictures releases *The Untouchables*, directed by Brian De Palma, and starring Kevin Costner, Sean Connery, and Robert De Niro.

Orion Pictures releases *House of Games*, written and directed by Mamet, and featuring Joe Mantegna and Lindsay Crouse. This film wins a Golden Globe nomination for Best Screenplay.

1988   *Uncle Vanya*, Mamet's adaptation of Chekhov's play, is staged at the American Repertory Theatre, Cambridge, Massachusetts, on April 16.

Speed-the-Plow, starring Joe Mantegna, Ron Silver, and Madonna, under the direction of Gregory Mosher, opens in May at the Royale Theatre, New York.

Where Were You When It Went Down? in *Urban Blight* is staged at the Manhattan Theatre Club, City Center, New York.

Mamet wins a Writers Guild Award nomination for Best Screenplay Based on Material from Another Medium for *The Untouchables*.

Columbia Pictures releases *Things Change*, directed by David Mamet and written with Shel Silverstein. *Things Change* stars Don Ameche and Joe Mantegna.

1989   Mamet's feature screenplay *We're No Angels* released by Paramount Pictures. Directed by Neil Jordan, the film stars Robert De Niro and Sean Penn.

Bobby Gould in Hell is produced with Shel Silverstein's *The Devil and Billy Markham* under the title *Oh Hell!* at the Mitzi E. Newhouse Lincoln Center Theatre in December. This production is directed by Gregory Mosher.

1990   Mamet's adaptation of Chekhov's *Three Sisters* is performed by the Atlantic Theatre Company, at the Festival Theatre in Philadelphia.

Mamet begins shooting his new screenplay, *Homicide,* with Joe Mantegna and William H. Macy in Baltimore for Cinehaus/Bison Films. Mamet directs.

Mamet completes work on several screenplays: *Ace in the Hole* and *The Deerslayer* for Paramount; *High and Low* for Universal; *Hoffa* for Twentieth Century Fox.

1991   British Broadcasting Corporation broadcasts a production of Mamet's adaptation of *Uncle Vanya*, directed by Gregory Mosher, with David Warner, Ian Holm, Rebecca Pidgeon, Mary Elizabeth Mastrantonio, Ian Banner, and Rachael Kempson on February 22.

Mamet's adaptation of Chekhov's *Three Sisters* to be produced off-Broadway in the spring by the Atlantic Theatre Company.

David Mamet

MAMET'S MIMETICS

Matthew C. Roudané

Mamet is an ethicist. From the initial plays—*Camel, Lakeboat*—to
those pivotal works that first brought him notoriety—*Sexual Perversity
in Chicago, American Buffalo*—from *Glengarry Glen Ross* to *Speed-
the-Plow* and *Oh Hell*—Mamet appropriates the play space with a
singular vision. This unity of vision most often finds its expression in
terms of an implicit social critique of a contingent and decidedly
ambiguous universe: a world from which Mamet eviscerates any moral
balance between public virtue and private self-desire. From such a
theater of disruption has grown Mamet's unique, and disturbing,
cultural poetics. His wit and comedy seem obvious, but beyond the
comedic witticisms lie darker visions. Mamet's ideographic backdrop
often concerns the near-complete separation of the individual from
genuine relationship. Mamet replicates human commitments and desires
in demythicized forms: commodity fetishism, sexual negotiations and
exploitations, aborted or botched crimes, brutal physical assaults,
fraudulent business transactions enacted by petty thieves masquerading
as businessmen, and human relationships whose only shared feature is
the presence of physical sex and the absence of authentic love.

A dialogist of poetic idiolect, Mamet spectacularizes his stage,
above all, through language, a riposte that lexically as well as
psychologically shapes his cultural poetics. Mamet's evolving *oeuvre*
spotlights not only the texture of his characters' language but, too, the
quality of human relationships defined (and confined) by that very
language. From Deborah's mocking reply to her temporary lover in
Sexual Perversity in Chicago, "Dan, I love the taste of come. It tastes
like everything . . . *good* . . . just . . . *coming* out of your cock . . ."[1]

and Kevin's reflection in *All Men Are Whores*, "She would suck me off
in taxicabs"[2] to Glenna's screams in *Edmond*, "GET OUT GET OUT!
LEAVE ME THE FUCK ALONE!!! WHAT DID I DO, PLEDGE MY
LIFE TO YOU? I LET YOU FUCK ME. GO AWAY"[3] and Charlie
Fox's proclamation to Karen in *Speed-the-Plow*, "[You're] A Tight
Pussy wrapped around Ambition. . . . He fucked you on a bet,"[3]
relationships are co-opted, defleshed, entropic.

The preceding four
exchanges (staged in 1974, 1977, 1982, and 1988 respectively) suggest
a fairly consistent ethical dilemma experienced by the characters, an
ethical quandary outlined by an inversion or distortion of what the
universalists would call "authentic" relationship. The following
meditation from *The Spanish Prisoner* epitomizes how Mamet
constructs a dialectic whose emotional poles are the ascendancy of
exploitation and the concomitant decline of eros. One character, simply
designated as *A*, says to character *B*, "all our life we were taught to
escape the teachings of our senses and accept a . . . to accept a . . .
unimpassioned view of the world," which *A* moments later concludes
banishes the force of love to the outer margins of human experience:
"And the rest, we say the test of *life*, the final: THE WILL TO
EXPLOIT."[5] Within Mamet's mimetics, relationships are reduced to a
terrible, competitive binarism, the women often being marginalized and
brutalized, the men left spouting what Sinclair Lewis in *It Can't
Happen Here* calls "orgasms of oratory," a rhetoric of near-illiteracy that
denies catharsis, purgation, and awareness. The option to "exploit"
appears as an inalienable right; the Mamet hero often feels *entitled* to
"exploit."

I
A Postmodern Cultural Poetics

If, however, we see Mamet as merely a leading proponent of "the
new realism" in American drama, a playwright of pornography,
patrism, or perversion, we risk oversimplifying what precisely
empowers his stage. In the pages that follow, I would like to consider
selected major features of his mimetics that, collectively, present
haunting images of what Stephen Greenblatt in *Shakespearean
Negotiations* would call "the cultural circulation of social energy."[6]
Mamet's cultural poetics intimate a broad range of human emotions,
emotions dramatized by his invoking traces of what I will term the

American view of Nature. As a shaping principle underpinning an indeterminate cosmos, Nature, as the Puritans and Emersonians conceived her, has for Mamet so lost her *energia* that the playwright must, if he is to be true to his art, re-figure, re-negotiate, re-furbish the stage into a postmodern secularism. At the center of Mamet's moral vision lies an amoral universe, a postmodernist American view of Nature spotlighting our organic disconnection from the historical, cultural, and mythic resonances of the past. As theatrician of the ethical, Mamet interfolds within his rather bleak topography a moral seriousness, notable within his characters by its traces, its absences, but nonetheless inscribed throughout every Mamet performance. The simultaneity of a Mamet performance—an amoral world juxtaposed with ethical boundaries no longer honored or even perceived—gives Mamet's theater its aesthetic empowerment.

But how does Mamet achieve aesthetic empowerment? What precisely defines his cultural poetics? What are audiences to make of Mamet's stagings of the kinds of "social energy" that have evolved into a stylistic feature of his dramaturgy? If we explore Mamet's choice of cultural objects and scenography, the *adiaphoria* as appropriated through language, his implicit reliance on and refiguration of the American view of Nature, we will discover the true source of Mamet's theatricality. Although I will exact what Jonas Barish would call "unwelcomed surgery" on selected Mamet playscripts, I am less concerned with his Sacred Texts than with their borders—the implied cultural and historical imprints inscribed in the margins of the texts. For in Mamet the subtext is everything. If there is a certain fixity to his text, there is also a destabilizing transference of spoken word to felt (mis)perception in performance. Mamet creates theater spaces of dislocation. And it is within the subtext, the marginalia of his carnivalesque play spaces, that we seize the horrifying beauty of *American Buffalo* or *Glengarry Glen Ross*. Herein lies, at least in part, the force of his cultural poetics.

II
Scenography

Mamet literalizes his theater in many ways, but one quality that
scholars, as far as I know, have yet to explore fully is Mamet's
scenography. The overwhelming majority of Mamet's plays are not
situated in the home. By contrast, those plays that traditionally define
American theatrical canonicity are mainly set at the home: Eugene
O'Neill's *Long Day's Journey into Night*, Thornton Wilder's *Our
Town*, Arthur Miller's *Death of a Salesman*, Tennessee Williams's
Streetcar Named Desire, Edward Albee's *Who's Afraid of Virginia
Woolf?*, and, say, Sam Shepard's *True West*.

And as we reconstruct our cultural notions of American dramatic
and literary canon formation, we see that a healthy number of those
plays produced by marginalized (but hardly minor) playwrights, too,
often are situated within or around the home. Susan Glaspell's *Trifles*,
Clare Booth Luce's *The Women*, Lillian Hellman's *The Little Foxes*,
Lorraine Hansberry's *A Raisin in the Sun*, Sonja Sanchez's *Sister
Son/ji*, Maria Irene Fornés's *Fefu and Her Friends*, Marsha Norman's
'night, Mother, August Wilson's *Fences*, and Ellen Sebastian's *Your
Place Is No Longer with Us* all are useful examples. Sebastian's play,
as Raynette Halvorsen Smith points out, "becomes the ultimate
manifestation of this shedding of theatrical machinery in that it takes
place 'on location' as it were, in an actual house."[7] This is not to
imply that American dramatists never situate their locales beyond a
living room. O'Neill, after all, went well beyond the horizon in many
of his plays, as do many contemporary playwrights, such as Lee Breuer,
Megan Terry, Ntozake Shange, Adrienne Kennedy, Joan Holden, and
Charles Fuller. However, any narrative history of modern American
drama reveals the (over)reliance on the primal family unit usually
embittered and embattled within the living room. Many of our
dramatists' works, Ruby Cohn suggests, "center on the American
family and are usually set in a middle-class home that proves to be a
jail for the sensitive protagonist. . . . But the minute we see a living
room in the scenic directions—whether in Texas, St. Louis, Queens, or
California—we are primed for an exposition, an action rising
remorselessly to climax, and an inevitable resolution (less resolved in
recent years) in the pattern designed by Ibsen a century ago."[8] So,
despite the heterogeneity of our playwrights, they share a homogenizing

feature: the home as the loci of spectacle. From Lanford Wilson, David Rabe, and David Henry Hwang to Beth Henley and Judy Grahn, American dramatists in many of their plays turn our spectatorial presence to the familiar "culturally demarcated zone"[9]—the home. Not Mamet. *Lakeboat*, one of Mamet's early plays (first staged in 1970), for instance, establishes a spatial ethos that will eventually grow into a stylistic feature of his corpus: a set whose location extends beyond the physical and psychological parameters of the home. *Lakeboat* enfolds within the "engine room, the galley, the fantail (the farthest aft part of the ship), the boat deck, the rail" of the *T. Harrison*, a Great Lakes boat that Dale, the young seaman, describes to the audience in some detail:

> That's the Lakeboat. Built 1938 for Czerwiecki Steel. Christened *Joseph Czerwiecki.* Sold to Harrison Steel, East Chicago, Indiana, 1954, renamed *T. Harrison.* Length overall 615 feet. Depth 321 feet. Keel 586 feet. Beam 60. The floating home of 45 men . . . . Gross tons 8,225. Capacity in tons 11,406. A fair-sized boat. A small world . . . . *T. Harrison.* A Steel bulk-freight turbine steamer registered in the Iron Ore Trade.[10]

Like Yank in O'Neill's *The Hairy Ape*, who initially calls the ship "home," Dale identifies with the boat and all it stands for: steel, strength, dynamism, all the elements from which he, as with Yank, ultimately feels alienated. But O'Neill was not reluctant, as Mamet apparently seems to be, to return to the home as the nerve center for his self-disclosing dramas: *Desire Under the Elms, A Moon for the Misbegotten,* and *Long Day's Journey Into Night* are performed within a domestic context. Significantly, the not-home play space of *Lakeboat* prefigures what will grow into a conspicuous feature of Mamet's dramatugy: a semiotic of decoration and play areas calling attention to an urbanized culture and its effects on its people: the dysphoria of his heroes. Amateurishly at first, but then with an emerging maturity, Mamet now in the 1990s brilliantly uses his sets to highlight his deeper cultural statements.

That the majority of his plays' action occurs *outside* of what has grown into a certain narrowness of play space for American playwrights and their valorized classics, the home, is central to Mamet's vision. But what characterizes his play spaces? His plays unwind in offices,

junkshops, pawnshops, hotels, coffeehouses, interrogation rooms, peep
shows, department stores, pornographic movie theaters, regular theaters,
whorehouses, automobiles, boats, health clubs, libraries, movie
houses, beaches, city parks, radio station studios, jails, missions,
subways, railroad parlor cars, restaurants, bars, woods, and various
unspecified (and often seedy) urban locations—usually Chicago,
sometimes New York City, and in *Speed-the-Plow*, Hollywood. In
Goldberg Street: Short Plays and Monologues, some nineteen of the
sketches do not carry any scenic description, and the few that do are
situated in country stores, a shopping mall, a radio studio, a shoe shine
parlor, and a subway station. Predictably, Mamet sets his 1989 play *Oh
Hell* in a men's club and his 1990 screenplay *We're No Angels* in a
penitentiary near the Canadian border.

Or in those rare instances when his plays are situated within the
home, the sets somehow underscore the temporaneousness and
uncertainty of their inhabitants: we usually see apartments whose
tenants often seem nomadic, cosmic waifs drifting with little discernible
purpose beyond getting laid, making a buck, or both. If there is a
genuine exchange of thought and feeling, it more often than not
spotlights the fragmentation of the home, as seen in the following
father-daughter scene from *Reunion*:

> CAROL: You know—when I was young they used to talk
> about Broken Homes.
> Today, nothing. Everyone's divorced. Every
> kid on the block's got three sets of parents.
> But . . .
> It's got to have affected my marriage . . . .
> I came from a Broken Home.
> The most important institution in America.
> BERNIE: Life goes on. Your mother and me . . ..
> CAROL: . . . Oh, yeah, life goes on. And no matter how
> much of an asshole you may be, or may have
> been, life goes on.[11]

In a sense, Mamet implies throughout much of his theater that many of
his characters come from "Broken Home[s]." Usually his apartment
dwellers appear as frustrated with their atomized setting as did Tom
Wingfield in Williams's *The Glass Menagerie*, whose apartment stands
as "one of those vast hive-like conglomerations of cellular living

units"[12] or as did Willy Loman in Miller's *Death of a Salesman*, whose once-brightly painted home has faded with Willy's dream into the "Bricks and windows, windows and bricks," a spatialization that prompts one of the salesman's many tirades: "The street is lined with cars. There's not a breath of fresh air in the neighborhood. The grass don't grow any more, you can't raise a carrot in the back yard. They should've had a law against apartment houses."[13] Like Tom Wingfield and Willy Loman, Mamet's heroes appear entrapped and frustrated by their settings; they often seem as confused about their place in the home as in the cosmos. However, whereas Tom and Willy exteriorize their inner frustrations and talk (usually ineffectually) about their environments, Mamet's heroes in many works lack the consciousness to perceive that the exfoliated urban apartment as setting even functions as an architectural monument to and psychological projection of their spiritual immobility. Such insight, Mamet implies, seems beyond their ken.

III
The Semiotic of Mamet's City

Mamet (like Eliot) presents unreal cities. Mamet's representations, accordingly, are less concerned with a meticulous staging of objective reality—the alluvia of urban existence—than with the social forces encoded within his cities. Roland Barthes, in *The Elements of Semiology* and in his other studies of architectural semiotics and urbanism, suggests that a "semiotic of the city" holds the city itself as a "text," a text scripted and enacted by the city's denizens.[14] For Barthes, the architectonics of the city are reflected, not merely in the styles of buildings and their immediate surroundings but, more importantly, in what transpires within the cityscape: the everyday life of the common person, the symbolic activities engendered in the commonplaces of a routinized life, the merchandise and exchanges, the whole social practice of the city dwellers. As Barth argues in his *Mythologies*, the commonplaces often invite a distortion of the social contract by blurring ethical distinctions between public virtue and private self-interest. Herbert Blau clarifies the point in *The Audience*: "This [the social distortion] is how relations that should be politically suspect are smuggled into the economic and social order as aspects of nature or natural law."[15] Barthes's theories, I believe, help place

Mamet's theater in a broader cultural perspective. As Marvin Carlson points out in *Places of Performance: The Semiotics of Theatre Architecture*, "Barthes calls particular attention to the center of the city as an area charged with signification, a 'ludic space' where the most concentrated encounters between inhabitants occur, and where, of course, theatres have often tended to gather."[16] Mamet scales down such "ludic space," his spectacles occurring most often in a locale that is *other*, rather than central, to the city's ludic space; but the encounters his characters experience are no less charged with "signification." If, as Carlson's study (echoing Barthes's diachronics) implies, examining "the components of a building and their interrelationships in terms of social and cultural messages" reveals a telling "articulation of space. . . through the choice of visual, decorative elements,"[17] then Mamet's sets—his "buildings"—provide audiences with a telling emblem of the playwright's cultural poetics.

A closer look at selected Mamet works suggests that the social semiotics encoded in his sets foregrounds for the audience a broader matrix of cultural and ethical associations. Hence Mamet's sets are central to his vision because, as Carlson observes, "Culturally we learn to read the messages of theatre spaces, locations, and decoration just as we do the many related architectural and urban codes by means of which we intellectually structure our environment."[18]

Mamet's theater spaces are characterized, as noted earlier, by places of work: the office or some other place where business deals are negotiated. For Mamet, such places of performance become what Walter Benjamin in *Illuminations* calls "cultural treasures." *Lakeboat, Sexual Perversity in Chicago, The Water Engine, Mr. Happiness, American Buffalo, A Life in the Theatre, Edmond*, and *The Shawl* all at some point (if not completely) take place within an urban place-of-work context.[19] The bars, whorehouses, or smoke-filled back rooms where ritualized poker games are played (as in Mamet's cinematic text, *House-of-Games*) become almost carnivalized parodies of Barthes's "ludic spaces." It seems clear, therefore, that Mamet's cultural objects shaping his sets may be "read" as signs, culturally encoded signals energizing his cultural poetics. Certainly in Mamet's world art and culture, as with human relationships and the environments in which those tragicomic relationships come into view, are devalued, exchanged, compromised: fiscal capital replaces cultural and spiritual capital. Thus Mamet's theater achieves its representations by verbal and nonverbal signifiers that dramatize (and traumatize), as Greenblatt puts it, "the collective dynamic circulation of pleasures, anxieties, and interests." Greenblatt, in his fascinating account of Shakespeare's cultural poetics, notes that there were many modes of cultural exchange from which Shakespeare drew his mimetic power, including appropriation, purchase, and symbolic acquisition. If in the English Renaissance "Money is only one kind of cultural capital,"[20] for Mamet living in a postmodern America, money becomes one of *the* driving cultural forces behind the circulation of social energy. In Mamet's Macbethean world, where "fair is foul and foul is fair," everything is negotiable. Thus for Teach in *American Buffalo*, free enterprise becomes a license to rob. The following exchange, laced with comedy and wit, reveals Teach's seemingly convincing argument. Its persuasiveness, of course, quickly dissolves when measured against his greediness, a selfishness that culminates with his ridiculous tirade near the end of the play when he becomes a shrill parody of the very ideals to which he professes to aspire:

TEACH:	You know what is free enterprise?
DON:	No. What?
TEACH:	The freedom . . .
DON:	. . . yeah?
TEACH:	Of the *Individual* . . .
DON:	. . . yeah?
TEACH:	To Embark on Any Fucking Course that he sees fit.
DON:	Uh-huh . . .
TEACH:	In order to secure his honest chance to make a profit. Am I so out of line on this?
DON:	No.
TEACH:	Does this make me a Commie?
DON:	No.
TEACH:	This country's *founded* on this, Don. You know this.[21]

The humor of watching small-time would-be thieves buffalo themselves darkens somewhat by the 1980s. Mamet's heroes still dazzle audiences with their skewed philosophical debates justifying some dimly perceived ideal or truth while trying to nudge their way past an "associate" (as Mamet often labels a business partner) to close a deal in such a way that plainly negates that ideal or truth. The comedy remains, and audiences still gaze at characters whose verbal wizardry seems to validate their business as sacrament mentality. But the comedy becomes more rarefied, the ironies more troubling. By the time Mamet composes *Glengarry Glen Ross*, entrepreneurial greed has devolved into a vaudevillian leitmotif; in this play, the pursuit of money under the guise of free enterprise becomes an excuse to deceive and steal. We see the unfettered pursuit of the Deal throughout Act II, but the point also surfaces at the end of the first act when Ricky Roma reinvents Teach's quasi-philosophical reasoning in his conversation with the unsuspecting James Lingk: "I do those things which seem correct to me *today*."[22] Such well-known rationalizations appear throughout Mamet's theater, as seen when Bobby Gould explains to Karen in *Speed-the-Plow* his views that plainly are extensions of ethical perversities reified in *American Buffalo* and *Glengarry Glen Ross*:

> KAREN: Is it a good film?
> GOULD: Well, it's a commodity. And I admire you for not being ashamed to ask the question. Yes, it's a good question, and I don't *know* if it is a good film. "What about Art?" I'm not an artist. Never said I was, and nobody who sits in this chair can be. I'm a businessman. "Can't we try to make good films?" Yes. We try. . . . The question: Is there such a thing as a good film which loses money? In general, of course. But, really, not. For *me*, 'cause if the films I make lose money, then I'm back on the streets with a sweet and silly smile on my face, they lost money cause nobody saw them, it's my fault . . . .You *see*? This is the way things are. (*SP* 41)

Indeed! To be sure, the theatergoer in all likelihood responds to Bobby Gould's street-wise savvy and wry sense of humor. But what makes the above exchange theatrically so powerful is that Mamet underpins the dialogue with a darker vision. Simply put, money, exchange, and commodity fetishism so pervade *Speed-the-Plow* as well as Mamet's theater as a whole that intimate relations seem like the buffalo alluded to in *American Buffalo*—on the brink of extinction. The humor remains. But in place of love we find sex, lies, and money, and if there's capital gain, such free enterprise-gain takes on any social form necessary for that moment. As Thorstein Veblen argues throughout

Theory of the Leisure Class, human desires are fulfilled only after the individual dons a predatory mask. Hence Edmond's monetary negotiations with the Girl at the peep show in scene five in *Edmond*, who quickly gets on with business, are symbolically much more than mere sexual negotiation; within Mamet's mimetics, the following exchange becomes an inverted cultural emblem for our collective loss of spirit, eros: "Take your dick out. (*Pause.*) Take your dick out. (*Pause.*) Come on. Take your dick out" (31). No wonder in a 1990 essay Mamet wrote, "the true nature of the world as between men and women is sex, and any other relationship between us is an elaboration, an approximation or an avoidance."[23] The three preceding examples from *American Buffalo*, *Glengarry Glen Ross*, and *Edmond* underscore the spiritual dislocation, of course, of Mamet's heroes. But Mamet pushes his aesthetic further by placing his characters in a world *bereft of Nature*. Near the beginning of this essay I alluded to the American view of Nature, and I would now like to consider the ways in which this paradigm relates to Mamet's vision.

IV
Mamet and the American View of Nature

Scholars of Early American Literature and the American Renaissance are all well aware of the particularly American way of regarding Natural phenomenon. Such classics as F. O. Matthiessen's *American Renaissance: Art and Expression in the Age of Emerson and Whitman*, Perry Miller's *Errand into the Wilderness*, *The New England Mind: From Colony to Province* and *The American Transcendentalists*, R. W. B. Lewis's *The American Adam: Innocence, Tragedy and Tradition in the Nineteenth Century*, and Leslie A. Fiedler's *Love and Death in the American Novel* in various ways explore the mythic impact Nature exerted on the American creative psyche. So, too, with many more recent studies, a few of which include Sacvan Bercovitch's *The American Jeremiad* and *The Puritan Origins of the American Self*, Andrew Delbanco's *The Puritan Ordeal*, Lawrence Buell's *Literary Transcendentalism*, Richard Slotkin's *The Fatal Environment: The Myth of the Frontier in the Age of Industrialization, 1800-1890* and *Regeneration through Violence: The Mythology of the American Frontier, 1600-1800*, Michael H. Cowan's *City of the West: Emerson, America and Urban Metaphor*, Ursula Brumm's *American Thought and*

Religious Typology, Annette Kolodny's *The Lay of the Land: Metaphor as Experience and History in American Life and Letters* and *The Land Before Her: Fantasy and Experience of the American Frontier, 1630–1860*, and James Hoopes's *Consciousness in New England: From Puritanism and Ideas to Psychoanalysis and Semiotic*. These studies differ greatly in methodology and emphasis, and they do not use Nature necessarily as their major critical theses; yet they underscore the extraordinary place of Nature as a divine and secular force within our writers and culture. These historiographic studies illuminate the ways in which, as Donald Weber observes, "the originating, generative power of the Puritan imagination continues to shape the way we tell the American literary story, indeed the way we explain the development of American culture."[24]

Interestingly, in reviewing the history of intellectual ideas relative to dramatic literature and theory, I found little to suggest that the critical discourse of contemporary drama takes into account this "American view of Nature." So at this point I would like to outline the major intellectual as well as artistic ideas underpinning this unique American view of Nature and then return to Mamet's plays and their relationship to Nature.

The nineteenth-century American writers we most often align with Romanticism were intrigued by the relationship between the individual and Nature. These writers presupposed the magical force of a personified Nature: she could *teach*, and her lessons metonymically as well as metaphorically encoded eternal truths that, once internalized, guided the individual through a Fallen world. Emerson and Whitman, for example, often present the human observer in some kind of dramatic encounter with Nature: the person sallies into Nature, alone, and typically experiences some kind of epiphany; above all, out of this dramatic encounter the individual discovers life-defining, significant facts about the self, the other, and the cosmos. Most American fictions, from the Puritans through the Transcendentalists, play off of this essentially Romantic paradigm: a vision of experience in which Nature's capacity to *teach* is linked with our ability to fathom Nature's meanings. Whether expressed through religious meditation, spiritual autobiography, or some version of the American Dream myth, our nation's literary canon often reflects this God-Nature-Human typology. Perhaps Arthur Miller places the role of the dream myth in perspective when he explains:

> The American Dream is the largely unacknowledged
> screen in front of which all American writing plays itself
> out—the screen of the perfectibility of man. Whoever is
> writing in the United States is using the American Dream
> as an ironical pole of his story. Early on we all drink up
> certain claims to self-perfection that are absent in a large
> part of the world. People elsewhere tend to accept, to a
> far greater degree anyway, that the conditions of life are
> hostile to man's pretensions. The American idea is
> different in the sense that we think that if we could only
> touch it, and live by it, there's a natural order in favor of
> us; and that the object of a good life is to get connected
> with that live and abundant order. And this forms that
> context of irony for the kind of stories we generally tell
> each other. After all, the stories of most significant
> literary works are of one or another kind of failure. And
> it's a failure *in relation to* that screen, that backdrop. I
> think it pervades American writing, including my own.
> It's there . . . an aspiration to an innocence that when
> defeated or frustrated can turn quite murderous, and we
> don't know what to do with this perversity; it never
> seems to "fit" us.[25]

Just as our dramatic literature from O'Neill to Shepard certifies Miller's observation, so our recent scholarly studies concerning American literary history confirm Miller's ideas.

In *The Frontier Experience and the American Dream*, for instance, Mark Busby, David Mogen, and Paul Bryant suggest that "historically the existence of a frontier settlement, and of unsettled and even unknown lands beyond, has generated in the American literary imagination a set of images, attitudes, and assumptions that have shaped our literature into a peculiarly American mold. The frontier experience has so profoundly altered our cultural history that it affects our sense of ourselves even today, and thus far its central importance to our literary tradition has not been fully recognized."[26] Indeed, the transference of Nature into myth, and myth into reality not only underscores the Bakhtinian dialogicism of the American view of Nature but also aesthetically empowers American literature—including our dramatic literature—from Mather to Mamet. In one sense, of course, this is nothing new. The Ancient Greeks, especially Homer and Sophocles, exploited the signifying elements of Natural phenomena to explain the Mysteries and the Furies. Or the medieval and Renaissance narratives and dramatic poetry clearly address this earthly and divine correspondence. As John M. Steadman argues in *Nature into Myth*, "As images, examples, hieroglyphs, types these natural phenomena point to an intelligible order beyond that of sense, or a spiritual order beyond that of reason. For a poet trained in this mode of sensibility, the simple objects of nature are usually only the starting point, not the end, of contemplation. A yellow primrose will be more than a yellow primrose to him; he will read it as a hieroglyph or signature of some moral or metaphysical truth. In an oak or rock he will see more than a tree or stone; he will recognize an emblem of constancy."[27] But in another sense, in American literature there is a unique "Americanness" to interpreting Nature that is at once indebted to ancient archetypes but at the same time expresses itself in a cadence and metaphysics defining a Puritan Christocentric universe as well as a large aspect of the American literary imagination. Mamet is acutely aware of this tradition. What follows does not to imply that this "American view of Nature" is the *only* paradigm suitable for understanding an all-ecompassing theory of American literature, but it sheds light on Mamet's re-historicizationist theater and may suggest further possibilities for future studies.

V
From Myth to Reality

Crossing the ocean will underscore the uniqueness of the American view of Nature. The English Romantic movement was largely inspired by man's desire to re-establish a passionate, felt kinship with his Natural world. Indeed, during and immediately following the age of Shakespeare and Donne, the human individual seemed to have gradually lost his way about and his role in the Natural rhythms of the universe. Toward the latter part of the eighteenth century, the connections linking the self to one's Natural surroundings had apparently collapsed. So, as Clark Griffith observes, for many of the initial writers we tend to associate with English Romanticism, the artistic goal was to reconstruct an aesthetic as well as psychological bridge, cross it more freely and with greater assurance, and thus re-enter into a more fulfilling relationship with Nature.[28]

But surveying the history of ideas, suggests Griffith, we find that "no such background precedes the rise of American romanticism." The new American, unsettled in his or her brave new world, was too exposed to Nature as a physical as well as metaphysical force to assume that the ways of man somehow run separately from the ways of Nature. As Griffith explains: "Set down face to face with Natural experiences at their most complex and demanding—dependent for his bare survival upon the behavior of forest and river, sea and soil—the American could hardly conclude that his physical surroundings were anything less than real and immediate. At a time when the European had sensed a wider and wider cleavage between Nature and himself, the American was scrutinizing events in Nature and finding them to be unquestionably *there* and unfailingly meaningful."[29]

For the Puritan struggling with the landscape in seventeenth-century America, then, Nature became a divine force, an enabling typological model. The immediacy, the presentness of the Natural surroundings for the Puritan was so palpable, so overwhelming that his struggle with the forests, rivers, and seasons prefigured a Darwinian world in which, indeed, only the fittest (and the elect) might survive in a determinist environment. Out of this Puritan ordeal came the possibility of grace and insight, for Nature embodied essential *Truths*.

These Truths, moreover, were signs, codes, clues sent from God: the rugged New England landscape; the brutal winters; the swollen rivers were not merely physical properties but divine reminders of humankind's hard life in a post-lapsarian world. Ever re-visioning an indeterminate universe, the Puritan viewed Cotton Mather's dog as more than an animal. When his dog urinated with him behind the same wall, Mather truly believed that this was a message from Heaven, a daily reminder that "the functions of the beast are likewise the function of depraved mankind."[30] For an audience nearing the twenty-first century, such correspondences surely seem trite, perhaps unbelievable. For the American settler, though, such signifiers confirmed the Puritan belief that Nature was a teacher whose lessons were designed by God for our profit and edification. Griffith places this attitude in perspective when suggesting that, "trivial or forced though they may seem to be, these readings of experience clearly indicate what Nature signified to the Puritan. Natural processes were his intimate and intimately known mentors. They supplied him with visible clues to which he might turn in order to spell out the wishes, the precepts and the chastisements of his invisible God."[31] Jonathan Edwards a century later essentially agreed with Mather. Nature was inescapably real, there, and the teacher of God's ways. The water, sky, rocks, snakes—Nature herself—overflowed with meaning, Truth, and were objects and elements whose "excellencies" reflected "divine excellencies." Mamet is, I suspect, too much the postmodern to accept these Natural correspondences, and he hardly celebrates the environment the way that the poet W. S. Merwin does, but when he talks about "the intrinsic soul of the culture" and our "economic system," we see that he links them to Nature:

> I think that human nature is altered by certain essential aspects of life in a given place, at a given time. For example, the same people live in California and Vermont, but the human nature is conditioned by such factors as the different flow of seasons, the difficulties of earning a living from the soil. So although human nature remains the same, it's tempered by different climates and different locales. The economic system is an outgrowth of this conditioning.[32]

Our earlier American literature, including Benjamin Franklin's practical ways to achieve salvation in *The Way to Wealth*, surely laid the ideological groundwork for Mamet's reflection.

By the time the Transcendentalists emerged, this attitude of looking at Nature as a teacher was, for many, a given. Thoreau saw in the pond ripples of water, but the concentric circles emanating became yet another connection with spirituality. Emerson's famous analogies comparing Natural experiences with religious insights reinforced the Puritan notion that Natural phenomena had direct symbolic equivalencies. The Puritans and the Emersonians, then, despite their theological differences, fostered for over two hundred years this unique American view of Nature. Not only was Nature most immediate and overwhelming and at times destructive, but Nature was personified and gender specific.[33] Nature was endowed with human intelligence, psychologized as a benevolent instructress, and most Americans, be they farmers or intellectuals, were inclined to accept this unique view of Nature. If the American commonfolk as for the greatest of our philosophers and writers sallied forth into Emerson's happy vision of Nature, these people would emerge from the forest with Providential lessons that would energize them. The pot of gold surely was just beyond the rainbow, a point Mamet indirectly alludes to in his essay, "Chicago":

> In our beloved Windville we curse the cold and revel in being the most senseless spot in North America to spend the winter in. But the air feels new, and all things still seem possible, as they did to Willa Cather and Sherwood Anderson and Willard Motley and Hemingway and Frank Norris and Saul Bellow and all the other Chicago writers who—when speaking of Home—finally wrote the same story. It was and is a story of possibility, because the idea in the air is that the West is beginning, and that life is capable of being both understood and enjoyed.[34]

Nearing the end of his career, Emerson himself knew that his All Seeing Eye theories connecting the Me to the Not Me would no longer harmonize with external reality, yet his optimistic Natural paradigm sustained a long-standing American tradition of bestowing upon Nature a religious value, and its mythic allure, its unstated but felt promise, may be located in Mamet's preceding remarks from "Chicago." Thus the physical landscape as a Natural objectification of this American view of Nature

> offered the possibility of new land, new resources, seemingly inexhaustible, yet to be gained. The frontier as the limit of existing society demarcated the line beyond which beckoned freedom from existing social and political restraints. In effect, the frontier was the gateway through which one might escape from time into space, from bounds to boundlessness, and from the works of corrupt and corrupting humanity to the works of God in uncorrupted time.[35]

If the Emersonians personified Nature *blessed* with human intelligence, by the mid-nineteenth century there emerged, too, a darker, more threatening interpretation of Nature. Nature, for Melville, Dickinson, and Twain may also be *cursed* with human personifications. For these post-romantic writers, Nature may be a helpful guide, a willing teacher, but she may also be malevolent, the saboteur, the one orchestrating evil in the world. Nature as malevolent instructress may deliberately withhold knowledge and truth from the human pupil. So the Emersonian notion that we glean from the environment Nature's deepest secrets becomes complicated, modified—modernized: the human searcher returns from his or her encounter with Nature, not with clear answers, but with crossed signals at the very least, and, at worst, with no answers at all. If for Melville and Dickinson, Nature imparts clues to experiences, those signs are too often ambiguous, vague, baffling. By the time American literature arrives at the turn of the century, the modernist sensibility first intimated by Melville in *Moby-Dick* and by Dickinson in such poems as "I heard a fly buzz when I died" and "A Light exists in Spring" was firmly ingrained in the psyches of Frank Norris, Stephen Crane, and Theodore Dreiser: Nature exteriorizes herself as the octopus, the menacing fire engine, and the safe that clicks shut. As American literature prior to World War II evolves, outer experiences confirmed the Naturalistic philosophy that was central to Ibsen, Strindberg, and Zola: the individual is reduced to an insignificant speck in universe with little or no control over the Natural forces overwhelming him or her. World War I, the Depression, the Dust Bowl, global starvation, World War II: these historical events only confirmed that humankind's separation from Nature was undeniable. Gertrude Stein was right when she told Hemingway that he and his fellow expatriates were "all a lost generation," but little did she know that other generations were soon to be lost, too, in Auschwitz and Dachau, or on the outskirts of Moscow or the jungles in Burma. Or try as Ibsen's Nora might, her "heredity," or so Torvald thinks, has polluted her and her children's existences in *A Doll's House.* Hemingway's famous "biological trap" in *A Farewell to Arms* only reinforced the givenness of Naturalism. So from the narrator in Charlotte Perkins Gilman's "The Yellow Wall-Paper" to the Bundrens in Faulkner's *As I Lay Dying*, from the alienated speaker in such Frost poems as "Design," "Bereft," or "Once By the Pacific" (speakers who wish to learn from Nature but can never venture far out nor in deep) to the arresting encounter Delia has with the snake in Zora Neale Hurston's "Sweat," Nature has appeared in our literary canon as an animating myth. Royall Tyler may be credited with Americanizing our native stage in 1787 with *The Contrast*, but his Sheridan-like satire in no way could anticipate the kind of contrasts that, by the 1990s, a Mamet would witness.

Mamet's theater measures the distance we have traveled from the classic American view of Nature. Essentially, a Romantic paradigm has gradually transformed through a cultural process of destabilization. If the American Romanticist perceived Nature as a benevolent instructress who was predictable and reliable, Mamet and the contemporary artist can no longer regard Nature with the divine simplicity that the Emersonians for the most part did. Beginning with Melville and Dickinson and continuing in the twentieth century with Frost, Eliot, and others, Nature *had* to be viewed as a much more ambiguous and sinister entity. Political, industrial, and cultural realities forced the modern writer to re-think Nature's capacities to yield Certainties. The ambiguity of the Natural (dis)Order of the universe, the social and mythic terrain upon which most if not all American fictions must be viewed, grows into an ironisised attitude that seems germane to most post–World War II writers, regardless of genre and cultural ideology.

By the time he emerges as a playwright in the 1970s, Mamet has inherited all of the historical and aesthetic traditions of his American literary past and therefore must reify his stage space in an image that is in harmony with the discordant timbre of the present American cultural landscape. What Griffith concludes about Frost's speakers applies to Mamet's characters as well. They are in the Emersonian sense "Men Seeing," but with "shrunken insight." They have become "Men Seeing," but in a context "when the gates of Nature have slammed nearly shut, all but closing out the human observer and rendering all but impossible the long and searching scrutinies of the American past."[36] But where Frost provides some respite for his speakers— through wit and irony his speakers keep their distance from a disillusioning Nature—Mamet plunges his players into a entropic present where Walter Cole—appropriately named *Teach* throughout a contemporary version of an American view of Nature in *American Buffalo*—has supplanted Nature as a "divine" teacher. Teach's self-serving attitude confirms the ontological split between man and Nature. In Mamet's cultural poetics, Nature has been sentenced to the outer margins of human experience, replaced by the non-Natural settings of offices, bars, prisons, automobiles, junkshops, and whorehouses and peopled with the Teaches of the world. If we now come back to see Mamet's didascalia as coded signs emblematizing such dislocation, we begin to realize the terrible beauty and veiled evil implicit in his dramatic theory and practice. In brief, Mamet's mimetics—sets, language, scopophila, the assertion of phallic power and then the annihilation of that very masculinization of space, his notion of the social contract—indicate just how far from the American view of Nature his characters have strayed. Too, the distancing from this Natural context historicizes his theater to a much greater degree than hitherto recognized.

VI
The Spiritual Profile of the U.S.A.

The ambiguity and implied evil inscribed in Mamet's performances certainly invite a number of possible ways to critique his dramaturgy, and I suspect that my American view of Nature argument ultimately breaks down when considering Mamet—or any contemporary writer. *But it must break down.* And this spiritual slippage of the body politic precisely shapes Mamet's lament for contemporary mores and ethics in the United States. In Heraclitean fashion, Mamet outlines the ideal by showing us what that ideal is not, by dramatizing the distance our culture—because of progress, technology, affluency, the atomic age, and an increasing impulse to call into question patriarchal hegemony—has fallen from a romanticized vision of the American mythic terrain. Mamet's characters and characterizations, their contradictory and frenzied actions, merely reflect what Saul Bellow calls the "spiritual profile of the U.S.A."

Mamet confirms the point in *Writing in Restaurants*, a collection of essays that clearly posits his dramatic theories. One can't help but be struck by the unity of *Writing in Restaurants* because in a majority of essays, Mamet always comes back to the same point: the moral imperative of the playwright is, as he argues in "Decay: Some Thoughts for Actors," "to attempt to bring to stage, as Stanislavsky put it, the life of the human soul" (*WR* 115). Too often, however, the audience sees the "death" of "the human soul" on the stage, and usually it is the set, its spacial impact, that not only provides the initial encoded signals that we see but also contextualizes such signals in the form of spiritual "death." The language that soon fills the stage intensifies the sense of spiritual "death" by suggesting that we must be on the brink of living in a dysteleological universe.

Still, viewing Mamet's stage at first glance seems fairly unremarkable. The audience is struck, I think, by the realism of the set: Mamet foregrounds his play space in contemporary dress that we all immediately recognize. As a place mirroring objective reality, there is something graspable about its overall arrangement. A restaurant, a bar, an office—they seem wedded to a truthful representation of the real world, founded on Mamet's meticulous perceptions of contemporary manners and life. In essence, Mamet's ordinary sets function as a culturally coded sign as well as a simulacrum, or mirror image, of outer reality: *The Duck Variations* or *Speed-the-Plow* are realistic plays set in realistic places, performed within a realistic time frame. In their straightforward spatial realism, these sets capture both Aristotelian unity and contemporary environments. All of the objects found in most Mamet plays—desks, chairs, file cabinets, lamps, tables, and so on—are props representative of the mimetic theory of art, a coherent and consistent formulation, a direct imitation of human places and possessions. Mamet deliberately chooses such stage props, for they create an overriding impression of contemporaneity: this is a play situated in the here and now by an artist who is of his time.

On the other hand, Mamet's sets and settings also embody striking nonrealistic qualities, qualities transferable mainly because of a shared understanding between actor, audience, and what the action and the *mise en scene* may signify about the play. Such a collaborative matrix adds to the *energia* of Mamet's plays. As Greenblatt observes, "We identify *energia* only indirectly, by its effects: it is manifested in the capacity of certain verbal, aural, and visual traces to produce, shape, and organize collective physical and mental experiences."[37] If Mamet's play spaces defamiliarize audiences minimally, they nonetheless invite theatergoers to question the hierarchical and patriarchal structures responsible for erecting such "realistic" performance environments— offices, bars, and so on—in the first place. Thus directors and scenic designers of a Mamet play contextualize performer, architecture, and performance space in a spectacle that, as architect Pauline Fowler claims, "embody the collective values of the society which these [architectural] forms represent."[38] Mamet, then, certainly on a psychological if not imagistic level, sabotages mere objective mimeticism. By melding the verifiable world with a figurative, imaginative world that's only hinted at, implied, identifiable by what visual artists call "negative space," Mamet's stages contribute to a nonrealistic atmosphere *and* call attention to the playwright's quarrel with American culture. This is not the blatant nonrealism of Shepard's *Operation Sidewinder* or Ionesco's *Amedee*, or the experimentalism found in, say, George Kaiser's *From Morning to Midnight* and his *Gas* trilogy, or the transformational stages of Megan Terry. Rather, Mamet's nonrealism encodes itself in the intertextuality of something as simple as a chair, or a scene enacted in a cafeteria. At least this is what the playwright would like us to believe; as he points out in "Realism":

> Why was that *particular* chair chosen? Just as that particular chair said something about the cafeteria *in* the cafeteria (its concern for looks over comfort, for economy over durability, etc.), so that chair, on stage, will say something *about the play*; so the question is: What do you, the theatrical director, wish to say *about the play?*
>
> What does the chair mean *in the play?* Does it symbolize power? Then have *that* chair. Abasement? Possession, and so on. . . . [S]houldn't that [director] *recognize* that he is consciously or unconsciously making a choice, and make the choice consciously, and in favor of an idea more specific to the play than the idea of "reality."
>
> A conscious devotion to the *Idea* of a play is a concern for what Stanislavsky called the Scenic Truth, which is to say, the truth *in this particular scene.* . . .
>
> So what if the play is set in a cafeteria? . . . Our question is *why* is the play set in a cafeteria, what does it mean that the play is set in a cafeteria, and what *aspect* of this cafeteria is important *to the meaning of the play?* (*WR* 131).

The answers to his questions bring us back, I think, to the larger cultural issues I've been exploring throughout this essay. One answer might be that Mamet's play spaces are much more complex than usually recognized: more than realistic-looking offices or clubs, these environments become subtexts themselves, implied playscripts which audiences may aurally and visually "read." This becomes a crucial element of Mamet's mimetics, his version of a theory of proxemics. And it is telling that Mamet's places of performance are not found in palaces, castles, or Trump Towers, but in junk shops and subways. Anthropologist Edward T. Hall defines proxemics as "the interrelated

observations and theories of man's use of space as a specialized
elaboration of culture,"[39] and in Mamet's theater we see that his play
spaces elaborate a culture whose denizens lead lives of reduced hopes in
marginal places. Further, his stages—the way in which his actors
perform visually, linguistically, sexually, and professionally within
these scaled down theater environments—dramatize humankind's
disassociation from home and Nature. Mikhail M. Bakhtin in *The
Dialogic Imagination* suggests that "Contemporary reality with its new
experience is retained as a way of seeing" in the novelization process,
but—and this is where Bakhtin's observations may relate to Mamet's
poetics—such reality "requires an authentic profile of the past, an
authentic other language from another time."[40] Mamet's strategy seems
to be based on invoking mythic *traces* of an American authentic past,
but he also stops short of providing a redemptive future based on the
pastness of the past. Mamet writes in "First Principles" that we live "in
a morally bankrupt time," but that "we can help to change the habit of
coercive and frightened action and substitute for it the habit of trust,
self-reliance, and cooperation" in a "society based on and adhering to
ethical first principles" (*WR* 27). One could argue that there is some
sense of affirmation at the closure of *American Buffalo* when Donny
and Bobby recover from Teach's explosion, or some hope at the end of
Edmond when Edmond responds to his cell mate. However, in the
majority of his plays he paints a much bleaker picture, dramatizing just
how far from Bakhtin's "authentic profile" we have drifted. If audiences
locate some degree of humor or redemption, such qualities must
compete with the tremendous sense of loss, irony, and satire that
threaten to vitiate consciousness.

I am not convinced Mamet would agree with my placing his
work in a mythologized context of the American view of Nature. On
the other hand, to read *Writing in Restaurants* is to see that he may be
closer to a shared, communal American literary theory than he might
admit. Throughout *Writing in Restaurants*, he laments the loss of our
mythic patterns. Thus Mamet in "Some Thoughts on Writing in
Restaurants" claims that we still need "True ritual . . . we still need the
gods." He further suggests that "'Is God dead?' and 'Why are there no
real movies anymore?' are pretty much the same question. They both
mean our symbols and our myths have failed us—that we have begun
to take them literally, and so judge them wanting . . . . When we
demand a rational and immediately practical translation of rituals, we

deny their unconscious purpose and power. . . . As these are the problems most important in our life, by denying their existence we create deep personal and communal anxiety" (*WR* 34–35). By the close of the essay, Mamet's acknowledgment of the necessity of our national myths becomes blatant. Whereas for Emerson Nature as a talismanic force was most real, for Mamet the "Emersonian belief in the concordance of the natural environment and consciousness," to use John L. Thomas' words,[41] has telescoped into a demythicized present, its magic long since buried in the conflagration of contemporary social forces. Still, the Romantic view of nature appears to intrigue the playwright; in "A Family Vacation" we learn that a Thoreauvian Mamet gazed at "a seashell and thought how very Victorian it looked, and wondered at the Multiplicity of Nature" (*WR* 63). He writes about feeling "naturally removed [from] the noise and distractions of a too-busy life," and, engulfed by Nature as any Emersonian would have been, experienced "the regenerating rhythm of the surf," an archetypal rhythm in which a person "could be healed because the natural order was allowed to reassert itself" (*WR* 64). Thus despite a semiotic that calls attention to an aleatoric and defleshed present, Mamet tempers his mimetics with a profound sense of history and myth. In "Concerning *The Water Engine*," he argues that "Myths and fables live on without advertising . . . with no one profiting from their retelling. The only profit in the sharing of a myth is to those who participate as storytellers or a listeners, and this profit is the shared experience itself, the *celebration* of the tale, and of its truth" (*WR* 107–108). Lest there by any doubt about his postmodernist American view of Nature, read "Decay: Some Thoughts For Actors," in which Mamet observes, "The problems which beset us are an attempt of the universe to, by natural selection, if you will, discover that one thing which will bring about a state of rest" (*WR* 113). As an essayist, he outlines a God-Nature-Human typology that sounds surprisingly close to the classic American view of Nature described earlier:

> If you can keep in touch with natural processes, with yourself and your God, with the natural rudiments of your profession—the human necessity to tell and hear stories—with the natural process of growth and decay, then you can, I think, find peace, even in the theater. (*WR* 116)

VII
Mamet as Ethical Theatrician

The detectable optimism found throughout much of *Writing in Restaurants*, however, is seldom found in his theater. In a Mamet play, "Things Change." Or perhaps Things Do Not Change, his characters remaining ossified spirits, divided against the self and the other, against home and Nature. At best, they reflect his indebtedness to Thorstein Veblen, whose *Theory of the Leisure Class* underscores human action and response in terms of "Pecuniary Emulation," imperialist ownership, sexual roles as first seen in tribal communities, honor, invidious comparisons, and the relationship between self-worth and wealth. Mamet *is* a theatrician of the ethical. But his characters, sets, and overall situations map out a predatory world in which "the slipstream of history, the narrativizing ground upon which all recognitions are made,"[42] remains forever a distant force. Juxtaposed with American history and its mythic implications, his plays outline a tragic world in which, perhaps, only the fittest (and surely the greediest) might survive. Hence Barker's lines in *The Water Engine* ratify, Mamet suggests, the gulf between idea and reality: "And now we leave the Hall of Science, the hub of our Century of Progress Exposition. Science, yes, the greatest force for Good and Evil we possess. The Concrete Poetry of Humankind. Our thoughts, our dreams, our aspirations rendered into practical and useful forms. Our science is our self."[43] Benjamin Franklin might have appreciated such comments, but I am less than convinced that Emerson, not to mention Mamet, would.

It seems appropriate to close with *Reunion*, a play whose title might better read as *Disunion*. Bernie tells Carol that he is "a happy man" who works at "a good job," but his uneasiness remains:

> People always talk about going out to the country or getting back to nature and all the time I say, 'Yeah, yeah,' and what does it mean?
> I see the logic of it, but it means nothing to me. Because my entire life I'm looking for a way around.
> Do you know what I mean?
> Like drinking, certainly, or with your mother, or my second wife. . . . Being in debt—there was never a reason for all that money trouble—and changing jobs all the

time . . . so what does it get me but dumber and dumber,
and I'm a cynic. (22–23)

The cause for his cynicism, his Heideggerian *angst* about his being-in-
the world, remains a mystery to Bernie, particularly when we see the
contemporary world in which he and Carol live: "It's a fucking jungle
out there. And you got to learn the rules because *nobody's* going to
learn them for you" (24–25). Thus true knowledge about the universe
can, in Mamet's world, only be purchased, as the almost poetic lines
continue:

> You wanna drink? Go drink.
> You wanna do *this?* Pay the price.
> Always the price. Whatever it is.
> And you gotta know it and be prepared to pay it if you
> don't want it to pass you by.
> And if you don't know that, you gotta find it out, and
> that's all I know. (24)

* * *

O'Neill would return to the home as set and setting for his richly
autobiographical plays and Miller to the primal family matrix within
his best works. So, too, with the best of Williams, Albee, Shepard, and
Lanford Wilson. But it is only fitting that Mamet's plays occur outside
the home, his characters left to experience what in *Reunion* is "the
fucking jungle out there" and their disconnection from both home and
Nature. Out of such experience emerges no epiphany. Rather, his
characters merely internalize the messy inconclusiveness of their
misspent lives, without the reassurances of some higher consciousness.
So Mamet's following observation is hardly surprising: "As the Stoics
said, either gods exist or they do not exist. If they exist, then, no doubt,
things are unfolding as they should; if they do *not* exist, then why
should we be reluctant to depart a world in which there are no gods?"
(*WR* 114). This stands as the metaphysical question Mamet raises, and
refuses to resolve, in his theater. The resolutions, whatever they may
be, are left for the audience to ponder.

Notes

I would like to thank two of my colleagues at Georgia State University, Robert Sattelmeyer and Janet Gabler-Hover, as well as Martin Jacobi of Clemson University, all of whom made intelligent suggestions for revising this essay.

1. David Mamet, *Sexual Perversity in Chicago and The Duck Variations* (New York: Grove Press, 1978), p. 40. All further references are to this edition and will be cited parenthetically in the essay.

2. David Mamet, "All Men Are Whores: An Inquiry," in *Goldberg Street: Short Plays and Monologues* (New York: Grove Press, 1985), p. 189.

3. David Mamet, *Edmond* (New York: Grove Press, 1983), p. 77.

4. David Mamet, *Speed-the-Plow* (New York: Grove Press, 1988), p. 40. All further references are to this edition and will be cited parenthetically.

5. David Mamet, *The Spanish Prisoner*, in *Goldberg Street*, p. 22.

6. Stephen Greenblatt, *Shakespearean Negotiations: The Circulation of Social Energy in Renaissance England* (Berkeley, Calif.: University of California Press, 1988), p. 13.

7. Raynette Halvorsen Smith, "Intersections Between Feminism and Post-modernism: Possibilities for Feminist Scenic Design," *Journal of Dramatic Theory and Criticism* 4 (Spring 1990): 163.

8. Ruby Cohn, "Twentieth-Century Drama," in *The Columbia Literary History of the United States*, ed. Emory Elliott et al. New York: Columbia University Press, 1988), p. 1117.

9. Greenblatt, p. 7.

10. David Mamet, *Lakeboat* (New York: Grove Press, 1981), pp. 24–25.

11. David Mamet, *Reunion [and] Dark Pony* (New York: Grove Press, 1979), p. 29. All further references are to this edition and will be cited parenthetically.

12. Tennessee Williams, *The Glass Menagerie* (New York: New Directions, 1970), p. 22.

13. Arthur Miller, *Death of a Salesman* (New York: Viking, 1975), p. 17.

14. Roland Barthes, *The Elements of Semiology*, trans. Annette Lavers and Colin Smith (New York, 1968), p. 63.

15. Herbert Blau, *The Audience* (Baltimore, Md.: The Johns Hopkins University Press, 1990), p. 346.

16. Marvin Carlson, *Places of Performance: The Semiotics of Theatre Architecture* (Ithaca, N.Y.: Cornell University Press, 1989), p. 11.

17. Carlson, p. 9.

18. Carlson, p. 206.

19. Even his children's plays, which for generic reasons I am not treating in this essay, fit a similar pattern: Mamet locates *The Poet and the Rent* in a theater and *The Frog Prince* in the woods. Although *The Revenge of the Space Pandas, or Binky Rudich and the Two-Speed Clock* ostensibly occurs in a house, Mamet again quickly transcends the home, allowing the imagination of Leonard Rudich, one of the lead characters, to move the setting to, among other intergalatic places, the "Fourth World in the Goolagong System." See David Mamet, *Three Children's Plays* (New York: Grove Press, 1986), p. 90.

20. Greenblatt, p. 12.

21. David Mamet, *American Buffalo* (New York: Grove Press, 1975), pp. 72–73.

22. David Mamet, *Glengarry Glen Ross* (New York: Grove Press, 1984), p. 49. (It's somehow fitting Mamet garnered the Pulitzer Prize for *Glengarry* in 1984: after watching the play during the Broadway run, I thought that maybe Orwell's vision did came true in Mamet's dystopian-like play.)

23. David Mamet, "In the Company of Men," *Playboy* 37 (April 1990): 173.

24. Donald Weber, "Historicizing the Errand," *American Literary History* 2 (Spring 1990): 101.

25. Matthew C. Roudané, "An Interview with Arthur Miller," in *Conversations with Arthur Miller*, ed. Matthew C. Roudané (Jackson: University Press of Mississippi, 1987), pp. 361–362.

26. Mark Busby, David Mogen, and Paul Bryant, "Introduction: Frontier Writing as a 'Great Tradition' of American Literature," in *The*

Frontier Experience and the American Dream, eds. Busby, Mogen, and Bryant (College Station: Texas A&M University Press, 1989), p. 3.

27. John M. Steadman, *Nature into Myth* (Pittsburgh, Pa.: Duquesne University Press, 1979), p. 3.

28. For a more comprehensive discussion of this point, see Clark Griffith, "Frost and the American View of Nature," *American Quarterly* 20 (Spring 1968): 21–37. Much of what follows in my discussion has been influenced by Griffith's various studies in American literature, and I gratefully acknowledge my indebtedness to him here.

29. Griffith, p. 23.

30. Griffith, p. 24.

31. Griffith, p. 24.

32. David Savran, *In Their Own Words: Contemporary American Playwrights* (New York: Theatre Communications Group, 1988), p. 141.

33. For further discussion of a gender-centered conception of Nature in American literature and the unique problems it presents for feminist critics in particular, see Annette Kolodny's *The Lay of the Land: Metaphor as Experience and History in American Life and Letters* (Chapel Hill, N.C.: University of North Carolina Press, 1975) and, relative to the American dramatic imagination, Linda Ben-Zvi's "'Home Sweet Home': Deconstructing the Masculine Myth of the Frontier in Modern American Drama," in Busby et al., pp. 217–225.

34. David Mamet, *Writing in Restaurants* (New York: Viking, 1986), p. 71. All further references are to this edition and will be cited parenthetically in the essay.

35. Busby et al., p. 6.

36. Griffith, p. 35.

37. Greenblatt, p. 6.

38. Pauline Fowler, "Women Building Culture: Architecture for Feminists," in *Work in Progress: Building Feminist Culture*, ed. Rhea Tregebov (Toronto, Canada: The Women's Press, 1987), p. 139.

39. Edward T. Hall, *The Hidden Dimension* (New York: Doubleday, 1966), quoted in Smith, p. 158.

40. Mikhail M. Bakhtin, *The Dialogic Imagination*, trans. Caryl Emerson and Michael Holquist (Austin, Tx.: University of Texas Press, 1981), pp. 29–30.

41. John L. Thomas, "The Uses of Catastrophism: Lewis Mumford, Vernon L. Parrington, Van Wyck Brooks, and the End of American Regionalism," *American Quarterly* 42 (June 1990): 223.

42. Blau, p. 251.

43. David Mamet, *The Water Engine [and] Mr. Happiness* (New York: Grove Press, 1978), p. 53.

"INTIMATE VOICES": *LAKEBOAT* AND MAMET'S QUEST FOR COMMUNITY

Michael Hinden

> Sunday nights we would go visiting. Coming home we'd
> play the car radio. It was dark and we'd be rolling through
> the prairies outside Chicago. CBS 'Suspense' would be
> on the air, or 'Yours, Truly, Johnny Dollar—the Man
> with the Million-Dollar Expense Account.' And the trip
> home always ended too soon; we'd stay in the car until
> my dad kicked us out—we wanted to hear how the story
> ended; we wanted the trip to be endless—rolling through
> the prairies and listening to the intimate voices.[1]

Mamet's essays are pungent and revealing. Here, in the opening paragraph of "Radio Drama," he distills a number of his favorite dramatic themes: nostalgia for family ties, the importance of the father-son relationship, the brooding loneliness of the midwestern landscape, a fascination with men whose lives are dedicated to dollars, suspense, dark journeys, and the mysterious intimacy of the human voice. Together these interests combine to form Mamet's continuing dramatic quest to establish the groundwork for a vision of community that could recreate the closeness of family life. The essential task of drama, he tells us elsewhere, is to duplicate the conditions of intimacy and enchantment that made those boyhood car trips seem so magical, and to recall for adult audiences "that which we desire most, which is love and a sense of belonging."[2] For Mamet, theater's purpose is to incarnate the "dream-life" of the nation;[3] its aim is "communion between the artist and the audience."[4] The playwright argues this point throughout his essays.

Through the intimacy of the human voice, theater affirms inter-
connectedness, as do certain other group activities, some as mundane as
poker-playing: "I have felt that *beyond* the fierce competition, there was
an atmosphere of *being involved in a communal* activity—that by
sitting there, we, these men, were, perhaps upholding, perhaps
ratifying, perhaps creating or re-creating some important aspect of our
community."[5]

Mamet's quest for community surfaces repeatedly in his plays.
His characters, like O'Neill's, want most of all to "belong," whatever
else may be the subject of their conversation. We might take a cue from
Mamet's discussion of *The Cherry Orchard*: no one in that play, he
insists, really cares about the orchard, although that is what the
characters mainly talk about. Rather, everybody in Chekhov's
masterpiece plays out the same scene, which concerns frustrated
sexuality.[6] So in his own plays, Mamet's characters care less about
sexual conquest and still less about business (the topics that preoccupy
them) than they do about loneliness and their failure to construct a
satisfying context for emotional security. This essay will explore that
premise, tracing the connection between intimacy, family, and
community in Mamet's work with reference to several of his plays,
primarily *Lakeboat*.

"The Most Important Institution in America"

In 1979, Mamet published two short plays in the same volume,
Reunion and *Dark Pony*. In *Reunion*, Carol, an insecure young woman
grasping for love, has an awkward meeting with her father, a recovering
alcoholic who smashed up the family twenty years earlier.

> CAROL: You know—when I was young they used to talk
> about Broken Homes.
> Today, nothing. Everyone's divorced. Every
> kid on the block's got three sets of parents.
> But. . .
> It's got to have affected my marriage. . . .
> I came from a Broken Home.
> The most important institution in America.[7]

In the companion piece, *Dark Pony*, an unidentified father and daughter—is it the same pair projected back twenty years in time?—share a lovely passage of intimacy as they drive toward home late at night. The father tells the sleepy little girl a story about an Indian brave and his loyal horse, Dark Pony, who saves the young brave from wolves. The tale is comforting and poetically embellished. Toward the end, the story's landscape (hills, prairies, valleys) blends with that through which the automobile passes in the enveloping night. The little girl knows that she is "almost home" because she remembers how the road sounds just before they get there. In the context of Mamet's *oeuvre*, this moment is a version of paradise regained: a picture of a secure relationship, an intimate voice telling a story in the night—and better than any car radio, it is the father who tells the story here—a satisfying return to home, and the message of the story itself, which promises the child that her powerful, loyal companion (Dad/Dark Pony) will always be there when needed. *Reunion*, though, reminds us that the story is made up, that the moment is transitory, and that the most important institution in America is the broken home.

Mamet himself is the child of divorced parents, which may suggest why this concern enters his work with such immediacy of feeling. In what may be his most revealing personal essay, he anatomizes the appeal of the comic book hero Superman who, far from being invulnerable as most boys imagine, is "the most vulnerable of beings, because his childhood was destroyed."[8] Mamet stresses that Superman is reduced to impotence in the presence of Kryptonite, found in fragments from his original home on the planet Krypton, which exploded. To foil his enemies who have access to Kryptonite, Superman must disguise himself; and because he cannot reveal his identity, he cannot be intimate with others.

> It is the remnants of that destroyed childhood home, and the fear of those remnants, which rule Superman's life. The possibility that the shards of that destroyed home might surface prevents him from being intimate—they prevent him from sharing the knowledge that the wimp and the hero are one. The fear of his childhood home prevents him from having pleasure.[9]

Mamet prefaces this brilliant analysis of a popular culture hero with the remark that he developed his insights while revisiting his childhood

home after an absence of twenty years. Thus the essay has
autobiographical interest, but it also sheds light on the psychology of
Mamet's male characters, who consistently adopt a pose of toughness
and aggressiveness in order to mask their own feelings of vulnerability.
We usually learn little concerning the early years of Mamet's
adult characters, but we *intuit* that few of them spring from secure and
loving families. Certainly they say little about family connections in
the present and seem pathologically afraid of intimacy. Yet they are
constantly jostling to position themselves in relation to rivals in
family-like configurations. It is interesting, for example, how in
American Buffalo three male rogues keep backing into each other until
they form an ersatz family circle. Bobby is the incompetent son
striving for paternal approval, while Teach and Donny compete for the
role of father surrogate.

> DON: You leave the fucking kid alone.
> TEACH: You want kids, you go have them.
>   I am not your fucking wife.[10]

The pseudo-family arrangement is a failure in *American Buffalo*, as it is
in Mamet's other plays, because the characters remain confused as to
the distinction between friendship and business, which in America is
the institution that governs adult relationships outside the family circle.
Consequently, the relationships are poised to unravel, because the rules
governing self-interest in the business world militate against communal
bonding. Teach's confused emotions focus the issue during his paen to
free enterprise, which he defines as the freedom of the individual to
"Embark on Any Fucking Course that he sees fit." Without this sacred
principle, he adds, Americans would still be "savage shitheads in the
wilderness . . . sitting around some vicious campfire."[11] However, the
dramatic context leads us toward the opposite conclusion—that,
compared to this, the old communal circle around the campfire was
anything but vicious, and that the substitution of the cash nexus for the
tribal unit, which functioned as an extended family, might have been a
retrograde development in human affairs.

Nowhere is Mamet's view on this subject expressed more
forcefully than in Richard Roma's monologue on individualism and
moral relativism in the opening of scene 3 of *Glengarry Glen Ross*. As
rhetoric, the function of this speech is to ensnare a prospective client

for a real estate deal, the unsuspecting James Lingk, who is sitting in an adjoining restaurant booth. Roma proffers business disguised as friendship, and Lingk indeed is drawn in. But the ultimate significance of the speech is embedded in its moral context, for Roma's virtuoso performance is bracketed by two references to excrement.

> ROMA: . . . all train compartments smell vaguely of
> shit. . . .There's an absolute morality? May *be*.
> And *then* what? . . . You ever take a dump made
> you feel you'd just slept for twelve hours. . .?[12]

To pervert intimacy by using friendship as a lure for business is to traduce communal values and represents for Mamet the key to Roma's self-disgust, his excremental vision of the world. The alternative might be defined as the communal vision, whose power is felt in Mamet's plays by its absence more often than its presence.

Community and "Communitas"

What precisely does Mamet mean by community? Perhaps his attitude may be clarified by Victor Turner's imaginative distinction between the flowing impulse toward human inter-connectedness and the actual form of social relationships as governed by time, place, and political organization. Turner uses the Latin term "communitas" to denote "a relation quality of full, unmediated communication, even communion" between human beings, whereas social structure (reflected in laws, codes, role-sets, and status distinctions) defines the formal relationships between human beings who live and work in an identifiable setting.[13] "Communitas" can be described as visionary, fleeting, or projected by desire. For Turner, it is "an essential and generic human bond, without which there could be *no* society."[14] In other words, "communitas" may be the experience that generates community, though it is not necessarily to be equated with any specific locale or institution. In fact, although community may evolve as an attempt to institutionalize "communitas," codification sooner or later degrades it, so that the emotion and the structure usually are found to be at odds. Turner theorizes that rituals, pilgrimages, and certain types of dramatic performances mediate these tensions by allowing their participants to reimagine "communitas" during a temporary break with social structure when rules of everyday interaction are suspended.

Turner's model may be useful in describing Mamet's vision of the theater as a site for family-like communion. It also may be useful in clarifying his particular concern with place. Mamet tends to see community as an idealized nexus of human relationships, not to be confused with the physical setting where his characters struggle for status and acceptance. As I have suggested, Mamet's quest for community is an extension of his mourning over family disintegration, and so the values that he ascribes to community are emotional rather than geographic or cultural. In this regard, some critics have exaggerated Mamet's self-identification as a "Chicago writer" and his attachment to the midwest as a setting for his work.[15] In actuality, the Chicago of Mamet's plays is a doleful metropolis of perversity and competition, whereas the midwest of his reminiscence is more the occasion for youthful nostalgia than the source of adult delight.[16] In his rosiest mood, Mamet perceives Chicago "not as an adversary, or as a random arena, but. . .as an extension of our dream-life"; for him, the city also represents the site of fellowship through his personal and professional association with several theater groups.[17] Of course, the playwright still recognizes the predatory nature of city life, with its economic hierarchies, class divisions, grime, and multiple anxieties: It is not so much *the* Chicago but a kind of Chicago that Mamet celebrates. Like Turner, the dramatist can tell the difference between an aggregation of people pressed together in the same geographical space and the mysterious intimation of "communitas" that sometimes thrills him when he is playing cards with friends, or mounting plays in concert with collaborators, or remembering with pleasure the disembodied voices that once linked a lonely kid to a family of radio listeners as his father's car sped across the darkened prairies of the Midwest.

Lakeboat

Lakeboat, Mamet's first play and still one of his best,[18] provides the most fully articulated perspective of his attitude toward community. The play offers a gritty depiction of the daily rounds of the crew aboard the *T. Harrison*, a merchant marine freighter out of Chicago plying a monotonous route around the Great Lakes. Life on board is repetitive, irritating, boring; yet it is close, providing the men with a substitute family structure. Here in the raw are Mamet's essential Chicagoans, sharing experience in close quarters. And here at the *margin* of the city, on a boat hugging the shore, are the makings of a true community. Unlike the hustlers of *The Water Engine, American Buffalo, Glengarry Glen Ross,* or *Speed-the-Plow,* men who are either entrepreneurs or in competition for commissions, these wage-earners are all roughly equal in status; they are all (figuratively as well as literally) in the same boat. However dissatisfied they may be with life on the lakes, life on land is even less attractive. Some of the men are married, but they rarely mention their wives or children. Shore life, as they recount it, consists of binging in bars, casual sex, and the excitement of occasional violence. It is telling that the plot of *Lakeboat* revolves around the disappearance of the ship's night cook, who may have been the victim of foul play when he left the boat in East Chicago. This is not to say that life on board is romanticized; on the contrary, the *T. Harrison* little resembles Melville's *Pequod* or the *S.S. Glencairn* of O'Neill's *The Moon of the Carribbees.* And "twenty years before the oil gauge" would be a more accurate description of life on board than "Two Years Before the Mast." Yet Mamet joins Melville, Dana, and O'Neill in depicting a rough comradeship on deck that goes some little way toward compensating the eight crewmen for their low pay, low status, and drudgery.[19]

The men of *Lakeboat* seek their closest relationships with their co-workers, and what we learn about their family lives suggests why they are driven to do so. Stan's father and mother both were alcoholics (a fact Stan cheerfully relates while drunk himself). The Fireman is divorced; so is the Cook (who, according to rumor, is able to afford two Cadillacs because he is disencumbered of family). Fred is divorced, too, although remarried. He speaks only of his "second wife," never mentioning her by name. His first wife he names in bitterness ("Denise ex-fucking Swaboda") for compelling him to pay alimony and child support. In an interesting slip he multiplies the number of his children:

JOE: You pay any alimony?
FRED: Yeah, ho, shit, did I pay? I was doing extra deck work and running to the track so that woman could fuck off and pamper the kids.
JOE: How many kids you have?
FRED: . . . . just one, actually. I don't know why I said 'kids.'[20]

This verbal tick suggests that Fred depersonalizes his family relationships—he speaks of "wife and kids" generically—while conveying to Joe his economic obligations. He does say that he visits his daughter when he can, but if he feels any real warmth for her, or for his "second wife," he conceals it. At the same time, he talks about the woman he used to smack around in high school and who still agrees to sleep with him whenever he commands, even though she is now married to someone else.

Like the other men on the boat, Fred disparages family life and expresses his affiliative instinct through contact with his fellow crew members. And like the others, Fred adheres to the code of rough talk that permits the men to vent frustration without openly discussing their sense of personal failure. It is Fred who explains the groundrule of the language used on deck to the neophyte Dale: "This is why everyone says 'fuck' all the time. . . .They say say 'fuck' in direct proportion to how bored they are." (scene 10, 27.) The allowable topics of conversation are restricted to sex, drinking, eating, fighting, shooting, mutilation, suicide, and gambling—which is to say, bodily functions, bodily harm, and chance. Almost every thought is punctuated with an obscenity; and yet there are moments of intimacy, too, and even crude attempts at transcendence, which testify to the thwarted creative energies of the men. One such flight is Stan's apostrophe to alcohol in scene 3—"Makes you an angel, A booze-ridden angel" (15)—another is Fred's ode to sex in scene 10: "I want to become one with ages of men and women before me down into eternity and goo in the muck from whence we sprung" (28). Still another is Fred's attempt to describe the poetry of horseracing (scene 13, 33), or Joe's loving description of a bridge (scene 21, 45). At these peak moments, the speakers reach through blunted language to express their deepest emotions, and their listeners seem eager to reciprocate and to affirm the bond of communication.

The men are at their liveliest when swapping stories, telling tall tales, or embroidering rumor. As C. W. E. Bigsby has observed, almost every encounter in *Lakeboat* involves story-telling, for the chief resource of these men lies in their fiction-making skills.[21] Indeed, in several instances it appears that the crew members have some difficulty separating fiction from reality. Fred and Stan argue hotly over movie heroes: which actor, they wonder, is more "stark," Johnnie Fast or Clint Eastwood? The crew's fictionalizing tendency is most pronounced in their collective myth-making in response to the fate of the missing night cook, Guigliani.

Each succeeding version of this story becomes increasingly detailed and dramatic, although (as typically happens during oral transmission of a legend) the name of the hapless crewman changes in some of the variations. In the first version, the Pierman reports that Guigliani was "rolled" by a prostitute while drunk and then fired for insubordination when he reported to the ship (scene 1, 9–12). In the next version, Collins says the nightman was "mugged" (scene 4, 17), and then adds in the retelling that the victim is now in the hospital (scene 6, 20). The Fireman invents a divorced woman as a substitute for the prostitute in his version of the tale in scene 8. In scene 11, Fred theorizes that the Mafia beat up Guigliani for welshing on gambling debts, and he embellishes his narration with a physical description of the wounds: "Ribs, back. The *back*. Hit him in the back. Left him for *dead*" (31). (Fred, it seems, is projecting his own fears, for he has gambling debts himself; later in the play he mentions a workman who was compensated by the company for losing two fingers in a winch, as if he were contemplating self-mutilation as a means of getting ready cash.) The saga of Guigliani continues in scene 23 (he is now called "Guigliami" or "Guiglialli"). The Fireman is convinced that the mysterious night cook was shot and killed by the cops or by the "G" men because he knew too much about politics (51). The final version of the story appears to be the prosaic truth: Guigliani missed the boat either because his aunt died or because he overslept; in any event, he will be picked up in Deluth. Mamet brilliantly develops the Guigliani story to dramatize the need of these men to imbue their routinized lives with adventure and melodrama. "The man lived on the sea, the man died on the sea," Fred intones, just before learning the dull truth (scene 28, 59).

Intimate Voices

The Guigliani story thus reflects the crew's communal endeavor to construct a myth that has the effect of glamorizing their shared fate. In the end, the tale remains an empty one, but it illustrates the potential of the crew to cohere through the shared medium of language. Throughout the play we glimpse additional signs of this potential through the eyes of an outsider, Dale Katzman, a middle-class college student who has taken a summer job on the boat. Dale stands in as Guigliani's replacement, which links him throughout to the crew's main object of concern. In many ways he remains on the fringe of the group, yet Dale's marginal status confers on him a special role: he becomes in effect the outsider's outsider, and as such, the men sympathize with him and take him under their wing. More importantly, they also permit themselves to confide in him, revealing intimate secrets that they hesitate to share with their grizzled companions. Indeed, there are three separate language codes operating in the play: (1) the crude, aggressive slang of the work-a-day world on deck, which sometimes can be stretched to express high emotion; (2) the formal posture of "correct" discourse reserved for boat-to-shore communication; and (3) the adjustment to intimacy made by some of the older crew members when speaking to Dale.

Dale's role on the boat, to employ a phrase that Victor Turner often uses in his anthropological studies, is "liminal" ("threshold-like") in relation to the rest of the crew.

> [Such figures] tend to be liminal and marginal people, "edgemen," who strive with a passionate sincerity to rid themselves of the clichés associated with status incumbency and role-playing and to enter into vital relations with other men in fact or imagination.[22]

According to Turner, one of the most significant functions of the marginalized individual occurs during initiation rites, when the subject typically is separated from the group prior to his readmittance in a new role (as adult, hunter, warrior, king, etc.). By virtue of some special test or experience, the initiate must discover what is most essential to the group ("communitas") during a period when his own relation to the social hierarchy is temporarily cast into limbo. Thus, the initiate is deprived of his former social status while his perceptivity is enhanced. In addition, his ulterior function is to "reinitiate" the community as a whole, which he can do by focusing the collectivity on its vital web of relationships: hence the initiation *ceremony*.[23]

It would be an exaggeration to claim that Dale successfully performs such a function for the crew of the *T. Harrison*—although in some respects his sojourn does resemble an initiation rite—or that he himself undergoes a learning experience of lasting importance. He seems largely unchanged at the end of the voyage, and so do the other men on board. Yet, as Turner points out, "communitas" often "breaks in through the interstices of structure, in liminality; through the edges of structure, in marginality;"[24] and it is through the chinks of Dale's conversations with various members of the crew that *we, the audience,* are encouraged by Mamet to glimpse the latent "stuff" of commonality that links the men, even if the vital flow between them remains partly dammed on stage.

The most intimate relationship developed in the play is that between Dale and Joe Litko, who is described in the stage directions as an Able-Bodied Seaman in his 40s or 50s. In the company of the other hard-bitten sailors, Joe's language is indistinguishable from theirs: "How the everlasting cocksucking FUCK do you know I never been to Italy?" (scene 8, 23.) But in Dale's presence he struggles to find the words that might enable him to articulate his aesthetic response to the bridge that he has been passing under once or twice a week for years: "And . . . you go underneath it and look up and all the same it's pretty. And you forget that it *does* something. But this beauty of it makes what it does all the more . . . nice. Do you know what I'm talking about?" (scene 21, 47.)

Of the permanent crew aboard the *T. Harrison*, Joe is the one most eager to share his emotions. He has been working on the lakes for twenty-three years. His father (like Stan's) died an alcoholic; his mother is blind (who takes care of her, we wonder?); there are no women in his life. To Dale he confesses that he once dreamed of becoming a ballet dancer, an admission that he carefully guards from the others. It appears that he is slowly going to pieces, for during the course of the play Joe complains of sleeplessness, tries to acquire morphine, and contemplates drowning. "I knew a guy who ate a chair," he remarks out of the blue. "Just cause nobody stopped him." (Scene 10, 30.) Joe claims that he is "sick of everything" (Scene 24, 53), and in the play's climactic scene, he confides to Dale that he once tried to commit suicide. The bungled attempt came when he grew depressed after practicing fast draws with a pistol in front of a mirror in a hotel room.

> JOE: And I . . . put the gun under my chin pointing at
>   my brain. But after a while I started feeling
>   really stupid. And I rolled over and put the gun
>   under my pillow, but held onto to it. I started.
>   You know, playing with myself, you know
>   what I mean.

DALE: I know.
JOE: A grown man. Isn't that something? (scene 26,
        58–59.)

Each element in this extraordinary confession suggests desperate
solitude, not to mention arrested development: cowboy fantasies,
pistols, masturbation, thoughts of suicide. Joe realizes the
unseemliness of the event as he narrates it to Dale, but in confessing
his most intimate secret, he reaches out to bridge a gap of loneliness
and manages, even if briefly and awkwardly, to establish a bond of trust
with his young listener.

For his part, Dale remains something of a cipher in *Lakeboat*.
His function is to elicit revelations, but he is not a fully developed
character with his own rich inner life or dilemmas. He is, after all, only
eighteen years old. In the fall he will be returning to begin his
sophomore year at a college near Boston, where he is studying English
literature, "a tough racket," as Joe drily remarks (scene 21, 45–47). A
self-effacing presence in the play, Dale falls in with the shipboard lingo
as he introduces himself to the Pierman, trades wisecracks with Skippy,
and responds sympathetically to Joe. He also listens without objection
to Fred, who describes how to brutalize women. Through it all, he
remains a passive facilitator of dramatic disclosure who discloses little
of himself. Mamet's design is to permit the audience to see with and
through Dale as a character, while the nascent community of the *T.
Harrison* tries to coalesce around him.

One reason for the ultimate failure of the community to gel is
that moments of true intimacy on board are rare. Emotion typically is
masked by undifferentiated, hostile verbiage that is inimical to precision
or self-discovery. As a consequence, the crew's impulse to collective
expression is severely hampered. The men will begin a conversation
only to turn away with a curse; or else they will fall silent, pick a
quarrel that can be resolved easily by shouting or intimidation, or divert
themselves with tall tales that may serve the function of localized myth
but which fail to provide any impetus for genuine solidarity.

This point is underscored by the new scene that Mamet added to
the play in 1983 (scene 9A in the Samuel French edition). Here the
issue of political consciousness is raised directly by Stan, as he banters
about Robin Hood and in doing so raises the issue of economic
injustice. According to Stan, people with money "want a piece of

everything" (26). Those who run the company remind him of Robin
Hood's nemesis, Bad Prince John. Fred, though, is innocent of history:
"Hey, fuck, the *past* is the past. I'm going to get a sandwich" (27).
He has no knowledge of Bad Prince John and no interest in Stan's analogy.
Mamet suggests that the Robin Hood legend carries more potential
information for the crew than the Guigliani myth of their own
invention, since the former embodies a debate over the distribution of
wealth, whereas the latter merely conveys the titilation associated with
gratuitous violence. Fred, however, turns away from Stan's discussion
and in the next scene takes solace in another social myth that allows
him to express his hostility toward women: "The way to get laid is to
treat them like shit" (scene 10, 29). In the Robin Hood myth, those
without economic power band together to strike out against the rich. In
Fred's myth, those with little economic power (working class men)
discharge their anger by striking out against those with even less power
(working class women). The pecking order is reaffirmed.

Mamet's implication here is that gender conflict is not only a
diversion from class conflict but absolutely self-destructive and abasing.
I do not wish to attribute a Marxist message to the play (Mamet's
political thinking, as far as I can gather, is fuzzy and disorganized); but
I do suggest that Mamet's allusion to the Robin Hood legend signals a
quarrel with social hierarchies and fixed status identities that he
intuitively senses are inimical to "communitas." The men of *Lakeboat*
have a similar quarrel with the world, although they fail to interpret (or
at least to articulate) the cause of their displeasure. But Mamet
interprets the quarrel for them, articulating a vision of communal
identity that the characters of *Lakeboat* struggle to perceive.

A Personal Quest

It is tempting to identify Dale Katzman as Mamet's
autobiographical emissary in *Lakeboat*. Mamet himself once spent a
summer working on a Great Lakes ore boat,[25] and the celebration in his
essays of working class tastes and masculine virtues links him to the
cast of *Lakeboat* by affinity as well as by experience. In his most recent
essay collection, *Some Freaks*, Mamet writes of his increasing desire
for communal solidarity, whether in the context of class, gender, or
ethnic affiliation. Yet as he continually reminds us, he tends to see
himself as an outsider (like Dale) who approaches solidarity only on the

fringes. Compulsively, he elbows himself into any group circle where
community is promised: he seeks out the company of men (through
such activities as card-playing, boxing, hunting, weight-lifting, and
target-shooting, not to mention battering opponents with pugil sticks
at paramilitary conventions). Apparently, he is equally sanguine in the
company of co-religionists, colleagues in the theater, families touring
Disneyland, and veterans who hang out at Harry's Hardware in Cabot,
Vermont. Were it not for the faint tone of desperation that shadows
these essays, some would appear ludicrous. Were it not for their
exuberance, even joyousness on occasion, some would appear mean-
spirited.

They are anything but that. In each of these essays Mamet
reiterates the demand for community that has driven his career. Men get
together, he keeps telling us, to play or to produce meaningful work in
concert: "The true nature of the world, as between men, is, I think,
community of effort directed towards the outside world."[26] In such
activities he delights, yet when Mamet contemplates the absence of an
overriding purpose in American life at large, he scowls. From this
concern he draws much of his authenticity and power as a writer. David
Mamet may not be a systematic thinker, but he is certain of one thing:
a vital community nourishes intimacy and dignifies the enterprise of
collective work. Surely Mamet would agree with D. H. Lawrence, who
argued in *Studies in Classic American Literature*: "Men are free when
they belong to a living, organic, *believing* community, active in
fulfilling some unfulfilled, perhaps unrealized purpose."[27] Mamet's
characters seek such freedom, but in the plays that he has written to
date, no one has found it.

Notes

1. David Mamet, "Radio Drama," *Writing in Restaurants* (New York:
Viking, 1986), p. 12.

2. Mamet, "Some Thoughts on Writing in Restaurants," *Writing in
Restaurants*, p. 36.

3. Mamet, "A National Dream-Life," *Writing in Restaurants*, 8.

4. David Mamet, "Stanislavsky and the Bearer Bonds," *Some Freaks* (New York: Viking, 1989), p. 71.

5. Mamet, "In the Company of Men," *Some Freaks*, pp. 89–90.

6. Mamet, "Notes on *The Cherry Orchard*," *Writing in Restaurants*, pp. 118–121.

7. David Mamet, *Reunion, Dark Pony: Two Plays* (New York: Grove Press, 1979), p. 29.

8. Mamet, "Kryptonite: A Psychological Appreciation," *Some Freaks*, p. 179.

9. Ibid., p. 178.

10. David Mamet, *American Buffalo* (New York: Grove Press, 1977), II: 98.

11. Ibid., pp. 72–73.

12. David Mamet, *Glengarry Glen Ross* (New York: Samuel French, Inc., 1984), p. 27.

13. Victor Turner, *Process, Performance, and Pilgrimage: A Study in Comparative Symbology* (New Delhi: Concept Publishing Co., 1980), "Appendix," p. 150.

14. Victor Turner, *The Ritual Process* (Ithaca, N.Y.: Cornell University Press, 1969), p. 95.

15. See, for example, Samuel G. Freedman, "The Gritty Eloquence of David Mamet," the *New York Times Magazine*, 21 April 1985, pp. 32–40; and C. W. E. Bigsby, *David Mamet* (London: Methuen, 1985), pp. 19–20.

16. See Mamet's essays "A Thank-You Note" and "When I was Young—A Note to Zosia and Willa" in *Some Freaks*.

17. Mamet, "A Community of Groups," *Some Freaks*, p. 100.

18. An opinion I share with Esther Harriott, who praises the play in *American Voices: Five Contemporary Playwrights in Essays and Interviews* (Jefferson, North Carolina: McFarland & Co., Inc., 1988), p. 63. Harriott's collection contains a substantial interview with Mamet.

19. Harriott suggests that *Lakeboat* parodies the classic seaboard adventure story: see *American Voices*, pp. 63–64. Bigsby mentions the possibility of Mamet's being influenced by O'Neill's early sea plays: C. W. E. Bigsby, *A Critical Introduction to Twentieth-Century Drama* (Cambridge: Cambridge University Press, 1985), p. 284.

20. David Mamet, *Lakeboat* (New York: Samuel French, Inc., 1983), Scene 15, pp. 36–37. Subsequent references are cited parenthetically. The Samuel French edition incorporates changes in the script made by Mamet after productions of the play in 1979, 1981, and 1982.

21. Bigsby, *David Mamet*, p. 23.

22. Turner, *The Ritual Process*, p. 128.

23. Victor Turner, *The Forest of Symbols* (Ithaca, N.Y.: Cornell University Press, 1967), p. 94.

24. Turner, *The Ritual Process*, p. 128.

25. Freedman, "The Gritty Eloquence of David Mamet," p. 40.

26. Mamet, "In the Company of Men," *Some Freaks*, p. 90.

27. D. H. Lawrence, *Studies in Classic American Literature* (New York: Viking, 1961 [1923]), p. 6.

DAVID MAMET AND THE METADRAMATIC TRADITION: SEEING "THE TRICK FROM THE BACK"

Deborah R. Geis

ROBERT: We *are* society. Keep your back straight, John. The mirror is your friend. (*Pause.*) What have we to fear, John, from *phenomena*? (*Pause.*) We are explorers of the *soul.* (*Pause.*)
JOHN: Is my back straight?
ROBERT: No.

—David Mamet, *A Life in the Theatre*

Metadrama, or drama that calls attention to its own status as theater or performance, faces some difficult demands for redefinition when it bumps up against the tenets of post-structuralist and post-modernist theory. On the one hand, self-referential theater from Sophocles to Beckett has been termed "metadramatic," and Lionel Abel and others have written studies of this phenomenon.[1] On the other hand, Derrida's insistence that a signifier is always only replaced by or defined through *another signifier* leaves us grappling with the possibility that "metadrama" is in effect a misleading formulation. Malcolm Evans explores this problem in "Deconstructing Shakespeare's Comedies":

> [T]he figures who speak and gesticulate on stage in the Comedies are much more than ordinary people. They are literally and ostentatiously 'characters'—hieroglyphs,

letters, elements in a signifying system which flaunts its
own abstractions against the claims of a *mimesis* which
strives for the unmediated *presence* of its represented
world.[2]

Evans goes on to argue that ". . . there is no 'meta-language' or 'metadrama' in the comedies, no level of representation which can fix 'what
is really going on,' only more production, more text."[3]

While theorists of the postmodern do not deny the existence of
the metadramatic, they point out that our traditional notions of
"framing" are necessarily limited by the ideology and aesthetics of the
"frames" themselves; for example, Jean-François Lyotard argues that
Freud's theory of the unconscious as *mise-en-scène* was circumscribed
by his dependence on the aesthetics of nineteenth-century Viennese
opera. Lyotard suggests that "[W]orks must not be taken as symptoms
symbolically expressing a concealed discourse, but as attempts to state
perspectives of reality. Interpretation must in turn give way to
descriptions of devices."[4]

We are faced, then, with a complicated situation when it comes
to accounting for the power and presence of metadrama in the works of
a contemporary dramatist such as David Mamet. Mamet's plays reveal a
passionate concern with the boundaries of the theatrical situation and
with the awareness that they are performed before an audience. In this
sense, we can see Mamet's indebtedness to the metadramatic legacy of
classical and Renaissance theater. But as postmodern drama, Mamet's
work cannot be regarded simply as part of the heritage of Shakespeare
and his forebearers or contemporaries. Like John Guare, David Rabe,
Maria Irene Fornes, and others, Mamet problematizes and even
stigmatizes the devices of the metadramatic tradition. Mamet's theater
owes a great deal to metadramatic "tricks" or strategies inherited from
ancient tragedy and comedy and from Renaissance drama, including
choral figures, soliloquy, storytelling, stock characters, and
manipulation of the audience. Yet he insists—continually and subtly—
on challenging us to rethink the directions in which the use of these
tricks will take a reader or spectator. Ultimately, he throws into relief
the ability of the theatrical work to "con" or persuade its audience.

* * *

In order to understand the shape and (re)definitions of the metadramatic impulse in Mamet's work, let us begin by examining two of his more explicitly "theatrical" plays, *Duck Variations* (1972) and *A Life in the Theatre* (1977). *Duck Variations* is naturalistic in its setting but formally theatrical in its structure; it is in some ways about the "performance" of nature.[5] *A Life in the Theatre*, on the other hand, involves two actors who play actors and is overtly concerned with the nature of performance.

As the musical conceit of *Duck Variations'* title (and subsequent scene divisions) suggests, the piece is intended to be a number of reworkings of a single theme; Dennis Carroll writes that Mamet was apparently influenced by Aaron Copland's *What to Listen for in Music* in structuring the play.[6] The central characters are Emil Varec and George S. Aronovitz, two elderly men who sit on a park bench near Lake Michigan and pass their time by talking about the life cycles of ducks (and related topics). It becomes evident in the course of the "variations" that the two men are using their observed world as the stepping-off point for their own mythology, a mythology based partially on vaguely remembered nature "facts" from *The Reader's Digest* and other sources, and partially on the unintentional poetry that arises from their commentary about the permutations of nature.

In the final scene, Emil creates an analogy (though not on a conscious level, one suspects) between his watching the ducks with George and the similar activities of the ancient Greeks:

> These were the ancient Greeks. Old. Old men.
> Incapable of working.
> Of no use to their society.
> Just used to watch the birds all day.
> First light to Last light.[7]

Emil's misreading of "Ancient Greeks" as "Old men" is comic, but the parallel to his and George's own status is also a poignant one. Emil's words resonate further in terms of Mamet's own sense of the storytelling in this play. The reference to the ancient Greeks evokes an image of the chorus figures in Greek drama—frequently, "old men"— whose role was to observe, narrate, and comment on the action of the play.[8] In Greek drama, the Chorus figures were in the position of

declaiming on the events of the play yet were powerless to act on these
events or to influence their outcome; so, too, have George and Emil
become marginalized "narrators" in a world that excludes them. Such an
allusion heightens *Duck Variations'* final affirmation of fiction-making,
and to do so is to anticipate *A Life in the Theatre* or *The Shawl*.
At the same time, there is a key difference between the
Emil/George tandem and the choral figures of Greek drama. The latter
react to the behavior of a central protagonist (e.g., Oedipus); in one
sense, Emil and George have taken over as the protagonists, but in
another sense, they *remain* choral figures, commenting on the ducks (or
on nature in general) as stand-in "protagonist(s)." One might take this
possibility one step further and suggest that this is, then, a play with
choral figures but *without* a protagonist. In other words, there is a
central void or absence in this play. Without a genuine protagonist, the
center cannot hold, and Emil's and George's "narrative" status as chorus
figures loses its authority. As a result, the exchanges between the two
men are tinged with a comic desperation; C. W. E. Bigsby characterizes
their interactions as "like a vaudeville act, each relying on the other to
keep the patter going, to avoid the dangerous silences."[9] Such an image
evokes Vladimir and Estragon of *Waiting for Godot*, or perhaps Tom
Stoppard's re-interpretation of *Hamlet*'s Rosencrantz and Guildenstern,
in the attempt to fill an increasingly threatening silence with words and
more words.[10]

   A Life in the Theatre, a slightly later play, is about an older and
a younger member of the acting profession. In the original production,
the stage was designed with two curtains so that the audience saw the
two players from the front during the backstage sequences and from the
back during their play-within-a-play sequences—"in effect," says
Mamet, "a true view from backstage."[11] Robert, the older actor, seems
to be caught within this double staging as if within a Pirandellian box:
even when he is offstage, he is always "acting." In what Pascale
Hubert-Leibler has pointed out is one of many teacher-student
relationships in Mamet's plays,[12] Robert instructs John, the younger
actor, that theatrical tradition needs to be passed from one generation to
the next; he feels that the theatre is "a closed society" (66) to such an
extent that he has virtually no life outside of the theater. Although he
tells John that "life on stage" is nothing but "attitudes" (67), these
"attitudes" sustain Robert in his everyday behavior.

As in *Duck Variations,* however, the two characters are not simply metadramatic commentators. A more traditional playwright's approach would culminate in a validation of Robert as a tragic hero of sorts, a representative of the generation that understood the "true" essence of the theater. However, the tensions between Robert and John which emerge in the course of the play suggest that even though John certainly may see Robert as a mentor—and even though Robert's speeches expressing his love for the craft of acting are indeed moving— Robert is in the process of becoming a cipher, a character, an empty sign that has a floating referent. His pursuit of "life" through the theater is ultimately an impossible one; the characters, like the stage open from both the front and the back on which they perform *A Life in the Theatre* itself, can rely only on illusory and invisible "backgrounds."

* * *

In a contemporary play, the indication that a character is "soliloquizing" risks sounding self-consciously quaint, yet Mamet uses this stage direction with relish throughout his plays. The tension between the Shakespearean command to "soliloquize" and the decidedly un-Hamletlike characters Mamet creates suggests an additional dimension to his metadramatic range. As we shall see, Mamet plays with and against the soliloquy form as it has emerged from the Shakespearean tradition.

A brief definition of the soliloquy may be useful at this point. A soliloquy is a kind of monologue that generally suggests introspection. In a soliloquy, the speaker addresses himself/herself or the audience but not another character—unless, as Erving Goffman reminds us in *Frame Analysis,* a character happens to overhear the soliloquizer's remarks to the audience.[13] A soliloquy usually involves the verbalization of the speaker's interior feelings or thoughts and often entails a revelation or decision which would typically not be expressed aloud but which is enacted this way for the benefit of the audience. Thus, even though a soliloquy may occur in a naturalistic play, it is inherently metatheatrical because it calls for the vocalization of thoughts and because the implicit or explicit acknowledgment of the audience as auditors may also work as a reminder that the speaker is a character in a play. Yet the soliloquy is indeed entirely "natural" insofar as the audience places it within the context of a necessary or expected device within the play.

A fleeting, but pivotal, moment of soliloquy in *A Life in the Theatre* occurs in scene 2 when Robert and John are on their way out of the wardrobe area and John hands Robert his hat; Robert looks down at it and pauses, then (the stage directions tell us), "*[s]oliloquizing,*" says, "My hat, my hat, my hat." He turns to John for approval: "Eh?", and John's reply is an ambiguous "*Mmm*" (27). Here, soliloquizing is the self-conscious impulse of an actor who is always "on stage"; it is a natural outburst for a histrionic character. When Robert extends the soliloquizing impulse into a speech about his makeup in the dressing room, John tells him in exasperation to "shut up" (65). But it is clear by the end of the play that Robert turns again and again to soliloquizing not simply because he is always "on," but because the form reflects his existential loneliness. The soliloquizer speaks to a captive audience yet dares not wish for a reply. In the final scene, a reversal of the earlier moment where Robert insisted on staying while John rehearsed his speech, Robert speaks to an empty house as John eavesdrops:

> You've been so kind . . . Thank you, you've really been
> so kind. You know, and I speak, I am sure, not for myself
> alone, but on behalf of all of us . . . (*composes himself*)
> . . . All of us here, when I say that these . . . *these*
> moments make it all . . . they make it all worthwhile.
> (94–95)

Robert's delivery of the speech to a theater full of empty seats adds an ironic downbeat to his insistence that "these moments" make it all worthwhile. Yet he *does* have not only John as a listener, but the filled seats (one would hope) of the actual theater in which the actor who plays Robert is performing. Thus, the moment embodies the paradoxical nature of the soliloquy: the presence of the audience is both ignored in the intimacy of the moment and acknowledged in the vocalization of the speaker's thoughts. Goffman's comments on this paradox are fascinating to consider in light of the "double staging" of *A Life in the Theatre*:

> . . . [In a soliloquy], instead of musing alone or silently,
> the individual addresses the whole house. And through
> this structural conceit his thoughts are opened up to the

audience. Of course, the peculiarity about such flagrant
exposure of self is balanced somewhat by the fact that
those to whom the revelation is made are not themselves
persons in ordinary participation status, but rather
individuals restricted to the capacity of theatrical
audience.[14]

In *Lakeboat* (1980), when Fred speaks alone on the deck in
scenes 11 and 13, Mamet specifically indicates in the stage directions
that he "soliloquizes."[15] Yet there seems to be something tongue-in-
cheek about the application of this consciously theatrical term to Fred's
remarks about Guigliani's mugging and about horseracing. It is true
that in both of these "soliloquies," Fred arrives at a decision or
revelation by voicing his thoughts aloud with no explicit audience
present, and so the speeches fit our original definition of the soliloquy.
Such a dramatist as O'Neill might write this type of scene to suggest,
with no intended irony, that Fred is indeed a "poet" of the ordinary.
Mamet, however, does not intend for us to see Fred as a possessing a
poetic voice but rather for us to appreciate our position as members of a
real audience who observe Fred as he speaks both to himself and to an
imaginary audience. Fred is no poet, but he is also a less distant relative
of *A Life in the Theatre*'s Robert than one might initially think.

Similarly, each of the four characters in *Sexual Perversity in
Chicago* (1974) delivers at least one soliloquy (or facsimile thereof) at
some point in the play. Bernie speaks to a set of imaginary companions
at the Health Club, Danny to an imaginary co-worker, Deborah to
herself, and Joan to her imaginary nursery-school students. In the stage
directions for Bernie's, Danny's, and Joan's "soliloquies," Mamet
suggests, by using the word "imaginary" in reference to their listeners,
that the characters have an actual audience which *we* must imagine
seeing. It is also possible, though, that they are pretending to speak for
an audience; in any event, there are no extra characters visible on stage.
The effect is to call into question the extent to which these speakers
find themselves in a "naturalistic" play, and therefore to heighten the
emphasis on fictionmaking or storytelling. Even if the characters are
holding forth for "invisible" rather than purely "imaginary" listeners,
we might conclude that their desire to do so is yet another sign of their
inability to engage in actual dialogue with one another. In Deborah's
brief soliloquy, which is the only one where the speaker is undoubtedly
onstage alone, she asks questions aloud ("You see? What is a

sublimation of what? . . . What signifies what?")[16] as *if* there were a listener present; her words evoke both the futile reaching towards dialogue which seems to be a way out of monologic isolation and the awareness on some level that she *is* addressing (the play's) spectators— but they are incapable of participating in dialogue.

* * *

In his analysis of Shakespearean soliloquy, Lloyd Skiffington labels one type of Shakespearean soliloquy as the "homiletic" speech.[17] This soliloquy may be only a few lines, or it may be relatively lengthy; in either case, the speaker delivers words which sometimes appear as "thoughts" and sometimes acknowledge the audience more directly, but which are in any event of a didactic nature and often provide the opportunity for Shakespeare to demonstrate his rhetorical skill. Although the homiletic soliloquy blends at times with the psychological soliloquy, it is frequently possible to distinguish the two by noting that the homiletic soliloquy involves more generalizations and less genuine revelation or self-probing on the speaker's part; Falstaff's "honor" speech in *Henry IV* (Part One) and Edgar's "Who alone suffers suffers most i' the mind" speech in *King Lear* are two examples of Shakespeare's use of homily.

Mamet's *American Buffalo* (1975) is a play that relies upon homily to create the growing awareness in the audience of the gulf between what the characters (particularly Don and Teach) claim to know and what little they actually know. Most of the homiletic speeches in *American Buffalo* issue from the ironically-named Teach, who attempts constantly to instruct the other characters, yet is utterly blind to his own shortcomings. For instance he confuses "free enterprise" with a more metaphysical type of freedom:

> You know what is free enterprise? . . . The freedom . . . of
> the *Individual* . . . To Embark on Any Fucking Course
> that he sees fit . . . In order to secure his honest chance to
> make a profit . . . The country's *founded* on this, Don . . .
> Without this we're just savage shitheads in the
> wilderness . . . Sitting around some vicious campfire . . .
> And take those fuckers in the concentration camps. You

think they went in there by *choice*? . . . They were
dragged in there, Don . . . Kicking and screaming.[18]

For Teach, such notions as "free enterprise" are the glue that holds
civilization itself together; from an individual perspective, too, he sees
himself as nothing if he is deprived of the chance to participate in this
enterprise as he defines it. At some level, Teach views himself as a
deeply moral human being; to find confirmation that the world does not
meet his expectations—as he does at the end of the play, when the
robbery plans go haywire—is, for him, to look into the abyss. Mamet
writes Teach's final litany of disavowal in the form of
"pronouncements":

> My Whole Cocksucking Life . . .
> The Whole Entire World.
> There is No Law.
> There Is No Right and Wrong.
> The World Is Lies.
> There Is No Friendship.
> Every Fucking Thing. [*Pause.*]
> Every God-forsaken Thing . . .
> We all live like the caveman. (103)

In Teach's didactic moral vision, the myths of freedom, profit,
friendship, and so forth are the principal forces of order in the universe
itself. Like Polonius, though, Teach lives in a world in which one's
survival cannot be assured merely through the formulation of
"principles" which one passes on to others. Dramatic irony tends to
demand, then, that a homiletic narrative will ultimately point the
spectators toward the shortcomings of the speaker rather than simply
toward a vision of his or her "wisdom."

The most striking innovation in the use of the soliloquy for
Shakespeare comes with his exploration of the "psychological"
soliloquy, particularly in plays like *Hamlet* and *Macbeth*. The
psychological soliloquy involves a speaker's expression of an inner
debate (perhaps a legacy of the *agon* of ancient Greek drama). This
interior debate is often followed with a revelation or act of self-
disclosure by the speaker. Perhaps the most illustrious examples are
Hamlet's soliloquies. As Francis Fergusson points out, Hamlet's
speeches serve as "cadenzas" which open up his character.[19]

Psychological soliloquies call for the temporary transportation of the audience and character from staged or visible space into the imagined, invisible, linguistically commanded space of the psyche. With the Shakespearean psychological soliloquy comes the ascendance of interiority coupled with the singular demands that its expression places upon the visual and narrative movement of the play.

Moreover, the psychological soliloquy represents a form of what Ken Frieden in *Genius and Monologue* calls "deviant discourse."[20] Lady Macbeth's sleepwalking speech is a vivid instance of this kind of discourse brought to its extreme, though Hamlet's soliloquies are better examples of the connection between "mad speech" and creativity or self-disclosure. The speaker of the psychological soliloquy teeters between rationality and madness; the eventual lapse into the language of soliloquy implies in itself a movement over the precipice into a frighteningly non-linear, illogical and monologic world. Historically, Frieden suggests, Shakespeare's creation of such worlds shows the dominance of characters' inner struggles over those created by supernatural or divine forces, though these forces continue to exert their influence (as in *Hamlet* or *Macbeth*):

> . . . [A]s the tensions between immanence and transcendence work themselves out in the dialectic of monological modes, the supposedly autonomous subject discovers its internal conflicts. To the extent that the soliloquy is coupled with relationships to society and divine beings, it never entirely loses the connection with otherness and transcendent *Logos* . . . [but t]he new poetic monologue, instead of interacting with supernatural powers, turns toward contemplation on the appropriate rhetoric for imaginative expressions of the self.[21]

Does Mamet use the psychological soliloquy? The issue is a complicated one because, as we return to the deconstructive and postmodern notions of character cited at the beginning of this essay, we recall the possibility that a sign always stands in for little more than another sign, or that character is formed through a series of tricks or devices. If this is the case, it may be that the psychological soliloquy as described above has been rendered an impossible creation for a playwright like Mamet: the artificiality or theatricality of the staged soliloquy would tend to eclipse our acceptance of it as a tactic for the (self-)revelation of a character. There *are* glimpses of the psychological soliloquy in Mamet's plays—in some of the sailors' speeches in *Lakeboat*, for example, or in moments of *Edmond* (1982). For the most part, though, the psychological soliloquy in Mamet has been replaced by *storytelling*. As in *Duck Variations* and as explored in such pieces as *The Sanctity of Marriage* (1979) and *The Woods* (1979), a character will turn toward *another character* rather than inward or toward the audience in order to express the crises of personal discovery and the self-disclosure associated with the psychological soliloquy—or in order to *deny* the possibility of the emergence of these impulses. As such, we might wonder how the search for "rhetoric for imaginative expressions of the self" described by Frieden takes shape in the Mamet canon. One answer is that the storytelling monologue/dialogue, taken to its extreme form (which occurs fairly often in Mamet, though not to the surreal extent that it does in Shepard's plays), begins to assume this role when it is spoken by one of Mamet's hucksters, charlatans, or salesmen. These figures, as we shall see, embody Mamet's version of the "manipulator," a character that goes all the way back to the comedies of Terence and Plautus.

* * *

Most often, the speakers of soliloquies in Roman comedies are the slaves who (behind the backs of their masters, the apparent protagonists) create the disguises and encounters that result in chaos and eventual reunion or marriage (cf. *Pseudolus, The Self-Tormentor, Phormio*, and others). In this respect, there is an obvious link between manipulation of the narrative and manipulation of the playing space. Though these characters are slaves, their command of the linguistic and of much of the physical action marks them as "directors" as well. In Terence's *Phormio* (IV.ii.), for instance, the following soliloquy by the slave Geta shows his role in the plot as well as his rhetorical stance:

> I've never seen a smarter man than Phormio. I came to
> the fellow to tell him we needed money and how we could
> get it. I'd hardly given him half the plan when he caught
> on . . . I told him to go downtown and wait for me there—
> said I'd bring the master down there to meet him. Oh-oh!

There he is! Who's that behind him? Great gods!
Phaedria's father is here! Well, why are you afraid, you
idiot? Why? Because you've got two to put over the
jumps instead of one? A lot better that way, I think; it
gives me an extra string to my bow. I'll tackle Demipho
first, as I planned. If he pays, that will be fine. But if I
get nothing from him, then, I'll go after our traveler
here.[22]

Geta puts on a mask of self-deprecation, yet the irony in a line like "I'd
hardly given him half the plan when he caught on" is evident.
Moreover, his desire to add "an extra string to my bow" shows the
transparency of the "amateur" mask. It is clear that Geta is not only in
control of the action, but he takes pleasure in his ability to master its
unexpected twists and turns with the assurance of a professional.

   Glengarry Glen Ross (1983) foregrounds the presence of the
manipulator or huckster in Mamet's plays, for the major characters in
this work are real-estate salesmen who attempt to pawn off worthless
pieces of Florida swampland on unsuspecting buyers. All of the
salesmen are storytellers, and their stories show their adeptness at
taking advantage of narrative (in monologue form) to "sell" an idea, a
dream, or a personality. Monologue is, after all, the consummate sales
pitch: not only does it preclude interruption, but it allows the speaker
to appear "personal" and "confessional" even when (s)he is only acting.

   Richard Roma, one of the upward-bound salesmen in the play, is
a prime example of a manipulator figure. The first time we see Roma,
he is seated in a Chinese restaurant, delivering a long and peculiar
monologue to James Lingk—a man alone at another table—and
moving almost undetectably into a sales pitch. He begins on a
perversely, abruptly personal level, telling Lingk that rather than being
hypocrites, people should live with their actions: "You fuck little girls,
so *be* it."[23] Lingk barely responds to Roma's questions, which seem
purely rhetorical, and so Roma continues by moving from a description
of his most memorable sexual encounter to a more "philosophical"
plane:

> . . . I do those things which seem correct to me *today*. I
> trust myself. And if security concerns me, I do that which
> *today* I think will make me secure . . . Stocks, bonds,
> objects of art, real estate. Now: what are they? [*Pause.*]

> An opportunity . . . They're an *event*. A guy comes up to
> you, you make a call, you send in a brochure, it doesn't
> matter . . . All it is is THINGS THAT HAPPEN TO YOU
> . . . Some poor newly married guy gets run down by a
> cab. Some *busboy* wins the lottery. [*Pause*.] All it is, it's
> a carnival. What's special . . . what *draws* us? [*Pause*.]
> We're all different . . . I want to show you something . . .
> [*Pause*. *He takes out a small map and spreads it on a
> table*.] What is that? Florida. Glengarry Highlands.
> Florida. "Florida. *Bullshit*." And maybe that's true; and
> that's what *I* said: but look *here*: what is this? This is a
> piece of land. Listen to what I'm going to tell you now:
> (49–51)

The scene ends, mid-sentence, with Roma's "now:"—and we can infer
that at this point, the monologue has Lingk transfixed, and so Roma
can move from there to the details of the sale. But Roma's monologue
itself is striking on several counts. As he draws his listener in, Roma
indicates that he *lives inside* his own fictions. His personal
"philosophy" and his need to sell are inseparable, for he has sold
himself on himself. C. W. E. Bigsby suggests that the audience, like
Lingk, has been seduced and then "betrayed" by the discovery that this
is a sales pitch where it has appeared that genuine contact was
occurring.[24] Roma's words, on the surface, indicate a philosophy of
passivity—"THINGS HAPPEN TO YOU"—but this is a mask for a
philosophy of gratification and acquisition, a capitalist *carpe diem*. "The
point," Mamet says in an interview with David Savran, "is not to speak
the desire but to speak that which is most likely going to bring about
the desire."[25] Certainly, Roma is creating a "character" for the purpose
of making a sale—but if he is an actor, he is a Method actor, and he has
internalized his role.

Indeed, Roma carries through with the theatrical aspect of his
salesmanship when Lingk comes into the office to try and cancel the
contract he has signed. Immediately and unflinchingly, Roma enlists
Levene (another, older salesman) in a "routine" in which Levene is an
out-of-town client whom Roma must rush to the airport so that he will
not have time to talk with Lingk. He follows this with a large dose of
"psychology" regarding Lingk's need to be able to do things
independently of his wife without feeling unfaithful, a tactic which is
on the verge of success until Williamson ruins it. We receive

confirmation in these scenes that Roma is intuitively connected to the procedures for deception; he slides from story to story so effectively that he even begins to persuade Levene to be his partner so that he will be able to profit from Levene's sales as well as his own. No "principles" of friendship or of business ethics, it seems, will prevent Roma from getting what he wants, yet he bases his persuasive narratives on the proposition that he is a man who has done a considerable amount of soul-searching. He does not have to play at being sincere, for he has made his world-weary cynicism into part of his routine—or, more aptly, he is entirely *sincere* about his utter immersion in deception. Thus, he is able to say in so many words that the Florida land is "bullshit," but his readiness to say this becomes part of the reason that his sales pitch is successful.

Roma succeeds where others (such as Levene) fail, then, because he has internalized the capacity for fraud, and so he can sustain the fictions he creates. In the world of these hucksters, the ability to maintain one's stories is a survival tactic, and the play—on one level— makes an obvious judgment about the unethical nature of those who rob others by practicing such deception. But it is crucial to realize that on another level, Mamet is *not without admiration* for the capacity that such a figure as Roma has acquired. The "D. Ray Morton" scene which Roma and Levene perform to save Roma's deal makes manifest the connection between the salesmen's fraudulent stories and the theater itself, for the sequence—even with its qualities of *shtick*—functions as a play-within-a-play, and we delight in seeing the two characters "act" under pressure. If storytelling constitutes a kind of fraud, Mamet seems to say, then to act in the theater is to seduce and persuade with one's stories in the same way that the salesmen use their narratives to lure customers (and indeed, to extend the metaphor of the real-estate salesmen, the actors, too, must sell the audience on the tangibility of their "properties").

* * *

The power of the sales contest board in *Glengarry Glen Ross*— or, for the customers, the descriptions of the real estate—resides in the promise that the characters will come one step closer to transforming their inner narratives of achievement into actuality; as a result of their readiness to believe in the viability of myth, though, the characters are caught in a matrix of self-perpetuating deceptions. Yet the theater itself is just such a matrix of *intentional* deceptions. The imaging of such characters as Roma and Levene as actors or as "directors" of others' theatricalized actions leaves us with the sense that Mamet's movement towards a validation of "fraud"—at least in theatrical terms—is perhaps inevitable.

The Water Engine was written as a radio play and then reshaped for stage production in 1977, but the staged version retains a great deal of the original reliance on verbal narrative rather than visual action.[26] Mamet notes of the first theatrical production that

> . . . many scenes were played on mike, as actors
> presenting a radio drama, and many scenes were played
> off mike as in a traditional, realistic play. The result was
> a third reality, a scenic truth, which dealt with radio not
> as an electronic convenience, but as an expression of our
> need to create and to communicate and to explain—much
> like a chainletter.[27]

This "third reality" operates in terms of multiple narrative levels; interwoven like musical themes throughout the play are the radio voices (e.g., the Announcer's), the interactions of Lang (the protagonist) and others, the chainletter, the Hall of Science voices, overheard conversations, a knife-grinder and train conductor, and the soapbox speakers. *The Water Engine*'s multiple voices thus offer us different "layers" of fiction, and Mamet plays with our (in)ability to determine which, if any, can be considered reliable or authoritative. In his discussion of the audience's role in Greek drama, Peter Arnott writes that frequently, the spectators served as an implicit "jury" whom the protagonist also addresses during the *agon* (even when the character seems to be speaking directly to others on stage). Arnott cites the examples of Medea's accusation of Jason and Theseus' accusation of Hippolytus.[28] As the spectators of *The Water Engine* are besieged with stories—some in the form of gossip (the stories in the elevator), and some in the form of declamatory address (the speakers in Bughouse Square)—they, too, fill the role of ostensible jurors as the central narrative undertakes the revelation of fraud. In Greek drama, though, a clear verdict is rendered; here, rather, the implication is that all of the ways we give and receive information involve a certain level of deception inherent in the act of transmission. Mamet writes, "The only profit in the sharing of a myth is to those who participate as storytellers or as listeners, and this profit is the shared experience itself, the celebration of the tale, and its truth."[29] In other words, the classical theater gives primacy to the power and inherent truth of the myth or narrative itself, viewing the storytelling characters as attorneys of sorts whose job it is to present a "case" to the audience. For Mamet, though, the *transmission* and *reception* of a narrative form the basis of a profitable communicative act, rather than the judgment of the narrative's essential plausibility. The *"celebration* of the tale, and its truth" (emphasis added) overrides the "objective" content of the tale itself.

The main character of *The Shawl* (1985), John, is apparently another one of Mamet's manipulators: as a "psychic" or "spiritualist," he professes to divine the answers to his clients' questions, insisting to Charles, his lover, that doing so is simply a matter of knowing how to read the signals that the client himself/herself provides unwittingly. When Miss A comes to John for advice, Charles convinces him (under duress) to try and use his "powers" to get her money; the scheme falls through, but as John continues to talk with Miss A at the end of the play, the possibility that John does indeed possess some type of psychic ability hovers over their closing exchange.

Early in the play, John tells Charles that the problem Charles has in accepting his techniques is due to his lack of experience in seeing the operation from the inside out, as it were:

> . . . I show you the trick "from the back" and you're
> disappointed. Of course you are. If you view it as a
> "member of the audience." One of the, you will see, the
> most painful sides of the profession is this: you do your
> work well, and who will see it? No one, really . . . To
> say, to learn to say, I suppose you must, to just say what
> separates us, finally, from them is this: that is we look
> *clearly.*[30]

In *The Shawl*, as in *A Life in the Theatre*, we see "the trick 'from the back,'" as John tells Charles. The implication is that to do so is to risk a split between one's immersion in and one's "disillusionment" in the "art" one is witnessing. In some respects, as Bigsby suggests, the passage thus stands as a justification of Mamet's *own* "art": ". . . [f]rom the deceits of art are born truths," but that realization should be combined with a sense of "the poetry that lies behind the calculation."[31] The magic that this art constitutes, John claims, comes simply from the ability to "look *clearly*"—but even these words suggest a pun which reaffirms the doubleness of his vision, for "look clearly" is also a translation of "clairvoyance"—which suggests the very psychic ability John seeks so ardently to deny. *The Shawl* tells a story, then, which Mamet feels can be seen "from the back" without losing the simultaneous acknowledgement of the unseeable, the intangible—in effect, it insists upon a recognition of theatrical narrative's power to "conjure" images.

If the traditional definition of metadrama presupposes that theater is capable of an internal *mimesis*, an ability to duplicate and imitate its own processes, then Mamet engages in the postmodern practice of "tricking" these processes. To leave us uncertain whether John is a charlatan or a spiritualist at the end of *The Shawl* is to play at the abstractions of theater's potential to "dupe" its audience. Yet Mamet's works do not demand the breaking of the fourth wall to call attention to the "trick from the back," nor does the rhetoric of theatricality in his plays remain self-enclosed as it does, for example, in *Hamlet*. Rather, Mamet foregrounds the existence of *devices* in his works and allows the energy of these devices to power his staging and characterization without being blocked by a concern with the extent to which the manipulation involved in these devices is *genuinely* "conning" the audience. If Mamet's latest play, *Bobby Gould in Hell* (1989) foreshadows an increasing preoccupation with the "trappings" of Renaissance drama (it contains everything from trap doors to lightning to an exit "pursued by a bear"), it may be because his next phase is an explicit test of what happens when metadrama turns to trick-playing— when the theater is a "house of games" which we enter with an awareness of our desire to watch ourselves being fooled.

Notes

1. For more information, see the following studies: Robert J. Nelson, *Play Within a Play: The Dramatist's Conception of His Art: Shakespeare to Anouilh* (New Haven: Yale University Press, 1958); Anne Righter, *Shakespeare and the Idea of the Play* (London: Chatto & Windus, 1962; rpt. Baltimore: Penguin, 1967); Lionel Abel, *Metatheatre: A New View of Dramatic Form* (New York: Hill & Wang, 1963); James L. Calderwood, *Shakespearean Metadrama: The Argument of the Play in Titus Andronicus, Love's Labour's Lost, Romeo and Juliet, A Midsummer Night's Dream, and Richard II* (Minneapolis: University of Minnesota Press, 1971) and *To Be and Not to Be: Negation and Metadrama in Hamlet* (New York: Columbia University Press, 1983); Robert Egan, *Drama Within Drama: Shakespeare's Sense of His Art in King Lear, The Winter's Tale, and The Tempest* (New York: Columbia University Press, 1975); June Schlueter, *Metafictional Characters in Modern Drama* (New York: Columbia University Press, 1979); Sidney Homan, *When the Theater Turns to Itself: The Aesthetic Metaphor in Shakespeare* (Lewisburg, Pa.: Bucknell University Press; London and Toronto: Associated University Presses, 1981) and *The Audience as Actor and Character: The Modern Theater of Beckett, Brecht, Genet, Ionesco, Pinter, Stoppard, and Williams* (Lewisburg, Pa.: Bucknell University Press; Cranbury, N.J.: Associated University Presses, 1989); Richard Hornby, *Drama, Metadrama, and Perception* (Lewisburg, Pa.: Bucknell University Press; London and Toronto: Associated University Presses, 1986).

2. Malcolm Evans, "Deconstructing Shakespeare's Comedies," in *Alternative Shakespeares* ed. John Drakakis (London: Methuen, 1985), p. 72.

3. Evans, p. 74.

4. Jean-François Lyotard, "The Unconscious as Mise-en-Scène," trans. Joseph Maier, in *Performance in Postmodern Culture*, eds. Michel Benamou and Charles Caramello (Madison: Coda Press, 1977), p. 98.

5. In the Piven Theatre Workshop's 1985 production of the play (in Evanston, Illinois), the extent to which this "performance" was emphasized became almost Brechtian: the characters "constructed" the set at the beginning of the play, and turned pages of a large book which announced the number and title of each "variation."

6. Dennis Carroll, *David Mamet* (New York: St. Martin's Press, 1987), p. 72.

7. David Mamet, *Sexual Perversity in Chicago* and *The Duck Variations* (New York: Grove Press, 1978), p. 124.

8. In Gerald Gutierrez' Acting Company production of the play, Emil and George wore three-quarter masks, thus creating an additional link between this passage and the characters themselves. See Carroll, p. 122.

9. C. W. E. Bigsby, *David Mamet* (London: Methuen, 1985), p. 31.

10. It is striking that Beckett is usually perceived as a figure whose works straddle the distance between the "modern" and the "postmodern," with the early, more explicitly metadramatic works [*Godot, Endgame*] perceived as "modern" and the later, minimalist works perceived as "postmodern." Yet one might argue that the way Godot, the apparent protagonist, never appears or even has his existence validated is an example of the postmodern "de-centering" technique being described here.

11. David Mamet, *A Life in the Theatre* (New York: Grove Press, 1977), p. 9. All further references are to this edition and will be cited parenthetically in the essay.

12. Pascale Hubert-Leibler, "Dominance and Anguish: The Teacher-Student Relationship in the Plays of David Mamet," *Modern Drama*, 31 (December 1988): 557–570.

13. Erving Goffman, *Frame Analysis* (Cambridge, Mass.: Harvard University Press, 1974), p. 233.

14. Goffman, p. 231.

15. David Mamet, *Lakeboat* (New York: Grove Press, 1981), p. 57.

16. Mamet, *Sexual Perversity in Chicago*, p. 58.

17. Lloyd A. Skiffington, *The History of English Soliloquy* (Lanham, Md.: University Press of America, 1985), pp. 76–87.

18. David Mamet, *American Buffalo* (New York: Grove Press, 1976), pp. 72–73. All further references are to this edition and will be cited parenthetically.

19. Francis Fergusson, *The Idea of a Theatre* (Princeton, N.J.: Princeton University Press, 1949), p. 113.

20. Ken Frieden, *Genius and Monologue* (Ithaca, N.Y.: Cornell University Press, 1985), p. 20.

21. Frieden, p. 133.

22. Terence, *Phormio*, in *The Comedies of Terence*, trans. Frank O. Copley (Indianapolis: Bobbs-Merrill, 1967), p. 89.

23. David Mamet, *Glengarry Glen Ross* (New York: Grove Press, 1982), p. 47. All further references are to this edition and will be cited parenthetically.

24. Bigsby, pp. 118–119.

25. David Savran, "Trading in the American Dream," *American Theatre* 4 (September 1987): 16.

26. For a fascinating description of the details of staging the play, see Carroll, pp. 134–136.

27. David Mamet, *The Water Engine* and *Mr. Happiness* (New York: Grove Press, 1978), note on production, n.p.

28. Peter D. Arnott, *Public and Performance in the Greek Theatre* (London: Routledge, 1989), p. 22.

29. David Mamet, *Writing in Restaurants* (New York: Viking Press, 1986), pp. 107–108.

30. David Mamet, *The Shawl* and *Prairie du Chien* (New York: Grove Press, 1985), pp. 26–27.

31. Bigsby, p. 128.

DOMINANCE AND ANGUISH:
THE TEACHER-STUDENT RELATIONSHIP
IN THE PLAYS OF DAVID MAMET

Pascale Hubert-Leibler

Although at first sight Mamet's urban microcosm—inhabited by rugged, unsophisticated, often inarticulate men—and the school world would seem to be poles apart, relationships of the teacher-student type appear in most of his plays. *A Life in the Theatre, Squirrels,* and *American Buffalo* for instance, are built around a master-disciple paradigm; the protagonist of *Mr. Happiness* is presented as an expert in psychology who dispenses guidance and words of wisdom to his eager listeners. In *Lakeboat,* young ordinary seaman Dale elicits a "teaching reflex" from several of the older crewmen, who take it upon themselves to teach him his job and initiate him into adult life (see scenes 10 and 21). The importance of the pedagogical relationship is also reflected thematically by the frequent occurrence of words like "learn," "show," "teach," "know," "lesson," or "school." Some details make direct references to institutionalized education: for instance, we learn that Dale is a college student and that he may go on to teach English; Joan in *Sexual Perversity in Chicago* is a kindergarten teacher.

We also find little vignettes that vividly conjure up the world of the school—re-enactments of typical classroom scenes familiar to all of us former students. *American Buffalo* is particularly rich in such echoes.[1] First of all, the two older characters—the owner of a junk-shop and his "friend and associate"—are called Don,[2] and Teacher (or Teach). Both act as instructors of Bobby, who is Don's gopher and protégé, but the relationship between Don and Teach is frequently patterned after the same teacher-student model too. In Act I, as the two older men are planning the theft of a coin collection, Teach asks for " [a] crash course. What to look for. What to take" (45), and later wants Don "to quiz me on some coins" (47). A moment later, Don expresses doubt about Teach's competence as a burglar and starts bombarding him with questions on how he plans to break into their intended victim's house (49–50); and Teach then sounds very much like a pupil who, having come to class unprepared, tries to cover up for his ignorance with self-assurance. He finally endeavours to break the cycle of questions with a cry of protest coming directly from school memories: " Hey, you didn't warn us we were going to have a *quiz*" (50). Having failed Don's test Teach will have to accept that a third, more efficient man, Fletch, join their team of robbers. Later, at the beginning of Act 2, Don is waiting for his two accomplices who were supposed to meet at the shop at eleven, before the burglary. When Teach arrives around eleven-thirty, he gets told off like a child late for class and comes up with the hackneyed excuse that his watch broke. He then complains of Don's favouritism towards Fletcher in a passage where Don is cast as the partial teacher, Fletch as the teacher's pet, and Teach himself as the victim of glaring injustice (68).

These evocations of the school world are not simply picturesque and comical; they also serve to throw into relief several essential aspects of the teacher-student relationship. For example, the scenes mentioned above emphasize questions such as competence and pretense, fairness and injustice. But certainly the most striking aspect of the relationship they underscore is that the character assuming the role of the teacher exercises the prerogatives of questioning, testing, and punishing, while the student has to submit to his probing and accept his decisions. In other words, it becomes apparent that the teacher-student relationship is first and foremost a power relationship.

The work of Michel Foucault can furnish us with useful tools towards the analysis of the teacher-student paradigm as a mechanism of power. In his article "The Subject and Power,"[3] Foucault examines the very same pedagogical relationship as an example of the tight power structures he calls "block[s] of capacity-communication-power" (426). The first constituent of the block, variously called "capacity," "objective capacities" or "finalized activities" (425), consists of the technical apparatus brought into play in order to achieve a certain goal. This goal, in actual pedagogical relationships, is to "ensure apprenticeship and the acquisition of aptitudes or types of behavior" (426),[4] and the activities which further it are in fact the second and third elements of the block: communication processes and control devices. The second element of the system, defined as an "ensemble of regulated communications" comprises in our case "lessons, questions and answers, orders, exhortations, coded signs of obedience, differentiation marks of the 'value' of each person and of the levels of knowledge" (426). In other words, and this is everywhere obvious in Mamet's plays, verbal tasks and the right to speak are assigned according to strict rules within the teacher-student model, the most important of which being that the teacher has an automatic right to speech. Foucault describes the exercise of power as "a mode of action upon the actions of others" (428). This definition readily applies to the professorial discourse, which is inherently directive—it determines the content of communication, initiates and terminates it, imposes silence or demands answers—and controls and acts upon the student's discourse. It also controls non-verbal actions to a certain degree, but its impact is limited by the teacher's primary role as a guide. Its sphere of influence then tends to be confined to the mode of execution of actions: the teacher does not primarily tell the student *what* to do, but rather *how* to do a certain task.

The professorial discourse can operate within two distinct modes, autonomous or interactive. In the former mode, the teacher assumes the pose of the lecturer and delivers the text of his lesson, gives orders and advice, without inviting any comment other than unconditional acceptance from his listener, whose role it is to commit his words to paper or memory and submit to his authority. Such is the kind of pattern Robert, Arthur, and Bernard—in *A Life in the Theatre*, *Squirrels*, and *Sexual Perversity in Chicago* respectively—consistently strive to force upon their younger associates John, Edmond and Danny.[5] Both Robert the actor and Arthur the writer delight in talking and their favourite mode of address is, naturally, the monologue. Robert's sermons are riddled with pompous generalizations, advice, exhortations, as at the end of scene 5, while the two men are exercising in the dance room: "We *are* society. Keep your back straight, John. The mirror is your friend. (*Pause.*) For a few more years. (*Pause.*) What have we to fear, John, from *phenomena*? (*Pause.*) We are explorers of the *soul*." (36); whereas John's lines in the same scene rarely exceed one word. The first episode of *Squirrels* opens on the same situation, with Arthur improvising wildly, unhampered by Edmond's timid monosyllables. Likewise, most of Danny's remarks and questions serve mainly to encourage and sanction Bernie's extravagant telling of his fabulous sexual encounters (7–14), and confirm him in his role of sex expert (17–18, 25, 26–28).

When the teacher chooses to operate within the question-answer structure, the student is granted the right to speak, but only in the form of the duty to answer. Questioning can fulfill two crucial functions. One consists in stimulating the student's intellect through the use of carefully oriented questions and aims at helping him find the answers himself (the Socratic method). This is exactly what Don is trying to do with Bob in the following exchange from *American Buffalo*:

> DON: I mean, Fletcher, he plays *cards*.
> BOB: He's real sharp.
> DON: You're goddam right he is.
> BOB: know it.
> DON: Was he born that way?
> BOB: Huh?
> DON: I'm saying was he born that way or do you think
>   he had to learn it?
> BOB: Learn it.
> DON: Goddam right he did, and don't forget it. (6)

The other use of questioning is the assessment of the student's competence. He who controls the operation of testing wields considerable power over the character in the student's position, as we can see in the above-mentioned passage where Don examines Teacher's claim that he is a competent burglar: not only does Don expose Teach's incompetence, but by deciding to add Fletch to their team, he further humiliates his associate and devalues his place in the economy of the play.

Besides these regulations of oral communication, there also exists a gestural code of obedience by which the teacher expects the student to abide. The relationship between Robert and John in *A Life in the Theatre* is based upon such an "etiquette"—Robert's expression (18 and 65)—which comprises, in addition to certain conventions of speech that John must observe (politeness, approval, etc.) an ensemble of physical signs of submission: for example, John has to go out with

Robert after work (sc. 1 and 6), light his cigarette (sc. 13), let him use his towels (sc. 22), and perform a variety of little favours for him.

The third element of the pedagogical block described by Foucault is a "series of power processes" consisting of "enclosure, surveillance, reward and punishment, the pyramidal hierarchy" (426). Foucault has in mind the actual institution of the school, but these power processes are also present in Mamet's plays. Enclosure in the school is mirrored by the constrictive settings which serve as places of teaching and apprenticeship: the lakeboat in the play of the same name, Arthur and Edmond's office (as well as the obsessional theme of their never-completed story, squirrels in a park), and the junk-shop Don never leaves. Similarly, the inquisitiveness of Mamet's teachers vis-à-vis their students can be regarded as a form of surveillance. In scene 6 of *A Life in the Theatre* for instance, we see Robert come upon John, who is on the telephone, and ask him to whom he is talking. Joan and Bernie's extreme curiosity about Deborah and Danny's love life amounts to a downright invasion of privacy (*Sexual Perversity*, 21, 23–24, 28, for instance). The problem of retribution plays an important part in the relationships between Don, Teach and Bobby (*Buffalo*), Edmond and Glenna (*Edmond*), and John and Charles (*The Shawl*).

We have now come to the question of hierarchy within Mamet's teacher-student paradigm. The hierarchical edifice, usually composed of only two levels, is mostly based on the age difference between the teacher and the student. Arguably, age may be the main distinctive feature of Mamet's characters. It is almost always mentioned in the lists of characters, often as the only element which distinguishes them, as in *Squirrels* or *A Life* ("Robert, An older actor" / "John, A younger actor"). In *Glengarry Glen Ross*, the characters are grouped according to age without any mention of their occupations (although the group of men in their early forties actually consists of a salesman, his customer, the head of the agency, and a detective). If age is an important factor in most of the relationships in the plays, its role in the teacher-student paradigm is a central one. Not only does it set up a hierarchy of power, it also motivates the very establishment of the relationship, directs its evolution, and determines its finality.

Most of Mamet's characters are mediocrities, losers who generally occupy the lower echelons of American society. Some of them hardly seem to have a place in it, like Bobby the junkie, Don and Teach who straddle the border between commerce and crime, the actors

of *A Life in the Theatre*, the writers of *Squirrels*, marginalized by their
occupations and their isolation. Whether they be casualties of
capitalism—those for whom the American dream never materialized—or
outsiders, it is clear that they do not have access to the power conferred
either by money, status, or, for that matter, love. Yet their profound
need for dominance is very much alive, and because of their
disempowerment, can only be expressed through a few particular
channels. One of them, as Christopher Bigsby has remarked, is the
making up of stories, a reappropriation of fate through imagination.[6]
Another—hardly less illusory and often found in conjunction with the
former—is the achievement of the position of teacher in a relationship
of a pedagogical type. This position holds a particular attraction for the
older characters, the most vulnerable of all, because it allows them to
transform what is actually a weakness into an instrument of dominance:
within the teacher-student relationship, age becomes equated with
experience and superior knowledge—either real or imagined—therefore
lending authority to their words and granting them control over
communication. The best and most moving example of this process
may well be the following exchange between Joe and Dale in
Lakeboat.[7] Joe Litko is a paradigm of disempowerment and failure.
Still only an able-bodied seaman after more than twenty years on the
lakes, unmarried and unloved, haunted by suicidal tendencies,
inarticulate, he hardly seems to occupy a dominant position vis-à-vis
Dale, an English major at a "good school" near Boston (83), who is
doing a stint on the lakeboat that summer. Joe's only way to achieve a
dominant position in his relationship with the young man is to avail
himself of the age difference between them. It seems at first that even
this kind of superiority is hard to claim, as Joe feels that Dale's
maturity is that of an older man (86): "You're a young guy for such a
. . . I mean, you're not that *young* but you seem . . . older, you know?
You seem like you wouldn't of been that young." Yet Joe is finally
able to hoist himself into the position of a teacher, by claiming that the
mathematical fact that he is older than Dale entitles him to teach the
young man something—anything, even a very simple prediction will
satisfy his tremendous compulsion to teach, that is, to feel that he is
"in control" (87–88):

> Ah, you know what I'm saying to you. I just wanted to
> tell you, Dale. I just wanted to let you know. So you'll

understand. I mean. I've lived longer than you have. And
at this stage one can see a lot of things in their proper
light . [. . .] I've lived a hell of a lot longer than you
have and I want to tell you, you're going to be Okay.

Within the teacher-student paradigm, Mamet can probe and
expose the motivations and the finalities underlying the exercise of
power. Through his portrayals of such relationships, he unveils the
desires and the deficiencies which his uncultivated, quasi-aphasic
characters are unable to express openly or even acknowledge to
themselves. We have seen that the pedagogical relationship was, for the
majority of the older characters, the only access to a dominant position
available to them. This therefore makes the relationship especially
valuable in itself, and power is exercised for its own sake, as a precious
and delightful rarity. But the pedagogical relationship implies more than
a distribution of power. It is also a structure of exchange, a contract
guaranteeing the two parties entering it a number of precious benefits.
Interestingly enough, the terms of this implicit agreement have been
defined by Roland Barthes in words which echo some of the major
themes of David Mamet's plays. In his article "Writers, Intellectuals,
Teachers," Barthes remarks that if the student expects to receive an
adequate professional training and acquire knowledge in the course of his
apprenticeship, the teacher essentially demands that the student "let
himself be seduced" and "assent to a loving relationship;" that he
"acknowledge him in whatever 'role' it may be"; and finally, that the
student "act as relay, . . . extend him, . . . spread his style and ideas far
afield."[8]
    On a psychological level, this contract can be extremely
advantageous for the teacher. In his plays, Mamet invariably deals with
his characters' difficulties with communication, and the obstacles they
meet and create when trying to establish intimate contact with each
other. Although their attempts are usually unsuccessful, they evince a
deep-seated desire to make contact with and elicit love from the other; as
Christopher Bigsby remarks, " [t]he primary fact of their lives is a
missing intimacy."[9] This need for affection and closeness seems to be
fulfilled in a version of the teacher-student model which we could call
the mentor-protégé variant. Here, as in the father-son relationship, the
exercise of power is mitigated by feelings of solicitude and love, and a
real concern for the other's well-being. The best illustration of this
variant is the bond uniting Don and Bobby in *Buffalo*. Don plays the

role of a protector as well as that of an educator. We see him instructing and mothering Bob from the earliest moments of the play, alternately lecturing and pampering him, as on page 8: "You don't have *friends* this life. . . . You want some breakfast?" Bobby depends on Don's help for almost everything—money, food, health, apprenticeship. Don's power over Bob is nearly absolute, but he uses it to obtain affection from him, and the young man's dependency on him is a warrant of his gratitude and faithfulness. Towards the end of the play, Don allows Teach to punish Bobby out of pain and bewilderment at having his affection betrayed (the two men think that Bobby secretly carried out the robbery with Fletcher). And when it turns out that Bobby has not betrayed Don for Fletcher after all, but is merely guilty of a lie which does not call his fidelity to Don into question, the latter forgives him immediately and apologizes to him.

Other relationships are based, at least in part, on a similar need for affection and intimacy. The longest scene of *Lakeboat*, evocatively entitled "The Bridge," deals with Joe's attempts to establish himself as Dale's teacher and protector. For instance, Joe offers Dale his help: "If he [the First mate] gives you shit, just let me know" (89). Joe needs this kind of relationship to demand sympathy as well as attention from Dale, whom he makes the confidant of his dead dreams and mounting fears. But when Barthes says that the student is expected "to let himself be seduced" and "assent to a loving relationship," he also evokes the pedagogical paradigm of Ancient Greece, in which the relationship between master and disciple is based on pederasty, on the exchange of knowledge for love and sex. The initial situation of *The Shawl* is reminiscent of this paradigm.[10] John, who is fifty, is trying to get Charles, a hustler, to stay with him. John knows that he somehow has to pay for Charles's presence and offers to trade his secrets—he is a clairvoyant—for Charles's love: "whatever I have is yours [. . .] Just now that's very little. In material things. Very little. What I *can* offer you is: a . . . a profession. The beginnings of a craft" (25–26). In Mamet's dramatic world, the rare heterosexual relationships, doomed from the start by male misogyny and the mutual incomprehension of the sexes, usually end in disaster. Latent or overt homosexuality is present in a number of relationships and frequently appears within the teacher-student paradigm. In *A Life in the Theatre* for instance, Robert and John symbolically act out homosexual fantasies. Their relationship, established in scene one, is sealed by an evocation of a kiss, when John

removes a spot of makeup from Robert's neck with a tissue moistened
with his own saliva (25). Scene 8 ends on a symbolic representation of
fellatio and an invitation to anal intercourse. Just as Robert is leaving
to go on stage, his zipper breaks: he refuses to call in the dresser ("You
don't want the woman?" "No. I don't want the woman.") and John
offers him his help. Robert then climbs on a chair, John pins his fly
after a few fumbling attempts, while Robert repeatedly enjoins him to
"stick it in" (44–45).

Barthes's remark that the student is "to acknowledge him [the
teacher] in whatever 'role' it may be" points to another vital need that
Mamet's older characters are trying to satisfy through their domination
of younger men. Although accession to the status of teacher endows
their experience with value, it cannot directly counter the destructive
effects of aging they dread, nor erase the reality of their mediocrity.
Their faculties are on the wane; Robert starts forgetting his lines
(scenes 9 and 24), Arthur (*Squirrels*) acknowledges to the cleaning lady
that he is in a rut and that maybe he has "lost the touch" (41), Levene
in *Glengarry* has not closed a sale in months. But they refuse to accept
the altered, diminished images of themselves reflected by mirrors (see
the episodes of Joe's suicide in scene 26 of *Lakeboat* and Robert's
remarks on mirrors in scene 5 of *A Life*), poor reviews (*A Life*, scenes
10, 21, 22), or statistics (in the case of the older salesmen of
Glengarry). The plays portray their desperate efforts to retain a grip on
themselves and recover a sense of the identity which eludes them; often
this is attempted through the establishment of a teacher-student
relationship. For example, when Levene is threatened with losing his
job in the first scene of *Glengarry*,[11] he assumes a professorial pose as a
defense tactic. Although on the one hand he is pleading with his boss
Williamson not to be fired, on the other he prevents him from speaking
and lectures him: "All that I'm saying, that you're wasting leads. I
don't want to tell you your *job*" (15)—exactly what he is doing, and
what the professorial discourse is designed to do. Levene is trying to
force Williamson to see him as he wants to be seen—as the student
must see the teacher: competent and irreplaceable.

The only way to reverse the process of disintegration which
destroys self-confidence and eventually identity itself is to replace the
terrifying image of one's decay by a positive image of oneself,
constructed and projected—principally in speech—to be reflected in the
admiring attitude of an "other." Indeed, if the other listens to me, my

discourse is validated, and so is the verbal self-image I have created through it.[12] This is the assumption underlying the relationship between John and Robert, who literally feeds on the young man's praise and silent approval. Similarly, the lesson in sexual education Fred gives Dale in *Lakeboat* affords the old seaman the opportunity to revise the details of his first sexual encounter, and to appear potent and masterful in his relationships with women—at least for the time of the narration. Yet if the pedagogical relationship seems a wonderfully seductive means of averting fate and reconstructing both present and past, it is also a knife that cuts both ways: the teacher becomes heavily dependent on the sanction of his student, which induces a transfer of power in the relationship.

Foucault says that the teacher-student relationship is oriented toward a goal: to "ensure apprenticeship and the acquisition of aptitudes or types of behavior." This can easily be read in conjunction with Barthes's remark that the teacher expects the student "to act as relay, to extend him, to spread his style and ideas." Ideally, the teacher can perpetuate himself through his student, whom he will have moulded in his own image. This is precisely what Robert claims he wants when he clumsily tells John of his ambition to "see the *young* of the Theatre . . . (And it's *not* unlike one's children) . . . following in the footpaths of . . . following in the footsteps of . . . those who have gone before" (82–83). Indeed, the older characters present themselves as role models for the younger ones, and urge them to emulate certain types of behaviour—Don promotes good eating habits (*Buffalo*, 8, 12–13, 21), Bernie and Fred, machismo. Yet difficulties are bound to arise when the student who follows in the teacher's footsteps actually achieves a degree of success. A successful student can no longer serve as a docile mirror reflecting the teacher's enlarged image and nothing else. His own self begins to show through and soon ends up cancelling out the reassuring reflection, exposing instead by contrast the teacher's own decline and mediocrity. This is precisely what Robert acknowledges in scene 23 of *A Life*, after having watched John rehearse on the empty stage: "Christ, but you make me feel small. You make me feel *small*, John. I don't feel good" (83). In addition to denying the teacher his customary dose of comfort and threatening to shatter his cherished illusions, the student can also become a dangerous rival, capable of relegating his master to an inferior position, or even to the vacuum of uselessness and non-being. Such is the fate of *Glengarry*'s Levene; and maybe of Robert who, in the last scene of *A Life*, takes his leave of the audience and possibly of his career too, foreseeing only darkness and loneliness for himself: "The lights dim. Each to his own home. Goodnight. Goodnight. Goodnight" (95).

The character in the teacher's position thus has to deal with the double threat of creating a rival for himself and losing his domination over the student. The only course of action open to him is therefore to deny the student self-expression and accession to independence, in order to extend the duration of the relationship and preserve the original balance of power as long as possible. Thus Joan and Bernie in *Sexual Perversity* try first to discourage Deborah and Danny from living together (see 25–26, 31, 37–38) and then to make them turn away from each other. Robert diminishes the value of John's achievements by dismissing the young man's good reviews as undeserved (*A Life*, scene 22). Arthur, in *Squirrels*, appears bent on preventing Edmond from actively participating in the elaboration of their story. This attitude, of course, constitutes both an abuse of power and a violation of the tacit contract binding teacher and student, as the latter is not allowed to experiment nor, ultimately, to learn. And since the teacher is not keeping his end of the bargain, the student is going to rebel.

All power relations, whether founded on consent or force, are by nature unstable, as Michel Foucault reminds us in "The Subject and Power."[13] The teacher-student relationship in Mamet's plays is especially susceptible to disruption because it is based on a very fragile agreement. Its main weakness is that the student's motivation for entering into the relationship is usually low—he consents to it rather than actively seeks it. And even if he hopes to learn from the teacher, he is mainly interested in getting fast answers, recipes, magic formulas (like Charles and Miss A in *The Shawl*, Edmond in the play of the same name, or Mr. Happiness's listeners), and he rejects the principle of a long-term apprenticeship. The tension caused by the conflicting interests of teacher and student is bound to come to a head eventually. As Mamet's is a closed world, the characters are often trapped as it were together, and the conflict is likely to develop as a struggle for domination rather than for independence or separation—a struggle for the empowering position within the relationship, which is that of the teacher. The student will therefore endeavour to beat the teacher at his own game. The first act of resistance will be to neutralize the teacher's words by refusing to listen—John's strategy in scenes 13 and 14 of *A*

Life, Arthur and Edmond's weapon during their duel for the monopoly
of speech in *Squirrels*—or resisting enquiry, as Danny does when Bernie
becomes too inquisitive about his affair with Deborah (28–29 of *Sexual
Perversity*). The student's next step is to claim his own voice, as
Edmond tries to do repeatedly in *Squirrels,* and finally to denounce the
contract entirely: first, Edmond dares to answer "No" to Arthur's
question "Have you learned nothing working here?" (33), then he
declares that he is "unhappy," that Arthur is "very overbearing," that
they "write the same thing all the time" (45). John's brutal injunction
to Robert to "shut up" in scene 17 of *A Life* and Deborah's sudden
announcement to Joan that she is "moving in with Danny" (38 of
Sexual Perversity) are likewise acts of open rebellion. Both *Squirrels*
and *A Life* end on a complete exchange of roles. The final scenes—
reversed images of the opening scenes—show us the former students in
control of the relationship, with Edmond directing the process of
literary creation, while John proclaims his independence by not inviting
Robert to dinner and now asserts his superiority by demanding in his
turn signs of submission of the old actor (lighting his cigarette, lending
him money). In other plays, it is the teacher who wins: Deborah and
Danny return to Joan and Bernie in *Sexual Perversity* ; the relationship
between Don and Bobby in *American Buffalo* is preserved, since the
suspicions about Bobby's alleged betrayal are proved unfounded.

In the course of this struggle for dominance, however, the teacher
may well resort to force as a last-ditch attempt to protect his privileges.
Violence can be verbal—it is the case with Arthur (46–47 of *Squirrels)*
and Robert, who calls John a "fucking TWIT" (79)—or both verbal and
physical, as in *Buffalo* and *Edmond.* In the former play, Teach viciously
abuses and hits Bobby for his imagined betrayal. He is also the one
who uses the verb "to teach" in a very revealing way: at the beginning
of Act I, furious against his friends Grace and Ruthie, he exclaims
"[t]he only way to teach these people is to kill them" (11). His remark
exposes the dark side of teaching, the possibility that its authoritarian
nature may be pushed to extremes of totalitarianism. It suggests that
when the pedagogical relationship can no longer be maintained by
consensus, when the student proves indocile or "unteachable," violence
and annihilation are the ultimate manifestations of the control device of
retribution originally inscribed in the relationship. Mamet illustrates
this point in *Edmond.*[14] In the first half of the play, the disoriented
eponymous hero in search of himself has been following the advice

haphazardly dispensed to him by a clairvoyant, a drunk in a bar, a leafleteer, a whorehouse manager. A few scenes later, broke and badly bruised, Edmond rebels, buys a knife, harasses a woman on a subway platform and beats up a would-be mugger. He then starts teaching, preaching, explaining life to the first person he meets, a waitress named Glenna: "We've bred the life out of ourselves. And we live in a fog. We live in a dream. Our life is a *school* house, and we're dead" (sc. 15, 67). But despite his liberating message, he does not want Glenna to leave the schoolhouse. In the following scene, his discourse becomes more and more authoritarian, his manner increasingly domineering. When Glenna refuses to obey him and rejects both him and his teachings, Edmond, unable to regain his position of dominance in any other way but force, tries to silence her, abuses her, and eventually stabs her to death.

This explosion of violence, as instinctive as it is absurd, occurs in a context of profound social crisis accompanied by a total confusion of values. Edmond's behaviour is an extreme manifestation of what for David Mamet constitutes the bane of contemporary society: a total self-centredness which profoundly alienates individuals from each other and undermines all relationships. Christopher Bigsby quotes Mamet himself on this subject: "Everyone tries to establish over others an *alien* power in order to find there the satisfaction of his own egoistic need." As a result, Bigsby adds, " [o]ne individual approaches another with a tainted bargain, an offer of relationship now corrupted by the values of the market."[15] The teacher-student model, as we have seen, is founded on a "tainted bargain," and serves the playwright's purpose well to retrace and expose the unravelling of the social fabric and the deterioration of human relationships. But it is also a remarkably productive ironizing device, which Mamet uses to bring out the deficiencies, inconsistencies, and paradoxes of the world he depicts in his plays.

First of all, the fact that he casts mostly uneducated and inarticulate characters in teachers' roles acutely underscores their profound ignorance and incompetence in all aspects of life. Knowledge, though a constant preoccupation in the plays, is conspicuously absent: this is a world without certainties, baffled, groping for meaning and purpose, inventing and faking definitions with mounting anxiety. It is the function of a teacher to pass on truth and provide answers; but in Mamet's plays, the lessons of the pedagogues—although delivered with due self-assurance—are incoherent (those of Bernie or Arthur), vapid

(Robert), or self-contradictory (Don and Teach). People turn to clairvoyants (*Edmond, The Shawl*) or radio psychologists (*Mr. Happiness*) for answers, reassurance, guidance, values. But values seem to have lost their substance, as a passage from *American Buffalo* makes clear. When Bobby returns to the junk shop with a buffalo nickel in the second act, he asks Don how much it is worth:

> DON: [. . .] You got to look it up.
> BOB: In the book?
> DON: Yes.
> BOB: Okay. And then you know.
> DON: Well, no. What I'm saying, the book is like you
>   use it like an *indicator* [. . .] you got an idea, Bob.
>   You got an idea you can *deviate* from.(61)

Like the traditional social and moral code, the old coinbook is outdated; but it can still serve as reference, and provide ideas to "deviate from." The use of the term "deviate" is not at all an innocent one, and reveals another irony: although they do yearn for certainty and stability, the inhabitants of Mamet's world would rather not have a "book" containing fixed meanings and values. They prefer, not just to extrapolate, but *deviate* from now uncertain definitions, distort them at their own convenience, as it happens to serve their purposes. Thus does Teach find himself caught in the contradictions of what he professes. When he declares that free enterprise is "The freedom [. . .] Of the *Individual* [. . .] To Embark on Any Fucking Course that he sees fit [. . .] In order to secure his honest chance to make a profit"(72–73), he fails to understand that the total egotism he is promoting also implies the frightening consequences he will bitterly deplore at the end of the play: "There Is No Law. / There Is No Right And Wrong. / The World Is Lies. / There Is No Friendship" (103).

The teachers in Mamet's plays all aim at teaching their students about life. Yet, if there are no longer any fixed values in this corrupt world, there remains little knowledge to pass on to future generations. It also follows that experience, which in traditional societies is valued and treasured, can be of little use here. The very notion of teaching therefore becomes obsolete, meaningless. Only occasionally do Mamet's characters become dimly aware that it may be so: in *Sexual Perversity* Joan acknowledges that "I don't know anything, Deborah, I swear to god, the older I get the less I know." (29). In Robert's confused statement in scene 17 in *A Life*, the idea remains subconscious: "One generation sows the seeds. It instructs the preceding . . . that is to say, the *following* generation . . . from the quality of its actions" (66). Robert's slip is revealing. Maybe it does not matter after all who is teaching whom since there is so little left to teach. There are messages that get across though; that women are " [s]oft things with a hole in the middle" (*Lakeboat*, 59) to be treated purely as sexual objects, that the individual can "Embark on Any Fucking Course that he sees fit," that "you don't have friends this life" (*Buffalo*, 71, 78), that betrayal and the breaking of contracts are purely a matter of convenience. Here, the irony is that the same characters who profess these principles of contempt toward others demand fidelity and respect from those whom they consider their students; that the teachers expect their students not to apply the only lesson they have learned to their relationship with their masters.

All the ironies and paradoxes Mamet thus unveils stem from the same tragic flaw of man as a social being—or rather, as an increasingly antisocial individual. His self-centredness makes him blind to the implications of his behaviour, indifferent to what is not the immediate fulfilment of superficial desires, incapable of recognizing that his egoism will only make him more lonely, confused, and frustrated, and leave his profound needs for contact and love forever unsatisfied. In Mamet's world, if man is shown as alienated and corrupted by the tainted value system of capitalism, he is not depicted as a victim of the economic order. Rather than bring out an external cause for man's alienation, the plays emphasize his responsibility in propagating and nurturing corruption: Mamet's moral, again and again, is that people are absurdly their own tormentors.

Notes

1. David Mamet, *American Buffalo* (New York: Grove, 1977). Page references to this edition are cited parenthetically.

2. The title of a professor at Oxford or Cambridge, and a term which also playfully evokes the privilege of the teacher to establish rules—that is, do's and don'ts.

3. Michel Foucault, "The Subject and Power," in *Art After Modernism*, ed. Brian Wallis (Boston: Godine, 1984), pp. 417–432. Specific references are cited parenthetically.

4. We shall see later that although the aims of the teacher-student relationships in Mamet's plays ostensibly correspond to the definition proposed by Foucault, their actual result is considerably different.

5. David Mamet, *A Life in the Theatre* (New York: Grove, 1978); *Squirrels* (New York: Grove, 1974), *Sexual Perversity in Chicago* and *The Duck Variations* (New York: Grove, 1977). All subsequent references to these editions are cited parenthetically.

In *Sexual Perversity*, the relationship between Joan and Deborah is a mirror image of that between Bernie and Danny, only less developed.

6. "For David Mamet, an admirer of Chekhov's work, storytelling also becomes fundamental, not only a central strategy of the writer . . . but also a basic tactic of characters for whom it becomes a resource, a retreat and ultimately the only available redemption . . . . [T]hey compulsively elaborate fantasies, create plots, devise scenarios or simply exchange rumour and speculation." Christopher Bigsby, *David Mamet* (London: Macmillan, 1985), p. 22.

7. David Mamet, *Lakeboat* (New York: Grove, 1981). Page references to this edition are cited parenthetically.

8. Roland Barthes, "Writers, Intellectuals, Teachers" (first published in *Tel Quel*, 47, [1971]), in *Images, Music, Text* (New York: Grove, 1977), p. 196.

9. Bigsby, p. 22.

10. David Mamet, *The Shawl* and *Prairie du Chien* (New York: Grove, 1985). Page references to this edition are cited parenthetically.

11. David Mamet, *Glengarry Glen Ross* (New York: Grove, 1984). Page references to this edition are cited parenthetically.

12. Roland Barthes equates self and discourse, and the audience's reception of that discourse with what constitutes the speaker's identity, when he describes the condition of the lecturer deprived of his audience's feedback or incapable of interpreting it: "I am the person who, under cover of *setting out* a body of knowledge, *puts out* a discourse, *never knowing*

how that discourse is being received and thus forever forbidden the reassurance of a definitive image—even if offensive—which would *constitute me.*" Barthes, p. 194.

13. "At the very heart of the power relationship, and constantly provoking it, are the recalcitrance of the will and the intransigeance of freedom. Rather than speaking of an essential freedom, it would be better to speak of "agonism"—of a relationship which is at the same time reciprocal incitation and struggle, less of a face-to-face confrontation which paralyzes both sides than a permanent provocation." Foucault, p. 428.

14. David Mamet, *Edmond* (New York: Grove, 1983). Page references are cited parenthetically.

15. Bigsby, p. 50.

POWER PLAYS: DAVID MAMET'S THEATRE OF MANIPULATION

Henry I. Schvey

One of David Mamet's least well known works, *The Shawl* (1985), is an unpretentious little play which attracted relatively little notice from the New York critical establishment when, performed together with the one-act reconstructed radio play *Prairie du Chien*, it reopened the Mitzi E. Newhouse Theater in Lincoln Center in December 1985. But if the bill proved modest to a fault when compared with successes like *American Buffalo* (1976) or *Glengarry Glen Ross*, the winner of the 1984 Pulitzer prize, the lesser play may nevertheless help to illumine something essential about the playwright's theatrical vision.

The Shawl, like many of Mamet's plays, is concerned with exploitation. Its subject is a small-time mystic who is out to con a bereaved woman out of her inheritance, while at the same time John, the medium, is trying to keep his homosexual lover Charles happy and teach him the rudiments of his "craft"—that is, to demonstrate how his "clairvoyance" may be used to inform the woman of whatever it is she wants to know and ultimately induce her to "Leave what you will. To aid us with our work."[1]

The first act of the play shows the mystic in action, intuiting and accommodating himself to the emotional needs of his prey. The second shows him with his amanuensis, who at the end of the act forces John to choose between taking his victim's fortune the next day during a seance with her dead mother or losing his lover. In the play's climactic third act, the dead woman is indeed "summoned" during the seance, only to have the hoax exposed when the young woman reveals

that the photograph of the dead woman with whom John has communed
is in fact not her mother: "THAT'S NOT HER PHOTOGRAPH. I TOOK IT
FROM A BOOK. You're all the same, all of you, god *damn* you! How
could you, 'I see her by the bed.' How can you *prey* on me? Is there no
mercy in the world . . . ?" (43).

The sudden dramatic reversal indicated in these lines is followed
by an even greater one in which John announces as if possessed, "Oh,
God help me. I see your sainted mother. Wrapped you in a shawl. A red
shawl . . ." (44–45), thus saving the situation and leaving the audience
in some confusion as to whether his vision (confirmed by the woman)
is indeed genuine.

The audience's bafflement at the end of the third act is apparently
resolved at the beginning of the final act when John announces to
Charles that his visionary experience was in fact the result of a visit to
the library: "Society files. Perhaps two pictures. Of a woman in a red-
fringed shawl" (47). But unexpectedly the tone of John and Charles's
relationship is altogether changed. Now, having explained "the
Pythagorean Mysteries" to his young protégé, he insists that he leave,
thereby reversing the earlier situation in Act Two in which Charles
threatened to leave John; "I TOLD YOU. IT WAS A *TRICK*. IT WAS A
TRICK. ARE YOU DEAF? Live in the world. Will you please? That's
what *I'm* trying to do. I'd *wished* that we would be something more to
each other. It was not to be" (49).

Following the young man's forced departure, the woman
reappears, ostensibly to thank John for helping her to make her decision
regarding her mother's will, but actually to authenticate the veracity of
the image of her dead mother that he has "seen"—their conversation
providing yet another reversal and the surprising conclusion to the play:

MISS A :   You must *tell* me. (*Pause*.) You *must* tell me.
           You saw me. You *saw* her (*Pause*).
JOHN: Yes.
MISS A :   You saw her wrap me in that shawl.
JOHN: Yes. (*Pause*.)
MISS A :   And you say I *lost* it.
JOHN: You, yes that is what I said. But you did *not*
           lose it. You *burnt* it. In rage. Standing
           somewhere by the water, five years ago.
MISS A :   Yes. And then I . . .?
JOHN: I do not know. That is all I saw. (53).

The Shawl, a play which appears to be built on deceit and betrayal, is actually concerned with the mystic's gradual awakening to a higher ideal. Having begun as an object lesson for his young protégé about how to inspire false trust and use that trust to steal an innocent woman's money, the play is really about a man's growth and capacity for self-knowledge in the midst of corruption. Faced with the choice of losing his young lover if he does not take the woman for all she is worth, John apparently experiences a moment of real self-awareness as a result of her anguished cry of betrayal. The ending of the play in fact confirms that the visionary experience of the shawl has been real, not part of the charlatan's con game, and John's decision to send Charles away is the logical outcome of that glimpse of a higher possibility in himself.

The Shawl is an instructive example of Mamet's theatrical mind at work because, within its fairly simple means, it reveals a situation which is repeated in other, more difficult plays. Most important is the element of economic exploitation which Mamet feels is rooted in the nature of American society:

> The American Dream has gone bad. . . . It was basically
> raping and pillage. The idea was that if you got out there,
> as long as there was something to exploit—whether it
> was the wild west, the Negroes, the Irish, the Chinese in
> California, the gold fields, or the timberland—one had
> the capacity to get rich. This capitalistic dream of wealth
> turns people against each other.[2]

In a revealing essay entitled "First Principles," Mamet describes at some length his views of American society—founded on democratic ideals and "first principles," but "when faced with discomfort, [ready] to discard any and all first principles of liberty; and further to indict those who do not freely join with us in happily abrogating those principles."[3]

It is entirely consistent with these views that Mamet sees his function as a playwright as a moral one "in a morally bankrupt time."[4] Consequently, for him "the theatre also has its First Principles—principles which make our presentations honest, moral (and, coincidentally, moving, funny, and worth the time and money of the audience)."[5]

But if Mamet has described a play as a "strict lesson in ethics"[6] it would be a mistake to view his work as political or "engaged" in the traditionally accepted meaning of the word. Indeed, Mamet, who began his career as an actor and director, is too much a man of the theatre to forget that "the purpose of the theatre is something completely apart from the purpose of literature." For him, "the traditional purpose of theatre is to celebrate. Which is to say it comes closer to the job of the church than the job of the publishing house."[7]

Elsewhere, he has stated that "the task of the theatrical creator is to bring the life of the human soul to the stage. We are driven to the theatre by our need to express and hear the truth, by our need to be united in this with others, with the audience."[8] But if Mamet has sought to reawaken the ancient function of the theatre as a communal celebration of truth, his excellence as a dramatist is even more beholden to another axiom of the stage—that "Drama is basically historically about lies. That is what drama is about, somebody lying to somebody."[9] Writing about people who are most often self-deceived or lying to one another, Mamet's plays paradoxically allow us to celebrate basic truths about ourselves and our society more adequately than if their moral message was explicitly conveyed through didactic speeches.

The prototypical situation encountered in most of Mamet's plays is a short, fast-paced accumulation of scenes usually between two characters, one of whom tends to dominate. It is the case in *The Shawl*, as previously noted, and it is also true of *The Duck Variations,* Mamet's first play, produced in 1972 while the playwright was teaching at his *alma mater*, Goddard College in Vermont.

However, *The Duck Variations*, despite its convincing mastery of the voices of two old men sitting in a park on the edge of a lake, speculating on the mysteries of the universe and the habits of the duck (matters about which they are both ignorant), betrays all too obviously the influence of Pinter and Beckett in its static plotlessness, and attempts to fill the time with meaningless banter. As in *Waiting for Godot*, there is also the attempt to create a kind of poetry out of fragments:

> EMIL: Where's the duck?
> GEORGE: The duck is dying.
> EMIL: Out in the marsh.
> GEORGE: Out in the marsh.
> EMIL: Oh no.
> GEORGE: In a flock of feathers and blood. Full of bullets.
>   Quiet so as not to make a sound. Dying.

EMIL: Living his last.
GEORGE: Dying.
EMIL: Leaving the Earth and sky.
GEORGE: Dying.
EMIL: Lying on the ground.
GEORGE: Dying.
EMIL: Fluttering.
GEORGE: Dying.
EMIL: Sobbing.
GEORGE: Dying.
EMIL: Quietly bleeding.[10]

The Duck Variations is weakened by the fact that its basically static situation is not compensated for by the *internal* energy and momentum of the characters as are Mamet's more mature efforts; yet there are certainly glimpses of the playwright's fine comic idiom, as in the fourth variation when the two old men pontificate with bluff self-assurance as to whether or not the duck is able to fly at birth:

EMIL: No, no. No. I must still stick to my saying no. No.
GEORGE: . . . Perhaps I misread it. What a thing, however. To be able to fly. In later life.
EMIL: Swimming ain't so bad either.
GEORGE: But any fool who knows how to swim can swim. It takes a *bird* to fly.
EMIL: Insects also fly.
GEORGE: But not in the same category.
EMIL: Insects . . . birds and insects and . . . I could be wrong but . . .
GEORGE: You are wrong. Nothing else flies. (89)

Here, we are very close to the verbal brilliance of Mamet's more recent plays where characters defend their utter ignorance with an intensity which is as passionate as it is pathetic.

Sexual Perversity in Chicago (1975), written when Mamet was only twenty-eight, shows us the playwright in full possession of his powers. The play is a hilariously funny treatment of contemporary notions of sex as seen from the vantage point of four frequenters of the singles bar circuit in Chicago. We laugh at the comic absurdity and ignorance of these young people's notions of human relationships:

BERNIE: The main thing about broads . . .
DANNY: Yes?
BERNIE: Is two things. One: The Way to Get Laid is to
Treat 'Em Like Shit. . . .
DANNY: Yea. . . .
BERNIE: . . . and Two: Nothing . . . nothing makes you
so attractive to the opposite sex as getting
your rocks off on a regular basis. (22)

But we are never allowed to forget how completely inadequate, empty, and dangerous these attitudes are. In a typical Mamet relationship, Bernie "educates" and indoctrinates his younger friend Danny in the ways of the world as he understands it. When Danny seems to question the gospel according to some outdated morality, such as not asking a woman her age, he is immediately slapped down: "Dan, Dan, these are modern times. What do you think this is, the *past*?" (30).

As Dan gravitates toward a serious relationship with Deborah, he is similarly subtly encouraged by Bernie to avoid a serious emotional entanglement: "I mean what the fuck, a guy wants to get it on with some broad on a more or less stable basis, who is to say him no. (*Pause.*) A lot of these broads, you know, you just don't know. You know? I mean what with where they've been and all. I mean a young woman in today's society . . . time she's twenty-two-three. You don't know where the fuck she's been. (*Pause.*) I'm just *talking to you, you understand*" (39).

It is not merely that Mamet has captured the rhythms and idiosyncrasies of American speech, with its casual obscenities and "you knows," just as eloquently as Pinter has the English, but that the play carries with it, for all its humor, an undercurrent of profound despair for the ugliness and sterility of what human relationships have become in our society of quick, casual sex without feeling.

An audience may laugh at Bernie's mock profundity in speaking about his friend's incomprehensible need for a more serious affair with Deborah: "So what does he know at the age, huh? Sell his soul for a little eating pussy, and who can blame him. But mark my words: one, two more weeks he'll do the right thing by the broad. (*Pause.*) And drop her like a fucking hot potato." (46). Yet when Dan succeeds in learning the lesson, and answers Deb's query, "Will you love me when I'm old?" with "If you can manage to look eighteen, yes" (51), the laughter is more muted and eventually dissolves altogether, as when we see Dan and Bernie at the beach at the end of the play, just as they were at the beginning, talking about girls in a perpetually adolescent quest for tits and ass."

If these characters seem without real identity to us, it is because in their isolation they have none, only the words and the shared values of a society which offers no possibility for real contact, a world "full of distorted wisdom, of lessons learned but learned wrong because of the unreasonable ferocity, the lack of shape or instruction of middle American life."[11]

In play after play such as *A Life in the Theatre* (1977), dealing with two actors, one old and experienced, the other young; *Reunion* (1976) about the meeting between a father and daughter who have not seen one another in nearly twenty years; and *Dark Pony* (1979), a brief fairy tale of a play in which a father tells his young daughter a story about an Indian boy and his magical pony, Mamet describes meetings between two characters who strive to make real contact with one another but cannot quite.

Their finger tips do not quite touch; the golden bracelet which the father gives his daughter in *Reunion* carries the wrong inscription ("It's my fault. It's not their fault. My threes look like eights"),[12] the story of *Dark Pony* is more a plea for reassurance to the father's own apparently weakened sense of self than it is a means of real security to his daughter, who is already thinking "We are almost home'; while despite momentary points of contact, Robert, the elder actor's final words—"The lights dim. Each to his own home. Goodnight. Goodnight. Goodnight"[13]—stress his isolation and sadness at not really having made contact with his young protégé. As Mamet has said, "What I write about is what I think is missing from our society. And that's communication on a basic level."[14]

Much has been written concerning *American Buffalo* (1975), and there is no question that it remains one of the central works in this playwright's already substantial canon. Set in Donny Dubrow's Resale Shop, it concerns the planned robbery of a coin collection from a man who has walked into Donny's store and bought a buffalo nickel for the astronomical price of ninety dollars.

The projected robbery by the three inept would-be thieves never takes place, and any description of the plot of the play tells us about as much as a similar description would reveal about Beckett's *Waiting for Godot*. Nevertheless, some critics have been put off by the lack of "action," an incomprehensible charge given the fact that *American Buffalo*, its plot notwithstanding, is full of activity, movement, and even violence. Mamet himself, commenting on this kind of criticism, ironically argues that "even after Beckett and Pinter, there are people . . . who think that three men talking for two acts about a break-in they do not commit does not constitute a plot."[15]

The issue of its plotlessness aside, *American Buffalo* is a play remarkable for its brilliance in capturing the basic inarticulacy of everyday American parlance, its subtle examination of the corruptive force of American society and its dreams, and the effect of this corruption on individuals.

The most significant and often-used word in *American Buffalo* (aside from the ubiquitous "fuck") is almost certainly "business." At the very beginning of the play, Donny, the shop owner, is instructing his young junkie friend, Bobby, on the meaning of this crucial concept. Discussing Fletcher's having brought (or stolen?) pig-iron from his friend, Ruthie, Donny delivers an important lesson on the way of the world:

> DON: He didn't steal it, Bob.
> BOB: No?
> DON: No.
> BOB: She was mad at him . . .
> DON: Well, that very well may be, Bob, but that fact
>   remains that it was business. That's what
>   business is.
> BOB: What?
> DON: People taking care of themselves. Huh?[16]

Near the end of this valuable lesson, which is at the heart of the play's theme, the third character, Teach, enters Don's junk shop. Teach, who later proclaims "I am a businessman, I am here to do business, I am here to face facts" (83), quickly ascertains that Don and Bobby are planning the robbery of the coin collection and wastes no time in trying to get a piece of the action for himself, even if it means pushing Donny's friend Bobby out of the picture:

> TEACH: He's a great kid, Don. You know how I feel
>   about the kid. (*Pause.*)
> DON: He's doing good.

TEACH: I can see that. (*Pause.*) But I gotta say something here.
DON: What?
TEACH: Only this—and I don't think I'm *getting* at anything—
DON: What?
TEACH: Don't send the Kid in.
DON: I shouldn't send Bobby in?
TEACH: No. Now, just wait a second. Let's siddown on this. What are we saying here? Loyalty. (*Pause.*) You know how I am on this. This is great. This is admirable.
DON: What?
TEACH: This loyalty. This is swell. It turns my heart the things you do for the Kid. . . . All I mean, a guy can be too loyal, Don. Don't be dense on this. What are we saying here? Business. . . . All that I'm saying, don't confuse business with pleasure. (33–34)

Teach worms his way in on the job, convinces Don to get rid of Bobby and later tries to oust Fletcher, who is supposed to be involved in the break-in as well. When Donny argues that Fletcher is necessary because he knows how to get in the coin collector's house, Teach disposes of the argument in the typically hard-headed fashion of this progressive man of business: "What the fuck, they live in Fort Knox? You break in a *window*, worse comes to worse you kick the fucking *back door* in. What do you think this is, the Middle Ages?" (77).

Earlier in the play, Teach has taken the trouble to define the capitalist system of which he considers himself such an outstanding representative:

TEACH: You know what is free enterprise?
DON: No. What?
TEACH: The freedom . . .
DON: . . . yeah?
TEACH: Of the *Individual*
DON: . . . Yeah?
TEACH: To embark on any fucking course that he sees fit.
DON: Uh-huh. . . .

TEACH: *In order to secure his honest chance to make a*
        profit. Am I so out of line on this?
DON: No.
TEACH: Does this make me a Commie?
DON: No.
TEACH: The country's founded on this, Don. You know
        this. . . . Without this we're just savage
        shitheads in the wilderness. (72–73)

In discussing *American Buffalo*, Mamet has stated that the play "is about the American ethic of business, . . . about how we excuse all sorts of great and small betrayals and ethical compromises called business. . . . There's really no difference between the *lumpenproletariat* and stockbrokers or corporate lawyers who are the lackeys of business . . . . Part of the American myth is that a difference exists, that at a certain point vicious behavior becomes laudable."[17]

Despite the forthrightness of Mamet's comments, only a small part of the play's success comes as a result of its explicit attack on American values through the mouths of three inept and semi-articulate grifters who cannot even pull off a simple robbery. Significantly, the play ends with an image of chaos as Teach explodes on stage, hitting Bobby viciously on the side of the head at a wrongly suspected betrayal of their plans by the innocent junkie, before finally trashing the shop with an iron "dead-pig sticker," screaming in frustration about the absence of the very values he has steadfastly discounted in the course of the play: "The Whole Entire World. There Is No Law. There Is No Right And Wrong. The World Is Lies. There Is No Friendship" (103).

Beyond the fine comic reversal of the cheap hoods who justify their planned crime with the logic (if not the precise diction) of Wall Street, the essence of *American Buffalo* lies in its notions of betrayal. We have previously observed that at the beginning of the play Donny presents himself as an instructor to his young ward, Bobby. He has taught him about the difference between business and friendship, cautioning him that "Things are not always what they seem to be" (8), before embarking on a fatherly lecture about Bobby's eating habits:

DON: . . . You want some breakfast?
BOB: I'm not hungry.
DON: Never skip breakfast, Bob.
BOB: Why?

DON:	Breakfast . . . is the most important meal of the day.
BOB:	I'm not hungry.
DON:	It makes no earthly difference in the world. You know how much nutritive benefits they got in coffee? Zero. Not one thing. The stuff eats you up. You can't live on coffee, Bobby. (And I've told you this before.) You cannot live on cigarettes. You may feel good, you may feel fine, but something's getting overworked, and you are going to pay for it. Now: What do you see me eat when I come in here every day?
BOB:	Coffee. (8)

The situation where one character offers well-seasoned and clichéd advice to an innocent partner is a recurrent one in Mamet's plays, but in *American Buffalo* it provides ample moral and psychological underpinning to the comedy. Seen in its simplest terms, the play is about the corruptive force the American business ethos has on human relationships.

At the opening of the play we see Don posing as a Bellovian "reality-instructor" and paternalistic adviser to Bobby, the reformed junkie, teaching him about business, breakfast, vitamins, and most important of all, friendship; "Cause there's business and there's friendship, Bobby . . . there are many things, and when you walk around you *hear* a lot of things, and what you got to do is keep clear who your friends are, and who treated you like what. Or else the rest is garbage, Bob . . ." (7–8).

When Teach appears on stage shortly after the above comments, Don's advice is put to the test, and ironically it is Don, the bluff and blustering Oliver Hardy to Bobby's Stan Laurel, whose perception of the difference between business and friendship is found to be sorely lacking. Using essentially the same street talk as Donny, Teach reverses Donny's lesson about the value of true friendship to impose himself between Don and Bobby, arguing that "Friendship is friendship and a wonderful thing, and I am all for it. I have never said different, and you know me on this point. Okay. But let's just keep it separate, huh, let's just keep the two apart, and maybe we can deal with each other like some human beings" (15).

After advising him to oust Bobby from the planned robbery, encouraging him to "take the time to go first class," he balms Don's conscience by saying "You're only doing the right thing by him, Don. (*Pause.*) Believe me. (*Pause.*) It's best for everybody. (*Pause.*) What's done is done. (*Pause.*) So let's get started" (44).

If the first of the play's two acts reveals Teach's ability to fast-talk his way into the job and come between Donny and Bobby, the second indicates the consequences of Teach's poison in human terms. When Fletcher's non-arrival, Bobby's "discovery" of a buffalo nickel for which he asks to be paid fifty dollars, and Bob's subsequent announcement that Fletcher has been mugged "by some Mexicans" and is in the hospital with a broken jaw convince Teach that he and Don have been double-crossed on the hold-up, he turns on the boy, reminding him that "Loyalty does not mean *shit* in a situation like this."

The violence which ensues as Teach picks up a piece of junk and "hits Bob viciously on the side of the head" is implicitly endorsed by Don who continues to play a paternalistic role toward Bobby: "You know, we didn't want to do this to you, Bob." Only when it turns out that Bob's story about Fletcher's mugging has in fact been true and that he has not found but bought the buffalo nickel "For Donny." does Donny begin to realize that it is not his naive young protégé who has deceived him, but that Donny has deceived himself.

Unlike Bobby, who has remembered who his friends are, Donny has allowed himself to be conned by the streetwise con man, Teach, whose desperate accusation—'You *fake*. You fucking *fake*. You fuck your friends. You have no friends. No wonder that you fuck this kid around"—contains, despite its self-serving aspects, a considerable measure of truth. Only at this point does Donny see Teach clearly as the deceiver he is: "You stiff this one, you stiff that one . . . you come in here, you stick this poison in me. . . . You make life of garbage" (100–01).

In the essentially comic world of *American Buffalo*, Donny's clownish deception by his foul-mouthed, streetwise Iago does not yield tragic results. Instead, Teach's crazed destruction of Donny's junk shop reveals the inchoate mess that believing in Teach's gospel has made of their world, and the play ends with quiet pathos as Teach, revealing the absurdity beneath his bravado in a homemade paper hat to protect himself from the rain, goes for his car, while Donny and Bobby apologize to one another, Bobby for apparently letting his mentor down, Donny for not following his own sage advice to the boy that "Things are not always what they seem to be" (8). In *American Buffalo*, Mamet attacks the materialistic ethos which dominates American society and comes perilously close to destroying the bonds of "family." For, despite appearances, *American Buffalo* is to its author a play about "life in the family."[18] Only at the end of the play does Donny undergo something of an *anagnorisis* whereby he realizes how close he as come to killing the one thing he loves for the sake of business, and that it is he rather than Bobby who is in need of lessons on how to live.

Stylistically a very different kind of play, *Edmond* (1982) pushes these lessons even further. Edmond is a dark and ugly play, devoid of the brilliant humor which illumines the sordid world of *American Buffalo*. It will never be a popular play, and was, I think, victimized by an embattled critical reception which insisted on comparing the work with the "openness and youthful euphoria" of the playwright's early work,[19] or rejecting it outright because its central character lacked credible motivation, or because its philosophical premises were made insufficiently clear.[20] In fact, *Edmond* is a remarkable work which, despite its manifest darkness and depravity, is arguably one of Mamet's best to date.

The genre to which *Edmond* bears most similarity is the morality play, and it reveals with a frightening explicitness Mamet's apocalyptic vision of a society bent upon self-destruction. If for Mamet the American dream ultimately turns men against one another in a frenetic pursuit of insatiable greed, *Edmond* begins at the point where the dream "has nowhere to go so it has to start turning in on itself."[21]

Having been vaguely informed by one of the author's unreliable Fortune-Tellers in the opening scene that "You are not where you belong," and that his lot is predestined in a "world [that] seems to be crumbling around us,"[22] the play's upwardly mobile protagonist suddenly breaks with his wife, embarking on a downwardly spiralling odyssey in the bowels of what Albee's Jerry called "the greatest city in world. Amen."[23]

In his plunge into the darkness of New York's filthy underbelly, Edmond visits bars, peep shows, whorehouses, massage parlours, card sharks, sordid hotels, pawnshops and pimps. Edmond's movements through these stages on life's way are accompanied by a gradual loss of innocence and rapidly mounting violence. At the start of his journey he is awkward and naive, saying to the B-Girl he tries to pick up at a bar in the fourth scene, "I'm putting myself at your mercy . . . this is my first time in a place like this" (27). By the time he is held up by the Pimp in Scene Fourteen, he is sufficiently experienced in the ways of the world to turn the tables on his aggressor who is holding a knife to his throat, unleashing all the pent-up violence, fear, and racial hate with which he has been indoctrinated by society's crooks and cheats in scene after scene.

In the coffee-house scene which follows, Edmond meets Glenna, a young acting student who responds to his advances. However, when at her apartment she refuses to accept the label that Edmond gives her ("Say it: I am a waitress"), he stabs her in a fit of confused, insane rage. Unable to make the human contact for which he has vaguely searched for on the streets of New York, he is finally imprisoned for his crime and, noting that "Every fear hides a wish" adds that "I think I am going to like it here" (89).

However, even this hoped-for peace beyond the pale of society ends in violence as Edmond is sodomized and beaten by his black cellmate, and his complaints to the prison authorities go unheeded, resulting merely in the acknowledgement that such things "happen." In the final, lyrical scene, Edmond and the Prisoner each lie on their separate bunks discussing the world around them. Edmond seems to have adopted a Hamlet-like position of acceptance, and following a conversation about who or what it is that rules the universe and whether or not they are in hell, Edmond goes over to the Prisoner to exchange a goodnight kiss before returning to his own bunk as the lights fade.

In *Edmond*, Mamet has tackled nothing less than the spiritual poverty and emptiness of our urban civilization, and far from approving or condoning Edmond's impulse toward irrational violence as in such popular films as *Taxi Driver* or Charles Bronson vehicles like *Death Wish*, Mamet's play shows in its episodic structure of short, staccato scenes preceded by an expressionistic *Aufbruch* that the descent into violence is inevitable and unremitting.

At the same time, the play's apocalyptic movement downward is counterpointed by the sense of Edmond's own unconscious spiritual quest. Like a contemporary of Büchner's *Woyzeck* (a play with which it has frequently been compared), *Edmond* reveals man trapped in an overturned world which he is powerless to fathom, let alone change. As also in *Woyzeck* (composed as it is of short, fragmentary scenes, and whose climatic episode depicts a man's irrational stabbing of a woman), Mamet's play speculates on a world in which the bestial in man has been allowed to run wild. In naming his central character Edmond Burke, Mamet is not indulging in deliberate mystification, or wishing, as one reviewer put it, to "fake pedantic critics into straining for a link between him and the 18th-century British statesman and orator, who happened to spell his name with a 'u.'"[24] Rather, he is reminding us quite deliberately of his namesake's obsessive concern with the partnership between the individual and the social order, a partnership which for all we know may be irretrievably sundered in our own violent age.

In writing about the *contrat social* of Rousseau, Burke thus observed that society is indeed a contract but not merely a contract upon for the gratification of individual desires:

> It is to be looked on with other reverence; because it is not a partnership in things subservient only to the gross animal existence of a temporary and perishable nature. It is a partnership in all sciences, a partnership in all art, a partnership in every virtue and in all perfection.[25]

In commenting on the French Revolution, Burke sensed one of the most powerful temptations of modern society, the indulgence in liberty for its own sake: "what is liberty without wisdom and without virtue? It is the greatest of all possible evils; for it is folly, vice, and madness, without tuition or restraint."[26]

Edmond, then, reveals the playwright's fear that modern American society, founded on Teach's belief in the individual's right "To embark on any fucking course that he sees fit," has lost hold of its moorings. Edmond, having shaken himself free of the merry-go-round of competition and acquisition, unconsciously hungers for spiritual contact in a spiritless world. But, as Mamet has said, "It's impossible to have spiritual empathy if you don't have spirit. *That* is what is lacking. That's the point. That is what each person has to discover in himself."[27] Inherent in Edmond's downward spiral through the circles of hell that is New York City is an internal quest to be part of a human community which counsels only sexual abuse to women, fear of homosexuals, and racial hatred. In the final scene of the play, having fallen about as far as a man can, Mamet's Everyman finally begins to

discern a meaning in life beyond violence and aggression. It is at this
point of self-discovery that real existence begins.

It is hardly surprising that Mamet chose the world of small-time,
cut-throat real-estate salesmen as the subject of *Glengarry Glen Ross*,
winner of the Pulitzer prize in 1984 and the playwright's most
celebrated work to date. It is only a small step from the seedy grifters in
American Buffalo to the real-estate salesmen trying to peddle worthless
Florida swampland (albeit with mellifluous sounding names like
Mountainview, Glen Ross Farms, or Glengarry Highlands), while the
card-sharks, pimps and conmen who are peppered through *Edmond* are
similarly related to the fast-talking hustlers who subdue their
unsuspecting prey and each other in *Glengarry Glen Ross*.

But in these desperate salesmen whose motto is "Always be
closing," Mamet has perhaps found his purest metaphor for a society
built on merciless exploitation. As early as 1951, in *White Collar*, C.
Wright Mills identified the image of the salesman with America as a
nation: "The Salesman's world has now become everybody's world,
and, in some part, everybody has become a salesman. . . . This is a
time of venality. . . . The bargaining manner, the huckstering animus,
the memorized theology of pep, the commercialized evaluation of
personal traits—they are all around us; in public and in private there's
the tang and feel of salesmanship."[28]

In writing *Death of a Salesman*, a play which obviously invites
comparison with *Glengarry Glen Ross*, Arthur Miller was acutely
sensitive to certain essential values in American life which he felt were
in danger of being sacrificed to the prevailing materialistic ethos
whereby "business is business." This is suggested in the opening stage
directions in which the salesman's house is surrounded on all sides by
"towering angular shapes,"[29] by the fact that (in the Requiem) Biff
informs us that "there's more of him in that front stoop than in all the
sales he ever made," and most clearly in Willy's lament to his young
employer about the passage of a bygone era:

> In those days there was personality in it, Howard. There
> was respect, and comradeship, and gratitude in it. Today,
> it's all cut and dried, and there's no chance for bringing
> friendship to bear—or personality. (p. 74)

Near the end of Mamet's play, Richard Roma, the most successful and
slickest of Mamet's salesmen utters a very similar lament: "I swear . . .

it's not a world of men . . . it's a world of clock watchers, bureaucrats, officeholders . . . what it is, it's a fucked-up world . . . there's no adventure to it. (*Pause.*) Dying breed. Yes it is. (*Pause.*) We are the members of a dying breed."[30]

But if both Miller and Mamet use salesmen to expose the vacuity of the American dream, the differences in their perspectives, separated by more than thirty years, are predictably more revealing than their similarities. If Miller is indeed critical of Willy's dreams in the play's Requiem, he also places in mouth of Charley, Willy's neighbour, a defense of Willy as a man who "don't put a bolt to a nut, he don't tell you the law or give you medicine. He's a man way out there in the blue, riding on a smile, and a shoeshine, And when they start not smiling back—that's an earthquake. . . Nobody dast blame this man. A salesman is got to dream, boy. It comes with the territory" (132).

Writing at a time when more people perhaps believed in the efficacy of the dream, Miller's primary purpose is not so much to attack social injustice as to illuminate the psyche of a man unable to partake in the riches—due to the combination of his own temperament and forces around him. As the playwright himself put it in his essay "Tragedy and the Common Man," this is a study of a man willing "to throw all he has into the contest, the battle to secure his rightful place in his world."[31] (It is interesting to be reminded of the play's original title, *The Inside of his Head*, suggesting that the form of the play was intended to "literally be the process of Willy Loman's way of mind.")[32]

In contrast to Miller's perception of his play as psychological tragedy, Mamet's is a "gang comedy in the tradition of *The Front Page* or *Man in White* or detective story."[33] It is perhaps for this reason that some reviewers refused to acknowledge the play's significance, referring to its "lack of breadth and vision . . . when . . . set next to *Death of a Salesman*,"[34] or commenting that "To elevate it to the status of a bitter comment on the American dream would amount to cosmic foolishness."[35]

Indeed, the scope of the play is deceptively slight, and the "contest" in which Mamet's protagonists are involved is not to secure their rightful places in the cosmos but to win a Cadillac car as a sales bonus. Nonetheless, in its roughly 75 minutes of running time, Mamet has created a small masterpiece which reveals with extraordinary perspicacity the treachery of the materialistic world we live in.

The first act, set in a sleazy Chinese restaurant the salesmen use as their hangout and "office" away from work, depicts three consecutive two-character confrontations of the type in which Mamet specializes. Far from demonstrating one critic's claim that Mamet (in *A Life in the Theatre*) "seemed to be waiting for Sophocles to introduce the third character into the drama,"[36] these scenes are miniature gems, each providing a necessary element to our understanding of a world that is based on power, greed, and manipulation, as well as acquainting us with the rules of the salesman's game in which those who sell the most "units" will receive a Cadillac, while those who are on "bad streaks" are deprived access to the premium "leads" or "sits" (contacts with likely customers).

In the first of these scenes we meet Shelly Levene, a Willy Loman of the 1980s, who is on a bad streak and is reduced to begging for some good leads from Williamson, the office manager who, while administering the business for its unseen owners, is clearly not averse to being offered substantial kickbacks from the less successful salesmen.

The second scene offers us another cameo of two disgruntled salesmen who complain about their work, until it gradually becomes apparent that one of them has used the meeting to set up his colleague to rob the company office while he reaps the benefits of the heist and avoids detection. Much of the brilliance of the dialogue hinges on the precise distinction made between "talking" and "speaking" about the planned theft and sale of the leads to a competitive firm headed by Jerry Graff:

AARONOW: How do you know he'd buy them?
MOSS: Graff? Because I worked for him.
AARONOW: You haven't talked to him.
MOSS: No. What do you mean? Have I talked to
           him about this? (*Pause.*)
AARONOW: Yes. I mean are you actually *talking* about
           this, or are we just . . .
MOSS: No, we're just . . .
AARONOW: We're just "*talking*" about it.
MOSS: We're just *speaking* about it. (*Pause.*) As
           an idea.
AARONOW: As an idea.
MOSS: Yes.

AARONOW: We're not actually *talking* about it.
MOSS: No.(38–39)

The final scene is the briefest and most insidiously brilliant. Still at the restaurant, we witness an apparently friendly conversation, full of banal "insights" about how to live, until suddenly at the end of the scene the entire conversation is revealed to be a carefully orchestrated sales pitch to the unsuspecting prey, as Roma takes out a small map. "What is that? Florida Glengarry Highlands. Florida. 'Florida. *Bullshit*.' And maybe that's true; and that's what *I* said: but look *here*: what is this? This is a piece of land. Listen to what I'm going to tell you now." (50–51).

The second act has as its location the burgled real estate office, and while outwardly resembling nothing so much as a cops-and-robbers farce as the investigation into the robbery is mixed with the tearful arrival of the bamboozled and victimized customer of the previous act, the play's comic surface conceals its grim depths just as adequately as its sweet-sounding title disguises the all-pervasive corruption which is the play's true subject.

Glengarry Glen Ross is concerned with a world of competition in which human feeling is completely absent; when Roma, the dapper and most successful of the salesmen, asks his less fortunate colleague, Aaronow, "How are you?," the latter responds politely until he realizes that Roma's question had nothing to do with Aaronow's health, but rather his standing in the sales competition for the Cadillac:

ROMA: . . . How are you?
AARONOW: I'm fine. You mean the *board*. You mean
            the *board* . . . ?
ROMA: I don't . . . yes. Okay, the board. (56)

Similarly, the apparently friendly relations between Roma and Levene extend only so far as to enable them to join forces in a brilliant improvisation to dupe their unsuspecting prey, who comes to the office to try and rescind Roma's deal. Although Roma tells Levene that "We are members of a dying breed. That's . . . that's . . . why we have to stick together" at the end of the play, he tells Williamson what this "partnership" really means: "My stuff is mine, his stuff is ours. I'm taking half of his commissions—now, you work it out" (107).

Remarkably, despite the play's excoriating attack on American business values, the characters retain both their fascination and charm for the audience. Levene's magnificent entrance as "The Machine"—as he strides into the burgled office having momentarily recaptured his former glory with a sale of eight units of Mountain View property—is cheering, and for the time being we overlook the implications of his wicked description of the couple as they are forced to sign the contract: "They signed, Ricky. It was great. It was fucking great. It was like they wilted all at once. No *gesture* . . . nothing. Like together. They, I swear to God, they both kind of *imperceptibly slumped*" (74).

The true villain of the play (and this accounts for its great success) is the *system*, not the tribe of hustlers who implement it by cheating others out of their hard-earned savings. Thus we are amused and delighted by the theatrical genius of Roma and Levene, the former because he is so good at what he does, the latter because he is sufficiently punished by the system itself. In the tradition of the gang comedy which Mamet employs, the real conflict and confrontation is between "individuals and their environment much more than between individuals opposed to each other."[37] Yet even as we laugh, we are unable to forget that these are peddlers of false dreams to those innocent or stupid enough to buy.

Mamet's work, from the early *Duck Variations* through *Glengarry* and *The Shawl*, is remarkably unified. Concentrating on the banal wisdom of American speech, he has forged a theatrical language amazingly close to everyday American parlance, laced with a profanity that is, remarkably enough, transformed into an extra-ordinarily precise tool.

Like his acknowledged mentor, Harold Pinter (to whom *Glengarry* was dedicated), Mamet is concerned with pauses and the spaces between what is actually uttered in conversation. Like Pinter, too, Mamet is concerned with the ways in which fragmentary utterances and obliquities may be used as part of a game involving manipulation or power. Most important, without ever preaching to his audience, or losing their power to move us, Mamet's plays are highly articulate expressions of an attack on the materialistic values of American society. Yet the vision they present is never wholly dark, but it is either illuminated by the pursuit of self-knowledge or by the extraordinary "wisdom" with which his characters cloak their empty, banal lives.

Notes

1. David Mamet, *The Shawl and Prairie du Chien* (New York: Grove Press, 1986), p. 25. Further references are in parentheses following quotations.

2. Quoted in Mimi Leahey, "David Mamet: the American Dream Gone Bad," *Other Stages*, 4 Nov. 1982, p. 3.

3. David Mamet, "First Principles," *Theater* (Summer–Fall): p. 51.

4. Ibid., p. 52.

5. Ibid., p. 51.

6. Leahey, p. 3.

7. "Talking about Writing for the Theater," *International Herald Tribune*, 21 Feb. 1986, p. 7.

8. Leahey, p. 3.

9. Quoted in "David Mamet: Celebrating the Capacity for Self-Knowledge" (Interview with Henry I. Schvey), *New Theatre Quarterly, 4*, No. 13 (1988): p. 91. Subsequently cited as Mamet interview.

10. Mamet, *Sexual Perversity in Chicago and The Duck Variations* (New York: Grove Press, 1978), pp. 122–123. Subsequent references are in parentheses following quotations.

11. Richard Eder, "David Mamet's New Realism," *New York Times Magazine*, 12 March 1978, p. 41.

12. Mamet, *Reunion and Dark Pony* (New York: Grove Press, 1979), p. 40. Subsequent references are in parentheses following quotations.

13. Mamet, *A Life in the Theatre* (New York: Grove Press, 1977), p. 95.

14. Quoted in Patricia Lewis and Terry Browne, "David Mamet," p. 69.

15. Lewis and Browne, p. 66.

16. Mamet, *American Buffalo* (New York: Grove Press, 1976), p. 7. Subsequent references are in parentheses following quotations.

17. Richard Gottlieb, "The Engine that Drives Playwright David Mamet," *New York Times*, 15 Jan. 1978, Sec. 2, p. 4.

18. Mamet interview, p. 93.

19. Mel Gussow, "Mamet Explores the Fall of *Edmond*," *New York Times*, 17 June 1982, Sec. C, p. 17.

20. See for example, Frank Rich, "Mamet's *Edmond* at the Provincetown," *New York Times*, 28 Oct. 1982; or Clive Barnes "Stark Telling of Mamet's *Edmond*," *New York Post*, 28 Oct. 1982.

21. Quoted in Leahey, p. 3.

22. Mamet, *Edmond* (New York: Grove Press, 1983), p. 16. Subsequent references are in parentheses following quotations.

23. Edward Albee, *The Zoo Story* (New York: Signet, 1959), p. 37.

24. Joseph Hurley, "Mamet's Tour of Urban Depravity," *Other Stages*, 4 Nov. 1982, p. 3.

25. Edmund Burke, *Reflections on the Revolution in France* (Penguin Books, 1969), p. 194.

26. Burke, p. 373.

27. Quoted in Leahey, p. 3.

28. Quoted in Howard Kissel, "Miller and Mamet," *Playbill*, 2, No. 9 (1984), p. 10.

29. Arthur Miller, *Death of a Salesman* (New York: Viking, 1971), p. 5. Subsequent references are in parentheses following quotations.

30. Mamet, *Glengarry Glen Ross* (New York: Grove Press, 1984), p. 105. Subsequent references are in parentheses following quotations.

31. Robert A. Martin, ed., *The Theater Essays of Arthur Miller* (Harmondsworth: Penguin, 1978), p. 6.

32. Ibid. pp. 135–66.

33. Mamet interview, p. 92.

34. Edwin Wilson, "Theater: Lives of Salesman," *Wall Street Journal*, 4 Apr. 1984.

35. Douglas Watt, "A "Death" of Honest Salesman," *New York Daily News*, 26 Mar. 1984.

36. Quoted in Richard Eder, "David Mamet's New Realism," p. 41.

37. Mamet interview, p. 92.

HOW ARE THINGS MADE ROUND?

Ruby Cohn

"A good deal of this play has been written in an 'invented language' derived from contemporary American idioms. . . ." These words are excerpted from Sam Shepard's note in the London program of his *Tooth of Crime*, but even though David Mamet has never dedicated a play to Sam Shepard—as he has to Harold Pinter, Richard Nelson, and Wally Shawn—he nevertheless dramatizes American business in an "invented language." Much nonsense has been written about Mamet's accurate ear for demotic Chicago speech, just as nonsense was written about the London ear of his mentor Harold Pinter, but both dramatists stand on native ground in order to nurture verbal hybrids. As Mamet plants deftly in what I will call his Business Trilogy, as he himself is aware: "It's not an attempt to capture language as much as it is an attempt to create language" (Roudané, 76).

Only the middle play of the trilogy, *Glengarry Glen Ross*, deals with salesmen, but the rhythms of all three Mamet plays hearken back to the American salesman of popular and literary culture, whose speech bristled with rhetorical questions, calculated repetitions, impatient interruptions. Like their ancestors, O'Neill's Hickey and Miller's Willy Loman, Mamet's businessmen thrive on slang and colloquialism. On the eve of the twenty-first century, however, the frenzied pace of contemporary life is echoed in the rapid rhythm of Mamet's dialogue, which he controls by various devices. More than any other playwright, but not unlike film writers, Mamet quickens stage speech with monosyllables. Seemingly careless of syntax, he channels the insecurity of his characters into streams of questions. A recurrent query is: "Am I wrong?"

From the first three minutes on stage, questions energize dialogue in Mamet's Business Trilogy. *American Buffalo* opens on Don Dubrow's: "So?" which is at once expanded to: "So what, Bob?" (*AM* 3). Levene's second speech in *Glengarry* protests: "Will you please?" (*GGR* 16). A quotation early in *Speed-the-Plow* probes monosyllabically: "How are things made round?" (*STP* 3). Interrogative rhythms are quickly set and pervasively maintained in each play—even when the questions are merely rhetorical. *American Buffalo* immerses us immediately in a catechismic conversation between Don Dubrow of the ReSale Shop and his gopher, the ex-junkie Bob. When Teach intrudes upon this pair, he cloaks his questions in surmise about "the thing," "the job," "the mark," "the shot," "business." In *Glengarry Glen Ross,* interrogation sometimes cedes to exclamation, but questions still govern the salesman Levene's pleas for leads to the office manager Williamson, and questions even punctuate the complaints about leads from the salesmen Moss and Aaronow, which mount toward the summit of an office trashing. After the crime, the detective questions the real estate salesmen offstage, but an interrogative cloud hovers over the ransacked room, and in the last moments of the play Aaronow phrases and rephrases questions as to the culprit, before he returns to business: "Did the leads come in yet?" (*GGR* 108).

In *Speed-of-the-Plow* questions function mostly climactically. Until the end of the play, rising reflections solicit exultation as often as information on the part of the two self-styled Hollywood whores, Bob Gould and Charlie Fox. Once this pair grasps that the reigning male star is willing to make a prison buddy movie for them, Bob rhapsodizes: "The question, your crass question: how much money do we stand to make . . . ?" (*STP* 20) But when Bob himself, skillfully manipulated by the temporary secretary Karen, betrays the "crass question" for a movie of edification, he awards Charlie the favor of "one question" (*STP* 74) to Karen: "If [Bob] had said 'No' [to greenlighting the movie], would you have gone to bed with him?" (*STP* 77). Karen's negative reply is Charlie's positive triumph. The plow will speed ahead, as Charlie closes the play in a return to rhapsodic rhetorical questions: "What are we put out on earth to do? . . . Whose name goes above the title? . . . Then how bad can life be?" (*STP* 82).

Rising interrogative rhythms—with or without question marks in the text—are only forms of Mamet's ubiquitous repetition, which can sound tattoos in single syllables or entire sentences. Most striking, of course, are obscenities, whose sonic resources Mamet exploits—the hard consonants and clipped vowels of cunt, fuck, suck, cock, and dick. Singly and collectively, they form a percussive background to the forward movement of Mamet's business plots, and they also propel that movement by frequent alliteration and occasional rhyme with more innocent words. In *American Buffalo* Teach inveighs against "Fuckin' fakes" in an off-rhyme, and he prods Don: "It's kickass or kissass" (*AM* 74). The hero-victim of *Glengarry* is nicknamed Levene the Machine because of his (former) sales prowess, but he pleads in present rhyme: "I need the leads" (*GGR* 18). In *Speed-the-Plow* rhyme connotes celebration; as producers of the Doug Brown buddy film, Bob assures Charlie that women will succumb to them: "It's Boy's Choice" (*STP* 23). Charlie flatters Bob: "You're Yertle the Turtle" (*STP* 7). And he bends patriotic slogans to the sport of money-making: "First in war. First in peace. First in the hearts of Pee Wee Reese." (*STP* 32). The two would-be producers produce a kind of couplet:

> CHARLIE: Drop a dime on Western civilization.
> BOB: . . . 'Bout time. (*STP* 24)

Sensitive as Mamet is to sound, deploying it strategically, he rarely resorts to *mere* sound, such as nonsense syllables. Nevertheless, the momentum of their discourse occasionally reduces loquacious characters like Teach, Roma, Moss, and Charlie to "blah blah blah."

The critic Ross Wetzsteon quotes Mamet: "I'm fascinated by the way, the way the language we use, its rhythms, actually determines the way we behave, rather than the other way around." I would argue, however, that the way Mamet's characters behave determines their language and nowhere more pungently than in the Business Trilogy. Skillful as Mamet is with controlling rhythms sonically, he is even more adroit with grammar and vocabulary to reveal the insecurity of his characters. Wetzsteon writes of Mamet's "utter clarity of total grammatical chaos," (39) but there is method in his chaos.

A sense of pressure compels Mamet's characters to omit prepositions, conjunctions, or relative pronouns. As though the conjunction "if" were absent from the English language, Don instructs his gopher: "You're s'posed to watch the guy, you watch him" (*AB* 3). A dour and misogynistic Teach threatens: "She walks in back of me I'm going to hide my hand" (*AB* 15) or "We don't care we wreck the joint up" (*AB* 46). In *Glengarry* Levene pleads with Williamson: "I don't get on the board the thirtieth, they're going to can my ass" (*GGR* 18). Implying a code of honor among salesmen, Moss threatens Aaronow: "They come to you. You going to turn me in?" In *Speed-the-Plow* the newly promoted Bob Gould crows to his underling: "Chuck, Chuck, Chuck, *Charlie*: you get too old, too busy to have 'fun' this business; to have 'fun,' then what are you . . . ?" (*STP* 4). But a chastened Bob is later instructed by Charlie: "You can't tell it to me in one sentence, they can't put it in T.V. Guide" (*STP* 72–73). Other words dropped in the verbal rush are with, in, to, of, what, who. Since nouns anchor the meaning of these sentences, the missing monosyllables are expendable. In *Glengarry* an occasional Yiddish word intrudes into such abbreviated English—dreck, mishagas, schmuck, and in *Speed-the-Plow* schtup and Baal Shem Tov.

As in colloquial speech, but more sharply and comically, Mamet's characters wrench syntax for emphasis. Teach declares: "A guy who isn't tense, I don't want him on my side" (*AB* 47). Levene mutters: "The Glengarry Highland's leads, you're sending Roma out" (*GGR* 15). Bob warns Charlie: "To your face they'll go, 'Three bags full'" (*STP* 27).

Although such gyrations occur in colloquial speech, Mamet's cunningly constructed run-on sentences are pure invention, never heard off the stage. Probably the most brilliant example in all Mamet is Teach's explosion: "Only, and I'm not, I don't think, casting anything on anyone: from the mouth of a southern bulldyke asshole ingrate of a vicious nowhere cunt can this trash come" (*AB* 10–11). It is quite a mouthful for an actor, and yet the syntax is relatively simple: the parenthetical apology separates the adverb "only" from the phrase it modifies ("from . . . cunt"); the run-on closes on a simple declarative sentence, with subject intervening between auxiliary and main verb— "can this trash come."[1] Less flashy with obscenities is Don's run-on sentence that explains to Teach the lure of items of the 1933 World's Fair: "The thing, it ran two years, and they had (*I* don't know) all kinds of people every year they're buying everything that they can lay their hands on that they're going to take it back to Buffalo to give it, you know, to their aunt, and it mounts up" (*AB* 18). "The thing," both "know"s, and the free floating "it"s are gratuitous to the sentence structure, and yet the meaning is clear. Even the choice of "Buffalo" is not fortuitous in a play where all three characters are buffaloed about a buffalo nickel. Mamet's characters can shift tenses—usually from past to present. Their subjects and verbs can disagree in number, and pronouns can run riot, as in the threnody of the unsuccessful salesmen, Moss and Aaronow, where "you" and "we" dissolve into "they"s without antecedent, climaxing in despair: "All of, they got you on this 'board' . . ." (*GGR* 31). With a grammatical subtlety, Mamet predicts the end of *Speed-the-Plow*. When Bob and Charlie are high on their buddy film, they are careless of grammar, slumming in language, but after Karen seduces Bob with purity, Charlie is careful in phrasing his crucial question to her: "If he has said 'No,' would you have gone to bed with him?" (*STP* 77). In the face of Karen's reluctance to reply, Bob repeats the question, but he amends it with the elision and mispronunciation that typified his earlier conversation with Charlie: "Would you of gone to bed with me, I didn't do your book" (*STP* 77). There is no question mark; Bob's rephrasing has answered his own question and brought him back to business as usual.

Mamet bases his grammatical chaos on the solecisms, digressions, and tautologies of everyday speech, but on stage they become symptomatic of the chaos in the seemingly different worlds of petty crime, real estate speculation, and film production. When Mamet wrote of *American Buffalo* holds for the three plays: "The play, to me, is about an essential part of American consciousness, which is the ability to suspend an ethical sense and adopt in its stead a popular, accepted mythology and use that to assuage your consciousness like everyone else is doing" (blurb in Methuen edition). At first glance, or rather on first hearing of a Mamet play, grammatical chaos reinforces lexical poverty to convey a general impression of illiteracy. In the speed of delivery, characters do not notice when they contradict themselves. Teach declares: "I am calm. I'm just upset" (*AB* 68). A little later: "And the odds are he's not there, so when he answers [the phone] . . ." (*AB* 10). In *Speed-the-Plow* Bob Gould pronounces a contradiction in terms: "Money is not Gold" (*STP* 21).

Not only are Mamet's characters unaware of these contradictions, they have no sense of the slippage of words. Given the dubious ethics of business, "right" and "wrong" are very slippery terms.

DON: I'm just saying, something goes wrong . . .
TEACH: Wrong, wrong, you make your own right and
        wrong. (*AB* 52)

In *Glengarry* Levene momentarily crows over Williamson and Roma
supports him: "He's right, Williamson" (*GGR* 77). Whereupon Levene
continues: "It's not right" (*GGR* 78). Thus words can shift their
meaning, even as the circumstances of his characters' lives.

In *American Buffalo* the gopher Bob confesses: "I only went
around to see he's coming out the back," and his employer Don
remonstrates: "No, don't go fuck yourself around with these excuses"
(*AB* 4). The first "around" is a directional adverb, but the second is an
intensifier of an obscene verb which seems to mean "reveal one's
inadequacies."[2] *Glengarry Glen Ross* enfolds a shift of meaning in a
sight gag. Central to the salesmen's life is the black*board* on which
their sales are graphed in chalk, but in Act II "*A broken plate glass
window [is] boarded up. . . .*" (*GGR* 52), to which Roma calls
attention: You've got a *board-up* on the window" (*GGR* 54). The two
different boards are visible to us, both boding ill for the real estate
salesmen.

In the three plays the all-purpose noun is the word "thing,"
which can serve as a conversational opener: "The [only, important]
thing is. . . ." Things are at times visible material objects, like Teach's
gun, the buffalo nickel, the clothes of the nickel opener, a book, a
movie, or wealth beyond imagining. "We're going to have to hire
someone just to figure out the *things* we want to buy . . . " (*STP* 19).
Sometimes things are words, but more often they are action. The
intended robbery of *American Buffalo* is usually referred to as "the
thing," as is the intended Doug Brown movie in *Speed-the-Plow*.
Things may be events that occur or qualities one possesses—"the one
thing she's got, her *looks*" (*STP* 71). Things may also be thoughts as
in "things on my mind," or abstract principles: "Things are not always
what they seem to be." "Things get set." "If you think that's the
thing." ". . . one thing changes you." At their most threatening, things
are akin to fate: "Things are going to fall around your head" (*AB* 75).
The three characters of *Speed-the-Plow* hammer at "things," ranging
over these meanings, and in that play the anonymous author of *The
Bridge* writes: "That things were ending. *Yes.* That things *must* end"
(*STP* 58). Within five minutes, we move down from these destiny-

laden phrases to mere items on Charlie's mental list: ". . . the one thing . . . And the other thing . . . those two things, only, what I wanted to say to you" (*STP* 61). Since the characters of the three plays are much preoccupied with things, it is entirely fitting that noun should embrace so much territory.

In the power ploys of the Business Trilogy, most of the characters are loquacious. Mamet differs from Pinter, whose quiet characters can dominate the talkers. Moreover, Mamet's characters talk about "talk," so that that verb can mean speak, ask, boast, chat, describe, explain, comfort, confide, bargain, deal, reveal, deceive, teach, intend, and even act. Don oxymoronically explains to Bob: "Action talks and bullshit walks" (*AB* 4), but in Mamet's drama "Talk acts." At its least devious level, talk is praise: "Now you're talking!" But it can also be dispraise: "I don't want that talk." Or "He talks a good game." Or "That's 'talk.' Our job is to *sell*." Talk as plan, is evident when Teach avers that it is good "to talk this stuff out" (*AB* 47), but Don insists on Fletcher's participation because Teach cannot "talk about how he will break in." For the gopher Bob, as well as Roma's client Lingk, talk denotes urgency: "I got to talk to you" (*GGR* 59) and the grammar improves somewhat for Charlie's repetitions to Bob: "I have to talk to you" (*STP* 4). Ironically, the effusive salesman Roma uses "talk" to mean "listen": "I can't talk now" (*GGR* 82). In Levene's pleas of *Glengarry* "talk" is request, which the office manager turns to threat: "You'll talk to me." Similarly, the detective's desire to talk to the salesman is a form of coercion: "Mr. Levene, I think we have to talk" (*GGR* 106). The salesmen are outraged at the way the detective talks to them; Aaronow sputters: "No one should talk to a man that way" (*GGR* 87). He himself later supplies the synonym of "mistreat" (*GGR* 88).

Of the three plays *Speed-the-Plow* sports "talk" least, substituting "say" and "tell," but "talk" still occasionally flexes muscles. Charlie's verdict about *The Bridge* is "A talky piece of puke" (*STP* 62), and the confession he elicits from Karen is punctuated by her repetitions of "We talked. . . ." When she shifts verbs from "We talked" to "We decided" (*STP* 79), Charlie wins his case against her.

Into the thicket of verbal repetitions—all-purpose or no-purpose—Mamet infuses variety. His characters disparage others in racist, sexist, homophobic colloquialisms—fruit, mooch, deadbeat, nigger, Jew, dyke, wog, fairy, Chink, Polack, chick, broad, and

Mamet's men scatter familiar blasphemies—God, Lord, Jesus, Christ, chrissake.

Each of the business settings is endowed with its own jargon:

American Buffalo—fin, lookout, kid's clean, set it up, mind the fort, a job cased, off the top, three-way split, up front—familiar from film.

Glengarry Glen Ross—the key leads, board, kicked out, sit, plat, closer.

Speed the Plow—bump, coverage, promote, cross the street, courtesy read.

In isolation, these terms are hardly original, but in avalanches they carry Mamet's signature.

Comically original, however, are Mamet's intrusions of another register into the dominant semi-literate discourse. Don lectures Bob on "nutritive benefits" (*AB* 8), Teach becomes lyrical: "They harbor *assholes* in there . . ." (*AB* 12) or "I am not here to smother you in theory" (*AB* 50). Unable to answer Don's questions, Teach stands on his dignity: "What am I doing demeaning myself standing here pleading with you to protect your best interests?" (*AB* 79). A lovely blend of Latinism and solecism is Teach's excuse for his gun: "All the preparation in the world does not mean *shit*, the path of some crazed lunatic sees you as an invasion of his personal domain" (*AB* 85).

Ineffectual as a thief, Teach is the champion verbalist of *American Buffalo*, but Roma of *Glengarry* excels in both verbiage, which we hear as a stream-of-consciousness monologue enveloping his victim in personal concern. Too long to quote, the shift in register is evident in his imagined reaction to a real estate brochure: "'Some schmuck wants to make a buck on me'; or 'I feel a vibration *fate* is calling.'" In *Glengarry*, too, Mamet contrasts his loquacious salesmen with the tight-lipped office manager Williamson, who, "marshalling his sales force," is more ruthless than they. Although Levene's vocabulary seems limited, he can describe his sales victims "perceptively slump[ing]" (*GGR* 74), and he feigns surprise at the "purloined leads."

Far more ambitiously in *Speed-the-Plow*, Mamet again introduces a contrasting idiom, that of Karen. Like their predecessors with lower incomes, Bob Gould and Charlie Fox stud their monosyllables with shards of education. Charlie utters the words "watershed," "pariah," and "a boon . . . to assuage guilt"; Bob preaches about "auspicious," "courage to embrace a fact." He teases Charlie about being "Master of the Revels" (*STP* 28). But it is Karen who never soils her lips with obscenity and who almost always obeys grammatical rules; she is comfortable with Latinisms like "degradation," "titillation," "companionship." Although Karen did not write the book sent for a courtesy read, she imitates its maudlin, mawkish, quasi-mystic tone. I believe that Mamet intended Karen and *The Bridge* to mock religious fundamentalism, but, lacking the comic energy of his business scenes, that satire falls flat.

Like most Mamet critics (as opposed to reviewers), I admire the playwright's language strategies, but unlike Bigsby, Carroll, Dean, and Wetzseon, I also view them critically, and in *Speed-the-Plow* Mamet's reach exceeds his considerable grasp. In the three business plays Mamet presents himself obliquely and sardonically: he gives his own nickname Teach to the least sympathetic character of *American Buffalo*; he gives his own name David to Moss, the least attractive salesman of *Glengarry Glen Ross*, and he assigns his own professional experience (and conduct?) to Williamson, its least sympathetic character. In *Speed-the-Plow* the unnamed "Eastern Sissy Writer" (*STP* 23) of *The Bridge* is none other than David Mamet, whose *Bridge* is not a novel but a six-page short story about a nameless protagonist haunted by nightmares of nuclear holocaust.[3] However, the resemblance ends with title and subject, for not a single sentence from Mamet's story is quoted in the play, where the putative novel is, I repeat, maudlin, mawkish, and quasi-mystic, but, alas, not funny. Despite the limitations of Mamet's Veblen-based social analysis, his most trenchant plays are redeemed by the comic brilliance of his invented language. But when so astute a reader as Anne Dean takes Karen seriously—"Her idealism and fecund creativity leave their mark on an otherwise barren and arid play" (66)— Mamet's own talk fails; he misses what I believe to be its mark.

Only in passing have I dwelled in Mamet's obscenities, but they are testimony to his fecund creativity. Sometimes they function literally, but just as often they embrace several meanings listed in Partridge, and they do so with comic and graphic color. "Balls" is of course slang for testicles, whence it connotes courage, as when Don instructs Bob at what is required to win a card game: "Skill and talent and the balls to arrive at your own conclusions" (*AB* 4). Partridge defines "to have someone by the balls" as "to have utterly in one's power," but Don's extension of the metaphor is hilarious, as he praises Fletcher to Bob: "You take him and you put him down in some strange town with just a nickel in his pocket, and by nightfall he'll have that town by the balls" (*AB* 4). Unlisted in Partridge is "busting one's balls" or "working against insuperable obstacles," and this is Roma's claim: "I'm busting my *balls*, sell your *dirt* to fucking *deadbeats* money in the mattress . . ." (*GGR* 62).

Less savory are the connotations of "shit," which means excrement and is therefore a term of abuse, either in itself or in the compound "shithead." On the other hand, shit can imply value, as in Teach's ". . . a guy's lookin' for valuable shit" (*AB* 34) or Bob Gould's "jolly shitloads of [money]" (*STP* 20). One of Partridge's definitions equates shit with blarney, and Mamet's characters express disbelief with the exclamation: "No shit." Related perhaps to this meaning is the amiable conversation connoted by "shoot the shit." In contrast, Partridge defines "shit-eating" as "sycophantic," but gopher Bob's repetitions of "I eat shit" imply a deeper self-abnegation, while in *Speed-the-Plow* variants on the consumption of excrement describe Charlie's position with respect to the executive Bob. (All three plays feature a business hierarchy.)

Mamet's favorite obscenity is "fuck," either as pleonasm—"How the fuck do I know?" (*AB* 50)—or, less often, in its literal meaning: "Guys like that, I like to fuck their wives" (*AB* 28). Don's pleonastic use is rousing: "The ass on this broad, un-be-fucking-lievable . . ." (*AB* 32). As "shit" can mean the opposite of excrement, so "fucker" can be a term of admiration (as can "son of a bitch"). Partridge defines "fuck about" as "to play the fool," but Mamet prefers "fuck around" which is closer to "waste time." Levene assures his client: "I don't want to fuck *around* with you" (*GGR* 73). On the other hand, "to fuck someone around" is "to destroy," as in Teach's accusation to Don: "No *wonder* that you fuck this kid around" (*AB* 100). Wasting time can also be conveyed by "fuck with," as in Teach's snarl: "You think that I'm going to fuck with Chump Change?" (*AB* 36). More often, however, the strong negative imperative implies menace: "Don't fuck with me"—Don to Bob, Don to Teach, Teach to Don, Roma to the detective, Charlie to Bob. For Partridge "to fuck up" is "to fail dismally," and Mamet's characters often chant that particular litany, either transitively or intransitively.

The trumpets for these obscenities give no thought to their semiotic slippage, but Mamet gives considerable thought to gathering them in bouquets at climactic moments. As Teach "*hits Bob viciously,*" he also beats him verbally: "Grace and Ruthie up your ass, you shitheads, you don't fuck with us, I'll kick your fucking head in. (I don't give a shit . . .)" (*AB* 94). Blows do not rain down in *Glengarry*, but when Williamson punctures Roma's lie to his client, the salesman explodes: "You stupid fucking cunt . . . I'm talking to *you*, shithead . . . What are you going to do about it, asshole. You fucking *shit*. Where did you learn your *trade*. You stupid fucking *Cunt*. You *idiot*. Who ever told you you could work with *men*?" (*GGR* 95-96). Similarly macho, a frustrated Charlie "*hits Gould*" in *Speed-the-Plow*, punctuating the blows with words: "I'll fucken' kill you right here in this office. All this bullshit; you *wimp*, you *coward* . . . now you got the job, and now you're going to *run* all over everything, like something broke in the shopping bag, you *fool*—your fucken' sissy film—you squat to pee. You old *woman* . . ." (*STP* 70). Tense moments in the theater, these outbursts evoke no smiles.

In the Business Trilogy Mamet implies that the foulest obscenity of all is the word "business."[4] Like four-letter words, this noun of twice four letters is occasionally comic, and it, too, undergoes slippage. Early in *American Buffalo*, Don defines business for Bob: "People taking care of themselves" (*AB* 7). In edging Bob out of the robbery, Teach admonishes Don: "All that I'm saying, don't confuse business with pleasure" (*AB* 34). Within a moment he expands: "And (and simply as a *business* proposition) you cannot afford to take the chance" (*AB* 35). Trying to edge Fletcher out of the robbery, Teach again invokes business to Don: "We're talking business, let's *talk* business: you think it's good business to call Fletch in?" (*AB* 52). The curtain line of Act I epitomizes Don's misgivings about the whole enterprise: "Fuckin' *business* . . ." (*AB* 55). In Act II Teach continues to invoke business, but the last sound of that particular obscenity comes from the gopher Bob, who has sensed that the way to Don's affection is through fraud and "business."

The word "business" is heard less often in *Glengarry Glen Ross*, where we see business in action. Levene and Moss mention "doing business," but the meaning changes as Moss involves Aaronow in the planned robbery: "That's none of your fucking business . . . My end is *my* business" (*GGR* 45, 46). In Roma's insult to Williamson, there is further slippage: "You know your business, I know mine. Your business is being an *asshole* . . ." (*GGR* 63). Roma can even disparage business when he presents the fictitious executive to his victim: "It's funny, you know, you get a picture of the Corporation Type Company Man, all business . . . this man, *no*" (*GGR* 82). Finally, Roma repeats obsessively that his victim has "three *business* days" (*GGR* 85) to annul the real estate contract; fittingly, "business" has become an adjective for fraud.

In *Speed-the-Plow* Bob and Charlie burble happily about the movie business, which Bob lauds as a "People Business" (*STP* 22). Charlie delivers a well-known one-liner, encapsulating his cynicism: "Life in the movie business is like the, is like the beginning of a new love affair: it's full of surprises, and you're constantly getting fucked" (*STP* 29). Karen, repetitively deprecating naiveté, announces her ambition "To think in a . . . business fashion" (*STP* 40). Obligingly, Bob instructs her: "This, in the business, is called 'a courtesy read'" (*STP* 42) and ". . . that's what we're in this business to do. *Make the thing everyone made last year*" (*STP* 56). During the purity quest with Karen, Bob mentions business less and less, but a victorious Charlie circles back to Bob's earlier ebullient phrase: "Because we joke about it, Bob, we joke about it, but it *is* a 'People's Business' . . ." (*STP* 81). And, implies Mamet, the more's the pity.

In the business worlds of the trilogy, business is presented as lethally circular; after shaking the characters to the depths of their insecurities, each play circles back to its beginning. *American Buffalo* begins and ends with Bob's apology to Don, for his ineptitude in a theft viewed as business. *Glengarry Glen Ross* begins and ends with the suggestion of twin-teaming Levene and Roma in their business of real estate sales, but the possibility of cooperation has been dramatized away by the cutthroat competition in the body of the play. Early in *Speed-the-Plow* Bob Gould reads a question from *The Bridge*: "How are things made round?" (*STP* 3) and the play itself circles round to Charlie's jubilant rhetorical questions, as the buddy prisoners of the Hollywood ethic happily clang the chain of their buddy prison film.[5]

How Mamet's things are made round is through his whittling ways with words.

Notes

1. See Dean, pp. 111-112, for a detailed commentary on what she calls an "aria of hatred."

2. Partridge's *Dictionary of Slang* is not helpful in this context.

3. I am grateful to the playwright Nicholas Wright for bringing this Mamet story to my attention as published in *Granta*, No. 16 (Summer 1985): 167-173.

4. Cf. Barbera, Schlueter, and Forsyth.

5. Many reviewers appreciated the irony of these buddy whores cooperating on a buddy film, but none noticed that the Hollywood buddies are also prisoners of "a popular, accept mythology."

Bibliography

Barbera, Jack V. "Ethical Perversity in America." *Modern Drama* (September 1981), pp. 270–275.

Bigsby, C. W. E. *David Mamet*. New York: Methuen, 1985.

Carroll, Dennis. *David Mamet*. Basingstoke: Macmillan, 1987.

Dean, Anne. *David Mamet: Language as Dramatic Action*. Cranbury, N.J.: Associated University Presses, 1990.

Mamet, David. Reviews of *Speed-the-Plow*. as published in *London Theatre Record* 1–28 January, 1989.

Partridge, Eric. *Dictionary of Slang*, London: Routledge, 1984.

Roudané, Matthew C. "An Interview with David Mamet." *Studies in American Drama* (1986), pp. 73–81.

Schlueter, June, and Elizabeth Forsyth. "America as Junkshop: The Business Ethic in David Mamet's "*American Buffalo*." *Modern Drama* (December 1983),pp. 492–500.

Wetzsteon, Ross. "New York Letter." *Plays and Players* (September 1976), pp. 37–38.

PHALLUS IN WONDERLAND: MACHISMO AND BUSINESS IN DAVID MAMET'S *AMERICAN BUFFALO* AND *GLENGARRY GLEN ROSS*

Hersh Zeifman

In an interview in 1984, David Mamet, deliberately echoing Calvin Coolidge, commented: "'The business of America is business. . . . We're a nation of entrepreneurs.'"[1] Precisely what Mamet thinks of American business is the business of his two most celebrated plays—as he himself has made abundantly, and repeatedly, clear. *American Buffalo* (1975), he has stated, "'is about the American ethic of business. About how we excuse all sorts of great and small betrayals and ethical compromises called business.'"[2] "'It's a play about honor among thieves and the myths this country runs on. . . . The ethics of the business community is that you can be as predatory as you want within a structured environment.'"[3] And of his Pulitzer-Prize-winning *Glengarry Glen Ross* (1983), written almost a decade later, Mamet noted: "'To me the play is about a society with only one bottom line: How much money you make.'"[4] "The play concerns how business corrupts," he told another interviewer, "how the hierarchical business system tends to corrupt. It becomes legitimate for those in power in the business world to act unethically. The effect on the little guy is that he turns to crime. And petty crime goes punished; major crimes go unpunished."[5] And he added to still another interviewer: "American capitalism comes down to one thing. . . . The operative axiom is 'Hurrah for me and fuck you.' Anything else is a lie."[6]

Mamet's anatomization of the apparently oxymoronic term "American business ethics" is dramatized in a number of ways in the two plays: critics have variously focused on the plays' metaphoric central actions, for example, or on characterization, or, most prominently, on the telling dynamics of the language characters use to define themselves and their nefarious activities. I'd like to take a somewhat different approach in this essay, however, by examining a dramaturgical strategy that has received surprisingly insufficient attention from Mamet critics. "'My job,'" Mamet once said to Mel Gussow during a discussion of his business plays, "'is to create a closed moral universe.'"[7] What's especially significant about this "closed moral universe" in both *American Buffalo* and *Glengarry Glen Ross* is that it is closed even more tightly by being portrayed as exclusively male. Mamet has written an astonishingly large number of such all-male plays; in addition to *Buffalo* and *Glengarry*, and ignoring for the moment his many monologues and short "sketches," the list includes *The Duck Variations* (1972), *A Life in the Theatre* (1977), *Prairie du Chien* (1979), and *Lakeboat* (1980). This insistent emphasis on an exclusively male world in so many of his plays clearly indicates Mamet's theatrical "fascination with the male tribe."[8] As Michelene Wandor has noted:

> The single-gendered play may be "unrealistic" in the sense that we all inhabit a world which consists of men and women, but it does provide an imaginative opportunity to explore the gendered perspective (male or female) without the complexities and displacements of the "mixed" play.[9]

In *Buffalo* and *Glengarry*, Mamet makes use of this exploration of "the gendered perspective" for specific thematic ends: a dramatic world in which women are marginalized to the point of literal exclusion provides *in itself* the most scathing indictment imaginable of the venality and corruption of American business.

The absence of women in *Buffalo* and *Glengarry* ironically underscores, as Christopher Bigsby has suggested, the pathetic impotence of Mamet's businessmen.[10] But it also has a much deeper significance: the exclusion of women from these plays implies that the values the male characters traditionally associate with the "feminine"—compassion, tenderness, empathy, spirituality—are seen as threatening to their business ethos; in the business world such values are characterized as weakness, "and weakness is despised as effeminate and dangerous."[11] By banishing women and the values they purportedly represent from these plays, Mamet thus shifts the focus to an examination of "the cocoon of the traditional American masculinity myths" inside which he himself was raised.[12] It is these values of machismo—toughness, strength, cunning—which have become appropriated and apotheosized by American business, alchemized into the fool's gold of power, greed, and competition. As Mamet has noted: ". . . the competition of business . . . is most times prosecuted for the benefit of oneself [i.e., the male] as breadwinner, as provider, as paterfamilias, as vestigial and outmoded as you may feel those roles to be."[13]

In an essay titled "In the Company of Men," Mamet wrote that men congregate under three circumstances:

> Men get together to do business. . . . Men also get together to bitch. We say, "What does she *want*?" . . . [And the] final way in which men get together is for That Fun Which Dare Not Speak Its Name, and which has been given the unhappy tag "male bonding."[14]

Buffalo and *Glengarry* mark the site where all three of the above circumstances conjoin: the bitchy business world in which men relate to other men, in which men *define* themselves as "men." The plays thus dramatize, to borrow Eve Sedgwick's term, a world of "homosocial desire":

> "Homosocial" is a word occasionally used in history and the social sciences, where it describes social bonds between persons of the same sex; it is a neologism, obviously formed by analogy with "homosexual," and just as obviously meant to be distinguished from "homosexual." In fact, it is applied to such activities as "male bonding," which may, in our society, be characterized by intense homophobia. . . .[15]

The homosocial world of American business so wickedly critiqued in *American Buffalo* and *Glengarry Glen Ross* becomes Mamet's theatrical "Phallus in Wonderland": a topsy-turvy world in which all values are inverted by characters who think with their crotch. Since machismo is the sole criterion of worth in the "closed moral universe" these plays depict, it therefore follows that the worst term of abuse in such a universe is one that questions masculinity. It's hardly surprising, then, that Mamet's businessmen are both deeply misogynistic and deeply homophobic. "[I]f you look around the United States of America," Mamet once noted in an interview, "you will see that we do have a certain amount of misogynistic men. For example, all of them."[16] A woman, by macho definition, is not a "man"; neither is a homosexual. In the values of a patriarchal culture which American business has internalized, misogyny and homophobia are inextricably linked; as Gayle Rubin suggests, "[t]he suppression of the homosexual component of human sexuality, and by corollary, the oppression of homosexuals, is . . . a product of the same system whose rules and relations oppress women."[17]

American Buffalo brilliantly exemplifies the debased values of an all-male business ethic in which the phallus reigns supreme. The epitome of macho business values in the play is Teach, whose total moral bankruptcy is deftly delineated in his succinct definition of free enterprise: "The freedom . . . Of the *Individual* . . . To Embark on Any Fucking Course that he sees fit. . . . In order to secure his honest chance to make a profit."[18] Indeed, like his counterparts in classical Greek comedy, this fumbling and incompetent petty crook might just as well be wearing his phallus strapped openly to his waist. But then the other characters could simply whip out a ruler and measure, which would bring the whole play to a crashing stop. Teach's self-preservation requires, instead, that the phallus be "covered," its presence less overtly—and less vulnerably—signalled in his physical and (especially) verbal swaggering. (Al Pacino, who played Teach in a series of revivals of *Buffalo* throughout the early 1980s, was constantly touching his crotch—as though talismanically touching base with the centre of his being, confirming that everything was still intact.)

Women constantly hover on the margins of *American Buffalo*—especially the "ghosts" of Ruth and Grace, ostensible friends of the three central male characters—but, though repeatedly invoked, their presence never literally materializes. There is no place for them on a stage where what they represent is debased and valueless, where women are routinely referred to as "cunts," "broads," "bitches," and "chicks." Value in *American Buffalo* is exclusively linked to testosterone: there are more reputed "balls" in this play than at Wimbledon. Since machismo is the coin of highest currency in the traffic of this business world, then its opposite—lack of "manhood"—signals utter worthlessness. Thus the off-stage Fletcher, having incurred the wrath of both Teach and Don, is repeatedly labelled a "cocksucker" (59, 72, 73); Teach calls Bob a "fruit" (94); and "(Fuckin' *fruits* . . .)" likewise becomes the dismissive term not only for the man whose coin collection the trio plans to rob but also for his sexy wife! (This same structure of abuse animates Mamet's *Speed-the-Plow* [1988], a further attack on American business—in this instance the film business. When Charlie Fox discovers he's been betrayed in a business deal by Bobby Gould, he explodes: ". . . you *fool*—your fucken' sissy film—you squat to pee. You old *woman*. . . .")[19] So ingrained in Mamet's businessmen is this specific vocabulary of abuse, and thus of the value system underlying it, that it extends, absurdly, even to women. When Don asserts that Ruth is a good card player, for example, Teach argues "She is *not* a good card player, Don. She is a mooch and she is a locksmith and she plays like a woman" (14). This kind of polymorphous misogyny and homophobia reaches the true heights of absurdity in Teach's hilarious indictment of Ruth as a "dyke cocksucker" (54). Never mind that the phrase is oxymoronic; for the moronic Teach it makes perfect emotional sense. The patently illogical has been transformed into the patently tautological: in Teach's pantheon of abuse "dyke" and "cocksucker" are simple equivalencies.

Mamet's attack on corrupt business ethics in *American Buffalo* is deepened through an implicit equation with other violent male "homosocial" institutions—specifically the military and the police. In all such institutions, lack of substance is shrouded in a linguistic fog; citing the sociologist and economist Thorstein Veblen, Mamet has noted that "the more that jargon and technical language is involved in an endeavor, the more we may assume that the endeavor is essentially make-believe. As in Law, Commerce, Warfare. There we were in Vietnam. . . ."[20] Buttressed by these institutions, people find themselves committing "gross acts of cruelty and savagery"; as Mamet has stated:

> We have it somehow in our nature, Tolstoy wrote, to perform horrendous acts which we would never dream of as individuals, and think if they are done in the name of some larger group, a *state*, a *company*, a *team*, that these

vile acts are somehow magically transformed, and
become praiseworthy.[21]

"A guy who isn't tense, I don't want him on my side . . ." (47), says
Teach while plotting his business heist; later he echoes Don's "You
want depth on the team" (51). This pathetic band of thieves huddling in
Don's junkshop sees itself as a beleaguered paramilitary unit: Don's
role in their incursion is to "mind the fort" (36); Fletch is brought in
because, as Don notes, "We can use somebody watch our rear" (52); and
Teach, having hocked his watch for the phallic extension and security of
a gun, defends his bearing arms like any good cop or soldier:
"Protection of me and my partner. Protection, deterrence" (85).

In the male homosocial institution of business depicted in
American Buffalo, "alien" values like loyalty, friendship and tenderness
have become inverted into obscenities. Thus Bob, having first been
betrayed in a business deal by Don with the Judas equivalent of thirty
pieces of silver ("I got to give you . . . thirty [dollars] . . ." [43]) and
then viciously beaten by Teach, is finally forced to admit that the
buffalo nickel he's been trying to sell Don throughout the second act ("I
like 'em because of the art on it" [64], this innocent confesses) was not
stolen from their mark but purchased from a coin store—not for profit
(Bob wants fifty dollars for it [66], the exact price he paid [99]), but as
a loving gesture toward his friend:

> TEACH: You buy a coin for fifty dollars, you come back
>   here.
>   *Pause.*
>   Why? . . .
>   Why would you do a thing like that?
> BOB: I don't know.
> TEACH: Why would you do a thing like that?
> BOB: For Donny. (99)

Teach's response to this, for him, utterly incomprehensible act of
selflessness and kindness is perhaps the saddest line in the play: "You
people make my flesh crawl" (100). "We all live like the cavemen"
(103), Teach later acknowledges, and for once what Teach teaches is
deadly accurate. In the brutally macho and materialistic dog-eat-dog
world of American business, values like compassion and spirituality—
implicitly inscribed as "feminine" and therefore, in the figures of Ruth

and Grace, devalued and excluded—are totally lacking. The world of *American Buffalo*—the world of American business—is thus *literally* ruthless and graceless.

Glengarry Glen Ross has been called by Mamet "formally a gang comedy in the tradition of *The Front Page* or *Man in White*,"[22] but, as in *American Buffalo*, the "gang" is exclusively male. The only real difference between the businessmen-thieves in the two plays is one of scale; as Anne Dean has commented: "In *American Buffalo*, Mamet portrays a group of small-time crooks who thought themselves legitimate businessmen; in *Glengarry Glen Ross*, his subjects *are* businessmen but they all behave like crooks."[23] In *Glengarry*, then, the gang's all here—wearing better clothes, certainly, and working out of an office rather than a junkshop, but still manoeuvring sharklike within the homosocial sphere of business deals in which phallus is always intended. "A man's his job,"[24] states salesman Shelly "The Machine" Levene reductively—and tautologically, for in the all-male world of *Glengarry* the job of selling worthless property through guile and chicanery both defines and is defined by the salesmen's concept of "manhood."

The sole criterion of worth here, as in *Buffalo*, is machismo. "I'm the *man* to sell" (19), Levene boasts in the play's opening scene, and later, congratulating himself on having brought off a stupendous sale, notes "I got my *balls* back . . ." (102). Lamenting the "degeneration" of business into "a world of clock watchers, bureaucrats, officeholders . . .," Roma, the gang's star salesman, hilariously complains to Levene ". . . it's not a world of men, Machine . . ." (105). Roma's concept of manhood is precisely that of a "machine"— sleek, heartless, devoid of conscience, designed simply to make money. So morally benighted is this macho world that when Aaronow, another one of the gang, sighs "I'm no fucking good" and is then consoled by Roma's "Fuck that shit. . . . You're a good man, George. . . . You hit a bad streak" (57), "goodness" is defined solely within the terms of business sales. We have now re-entered the commercial world of Shakespeare's *The Merchant of Venice*; when Shylock comments that "Antonio is a good man,"[25] he means only that Antonio is a "good" financial risk. Human worth has been relegated to the demeaning context of a commodity exchange.

Again as in *Buffalo*, the only unforgivable failing in this macho world, and therefore the worst epithet one can hurl at another, involves failing the test of manhood. Customers, by definition, are there to be screwed and, thus, again by the salesmen's definition, not "men": Levene repeatedly refers to them as "cocksuckers" (16, 21, 63). Similarly the disgruntled salesman Moss, complaining of the sales competition which will result in the losers being fired, vents his spleen at his bosses' treatment of the salesmen as less than men: "Look look look look, when they *build* your business, then you can't fucking turn around, *enslave* them, treat them like *children*, fuck them up the ass . . ." (36). In Moss's lexicon—in Moss's value system which that lexicon reflects—slaves are equivalent to children are equivalent to homosexuals. (The mention of "slaves" in Moss's litany reminds us, of course, that within this homosocial world racism is merely another cognate of misogyny and homophobia. Thus when Teach attempts to defend his masculinity against Don's jibes in *Buffalo*, he does so by telling Don "I am not your nigger. I am not your wife" [100]. Similarly the eponymous hero of Mamet's *Edmond* [1982] strikes out at a black pimp by shrieking "You *coon*, you *cunt*, you *cock*sucker. . . ."[26] For Edmond, all three insults are not simply alliterative but, more important, interchangeable.)

The most sustained torrent of abuse in *Glengarry*, however, is reserved for Williamson, the despised office manager who sits behind a desk and so, unlike the salesmen, never tests his manhood in the arena of "battle." Predictably, the terms of that abuse are misogynistic and homophobic. Levene's scorn for him is withering: "You don't know what it *is*, you don't have the *sense*, you don't have the *balls*. You ever been on a sit? *Ever*? Has this cocksucker ever been . . ." (76). (In the rehearsal typescript of the play, Levene further accused "You don't have the *blood*, John. You don't have the *blood* . . . ,"[27] thus emphasizing the sheer animal savagery of the business world; as one of the characters in Mamet's *Reunion* [1976] comments: "It's a fucking jungle out there.")[28] But the strongest abuse of Williamson is unleashed by Roma, livid with rage that Williamson has blown one of his deals:

> You stupid fucking *cunt*. You *idiot*. Whoever told you you could work with *men*? . . . I don't care . . . whose dick you're sucking on. You're going *out*. . . . What you're hired for is to *help* us—does that seem clear to you? To *help* us. *Not* to fuck us up . . . to help *men* who are going *out* there to try to earn a *living*. You *fairy*. . . . You fucking *child*. . . . (96–97)

For Roma, as for Moss and indeed *all* the characters of this exclusively male world in which machismo rules, "cunt," "fairy," and "child" are synonymous terms of abuse; each is equivalent to "non-man," and thus to nothing, to worse than nothing. The arena of "battle" entered into by the salesmen of *Glengarry* reminds us that, once again, Mamet is linking business with other traditional male homosocial institutions. When Moss turns viciously on Roma, for example, the invective spewing out of him in great bursts of bile, Roma retorts: "What is this, your farewell speech? . . . Your farewell to the troops?" (71). Similarly, Levene's boasting of his incredible sale is interrupted by Moss's "Hey, I don't want to hear your fucking war stories . . ." (67). Levene's description of closing that sale is, indeed, very like that of a military engagement; the language he uses suggests both an epic battle and, in its compulsively orgasmic rhythm, a sexual conquest, casting his customers in the role of the enemy who must at all costs not simply be defeated but *annihilated*. "They signed, Ricky," he exults to Roma. "It was *great*. It was fucking great. It was like they *wilted* all at once. . . . They, I swear to God, they both kind of *imperceptibly slumped*" (74). A businessman, Levene implies, is constantly putting his life on the line—like a soldier, like a cop. "You can't learn [what it takes] in an office . . .," Levene instructs the desk-bound Williamson. "You have to learn it on the streets. . . . 'Cause your partner *depends* on it. . . . Your partner . . . a man who's your 'partner' *depends* on you . . . you have to go *with* him and *for* him . . ." (97–98).

Levene's mock-heroic rhetoric, however, is belied by the play's action. There are, finally, no "partners" in *Glengarry Glen Ross*, nor—given the "values" of this world—could there be; each salesman is out strictly for himself. Don's definition of business in *Buffalo*—"People taking *care* of themselves" (7)—is dramatized with a vengeance in *Glengarry*, where the Practical Sales Maxim "ALWAYS BE CLOSING" (13), used by Mamet as the play's epigraph, applies to *all* relationships. Everyone in *Glengarry* exists potentially to be "sold": the customers, the salesmen, even the audience. Thus both acts end with a magisterial "selling" job by Ricky Roma, in which the audience too is "buffaloed": in act one when we ultimately realize that Roma's conversation with James Lingk is not simply a philosophical chat with a stranger over a drink but the cunning seduction of a sales pitch, and more lethally in act two, when "tricky Ricky" suddenly and viciously betrays his self-proclaimed "friend" and "partner" Levene.

"ALWAYS BE CLOSING" might also stand as *Mamet's* credo in *Glengarry*. For Mamet has once again "closed" this play about American business to women, excluding the "feminine" and its reputed values from the sphere of dramatic action; once again there is no place for such values in a world ruled by machismo. As in *Buffalo*, women haunt the margins of the text but never break through to the stage. Their presence is evoked only metonymically, as terms of abuse, or else in the form of "spirits" whose essence threatens male values. The most prominent of these off-stage women is the wife of James Lingk, who has ordered her husband to cancel the business deal into which Roma has "suckered" him. Roma tries desperately to change Lingk's mind, predictably lapsing into the language of commerce in characterizing Lingk's relationship with his wife—predictably, because Ricky can conceive of human intercourse only in commercial terms: "Come on, Jim. (*Pause*.) I want to tell you something. Your life is your own. You have a contract with your wife. You have certain things you do *jointly*, you have a *bond* there . . . and there are *other* things. Those things are yours" (93). Although Roma ridicules and attempts to dismiss her "prudence" as "something *women* have" (83)—akin to menstrual cramps, perhaps—Mrs. Lingk in fact implicitly challenges his macho code of behavior; she has a different agenda from his, a far less cutthroat one. Excluded from the stage, she is the "missing Lingk" whose values could destroy Roma's very existence.

Mamet once declared in an interview that he views his plays as "iconoclastic," "in the sense of tearing down the icons of American business, and some of the myths about this country."[29] In *American Buffalo* and *Glengarry Glen Ross*, one of the most powerful ways in which this iconoclasm is dramatized is through the exclusion from the stage of women and of the values traditionally associated with them. There are, of course, a number of potential problems here. First, to characterize women *as a gender* as compassionate, tender, empathetic, etc., is a remarkably sentimental notion; Mamet certainly doesn't sustain this view in his critical writings, say, or more significantly in those plays of his in which women actually appear.[30] Second, and far more serious, to use women metaphorically in this way, to inscribe them with certain values (however "positive" those values might be), may itself be a form of misogyny. Thus Michelene Wandor has noted that, even in plays by male dramatists in which women become "the conscience of humanity, . . . the perspective still remains male-determined . . .":

> What is interesting is that these plays simply represent variants on the "feminine." . . . Using woman as a metaphor may look like a compliment, but it is an unconscious way of denying her a real part of the stage action.[31]

Mamet has himself partially acknowledged this danger: "Men *generally* expect more of women than we do of ourselves," he has written. "We feel, based on constant evidence, that women are better, stronger, more truthful, than men. You can call this sexism, or reverse sexism, or whatever you wish, but it is my experience."[32] If there's a sense in which Mamet might be accused of misogyny in *Buffalo* and *Glengarry*, it's in this latter sense only—not that he shares the crudely misogynist views of those plays' male characters (which both plays clearly and explicitly condemn), but in this far more subtle essentialist reduction of women to a gender stereotype. Yet whether suspect in these ways or not, Mamet's insistence on all-male casts in *American Buffalo* and *Glengarry Glen Ross* makes his thematic point crystal clear. Both plays could thus have been titled *Sexual Perversity in Chicago*, for the perverse denial of an entire gender and its metaphorical import brilliantly exposes the moral wilderness of a business "ethic" ruled solely by the vile and violent values of a debased machismo.

Notes

1. Jennifer Allen, "David Mamet's Hard Sell," *New York*, 9 April 1984, p. 40.

2. Richard Gottlieb, "The 'Engine' That Drives Playwright David Mamet," *The New York Times*, 15 January 1978, Sec. 2, p. 4.

3. William A. Raidy, "Will Success Buffalo David Mamet? Are You Kidding?," *Chicago Daily News*, 2–3 April 1977, cited in Dennis Carroll, *David Mamet* (London: Macmillan, 1987), p. 32.

4. Mel Gussow, "Real Estate World a Model for Mamet," *The New York Times*, 28 March 1984, Sec. C, p. 19.

5. Matthew C. Roudané, "An Interview with David Mamet," *Studies in American Drama, 1945–Present*, 1 (1986): 74.

6. John Lahr, programme notes for *Glengarry Glen Ross* (London: National Theatre, 1983), cited in Anne Dean, *David Mamet: Language as Dramatic Action* (Rutherford, NJ: Fairleigh Dickinson University Press, 1990), p. 190.

7. Gussow, Sec. C, p.19.

8. See Samuel G. Friedman, "The Gritty Eloquence of David Mamet," *The New York Times Magazine*, 21 April 1985, p. 40.

9. Michelene Wandor, *Look Back in Gender: Sexuality and the Family in Post-war British Drama* (London and New York: Methuen, 1987), p. 140.

10. C. W. E. Bigsby, *David Mamet* (London and New York: Methuen, 1985), p. 76.

11. Ibid., p. 81.

12. See C. Gerald Fraser, "Mamet's Plays Shed Masculinity Myth," *The New York Times*, 5 July 1976, Sec. L, p. 7.

13. Mamet, "In the Company of Men," in *Some Freaks* (New York: Viking, 1989), p. 90.

14. Ibid., p. 87.

15. Eve Kosofsky Sedgwick, *Between Men: English Literature and Male Homosocial Desire* (New York: Columbia University Press, 1985), p. 1.

16. Esther Harriott, "Interview with David Mamet," in *American Voices: Five Contemporary Playwrights in Essays and Interviews* (Jefferson, N.C. and London: McFarland, 1988), p. 84.

17. Gayle Rubin, "The Traffic in Women: Notes on the 'Political Economy' of Sex," in *Toward an Anthropology of Women*, ed. Rayna R. Reiter (New York and London: Monthly Review Press, 1975), p. 180.

18. Mamet, *American Buffalo* (New York: Grove, 1977), pp. 72–73. All further page references will be cited in the text.

19. Mamet, *Speed-the-Plow* (New York: Grove, 1988), p. 70.

20. Mamet, "Capture-the-Flag, Monotheism, and the Techniques of Arbitration," in *Writing in Restaurants* (New York: Penguin, 1987), p. 5.

21. Mamet, "Concerning *The Water Engine*," in *Writing in Restaurants*, p. 109.

22. Henry I. Schvey, "Celebrating the Capacity for Self-Knowledge" [an interview with Mamet], *New Theatre Quarterly*, 4, No. 13 (February 1988): 92.

23. Dean, pp. 195–196.

24. Mamet, *Glengarry Glen Ross* (New York: Grove, 1984), p. 75. All further page references will be cited in the text.

25. Shakespeare, *The Merchant of Venice*, in *Shakespeare: The Complete Works*, ed. G. B. Harrison (New York: Harcourt, Brace & World, 1968), I.iii.12.

26. Mamet, *Edmond* (New York: Grove, 1983), p. 64.

27. See Bigsby, p. 120.

28. Mamet, *Reunion*, in *Reunion and Dark Pony* (New York: Grove, 1979), p. 23.

29. Schvey, p. 96.

30. See, for example, such plays as *Sexual Perversity in Chicago* (1974), *The Woods* (1977), and *Speed-the-Plow* (1988). See also Mamet's description of women in the business world he knows best, that of theater and films: "The coldest, cruelest, most arrogant behavior I have ever seen in my professional life has been—and *consistently* been—on the part of women producers in the movies and the theater. I have seen women do things that the worst man would never entertain the thought of—I do not imply that he would be stopped by conscience, but he *would* be stopped by the fear of censure, which takes us back to [women's] inability to compromise." Mamet, "Women," in *Some Freaks*, p. 28.

31. Michelene Wandor, *Carry On, Understudies: Theatre and Sexual Politics* (London and New York: Routledge & Kegan Paul, 1986), p. 157.

32. Mamet, "Women," in *Some Freaks*, p. 24.

PLAYING TO WIN: SEXUAL POLITICS IN DAVID MAMET'S *HOUSE OF GAMES* AND *SPEED-THE-PLOW*

Ann C. Hall

In David Mamet's *House of Games* (1985) and *Speed-the-Plow* (1987), women enter two of the most macho sanctuaries in American culture: poolrooms and the Hollywood film industry. To some extent the plays are complementary. *House of Games* presents the effects of men upon a woman, and *Speed-the-Plow* illustrates the effects of a woman upon the company of men. In both plays, the male characters view women dualistically; they are either Madonnas or whores. The female characters, however, persistently violate such codification. As Charlie Fox in *Speed-the-Plow* notes, their secretary is a rare specimen of femininity, for "she falls between two stools"; she is neither a dumb but innocent floozy nor an ambitious castrating whore.[1] Though Fox concludes that she, to continue his metaphor, does not have a leg to stand on, her ambiguous status causes a great deal of conflict between Fox and his buddy, Gould.

In the light of psychoanalytic, feminist theory, the Mamet plays accurately depict gender relations. According to Jacques Lacan, Luce Irigaray, and others, the mutually exclusive categories of femininity oppress women in profound ways. Within a male-dominated culture, most female behavior is classified according to this binary system, so confronting the oppression becomes a Sisyphean-like task for women. Almost any behavior they exhibit is dismissed or labelled under these terms. These theorists, however, articulate a strategy for revolutionizing female representation, a strategy which parallels the behavior of

Mamet's female characters. By "falling between two stools," by constantly moving out from under the labels, Mamet's female characters expose the male system of oppression as a house of cards. Mamet has clearly established himself as a playwright of male experience. In his recent collection of essays, *Some Freaks*, he not only defends the company of men from the "odious phrase male bonding," but he also describes male communities in spiritual terms. When two or more heterosexual men are gathered together in the name of fun, they create a mystical body of masculinity, an environment where "one [man] is understood, where one [man] is not judged, where one [man] is not expected to perform—because there is . . . room and encouragement for all [men] who wholeheartedly endorse the worth of the activity." [2] Throughout the essay, however, Mamet does not disassociate "fun" from more serious activities, implying that this sacred relationship occurs whenever men cluster. It is no surprise, then, that feminist viewers may be a bit skeptical when Mamet begins to create female characters.

Overall, however, Mamet characterizes his males ambivalently. In *American Buffalo* (1975) and *Glengarry Glen Ross* (1983), for example, the male characters are liars, cheats, or, at best, comically inept. Such characterizations persist in *House of Games* and *Speed-the-Plow*, but in these plays, the representation of men is complicated by the fact that important female counterparts are also present. Furthermore, what differentiates these plays from Mamet's early depictions of heterosexual relations as well as most twentieth century dramatic depictions is that romance is not the major concern of these two plays. Unlike Mamet's *Sexual Perversity in Chicago* (1975) and *The Woods* (1977), the battle of the sexes in *House of Games* and *Speed-the-Plow* occurs in the context of business, power, and wealth.

In psychoanalytic theory, sexual politics, power, and existence are also closely aligned. In simple Freudian terms, men "have" what women do not—the penis. Women are defined as "not-men." Freud's revisionist, Jacques Lacan, however, argues that all human subjects "lack": "In any case man cannot aim at being whole (the 'total personality' being another premise where modern psychotherapy goes off course)." [3] The discrepancy between the sexes occurs because women know that they are fragmented, while men understand themselves as self-reliant, autonomous. For men, existence is a "confidence game."

And this game leads them to objectify and oppress women in order to support their existential illusions.

According to Lacan, men paradoxically need an "Other," a mirror, a *petit objet à*, in order to feel complete.[4] For most men, this "other" is a woman who will reflect male desires. Women serve as "the place onto which lack is projected, and through which it is simultaneously avowed."[5] Rather than recognizing their own lack, men will turn to "an other" indefinitely, moving from woman to woman, never correcting their misreading.[6]

Despite their status as "not-men," however, women in the Lacanian scheme possess something extra. Their ability to change is not a liability entirely. They embody *jouissance*, a disruptive excess.[7] Luce Irigaray concludes similarly, arguing that female power and desire may appear under erasure, as hints, or traces which are subtly subversive:

> the issue is not one of elaborating a new theory of which women would be the *subject* or the *object*, but of jamming the theoretical machinery itself, of suspending its pretension to the production of a truth and of a meaning that are excessively univocal.[8]

Women need not merely function as mirrors, as objects of male desire; they have access to a revolutionary method which violates the dialectic designs of their male oppressors. By challenging the power structures established in the plays, and, more importantly, by challenging the expectations of other characters and their audiences, Dr. Ford in *House of Games* and Karen in *Speed-the-Plow* embody this revolutionary femininity.

Mamet's own introductory explanations concerning the filming of *House of Games* indicates that he, too, is consciously jamming the machinery of traditional Hollywood representation. He admits his indebtedness to Sergei Eisenstein, whose techniques suggest rather than legislate narration:

> The shot should stand as one unemotional term of a sequence, the totality of which should create in the mind of the audience a new idea, e.g., rather than the shot of a distraught woman crying, or the same woman describing to her friend over the telephone how she found out her

husband was cheating on her, Eisenstein would suggest
the following: (1) shot of woman reading a note; (2) shot
of the note, which reads, "Honey, I'll be home late
tonight. Going bowling, I love you;" (3) shot of woman
putting down note, looking down at something on the
floor; (4) her point of view, shot of the bowling ball in
the bowling bag.[9]

Of course, all readers attempt to make meaning, to solve the puzzle, or
to translate the "tells" in the Mamet film and play, but Eisenstein's
method and Mamet's mimicry of that method are more "readerly" than
"writerly," to borrow from Roland Barthes' terminology. Eisenstein,
Mamet, and Barthes foster a dialogue between text and viewer. Without
resorting to relativism, Barthes proposes that the "readerly text" is a
plural text:

> In this ideal text, the networks are many and interact,
> without anyone of them being able to surpass the rest;
> this text is a galaxy of signifiers, not a structure of
> signifieds . . . we gain access to it by several entrances,
> none of which can be authoritatively declared to be the
> main one. [10]

Such an approach accounts for the *jouissance* of the text, the "extra"
which eludes even careful readings. And though the psychoanalytic,
feminist approach could be defined as yet another entrance, this
theoretical model accounts for the excesses of representation Mamet and
his plays encourage.

   House of Games opens with a lure, a *petit objet à*, a sphinx-like
woman, Dr. Ford, who appears to have the secrets of the narrative at her
disposal. She is precise, professional, mannish. Close-cropped hair and
masculine clothes lead us to ask: what is this man/woman about? Lacan
describes all femininity as a masquerade, whereby women actually
signify the Phallus:

> Paradoxical as this formulation might seem, I would say
> that it is in order to be the phallus, that is to say, the
> signifier of the desire of the Other, that the woman will
> reject an essential part of her femininity, notably all its
> attributes through masquerade. It is for what she is not
> that she expects to be desired as well as loved. [11]

Through masquerade, women become desirable on the sexual marketplace, as we shall later see in the discussion of pop star Madonna, who starred in the New York City production of *Speed-the-Plow*. Ford, however, does not flaunt the excess or the lack but instead disguises herself as precisely the male, desiring subject, not the autonomous and mythical Phallus. While Lacan solves this riddle of femininity by asserting, "there is no sexual relation,"[12] the convolutions concerning gender in this play simultaneously assert and deny Dr. Ford's position as "the subject supposed to know." She is the master and victim of the male "confidence game."

We soon learn that Ford is an important personage: a young disheveled woman asks for her autograph, so we see the book title: *Driven: Compulsion and Obsession in Everyday Life*. The similarities between Freud's *The Psychopathology of Everyday Life* cannot be ignored, so in some way the film asserts Ford's power by her association with a prominent male thinker in the twentieth century. Of course, at the same time the title is derivative: Ford had to borrow a title from a man, symbolically and traditionally taking a title, a name, and an identity from the father of psychoanalysis. The woman, moreover, admits that she has purchased two copies. Again, ambivalence. Ford's successful advice is undercut by the suggestion that the woman compulsively bought a second copy.

In the next scene, we see Ford with her client, a young murderer. While Ford meticulously documents the speech of the woman, the patient challenges her ability to cope with experience. Ford deftly handles the situation, but the question is still "in the air." Much of Lacan's work began through his investigation of the analyst-analysand relationship. While many early Freudians saw the doctor-patient relationship as a master-slave dialectic, Lacan's concept of a divided subject exposed such a construction as just that, a fabrication, "subjected" to the same illusions and misreadings which characterize existence. In the case of the Mamet script, the separation between Ford and her patient also diminishes; the hierarchy established between patient and doctor blurs, since both are finally murderers.

Dr. Ford's mentor and colleague, Maria, protects the script from depicting all women as killers. As far as we know, Maria murders no man, and she offers Ford sound advice, thereby helping Ford to reestablish her mastery momentarily. She praises Ford's analysis of the patient's Freudian slip: "And now someone has heard her. Good

Maggie, good for you" (8). Of course, Ford herself immediately slips, substituting "pressures" for "pleasures" in her life. Maria admonishes her:

> Your book is a best seller, your income jumps up, people look at you differently, perhaps. This is confusing. Listen to me: Slow Down. Give *yourself* all those rewards you would like to have. You see a beautiful gold lighter, *buy* one for yourself. Your friend asks you to lunch, go and *eat* lunch with her. (8)

Though the advice concerning other people's responses to Ford's success is important, Maria stops short of a full Freudian reading of Ford's fascination with the little box. Freud reads such toying sexually. In his famous case history, his patient Dora plays with a similar trinket. He concludes:

> Dora's reticule, which came apart at the top in the usual way, was nothing but a representation of the genitals, and her playing with it, her opening it and putting her finger in it, was an entirely unembarrassed yet unmistakable pantomimic announcement of what she would like to do with them—namely to masturbate.[13]

By applying the analysis to Dr. Ford, it is Maria's "hot box" that she plays with during lunch, not her own. Admittedly, the act reflects Ford's need for intimacy, but given the bisexual libido and Ford's flight from Maria, this action may hint at lesbian desires or Ford's fear of such feelings.

Maria's appearance, too, offers an alternative to the sartorial preening traditionally demanded in order to assure a woman a place on the sexual market. Luce Irigaray argues:

> Psychoanalysts say that masquerading corresponds to woman's desire. That seems wrong to me. I think the masquerade has to be understood as what women do in order to recuperate some element of desire, to participate in man's desire, but at the price of renouncing their own. In the masquerade, they submit to the dominant economy of desire in an attempt to remain "on the market" in spite

of everything. But they are there as objects for sexual
enjoyment, not as those who enjoy.[14]

Maria's clothes, moreover, are not as masculine as Ford's attire. She
has found a way to dress comfortably, to recognize her own desire
within a system which constantly dismisses female wants. Through her
dress, she successfully "falls between" the "two stools" of feminine
representation.

Ford, however, does not remain with Maria long enough to learn
the manner in which she accomplishes this task. As a matter of fact,
during the screenplay's opening scenes, Ford continually runs away
from women. After leaving her unidentified "fan," her murderess, and
her mentor, Ford runs to Billy, her next client. Like her earlier patient,
Billy challenges Ford's position of power by questioning her "real-life"
experience. Ironically, he uses his losses to claim that he has more, a
tactic the young murderess did not resort to:

> I lost, what do *you* care maan, you're rich, you're
> comfortable, you got your goddamn *book* you wrote, you
> don't do *dick*, you don't do *nothing* maan, it's all a con
> game, you do nothing. . . . What do you think this is?
> Some "dream"? Maan *you're* living in a dream, your
> "questions," 'cause there. is. a. real. world. (10)

Through Billy, we see Ford in an unsympathetic light: she is a
frustrated, compulsive, protected, and pampered woman who knows
nothing about reality "period." Words, the scripts of others, create her
life. We later learn that Billy, also works from a script, crafted by the
con men who are about to hook Ford in a costly con game. At this
point, however, Ford apparently retains her control, because she takes
the gun away from the hysterical Billy. Symbolically and momentarily,
she recuperates her power with the phallic gun.

With such signifiers in her possession, she can enter the "house
of games." Sociologist Ned Polsky describes such establishments as:

> the exact center and veritable stronghold of a special
> kind of subculture that has become increasingly rare and
> unimportant in America—the heterosexual but all-male
> subculture, which required that certain gathering places
> (clubs, barber shops, taverns) serve as sacrosanct refuges

from women. The poolroom was not just one of these
places: it was *the* one, the keystone. [15]

Ford, however, is quickly taken into this world. Through a brief
exchange during which Mike does not "tell" her about "tells" but
instead shows her, Ford is in the game. This master "teller," this
"author," flatters her by informing her that she has the gift, too: "How
come you *made* me so quick? I'm not a hard guy? How did you size me
up so quick?" (14). Ford stammers, nearly betraying herself, almost
giving herself away in the face of phallic bravado. She recovers and
joins the card game. Since Mike has shown and told her that the
poolroom and her work, her psychoanalytic training, are equal, Ford
enters the male world with confidence. She has not left the world she
understands, a world in which people "tell" secrets without words.
According to Freud:

> There is a great deal of symbolism of this kind in life,
> but as a rule we pass it by without heeding it. When I set
> myself the task of bringing to light what human beings
> keep hidden within them, not by the compelling power
> of hypnosis, but by observing what they say and what
> they show, I thought the task was a harder one than it
> really is. He that has eyes to see and ears to hear may
> convince himself that no mortal can keep a secret. If his
> lips are silent, he chatters with his finger-tips; betrayal
> oozes out of him at every pore. And thus the task of
> making conscious the most hidden recesses of the mind
> is one which it is quite possible to accomplish.[16]

When Mike denies that he is an expert gambler, by admitting that his
gambling is not a hobby but a disease, Ford is hooked. Here is a man
she can help. She "assumes" control.

During the card game, however, it appears that Ford loses power,
since she and Mike have misread the Las Vegas man's "tell." Ford
quickly recovers. She is an expert reader; she realizes that the gun the
Las Vegas man has been using is not real—it "weeps." It is a false
phallus. Her own role as a woman pretending to be a man has prepared
her to sense and read such "holes" in texts. David Maurer argues that
part of a game of this sort entails granting the victim a sense of
"confidence." Marks feel secure in their abilities to discern reality:

> The mark is thrown into an unreal world which very
> closely resembles real life; like the spectator regarding
> the life groups in a museum of natural history, he cannot
> tell where the real scene merges into the background. . . .
> They see though the deal which is presented, analyze it,
> and strike the lure like a flash.[17]

Later when Ford discovers the con, it appears that the men did not have the entire con planned at this time. Instead, it may have been her reading here, her confidence and ability at this point in the game, which made the men decide to take her for eighty thousand, not six (60–61).

In either case, Ford is in the game. The men give her what she wants—to be treated as one of the boys, initiated in the male world. When she leaves the evening's game, not only armed with new, male knowledge but also a poker chip, Mike watches her departure and predicts her return through his own manipulation of a coin. Just as he coughs up the piece, so will he cough up Ford. Her treatment of her chip illustrates that she is not accustomed to this type of power, for while Mike lets go of the coin in order to have it return, Ford clings to it tightly, laughingly assuming power.

The evening affects Ford the next day. She does not have an answer for the murderess when she asks, "how can you live, when you've done something . . . when . . . ?" (29). Ford may express herself more during this meeting by giving the woman a hug and letting go of her pen, which previously never left her hand, but when she meets Maria, she describes herself and her profession in the same way that Billy did: "It's a sham, it's a con game" (30). She also slips, saying that her father called her a whore. Ford begins to believe the fantasy the men are constructing—her life and her desires are meaningless. Maria counsels Ford to relax, but once again Ford chooses the company of men, not women.

Her fatal error comes when she decides to "study" Mike and the other con artists. She, a commodity on the sexual marketplace, must be punished for not only behaving like a man but also trying to objectify them as "studies" for a book. In the tragic tradition of *hubris*, Ford does not even believe Mike when he tells her that he is a con man and thief. She believes that not only can she enter the house of men but that she is exempt from their usual manipulations of "marks." She is one of them.

Her first lesson is the "short con." According to Maurer, the only difference between a "short" and a "long" con is that the "long" or "big" con forces the mark to go to the bank to withdraw funds.[18] Mike, of course, does not tell Ford about the longer version but instead "tells" her what she wants:

> MIKE: Be *real*, Babe, let's up the ante here. (*He stops.*)
>   Do you want to make love to me . . . ?
> FORD: *Excuse* me. . .?
> MIKE: Because you're blushing. *That's* a tell. The
>   things we want, we can do them or not do them,
>   but we can't hide them.
> FORD: And *what* is it you think I want?
> MIKE: I'll tell you: someone to come along, to take
>   you into a new thing. Do you want that? Would
>   you like that?
>   *Beat.*
> FORD (*softly*): Yes. (38)

Through this interchange the shifts in power occur rapidly. Ford initially retains her mastery, even in the face of the famous Freudian question, "what do women want?" But by the end, Mike has won her over, objectifying her, "telling" her he knows better. After their romantic encounter, Mike gives her another lesson, this time in the intricate art of subtle subversion: "if you're fired from your job, take something . . . something to assert yourself, take something from life" (41). While he is out of the room, she takes a pocketknife.[19] After their stolen love in a stolen hotel room, Ford steals. Because Mike has told her to take something after she has lost something, it appears that on some level she knows that she has been objectified. With knife in hand, she asserts her authority.

Characteristic of con games, Ford is given a number of opportunities to leave. Maurer notes that con men never actually take the money or directly force their victims to comply:

> Of all the grifters, the confidence man is the aristocrat.
> Although he is sometimes classed with professional
> thieves, he is really not a thief at all because he does no
> actual stealing. The trusting victim literally thrusts a fat

bankroll into his hands. It is a point of pride with him
that he does not have to steal.[20]

Ford remains, and the men apparently con an unsuspecting traveller. As
was the case with the squirt gun at the poker game, Ford assumes she
has correctly interpreted the complexities of the text. The mark is a
"cop," and while Mike tries to protect her from detection, the
"policeman" is apparently killed in a scuffle. Escaping without the
"mob money," Ford gives the men eighty thousand dollars. She aids the
men who took her into their confidence.

Despite the frequent "telling" throughout the play, Mike warns
her not to confess this act. Ford's first destination, however, is Maria.
Glass separates the two now, but when a student opens the door, her
mentor lectures about jokes. The juxtaposition of Ford's pain and the
joke lecture emphasizes not only the close relationship Freud saw
between dreams and jokes, but it also highlights Ford's detachment
from the world. As a result of her association with men, she has
isolated herself from the world, not entered into it more fully. Amidst
the chaos of the class changes and Ford's own mental state, Maria tells
Ford to forgive herself.

Ford does not hear and so withdraws herself further. Her life, like
her diploma, shatters. While trying to dispose of the evidence which
could link her to the men, Billy reappears. She terminates her
relationship with him, but she coincidentally leaves the building at the
same time as Billy. She sees the car that she thought she had stolen
during their escape from the police. As a result of this slip, Ford
catches on to the con, and spies on the men later that evening. Here, the
screenplay almost goes out of its way to confirm their cruelty. The con
men refer to her as an "addict," a term of derision used to describe a
hooked mark and a "booster," a thief, since she stole Mike's lucky
pocketknife.[21] Much worse, however, she learns that Mike only slept
with her to get her money, "a small price to pay" (62).

Ford then seeks revenge, meets Mike at the airport, and hooks
him into her own con game by promising him greater wealth. Mike
takes the bait, proving his greed and lack of feeling for Ford. He risks
everything for the opportunity to leave her penniless and humiliated.
Ford, however, slips, betraying her game. Without skipping a beat,
Mike taunts her error: "Whattayagonna tell 'em, Stud? That the author
of the best-selling *Driven*, 'A Guide to Compulsive Behavior,' gave her

cash away to some con man?" (67). Mike's use of the word "stud" is an ironic and cruel reminder to Ford that she may have wanted to become a man, but she never can, no matter how many cons she pulls or con men she knows. Ford's response to Mike's insults indicate that he is wrong, for she has the gun, the phallus, and he is soon filled with holes. Symbolically, she has violently overturned the sexual relationship.

If the screenplay ended here, the inversion might be interpreted as a feminist triumph: a woman oppressed by men takes over and now rules her oppressors. Such a conclusion, however, is problematic, for in this reading Ford actually becomes one of the men, characters who overpower anyone in their way. The play itself does not leave us with this inversion only. Ford does not escape entirely; she returns to work and her life before the con.

In the final scene, it is clear that she has been away, and her tropical attire signifies a change in the rigid Dr. Ford: she is casually attired and more at ease. Here an unknown man, not a woman, asks her to sign his copy of her new book, entitled, *Forgive Yourself.* During her lunch with Maria, she admits that she has forgiven herself. And unlike the early scenes of the film, it is Maria who must leave the table to answer a phone call. Ford may have returned, but she is not the same woman. Apparently, she has discovered a way to "fall in between two stools."

While Maria is out of the room, however, Ford takes more than her own advice. She steals a lighter from a nearby female patron. We know that the lighter is significant, so this cryptic gesture calls the screenplay and Ford's position in that text into question. On the one hand, the gesture could indicate her guilt over Mike's murder. In a strict Freudian sense, her actions would betray her; she is living like Mike now. On the other hand, the theft assures her mastery within the text; she remains the sphinx. Her gesture is mysterious, and we are the inquisitors.

The theft ruptures the closure of the text through paradoxes: as a master, Ford steals. As a criminal, Ford is free. Jane Gallop writes:

> one can effectively undo authority only from the
> position of authority in a way that exposes the illusions
> of that position *without renouncing* it, so as to permeate
> that position itself with the connotations of its

illusoriness, so as to show that *everyone*, including the "subject presumed to know," is castrated.[22]

By the end of the play, Ford is enigmatic, but in charge, "gotten-away-with," illegal, neither idealized nor condemned. The woman who became a man and who is now a woman sets off alarms with her box of fire. We cannot read complacently, for this gesture forces us to reconsider, reread, and reevaluate. The play concludes with Ford remaining exuberantly and defiantly enigmatic, violating our own tendency to place female characters on one of two stools.

Speed-the-Plow also illustrates that such disturbances occur, but its conclusion is not as joyously subversive. It is, however, a more accurate portrayal of the placement of women in our culture: Karen signifies something more, but she is dismissed, leaving only a trace of that potential. With the shift in perspective—from a main female character's to two male characters' view—this play subjects Karen to more female stereotypes than Dr. Ford. Through her, however, the play exposes the constant categorizing exhibited by Fox and Gould. Fox makes it clear that she is unusual because she cannot be classified as either a Madonna or whore. Gregory Mosher, the director of the New York production, says that audiences should, in fact, leave the play asking "Is she an angel? Is she a whore?"[23] This separation, moreover, occurs throughout the play during almost every situation the men encounter. Such labelling characterizes phallic discourse; men wield the power to label women as either worthy or unworthy on the sexual marketplace.

Mamet's mixed feelings concerning Hollywood are well-documented in his collections of essays. He claims that film writing "taught me (for the moment anyway) to stick to the plot and not to cheat." He simultaneously notes, however:

> When you write for the stage you retain a copyright. The work is *yours* and no one can change a word without your permission. When you write for the screen you are a *laborer* hired to turn out a product, and that product can be altered at the whim of those who employ you.[24]

In his most recent collection, he is more hostile: "Film is a collaborative business: bend over."[25] He continues to make movies, however, and though *Speed-the-Plow* is not a flattering representation of the industry, it presents a sympathetic picture of male subjectivity and the motivation underlying the bravado.

Casting rock star Madonna in the role for *Speed-the-Plow's* Broadway premiere is another contradictory gesture. Since the play criticizes glitz, it is difficult to imagine why this master media manipulator played the role, box office considerations aside. Some critics assumed that the role itself was weak, so it needed a big star; others thought that both the star and the part were weak.[26] Madonna, however, was considered for the role as a result of her praiseworthy letter to Mamet after *House of Games*.[27] Her own image and her use of the media indicate that she is keenly aware of the dialectic mode of oppression employed in a male-dominated culture. She often reappropriates male fantasies in order to undercut them or make them female fantasies. Most clearly, she violates the mother/whore division by casting herself in the role of a virgin, material girl, who runs her own career as effectively and perhaps as ruthlessly as any Mamet male character. Like Karen, Madonna "decorates herself to court male eyes."[28] She masquerades. By casting Madonna, the audience is forced to ponder another enigmatic, Mamet female character. Is she Virgin or whore? Madonna or Karen? Given the star's reputation and the audiences she has trained to read her, audiences can answer "yes," "both," "neither"; that is, they answer correctly.

The play begins with a quote from Thackeray's *Pendennis*, a section which perhaps serves as a mirror to the play's source of philosophical tension: while deterministic, the epigram asserts that there are people who would flee the world and those who would remain in it; in either case "to each some work upon the ground he stands on until he is laid beneath it." The title, too, has spiritual overtones. According to John Simon it "derives from the fifteenth-century phrase, 'God speed the ploe,' i.e., grant success to your enterprise."[29] The battle between the practical-minded Hollywood producers and the unorthodox but spiritual text, *The Bridge*, does not conclude so magnanimously: a choice must be made; both cannot exist.

Mamet's own attitudes toward religion and social change are also at odds. In his entry in *Contemporary Authors*, for example, he lists politics as "the last refuge of the uninspired" and religion the "second-to-last." But at the same time he laments the fact that:

> We are spiritually bankrupt—that's what's wrong with
> this country. We don't take Sundays off. We don't pray.
> We don't regenerate our spirit. These things aren't
> luxuries. . . . The spirit has to be replenished. There has
> to be time for reflection, introspection, a certain amount
> of awe and wonder.[30]

Lacan, not surprisingly, associates religion with the *petit objet à,* another mirror which will make the subject feel "whole and complete." There is, however, a similar tension in his writings, so much so that he had to resort to an explicit defense. He argues that "I believe in the *jouissance* of the woman only in so far as it is something more. . . . And why not interpret one face of the Other, the God face, as supported by feminine *jouissance?*"[31] Rather than entirely oppressing religion, Lacan resurrects it through the concept of *jouissance.* Given the literal meaning of *jouissance,* a female orgasm, it is difficult not to read these conclusions comically. The joke, however, keeps the text open. We are left wondering here, as we are in the Mamet texts and biography.

Perhaps more than any other Mamet play, *Speed-the-Plow* is filled with religious imagery and syntax. Like his early works, however, in which the rhetoric of the American business dream was uttered by junkshop owners or shady real estate salesman, these religious references incongruously appear in this play through the dialogue of sleazy Hollywood producers. The play opens with Gould responding to Fox's entrance by saying, "when the gods would make us mad, they answer our prayers" (3). This opening sets signification in motion. Gould probably utters it to make himself feel powerful; he pontificates. But the cliché itself calls closure, meaning-making, into question: an answer brings madness, not joy. Here and throughout the play, the characters spew the rhetoric of redemption but do not heed its direction. Gould immediately resorts to dialectical judgments, disdaining the text he reads because "it's not quite 'Art' and it's not quite 'Entertainment'" (3). The work's title, *The Bridge,* offers a solution to the binary mode of existence, but Gould and Fox blithely label the book "trash."

Thrown into the abyss of signification, they try to create a sense of closure in order to overcome feelings of doubt or lack. The real estate maxim which opens *Glengarry Glen Ross* is appropriate here: "always be closing." Gould wants to "play" with the radiation text, to ridicule it, but Fox does not: "I have to talk to you" (4). Fun truncated, he pitches his deal, the script that Doug Brown has agreed to shoot. Fox begins the story seriously, and Gould finishes it: "a buddy film, a prison film, Douggie Brown, blah, blah, some girl. . . . Action, blood, a social theme" (13). This film will succeed because it is predictable. What is more, it is a white man's fantasy. Threatened by homosexual rape by black men in prison, the white man triumphs by showing the African Americans that they really do need him; oppression actually liberates them.[32]

In a matter of moments, the deal is solidified. Any doubts are smoothed over because they have the script, the star, and the means of production: "What's Ross going to say. . . 'No'? It's *done*" (19). This is the American dream: two mail room clerks who rise to the level of producers, make deals in minutes, and spend the rest of the day at lunch. In a classic Mamet dialogue, Gould asserts that "money is not the important thing." Through the call-and-response technique so common among Baptist preachers, the play undercuts the characters' sincerity. Their hypocrisy is highlighted by their use of a traditional religious preaching style:

> GOULD: What can you do with Money?
> FOX: Nothing.
> GOULD: Nary a goddamn thing. . . . *Fuck* money . . . But
>   don't fuck "people."
> FOX: No.
> GOULD: 'Cause, people, Charlie . . .
> FOX: People . . . yes.
> GOULD: Are what it's All About. . . . it's a People
>   Business.
> FOX: That it is.
> GOULD: It's *full* of fucken' people . . .
> FOX: And we're gonna kick some ass, Bob.
> GOULD: That we are.
> FOX: We're gonna kick the ass of a lot of them
>   fucken' people. (21–22)

Gould, clearly establishing himself as the "subject supposed to know," makes claims which Charlie follows. Both reverentially place themselves, their morals, and their mission above mere money. The use of the word "nary" makes them feel traditional, rooted, eternal, and right. Fox and Gould, however, conclude that film is the business of beating people, winning. Neither character notices the moral decline throughout this speech: they have moved from self-sacrifice to self-aggrandizing oppression. This speech makes it clear that words require no content in this Hollywood setting; they need only sound good. Unlike *House of Games* in which the men used a female mark to advance, to feel complete, Fox and Gould during the opening of this play reproduce the female mirror through their contracts, their loyalty to one another, and their stories. Since we see this process in action, however, we are not taken in by them, as we were in *House*. And to some extent, the play places us in the position of mastery. We, too, may "always be closing." They are "sleazy." They are "Hollywood." They are "not us." And for some, they are not as interesting as the mysterious Mike and his con men.

When Karen enters the room, the men immediately begin to perform. They even pretend to be women, calling themselves "old whores." On the sexual marketplace, such women have no value—they fulfill no desire, but when these men play at the game, whores suddenly take on noble significance. Says Gould, "I'm a whore and I'm proud of it. But I'm a secure whore" (26). Again, the term closes off ambivalence: an insecure whore, in Gould's mind, would be unthinkable; it would be a woman.

Karen, as audience, is in a position of power. As a "temporary," though, she does not remain there for long. The men begin to educate her in the ways of Hollywood. Fox tells her:

> Life in the movie business is like the, is like the beginning of a new love affair: it's full of surprises, and you're constantly getting fucked. . . . Everybody says "Hey, I'm a maverick." . . . But what do they do? Sit around like, hey, like Pancho-the-dead-whale. (29)

Gould's behavior proves this conclusion. He states that his "new job is one thing, the capacity to make decisions" (24). Through their discussion of the Brown film and the rest of the play, it becomes clear that there is no room for decision-making, even though the system creates the illusion that such challenges can and will be possible. Fox concludes: "You wanna *do* something out here, it better be one of Five Major Food Groups" (30). In this script, Hollywood is filled with "powerful hacks," who know nothing except syntax, structure, signifiers, and surface.

Karen's entrance almost immediately causes a disruption. Looking for male definitions of femininity, she is the perfect woman: "I don't know what to do. [*Pause.*] I don't know what I'm supposed to do." (31). Without male definition, Karen is nothing. After she has left the room, however, this nothing causes friction between the two men. Fox does not think Gould would have any luck with her because he says ominously, "she falls between two stools . . . she is not, just some, you know, a 'floozy'. . . . on the other hand, I think I'd have to say, I don't think she is so *ambitious* she would schtup you just to get ahead" (35). This combination is dangerous in a world which is "always closing," because she violates categorizing. In order to minimize the threat Karen signifies, Gould wages a bet with Fox: he will sleep with Karen that night. Fox is relieved. After all, this is the manner in which women should be treated. Luce Irigaray argues that such bets reveal more about the men than the women. She asserts that all:

> economic organization is homosexual. That of desire as well, even the desire for women. Woman exists only as an occasion for mediation, transaction, transition, transference, between man and his fellow man, indeed between man and himself.[33]

In this way, the bet secures an intimate relationship between Gould and Fox, not Karen and Gould.

At this point in the play, however, Fox albeit reluctantly permits his friend to pursue the woman, reassured that he will treat her just like a contract, something to be won, a commodity, just like the films he sells and makes. As he explains his job, the "courtesy read," and the industry to Karen, she asks him about "principles." During this exchange, Gould actually claims that without principles "all you've got is 'good taste'"(45). Implying that he possesses principles and that Karen has a fresh eye, he makes a date with her to discuss the script. The first act concludes confirming that he has neither principles nor good taste: he tells her to call Fox "and tell him he owes me five hundred bucks" (46).

While the prison film script took a matter of moments to discuss, the second act focuses predominantly on the play that the producers do not wish to film, stage, or even read. As a result of this second act, then, the script of *The Bridge* is, ironically, outlined, performed, and presented in great detail. Because it is embedded in

Speed-the-Plow, The Bridge is produced, despite Fox's and Gould's conclusions that it will never be a hit on screen or stage, for that matter. New York critic Clive Barnes impatiently writes about this section:

> Revealingly, Mamet never gives art an even break against mammon. The novel he has suggested, "The Bridge," is not only ludicrously pompous in its theme, but the lengthy passages interminably read to us are neither satirically funny nor conceivably convincing.[34]

Because of the play's extended focus on the book, however, the play appears to endorse the "radiation" script. Admittedly, the idea is interesting: radiation, like the workers in the Thackeray epigram, has a purpose, to make us better. As Karen tells Gould, the radiation comes "To change us. Constantly. . . . To this new thing. And we needn't feel frightened. That it comes from God. And I felt empowered" (48). On the one hand, *The Bridge* makes the same point as the prison script: do not worry about change, you are the Phallus. Neither black men nor radiation can harm you. On the other hand, the script offers optimism without exploitation, change without fear: the Dark Ages "aren't to come, the Dark Ages—they are now. We're living them" (49).

Gould, however, is practical. The idea may be good, but people do not want change or new ideas. His business is to "*make the thing everyone made last year. Make that image people want to see.* That *is* what they, it's more than what they want. It is what they require" (56). Here, the repetition of images creates the illusion of autonomy *en masse*.

Up until this act, Gould is in power, masterminding the scripts, Fox, and Karen. Karen changes this balance of power by admitting that she knew "what the deal was" when Gould asked her to read the book and then report to him later that evening. Unlike Dr. Ford in *House of Games*, Karen has not been conned. She is a woman, not a man-woman, and to some extent, she may know more about the masquerade of sexual desire and its rituals than the successful Dr. Ford. This understanding not only helps her to retain her desire, but she becomes the "subject-supposed-to-know." Like Dr. Ford, she also momentarily inverts the patriarchal system by telling Gould what he wants. Like Mike in *House of Games*, she tells her partner what he wants:

I know that you are [frightened]. I would have come here
anyway. Is that depraved? *I* know that it is to be bad. I've
been bad, I know what it is to be lost, I know you're lost.
I know that . . . How we are afraid . . . to *"ask,"* to even
"ask," and say in jest, "Yes. I prayed to be pure" . . . but
it was not an accident. That I came here. Sometimes it
reaches for us. And we say "show me a sign." And when it
reaches us, then we see we *are* the sign. And we find the
answers. (58)

The mastery is quickly complicated. Not only does Karen assert the
linguistic nature of subjectivity through the use of the word "sign"—we
are signifiers of the Other, constantly lacking, always waiting—but her
role is easily that of a Madonna, a saint who leads the way, a woman
who offers completion, a sense of autonomy: "What if your prayers
were answered? You asked me to come. Here I am" (60). At this point
in the script, it is easy to cast Karen in the role of the Madonna, female
stereotype, for she offers salvation, the healing word, to Gould.

But Karen's relationship to Gould has become more complicated
than a wager between men, than a homoerotic encounter, and more
complicated than a virtuous woman offering a new way of life to a
needy man. These shifts in her presentation and her characterization
bring conflict and hostility to Gould's relationship to Fox. The third act
opens with Fox assuming that they will make the prison film deal
soon. Gould bluntly tells Fox he will not do the film, and Fox thinks
he is joking. Their intimate level of communication has broken down;
their ability to play, complete each other's thoughts, or to engage in
the call-and-response ritual is gone.

Fox is enraged. He attacks the book: "Hey, I believe in the
Yellow Pages, Bob, but I don't want to *film* it" (67). Then Gould reads
a passage from the book which interprets even decay as divine. Gould
concludes "my life is a sham" (69). Fox, of course will have nothing to
do with this narrative. In response, he attacks both Karen and Gould:

You were up all night boffing the *broad*. Are you getting
old? What is this? *Menopause*? Your "life is a sham'?
Two days in the new job, you can't stand the strain
. . . .You're throwing your life away. [*Pause*] Listen to
me: Bob [*pause*]: Bob [*pause*]: I have to tell you
something . . . It's the secretary. She, what did she do to
you . . .? (69)

Ironically, while Fox argues that the book is "Little Lambsy Divey," a fairy tale, he is in the process of creating an equally preposterous fiction to explain reality. Like the con artists, he creates an unreal world that appears more palatable than the victim's actual life: Karen has infiltrated their office as a "temporary" in order to wreak havoc upon the Hollywood film industry. Of the book, he tells Gould, "I wouldn't believe this shit if it was *true*" (73). Through these complicated maneuverings regarding mimesis, *Speed-the-Plow* illustrates the tenuous nature of our meaning-making faculties.

Like Iago in Shakespeare's *Othello*, Fox leads Gould to misreading, and Gould, like Othello, is only too willing to read a woman as unfaithful. Gould, however, will not give in, so Fox tries one last tactic: he asks Karen into the office. Gould's patience and resistance wears thin, so he asks Karen if she would have slept with him if he had not agreed to do the book. She answers negatively, and the whole script unravels. Fox throws Karen out, and he and Gould are "buddies," together again, doing a "buddy" film.

Karen as neither saint nor whore has faults, and she has admitted them from the beginning of the play. Unlike Mike in *House of Games* who uses honesty in order to deceive, Karen is sincerely straightforward. In this world, however, women are not permitted any flaws. Gould wants a saint. In order to have an opinion, in order to make any changes or even think about making them, Karen must be pure. The play concludes with a hierarchy reestablished. Fox tells Gould, "And what *if* this fucken' 'grace' exists? It's not for you. You know that, Bob. You know that. You have a different thing" (81). In the end, however, all that matters is that their names appear on the marque, one above the other. In this case, Fox has won. Through Gould's relationship with Karen, however, we have seen his insecurity, the lack which he tries to disguise. Even though Fox reestablishes the patriarchal structure in the end, his relationship with Karen has created a place in the text for something more, feminist disruption.

Throughout *House of Games* and *Speed-the-Plow* the battle between the sexes has been a battle for power. While the scripts appear to grant power to the male characters, the women in these plays are the blind spots which violate our sense of closure. The female characters in the plays create disruptions in the lives of their male counterparts by specifically violating their stereotypes. Phallic power, characterized by the oppression of women by men, is overturned in both plays by the female characters' subtle subversive strategies. Neither play concludes with a triumphant feminist taking charge; instead, the females are enigmatic, a conclusion which may be more effective in creating changes concerning the representation of women. According to Luce Irigaray, such subtle disruptions have profound consequences:

> When women want to escape from exploitation, they do not merely destroy a few "prejudices," they disrupt the entire order of dominant values, economic, social, moral, and sexual. They call into question all existing theory, all thought, all language, inasmuch as these are monopolized by men and men alone. They challenge *the very foundation of our social and cultural order,* whose organization has been prescribed by the patriarchal system.[35]

Mamet's texts mimic the patriarchy and the role of women in them. His female characters create disturbances, admittedly behind the scenes, in effect behind the "yellow wallpaper," but they succeed in creating subtle disruptions in these texts which tempt us to return, rethink, and reconsider.

Notes

1. David Mamet, *Speed-the-Plow* (New York: Grove Press, 1987), p. 35. All further references are to this edition and will be noted parenthetically throughout the essay.

2. David Mamet, *Some Freaks* (New York: Vintage, 1989), p. 88.

3. Jacques Lacan, *Feminine Sexuality*, trans. Jacqueline Rose, eds. Juliet Mitchell and Jacqueline Rose (New York: Norton, 1985), pp. 81–82.

4. Lacan, pp. 74–85.

5. Juliet Mitchell, "Introduction I," *Feminine Sexuality*, by Jacques Lacan, p. 43.

6. Lacan, p. 84.

7. Lacan, pp. 144–145.

8. Luce Irigaray, *This Sex Which Is Not One*, trans. Catherine Porter (New York: Cornell University Press, 1985), p. 78.

9. David Mamet, *The House of Games* (New York: Grove Press, 1988), p. vi. All further references are to this edition and will be cited parenthetically throughout the essay.

10. Roland Barthes, *S/Z*, trans. Richard Miller (New York: Hill and Wang, 1974), p. 5.

11. Lacan, p. 84.

12. Lacan, pp. 138–148.

13. Sigmund Freud, *The Standard Edition of the Complete Psychological Works of Sigmund Freud*, trans. James Strachey (London: Hogarth Press, 1971), Vol. 7: p. 77.

14. Irigaray, pp. 133–134.

15. Ned Polsky, *Hustlers, Beats, and Others* (Chicago: Univ. of Chicago Press, 1985), p. 21.

16. Freud, pp. 77–78.

17. David Mauer, *The American Confidence Man* (Springfield: Charles Thomas, 1974), p. 90.

18. Mauer, p. 270.

19. In *The Psychopathology of Everyday Life*, Freud notes in a footnote that one of his patients made a slip of the tongue regarding a pocket-knife, the name of which coincided with a contraceptive manufacturer. Freud concludes, "in fact she turned out to be under the influence of unconscious thoughts about pregnancy and contraception" (*Standard Edition*, Vol. 6: p. 62). Dr. Ford does not seem to entertain such thoughts, however.

20. Mauer, p. 3.

21. Mauer, p. 269.

22. Jane Gallop, *Reading Lacan* (New York: Cornell University Press, 1985), p. 21.

23. Gregory Mosher, "Madonna Comes to Broadway," by William A. Henry, *Time* 131 (16 May 1988): p. 99.

24. David Mamet, *Writing in Restaurants* (New York: Viking, 1986), pp. 75-77.

25. Mamet, *Some Freaks*, p. 134.

26. See Gerald Weales, "Rough Diamonds," *Commonwealth* 115 (17 June 1988): p. 371. Moira Hodgson, *"Speed-the-Plow," The Nation* 246 (18 June 1988): pp. 974–975. Clive Barnes, "A Harvest of Riches," *New York Post*, (4 May 1988). Rpt. in *New York Theatre Critics Review*, 49 (1988): pp. 274–275. And Howard Kissel, "No She Can't Act," *New York Daily News*, 4 May 1988. Rpt. in *New York Theatre Critics Review*, 49 (1988): p. 277.

27. Madonna in William A. Henry, p. 99.

28. Nicholas Jennings and Marilyn Becker, "The Spell of Pop's Unstoppable Siren," *MacLeans*, 13 July 1987, pp. 40–41.

29. John Simon, "Theatre," *New York*, 21 (May 16, 1988): p. 106.

30. Gerald Weales also notes that another novel, *Speed the Plough* (1800) by Thomas Morton was also about guessing what people want. No one seems to know what Mamet indicates by the hyphenated title. See Mamet's thoughts on spiritual bankruptcy in *Some Freaks*.

31. Lacan, p. 147.

32. Mamet himself wrote a script somewhat similar to the one that Fox and Gould wish to market. In *Edmond* (1982) a white man leaves his suburban home, only to wallow in sin and crime. Unlike the white man in the Douggie Brown script, Edmond is jailed, takes the black, male lover, and some would say, he is happier for the choice.

33. Irigaray, p. 193.

34. Barnes, p. 274.

35. Irigaray, p. 165.

DAVID MAMET'S *THE VERDICT*: THE OPENING CONS

Steven H. Gale

David Mamet's *The Verdict* (Twentieth Century-Fox, 1982) is generally considered the writer's best screenplay.[1] Directed by Sidney Lumet, the 128-minute-long film contains Mamet's typically well-wrought dialogue, carefully drawn characters, and an entertaining, arresting, and tension-filled plot. These are elements that have been an integral part of his canon from the beginning of his career.

There are two elements in the filmscript that reflect characteristics of the author's writing as it has evolved since *The Duck Variations* was first staged in 1972. From the start Mamet's dialogue has been compared with that of Harold Pinter. Unlike Pinter, however, Mamet has developed an interest in his characters' professions as professions. Obviously what happens in *Glengarry Glen Ross* has meaning that extends beyond selling real estate, for instance, just as *Speed-the-Plow* is not limited in application to the Hollywood film scene and *The Untouchables* and *Things Change* are not merely motion pictures about gangsters. *The Verdict* clearly is about lawyers on one level, though on the most important level it could have been about psychiatrists (vide *House of Games*). While professions seem to have caught Mamet's attention in his later writing, then, the significance of these works is that they are about human beings in certain situations, and the general lessons extolled in them are universally applicable regardless of the characters' special occupational circumstances.

Still, even though the professions themselves may be used metaphorically by Mamet and are important specifically because of this,

The Verdict is about lawyers, a fact that is related to the second characteristic of Mamet's more recent dramas and films. The confidence game, or con, has become increasingly important as both a topic and a structural device for Mamet—what better example than *House of Games*—though the trick and the twist are prevalent throughout his writing in the 1980s. The law profession and the con come together nicely, and meaningfully, in *The Verdict*, particularly in the opening segment.

One critical theory contends that the opening shot, certainly the opening segment, of a film should contain the essence of what that film is about. Thus, an analysis of the beginning of a movie provides for an insight into the meaning being expressed and an understanding of the techniques utilized to express that meaning. There are literary parallels, of course: the importance of "Air #1" in John Gay's *The Beggar's Opera* and of Act I (even scene one) in Oliver Goldsmith's *She Stoops to Conquer* are obvious theatrical examples. Edgar Allan Poe understood this principle when he wrote a book review of one of Charles Dickens' novels after reading only the first chapter. The nine-minute, fifteen-second-long, thirty-six shot opening segment of *The Verdict*[2] (that is, approximately seven percent of the film's running time), sets up the character of the protagonist, Frank Galvin, finely portrayed by Paul Newman, so that a benchmark is established against which his actions can be measured. The segment also introduces the movie's plot line.

There are three basic types of lawyers depicted in *The Verdict*: ambulance chasers, large-firm attorneys, and honest, sincere, hard-working professionals. As the opening segment demonstrates, Galvin is an ambulance chaser. An essential component in Mamet's portrayal of his hero is the serious game, the con. Indeed, the first sounds in the movie are the non-synchronous pinball machine bells heard over the Gothic lettered titles (amusingly in connection with the names of the producers, Richard D. Zanuck and David Brown), and the first image is of Galvin playing the game (old-fashioned in a time of video arcade games).[3] Galvin is silhouetted on the right side of the frame, the machine extends across the lower quarter of the screen, and the lighted score board is on the left side of the frame facing Galvin in a relatively equal position. The shot is backlighted by light coming through the windows behind Galvin and the machine, so most of his figure is in shadow, framed by the dark room and machine. There is a tinsel Christmas garland stretched across the window, and leafless trees can be seen behind an iron picket fence across the street. Galvin shoots the ball, takes a drink of beer from a mug, and puffs on his cigarette as the camera pushes in to a close-up of his partially lit silhouetted face, still on the right of the frame, the light windowpanes seen behind him. This minute-and-twenty-second shot ends abruptly with a fade to black.

Already a number of components have been signified. Galvin is a solitary, somber character in a bleak landscape. He has minor vices and is isolated in dismal surroundings in the middle of the day unemotionally playing a mechanical game. He is dressed in a dark overcoat. Except for a brief moment during which someone can be seen walking through the woods in the deep background there is no connection between Galvin and humanity. Apparently even the bar is virtually empty, for no sounds other than the bells are heard. Furthermore, Galvin seems trapped, with the lines of the window frames, iron rod fence, and tall, straight, barren tree trunks forming the many lines of bars of his cage. This is especially emphasized when his head is framed by the window cross bars (the mullions) for the instant or two before the screen goes black.

In terms of cinematic techniques it is easy to see how Mamet has employed the camera eye, sound, and lighting to portray the nature of his protagonist before a single word of dialogue is spoken. Because, in the West at least, the natural movement of the eye is from left to right, the tendency would be to see the machine and then Galvin's figure—but this is balanced by the realistic *mise-en-scène*, the eye-level shot, and the high contrast lighting. Because the frame is lighter at the top and in the center frame, the bottom and right-hand side of the composition is heavier, a structure that suggests a combination of subservience and insignificance. The dominant contrast of the window catches our eye first, then the subsidiary contrast of the lighted face of the machine, and only after the eye tracks back across the screen to the right does Galvin become apparent. In fact, the movement of the indistinct figure across the street draws our attention before we focus on Galvin. All of this diminishes the protagonist's importance in the composition of the shot. When Galvin's face finally does emerge out of the murky darkness, the lighting is such that only the front edge of his profile is distinguishable. The effect of this is to create a feeling that he is hiding, perhaps even ambivalent and divided in his perception of his own self. His profile position underscores his remoteness from the audience and his surroundings (he does not notice, or pay attention to, the person in the far background of the shot). His confinement is stressed not only by the bar-effect of the window crosspieces, fence, trees, and shadows, but by the tight framing of the shot as well. This combination of image patterns and framing also serves to create a closed form, which again reinforces the sense of confinement and suggests the character's inability to control his own destiny. The opening shot contrasts markedly with shot number thirty-seven, in which Galvin has been galvanized into action by Mickey Morrissey, the Jack Warden character, and begins to move crisply and purposefully as opposed to the slow, lethargic, hesitant movements in the opening sequence. Most notable is the bright, white lighting of shot thirty-seven as it opens the next segment of the film, the centering of Galvin in the frame, and the extremely open form of the shot. Awash in light, almost nothing is visible in an eye-level medium shot except for Galvin, who moves from the center of the screen toward the right—the left-to-right horizontal movement is natural, and the lateral movement emphasizes his speed and efficiency.

According to some screenwriters, just as there is a classical model for dramatic structure (exposition, rising action, conflict, climax, denouement), so is there a traditional paradigm for feature-length films.[4] This paradigm consists of three "acts": the setup, the confrontation, and the resolution. Typically, the first and third parts are thirty minutes long and the second segment is sixty minutes long. At the end of the first and second sections normally there are "plot hooks," major twists in the plot designed to move the action forward in a new direction. There may be any number of minor plot hooks as well. Clearly, Mamet's screenplay loosely follows this pattern. The first nine minutes and fifteen seconds is certainly a setup, and the first plot hook comes at the end of this section through the mechanism of the information regarding the case that supplies the plot device that will lead to the confrontation.

Although Mamet laments in "A First-Time Film Director" that he was "completely ignorant" about the "visual" area of directing films and relied on Sergei Eisenstein's theories while preparing for his directorial debut (*House of Games*, 1987),[5] the opening sequence of *The Verdict* demonstrates that he is able to create a successful montage of "uninflected" shots. According to Eisenstein, a shot must not be evocative. That is to say, the meaning of the shot does not derive from narration but rather from its juxtaposition with other shots in a series, the effect of which is to transmit meaning visually based on information determined by the relationship of the shots in the series. Christian Metz contends that a cinematic shot is "not comparable to the word in a lexicon; rather it resembles a complete statement (of one or more sentences)." Given that the majority of Mamet's prior work is in the theatre where the word is predominant, his plea of ignorance is understandable and sympathy eliciting. In "Encased by Technology" Mamet notes that "movies are the first art to link the plastic and the temporal. They take place both tangibly, in the image, and continually, in the juxtaposition of those images."[6] Obviously he is attracted to the essence of film as "Art" and its suggestive nature—which is the creation of an image "not on *the screen*, but in the mind of the beholder." Later, he elaborates when he states that "Lumière et al." were "juxtaposing pictures *to create an idea in the mind* of the audience" (emphasis mine).[7]

Thus, most of the first segment of *The Verdict* contains no dialogue, yet the images provided convey a clear picture of Galvin's character and the nature of the life that he is leading, and this initial sequence illustrates how well Mamet understands and can realize the combination of the concepts of the opening segment and the uninflected components of montage in actual practice. In fact, the filmscript as a whole was so well conceived and executed that Mamet received an Academy of Motion Picture Arts and Sciences Oscar nomination in 1983 in the best-adaptation category (the movie was based on Barry Reed's novel of the same name), and his effect on his audience was equally impressive for, the author recalls, lawyers "wrote in droves to say that real lawyers don't behave that way."[8] Which kind of lawyer they do not act like—the ambulance chaser, the amoral big-firm, corporate attorney, or the honest, idealistic champion of truth and justice—is not identified.

In the final shot of the film there are obvious parallels with the movie's initial shot and some important differences. Ironically, as *The Verdict* ends, Galvin is again alone and in a darkened room. Even the composition of the shot in which we see him for the last time is vaguely similar to that in which we had our first sight of him. He is centered in the frame and a machine with a ringing bell, a telephone, evoking echoes of the opening sound of the pinball bells, is situated in the left corner of the frame. This time, however, Galvin is in a different environment. He is seated at his desk in his office. Wearing a vest, his collar open and tie loosened, he has his feet on the desk; his head is tilted back, his eyes closed. The windows behind him are high and to the left rather than framing him from behind, and the light that comes through is diffuse and offset by the brightness of the lamp on the desk that clearly illuminates him and the tools of his trade, a law book and a cup full of pencils. His features are distinct, and he is seen in a medium shot, straight on. The full-front position is the most intimate position for an actor, and the contrast between Galvin's lighting and position in this shot contrasts markedly with the remoteness expressed in the first shot. It simultaneously demonstrates and symbolizes the psychological distance that he has traveled in the interim. The lines formed by the window casements, massive support beams, and arches of the geometrically patterned carved concrete walls convey a sense of strength and upward movement as opposed to encaging bars, and Galvin is at the center of an almost pyramidal conglomeration. The ringing telephone is in the shadows. Whereas in the opening shot he was engaged in the mindless physical activity embodied in the pinball game, as the film ends, Galvin is motionless on the outside but his lack of physical action derives from a conscious mental decision.

Between the first and last shots, of course, is the movie, including the important opening sequence. There is an adage among filmmakers that the audience is either engaged in the film in the first ten minutes (they are involved with the characters or interested in finding out the outcome of the action) or they are disinterested. In *The Verdict* the law profession, the con game, the Eisenstein concept of uninflected shots, the cinematic paradigm setup establishing the protagonist's character and the premise on which the conflict/confrontation is to be based, and the reliance on the ten-minute maxim all combine effectively. An analysis of the shots that compose the opening segment montage illustrates how Mamet has effectively and efficiently manipulated his material to these ends.

Shot number two is an extended follow that opens focused on two men's hands as the one on the left (moments later discovered to be the funeral director) uses body motions to urge the one on the right to produce a ten-dollar bill from a roll of money. After the exchange of the bribe the camera pans up to reveal that it was Galvin who passed the money to the other man. He uses a breath spray and then trails after the funeral director, who is already approaching a grief-numbed widow in order to introduce Galvin to her. Galvin, kneeling beside the woman's chair, claims to have known the deceased husband "vaguely at the lodge." He offers to help her in "any way" and presses his business card into her unresponsive hand. The camera tracks Galvin as he moves across the room past the open casket (which he ignores) and out the front door—his card has fallen unnoticed into the widow's lap.

There is a dissolve to an extreme close-up of Galvin's hand holding a pen with which he is marking the obituary section of a newspaper that lies open on a bar table. A full whiskey glass sits next to the paper and two halves of a powdered sugar donut lie on it. Galvin is crossing out some of the notices and underlining parts of another.[9] Presumably those that he has crossed out are ethnically or geographically too distant to interest him or he has already visited them, and the underlining indicates the address that he will visit next. The hand drops the black pen and moves to pick up the whiskey glass. The hand begins to shake so much that the liquor starts to spill, and the glass is put back down.

There is a cut to shot four, a medium shot of Galvin looking about, then leaning over and taking a sip from the glass.[10] The emphasis on the protagonist's hands in these first three shots indicates that he is not leading a life of the mind, and the shaking denotes a physical deterioration as well. Having taken a sip, Galvin is now steady enough to pick up the glass. Before he takes a gulp of the liquor, though, he sits pensively for several moments, apparently bothered by what he is doing. His black suit, and the grey sky, somewhat older automobiles, and blocky, lower-class business buildings visible through the windows behind him reflect the murky and squalid tone that has been established in the first set of shots.

Another dissolve finds Galvin in line to introduce himself to another widow in another room with an open casket and assorted mourners. Presumably this is the wake that he noted in the obituary section. The people in the scene are situated at the back of the room, and there is open space at the center and bottom of the screen. This creates an elongated, panoramic view of a group of unknown people with Galvin in the middle of the plane of objects, conveying the sense that he is engaged in a long series of these kinds of experiences. But, in the next ten quick shots the events are very different from those depicted in the earlier wake scene. Shot five is a close-up of Galvin, leaning into the camera to hand his card to the widow. Then the shots alternate between Galvin in line and the widow and her son. The son states that

Galvin never knew his father (Galvin has claimed to, as before, and raises a handkerchief to his mouth as he is challenged) and demands that he leave. The funeral director's hand comes into the frame to grab Galvin's arm, and the camera pans to show the lawyer being escorted out. This entire sequence takes only fifty-four seconds.

There is a cut to an exterior shot (number fifteen) of the funeral parlor door, through which Galvin and the funeral director can be seen approaching. The door opens and the muffled sound of Galvin protesting, "Hey, you know me," can be heard. As Galvin is forcibly ejected, the funeral director tells him to never come back (has Galvin been betrayed? We do not know whether he paid a bribe this time). The lawyer insists that he "was just talkin' to the guy," but the funeral director counters that "Those are bereaved people in there" and goes back inside. The camera holds on Galvin's face in a quarter-turn close-up. Up to this point most of the sound heard has been synchronous, with the exception of a few scattered incidences of background noise (cars outside while Galvin is checking the obituaries, for example). There has been no music. Now a French horn begins a dirge-like melody as Galvin seems to comprehend the significance of what has happened to him (he frowns and bites his thumbnail). This is a minor plot point, certainly not an epiphany. The music (by Johnny Mandel) continues, with additional instruments, including chiming bells, and the shot becomes a crane shot. As Galvin walks down the street away from the camera, the camera rises into the air. The funeral home sign comes into view and ultimately takes up most of the right side of the frame, looming over Galvin's figure, which is small and dwarfed by virtue of perspective and the juxtaposition of the sign. The grey sidewalk and cold, dirty snow piled in the street balance the funeral home sign as a comment on what Galvin has been doing. Galvin walks out of the frame to the left, and there is a dissolve to the interior of the bar in which he was first seen. Shot from a different point of view, it is warmer looking and more plush than before with the intruding light from the windows having been replaced by wood-paneled walls, and there are nine other people present, listening to Galvin tell a Pat-and-Mike joke. The music has been used as a transition, though in the bar it becomes lighter in tone with the addition of a harp.[11] There is general, convivial laughter at the end of the joke, and, having been held to his offer by the bartender, Galvin buys a round of drinks for everyone. The use of music as a transitional device linking shots fifteen and sixteen reenforces the idea

that he has sought out the bar as a way of escaping the significance of
the funeral parlor incident. He avoids facing the consequences by
drowning himself in a combination of alcohol and the companionship
of a boisterous, animated group that differs dramatically from those in
the funeral scenes. That he tells a Pat-and-Mike joke after being ejected
from an Irish funeral (the Cleary's) may be his attempt to
simultaneously avenge himself and to diminish the effect of his
embarrassment by denigrating the ethnic background of those who have
unmasked him. The scene closes on a somber note, literally, when the
music turns ominous in tone with the insertion of a bassoon, strings,
and bass voices. Again there is a dissolve, and again the music serves as
a transitional device carrying over to shot seventeen where it becomes
discordant.

Shot seventeen begins the penultimate montage in *The Verdict*'s
opening section. Contemporaneously with the fade-in of shot seventeen
the funereal music becomes more discordant. It continues over the
subsequent six shots, though it becomes quieter and a bit more lyrical
with the arrival of Mick Morrissey (the dark, heavy undertones continue
to reverberate and echo). When Galvin and Morrissey, sitting and facing
one another in shot twenty-two, nod to signify their acceptance of each
other's presence, what is happening, and the initiation of their
conversation, the moody music ends.

A low-angle shot, shot seventeen signals that Galvin has about
reached bottom. The perspective of him washing his hands at the sink
in the cluttered washroom of his office makes things look distorted. The
jumble of intersecting lines and planes of window sills, piles of
cardboard boxes, wall moldings, and Galvin's figure are reminiscent of
the expressionistic production design of *The Cabinet of Dr. Caligari* and
reflective of the disordered state of the protagonist's mind. He cannot
even wash his hands. He grunts and shakes his hands in a display of
impatient, resigned self-disgust—an action recalling Lady Macbeth's
inability to remove the signs of her transgressions from her hands.
Galvin wobbles into his office on unsteady legs, the tracking shot level
with his feet and his legs filling and darkening the screen at one point.

It is significant that the transitions between the following group
of shots are composed of jump cuts rather than the dissolves that have
been the norm so far. In shot eighteen Galvin is standing behind his
desk, dumping the contents of a drawer on the floor, then staggering
from the impetus of his exertion. Shot nineteen finds him at a file

cabinet which he pulls over. This time the action results in his tumbling to the floor. A close-up of the back of Galvin's head as he looks at a framed diploma hanging on the wall comprises shot twenty. The diploma is partly seen over his shoulder. Next we see him taking the diploma down, pondering it blankly for a moment, and then smashing it against the corner of his desk. A piece of flying glass hits him above the left eye. Finally, Galvin is seen sitting on the floor in the narrow passageway to his office. His back is against one wall, his feet against an open door pushed up against the opposite wall. The image produced creates a boxed-in effect. Above him in the background on the wall above his law books is a crucifix. Through the open door Morrissey arrives—Galvin's personal savior.

This sequence exactly mirrors in practice Mamet's description of how Eisenstein's montage theory operates. The disjointed, jerky linking of these six shots emphasizes Galvin's fragmented mental condition. He is out of control physically and emotionally. He dumps the cluttered minutiae of his life. He stumbles, pulled down by the weight of his own actions. He attacks the symbol (the diploma) of a logical, orderly, and meaningful past life with which he no longer identifies. His violence and destruction are basically random and accidental, and in a mechanical universe a shard of glass is just as likely as not to strike him as a result of his wanton act. Enough is seen of the office to reenforce these impressions: an overflowing wastepaper basket sits on the desk; a chair lies on its side; the walls are dirty and cracked; the furniture is mismatched (metal and wooden file cabinets stand side by side); a desk lamp lies on the floor; a table lamp's shade is askew; litter lies everywhere. The details are abundant and convincing.

When Morrissey enters things change. He expresses the audience's appalled reaction to Galvin and the situation as he drags the protagonist bodily into his office (the camera, at floor level, follows). Morrissey berates Galvin, and he discloses information about the Sally Doneghy case that he has secured. The information about the case serves as a plot hook for it provides for Galvin's change in direction; Dr. Gruber's name is also mentioned, which prepares for a later plot point/sub-plot (Gruber's paid for disappearance) that forces Galvin to depend upon himself instead of relying on con games.

Previously the arched window in Galvin's office has only been seen piecemeal, in shadow, partly out of the frame, and so on. Now it is seen in full with Morrissey standing in front of it. Part of the arch is dissected by the office's back wall, but the fullness of the arch is evident. Furthermore, the shape is repeated in the view through the window, for a cathedral-like vaulted ceiling with a repeating rectangular box design is visible, as are arches over small windows on the building across the way. The lighting is such that the outside opening of the arch is the brightest feature in the frame, is centered, and provides a dominating effect of hope symbolized. At first the hope is associated with Morrissey because of his positioning in front of the window so that he is backlighted and the contrast emphasizes his figure. This emphasis is underscored in comparison to Galvin because the standing Morrissey is wearing a light colored overcoat and Galvin, slumped on the couch, is dressed in black. When the two men face one another and engage in conversation about the case, as one-sided as the dialogue is, the symbolic presence of hope expands to encompass Galvin by virtue of the fact that Morrissey takes a seat on the left side of the frame and Galvin is on the right, with the bright arch, like a rising, renewing sun, between them, filling the center half of the screen. In the eleven alternating one-shots used in the conversation, the background behind Morrissey includes another framed diploma hanging on the wall and several large law volumes and an index-card holder on the desk top. Galvin is framed by the peeling paint on the wall behind him. With Morrissey's exit Galvin is left alone. Up to this point, in the majority of shots in which Galvin is alone the lighting has been distinctly low key. Here it is normal. Moreover, the curve of the arch blends with the curve of his profile, the lines of the desk, chair, and an end table point toward him, converging on him, and the compositional weight of his dark clothing in the lower right quarter of the frame makes Galvin's illuminated face the dominant image, the light of hope from the window highlighting it. There is a jump cut to shot thirty-seven in which Galvin is now acting purposefully, but, as the note that he signs "Clare" reveals in shot thirty-eight—"Judge Geary called. Lunch tomorrow? Back soon."—he is still relying on a con.

By the end of the opening section of *The Verdict,* Mamet's audience understands that Frank Galvin is an ambulance-chasing lawyer, and apparently not a very successful one at that (we never see him working for a client, much less with one, and he has to resort to scanning newspaper obituary columns in his pursuit of business contacts). As evidenced by his willingness to pay for introductions, to intrude on others who are grieving, and to lie ("I was a friend of your father's"), his code of ethics is questionable, too. While he dresses well, his current environment is solitary, sterile, and seedy. Overall, then, Galvin has not been portrayed as a very admirable or sympathetic character. Still, he is seen as having some qualms about his position and his actions, and with the entrance of Morrissey there is an indication both that Galvin is salvageable and that there is an appropriate mechanism available that might lead to his salvation. That Morrissey appears, after all, demonstrates that he sees something of value in Galvin, and the case referral offers Galvin a potential first step toward fiscal recovery. Since Morrissey has made the referral, there is also an implication that Galvin has the potential for a moral and spiritual recovery as well. Later in the film key elements in Galvin's past will be revealed that explain how he came to be in the condition that he is discovered in at the beginning of the movie and that reenforce the implications in Morrissey's actions. More importantly, a benchmark for Galvin's character has been established. It is this standard against which the development of his character is to be measured.

In commenting on his cinematic adaptation of Nicholas Mosely's novel *Accident*, Pinter says, "In this film everything happens, nothing is explained. It has been pared down and down, all unnecessary words and actions are eliminated. If it is interesting to see a man cross a room, then we see him do it; if not, then we leave out the insignificant stages of the action."[12] Obviously the success of Mamet's screenplay for *The Verdict* is a result of the same approach to his material, and his techniques and delineation of his lawyer-protagonist's cons in the film's opening segment illustrate his screenwriting ability.

Notes

1. Among the popular movie reviewers, for example, Roger Ebert, in *Roger Ebert's Movie Home Companion 1989 Edition* (Kansas City: Andrews and McMeel, 1988), pp. 694–695, gives the film four stars, his highest rating, and says that Mamet's screenplay "is a wonder of good dialogue, strongly seen characters, and a structure that pays off in the big courtroom scene—as the genre requires. As a courtroom drama, *The Verdict* is superior work." On NBC's "Donahue" (12 April 1990) producer David

Brown said the *The Verdict* was the "best" film that he had ever produced—and his films include *Jaws, The Sting,* and *Driving Miss Daisy.*

2. Timed from the first sounds of the pinball bells heard over the titles.

3. Because the filmscript has not been published, my observations are based on a shot-by-shot close analysis of the film itself. A video-tape version was released by CBS/Fox in 1986.

4. For example, Syd Field in *The Screenwriter's Workbook* (New York: Dell, 1984), p. 8, discusses the standard screenplay's tripartite structure.

5. Mamet, "A First-Time Film Director," in *Some Freaks* (New York: Viking, 1989), pp. 119–120.

6. Mamet, "Encased by Technology," in *Some Freaks,* p. 160.

7. *Ibid.,* p. 161.

8. Mamet, "Notes for a Catalogue for Raymond Saunders," in *Writing in Restaurants* (New York: Penguin, 1987), p. 51.

9. It is interesting to note that when Galvin first sees Laura (Charlotte Rampling) it is in the bar, and she is situated in approximately the same position that he was in the opening scene, on the left side of the frame, though she is highlighted in the relative darkness of the room and that, together with the red scarf that ties her to the bishop's colors which were seen previously, makes her the dominant object on the screen. As part of setting up her con, Laura is seen with a pencil and a glass of liquor in her hand as she studies newspaper advertisements for apartments for rent—an action that is reminiscent of the attorney's studying of the obituary columns earlier as part of his con.

10. There is a "magic bunny" here—a mistake in the continuity from one shot to the other that is amusing though not significant. Galvin has put down his pen in the previous shot, yet he is holding it now.

11. The image of the bar is utilized as a transitional device later, at the beginning of Galvin's transformation after Mick's visit, for the next shot after he tapes the "secretary's" note to his office door is similar to the film's opening shot—he is standing at the pinball machine. He leaves the game machine to drink another beer, but this one has a healthy addition, a raw egg, and when he is finished consuming the drink, Galvin proceeds out the door, briefcase in hand, on his way to work on the Doneghy case.

12. Quoted in Martin Esslin, *Pinter, A Study of His Plays* (New York: Norton, 1976, expanded edition), pp. 204–205 (originally in John Russell Taylor, "Accident," in *Sight and Sound*, Autumn 1966).

THE RECENT MAMET FILMS: "BUSINESS" VERSUS COMMUNION

Dennis Carroll

The plays of David Mamet can be viewed as a shifting demonstration of the way that the pejoratives of "business" battle impulses toward "communion" in friendship or love. For Mamet, "business" is a euphemism for the selfish propagation of one-upmanship for personal advancement or profit—and the imperatives of "business," in a criminal context, are the source of both the comedy and the metaphoric power of his first Broadway play, *American Buffalo* (1975). Mamet's most acclaimed plays—*American Buffalo*, *Glengarry Glen Ross* (1983), and *Speed-the-Plow* (1988)—are "negative" in the sense that nascent connections between people are destroyed by the self-interest epitomised by "doing business." But some of Mamet's most interesting and variegated plays—*Reunion* (1976), *A Life in the Theatre* (1977), and *The Shawl* (1985)—give a sense of communion winning out in various relationships, whether they are those of friendship, mentor-protégé, sexual or familial; and a related group of works focuses on a single individual undergoing various trials which prepare him or her for such communion—*Lone Canoe* (1979), *Edmond* (1982), and the film *The Verdict* (1982). I have explored in detail the tensions between the spirit of "business" and communion in the plays and earlier films in my study *David Mamet* (London: Macmillan, 1987).

It is interesting to note a similar dialectic operating in the several films written, and sometimes directed, by Mamet since 1985. The screenplays of several of these have been published; even more with screenplays than playtexts, one could agree with John Lee Beatty that there is a dimension in Mamet that "doesn't come through when you're just reading it" (quoted by Richard Christiansen, *Chicago Tribune*, 15 June, 1979, Sec. 3, p. 10). Some of the realized films satisfyingly develop the published blueprints, others seem to diminish them. Of the films under consideration here, three are directed by Mamet: *House of Games* (1987), from a screenplay by Mamet and story by Mamet and Jonathan Katz; *Things Change* (1988), from a screenplay by Mamet and Shel Silverstein; and *Homicide*, currently in production in fall 1990, from an original screenplay. The other two films were written by Mamet but directed by others: *The Untouchables* (1987) by Brian De Palma and *We're No Angels* (1989) by Neil Jordan.

On the face of it, *The Untouchables* is an updated genre film in which a group of law-enforcers, led by Department of the Treasury officer Elliott Ness (Kevin Costner), brings down the criminal "business" empire of gangster Al Capone (Robert De Niro) in 1935 Prohibition Chicago. Under the surface, many of Mamet's key concerns, familiar from the plays, are again working. The film could be compared to *The Water Engine* (1977) in locale and period—here, though, "good" wins out, whereas in the play—albeit distanced by the radio-drama framing format—darkness is victorious even though the murdered inventor gains a small victory in passing his invention on to a promising young protégé. Teaching, learning and discipleship are also central to *The Untouchables*. But the "education" of Elliott Ness is a process that is equivocal and flecked with darkness. After Ness's mentor the Irish street-cop Malone (Sean Connery) is murdered, the thrust of his tutelage lives on, as Ness makes the personal compromises in his idealism to ensure the success of his aims.

Capone's "business" empire is founded on the coercion of forced "teamwork" and on the manipulation of ethnocentric identity and its hatreds. Capone, introduced at the beginning being interviewed in a barber's chair, insists that his prosperity and power are based on sound "business" principles—and we are immediately reminded of the character Teach in *American Buffalo*, except that Capone is of course vastly more successful than the small-time hood of the play, his viciousness differing less in kind than in scale. Capone's violence is not the spontaneous, frustrated trashing of a junk shop. It is introduced in the initiating sequence in which an innocent little girl is killed in a speakeasy explosion—detonated when the owner rejects a "deal" of forced sales from Capone. It is further exemplified, and personalized, by

Capone's bludgeoning to death of an erring lieutenant with a baseball bat at a formal banquet, prefaced by his lecture about the importance of "teamwork" and the threat posed to it by irresponsible individualism. Capone has total control of Chicago through his infiltration of the police force, the judiciary, and city hall—and the full extent of that power only becomes apparent as the film progresses.

Capone's "team" is founded on ethnic homogeneity—and fear. His most ruthless agent is the killer Nitti—the man who leaves the briefcased bomb in the speakeasy and who later lures Malone outside his apartment to cut him down with a machine gun. However, we rarely see Nitti and Capone together; they have no "relationship." In the murder banquet scene and elsewhere, Capone's "team" is seen as a backup group arranged around him in deferential cluster-formations with little human personality. Capone himself is parodied as a sort of latter-day Louis XIV, his Versailles the Hotel Lexington, where he lounges in bed as a butler opens multiple doors for his breakfast tray, and marble staircases at the hotel and the opera provide significant *mises en scène* to stress his potent yet grotesque elevation. But, willing to be raised and regal, Capone can complain of being alone in the world when he is crossed or stymied or when he wants dirty work done. The most disturbing alliance between ethnicity and "business" corruption comes in the murder scene of Malone: Nitti is luring the policeman to his death as DePalma cuts to the opera house; Capone is crying at the tragic climax of Leoncavallo's *Pagliacci* in a box surrounded by his henchman as an Italian tenor, seen in an ugly profile closeup berouged and in white makeup, sings. Later, when Nitti arrives to tell Capone of the murder, Capone's tears become laughter. Of course, though Capone's "team" has an ethnic core, it has attracted scores of hirelings and hangers-on of all ethnicities and backgrounds—bonded together solely for "business" profit in Capone's illegal Prohibition concern and protecting its business "viability."

Against this machine, Ness at the beginning of the film is alone—he is newly arrived in town and must first win over a corrupt police force, as well as the press, before even the slightest dent can be made in Capone's position. He has his own strength of will and courage and sense of moral principles—and his respect for the law—to help him bring Capone to heel. His family life provides a satisfying center for his work; his marriage and family bonds are strengthening forces, which De Palma underlines by often including Ness's wedding-ring hand in facial closeups, when Ness is depressed or exhausted. This resolve is strengthened further by the appeal of the murdered girl's mother, by his early sense that all kinds of family communal ties are threatened by "business" criminality, and by the later direct threats against his family. His innocence, however, is underlined by his naive response to the little girl's mother's appeal to him to bring Capone to justice. He does not know what we know—that the mother used what was probably an excuse, that she had a cold, to justify sending her child to the speakeasy with a beer pail, instead of going herself. Mamet, in this minor but telling detail, underlines the fact that "business" corruption thrives not only because of large-scale conscious complicity but of white lies and minor complicities as well. Ness himself refuses to take a drink. And in the screenplay, when his newly fledged "team" celebrates in an Italian restaurant their first successful strike against Capone, he refuses to let them drink as well.

But it is the bond with Malone that ensures that Ness's resolve is effective, because it is through this bond that a law-enforcement team is created and through it that Ness's own process of dark "learning" can begin. From a reading of the script alone it seems that Malone is about the same age as Ness; in the film, however, the air of innocence and untried boyishness that Kevin Costner projects is in sharp contrast to Connery's seasoned toughness—so that the relationship is less one of partners than of protégé and mentor. Malone first makes Ness aware of his street-smart expertise when he recognizes merely by looking at him that Ness is carrying a gun under his jacket—a skill which Ness also then acquires and puts to crucial use in the climactic courtroom scene.

For it is Malone who knows, far more than Ness, what the cost of defeating Capone will mean—and the tactics necessary to be successful. So the idealistic concern of Ness for staying within the law is immediately challenged by the assertion that much more is needed beyond that. It is significant that, at the end of the three crucial "bonding" scenes between Ness and Malone, Ness does not give Malone any guarantee that he is prepared to go beyond the law to "get" Capone. However, Malone without that assurance seals the "deal," and, shaking Ness's hand, tells him that he has just signed a blood oath.

A significant characteristic of Ness's and Malone's team is that it is composed of a larger American brotherhood of mixed ethnicities working together for an altruistic ideal and not a more ethnically homogenous group—like Capone's—working for criminal self-interest.

The team of "untouchables" is initiated by Malone's advice to Ness to trust nobody on the force; to go to the "apple tree" and not the "barrel"—the training-range of new recruits rather than the rookies already in the precinct house. This ensures the best possible chance that the team will be founded on the right principles and not corrupted self-interest. The first man to be signed on is the trainee "Stone," whom Malone baits with an ethnic slur to determine his spirit and his true ancestry. It is significant that "Stone" is of Italian ancestry and hates the Irish—but is nevertheless willing and able to ally himself against Capone. Once formed, it is the team's variegation of interests and skills that give it the strength and resources that a more homogenous group would not have had. The arrival from Washington, the accountant Wallace, proves a vital member of Ness's team after Ness initially fears that he will be useless. For it is Wallace who devises the legal strategy which will get Capone into court for tax evasion, if a ledger detailing payments to Capone from "phantom" companies and criminal transactions can be found. But it is Malone's street-smart skills and contacts that make it possible for Wallace's strategies to pay off— especially the determination with which he proves material witnesses who can explain and validate Capone's coded ledger.

It is Ness's "education" by Malone into the moral and strategic realities needed to defeat Capone that constitutes the more important result of their bond—and Mamet's dramatic spine in *The Untouchables*. Malone's contacts, again, make possible the first successful strike against Capone; it is Malone who gets the information about the large shipment of liquor coming through Canada; it is Malone who gets a stooge's cooperation by going "beyond the law." He scares the man into cooperating by "executing," with a shot through the head, the Capone lieutenant lying outside on the porch, whom the stooge does not know is already dead. In this sequence, the three younger men get bloodied. Stone gets wounded in the fray, and Ness and Wallace kill for the first time. Earlier, while waiting for the shipment to arrive, Ness gets nervous and asks Malone somewhat sardonically whether he is his tutor. Malone says, in all seriousness, that he is.

The second stage of Ness's education lies in Malone teaching him the power of ethnic loyalties and xenophobia and how these can sometimes be manipulated. This is introduced in the "testing" of Stone mentioned earlier; Malone uses it more seminally in finding the whereabouts of Capone's bookkeeper, potentially a crucial witness in

court. A corrupted fellow Irish cop is finally induced to betray Capone
on the basis of ethnicity—the Irish against the Italians—and tells
Malone that the bookkeeper will be leaving the city by train. But then
Malone, in the following scene, gets his comeuppance. Stalked by an
intruder in his home, he imagines that he is superior to this "wop" who
brings a knife to a gun fight and sneers at the man, crowing at him on
his fire escape—only to be machine-gunned to death there by the
murderous Nitti—the "wop" who has brought a machine-gun to a gun-
fight and has won. But in the climactic court room sequence Ness
discovers, too, that an ethnic slur can lead to unguarded, hair-trigger
emotional reactions. Ness has chased Nitti onto the rooftops during the
trial after he has found written evidence that he is Malone's killer. After
Nitti fails to escape by rope, Ness helps him back to safety, intending
to prosecute him through the regular legal channels of the criminal
justice system. But then Nitti brags that he'll beat the rap for the
murder and sneers that the dying man squealed like an Irish pig. It is
this that causes Ness to lose control and carry out revenge justice. He
hurls Nitti to his death off the courthouse roof—the penultimate stage
in Ness's "education" in going "beyond the law."

That act of unpremeditated killing, it is implied, gives Ness the
ruthless spirit needed to go further. He brings about Capone's downfall
only by inventing evidence that does not exist when he tells the
presiding judge at the trial that his name is on Capone's ledger—when
in fact it isn't. This stratagem leads to the judge switching the bribed
jury in his courtroom with the adjoining one next door. Only by this
measure is Capone successfully brought down.

The Untouchables suggests, more unequivocally than any of the
plays, that in order to thwart "business" one needs not only upstanding
moral righteousness to effect its downfall—but that kind of amoral,
knife-blade pragmatism necessary to create "business" advantages.
Mamet implies that, in a society such as early 1930s Chicago, moral
ends justify, indeed necessitate, immoral means. In the course of the
film, then, Ness becomes "corrupted," and the "mentorship" process he
undergoes contains a major modicum of groin-kicking ruthlessness.
Nevertheless, justice has won—even though the law has not always
been unequivocally upheld.

House of Games is a much darker work and the first (and so far
the only) Mamet work in which the main character is a woman.
Margaret Ford is a psychiatrist and a celebrity because of her best-seller

Driven: Compulsion and Obsession in Everyday Life. Of course, Ford is herself driven. Like Edmond in the play of that name, she is disturbed by the insufficiency of her inner life and the straitjacket of her social and professional role. She is also depressed by her failures to help the most troubled and "criminal" of her patients. She confronts a gambler confidence-man in a pool hall called "The House of Games," thinking to try to talk him out of a debt that a desperate young patient owes him. Instead, she becomes the dupe of this man and his clutch of cronies, of whom her patient is one. The confidence man Mike recognises her need to taste in her own life the sense of danger and the "forbidden" that has brought so many of her patients to a state where they need help. He persuades her into a sexual encounter in an appropriated hotel room and bilks her of $80,000 of her savings in an elaborate hoax. She eventually learns the truth, confronts him in a deserted airport loading area, and, after he rebuffs her, shoots him to death. At the end of the film, she resumes her former life—but in the final frames it is revealed that she has become a compulsive thief.

The darkness of Mamet's vision here yokes this work not only to the plays where "business" is triumphant over communion but also to *Edmond*—that equivocal and underrated work in which the hero undergoes a savage rite-of-passage, a Joseph Campbell-like "departure, initiation and return" (Campbell 105, 162) But here again, as in *Edmond*, the process unmakes and then re-makes the psyche in a truer but bleaker image of human possibility—and "self-knowledge" is achieved only in the most ironic context.

In *House of Games*, "business" wins out because of a betrayal of genuine "communion" and attraction on Mike's part—at least the realized film, far more than the screenplay, suggests this. Mamet's direction elicits a chemistry between Ford (Lindsay Crouse) and Mike (Joe Mantegna) throughout their encounters, present in subtext, but set in motion by a long gaze between them—not specified in the screenplay—during the initial cardgame in which she has agreed to act as his "girlfriend" and "partner." When she sees through this first attempt to bilk her, Mike defines his terms and possibly betrays his nascent feelings in an unequivocal foreshadowing of what is to come:

> MIKE: You aren't miffed with us, are you, I mean,
> nothing personal.
> FORD: You were going to con me out of my money.
> MIKE: It was only business.

> FORD: It was only business, huh?
> JOEY: It's the American Way. (25)

In his direction of Joe Mantegna, Mamet achieves the effect of a slight italicisation, a roboticisation of speech, as if the character is guarding his litany of statements against an underlying feeling which might betray them—and later, in the climactic scene, Lindsay Crouse's acting manifests a similar quality, as if her actions are dictated by principles unleashed in her by Mike's betrayal of his—and her—feelings. Ultimately, it is Mike's professional pride, his refusal to acknowledge any sexual or personal attraction, that leads to his death. This denial emerges clearly in the climactic scene:

> FORD: I gave you my trust.
> MIKE (*laughs*): Of *course*, you gave me your trust. That's
> . . . You asked me what I *did* for a living...this is it.
> (67)

And a little later:

> FORD: I want to know how you could do what you did to
> me.
> MIKE: It wasn't *personal*. Okay? (68)

Just before she shoots him, Ford orders Mike to beg for his life. Ford, having been "personally" rebuffed, now wants the kind of power over Mike that he has had over her, the power of "business" advantage. He refuses her this as well—and loses his life as a consequence.

But ironically, at the very end, Ford has been transformed by a process different from those compulsive scenarios dictated by both "business" and sexual attraction. As Ness is "educated" by Malone, so Ford is by Mike, who as "mentor" gradually replaces Maria, Ford's older psychiatrist colleague. The way that Ford steals a gold cigarette lighter in the final sequence underlines the dead Mike's power over her. Apparently relaxed and newly sensual in clothes and manner, Ford is lunching with Maria in a posh restaurant. Maria has been called away to the phone on a professional matter. Maggie makes a "mark" of the lighter's owner before she steals it—and the "mark" is a tweedy woman with a distinctly underlined interest in Maggie in their first exchange of glances, a moment pointedly and suggestively timed in Mamet's direction. Ford "becomes" Mike—and uses the women's attraction to her to proceed. Maggie asks her, politely, if she can tell her what is on the buffet. As the woman turns away and cranes to look, Maggie deftly lifts the lighter from her handbag. Mike's lesson has been well learned—the "short con" has been accomplished because Maggie has made the woman "feel good" in serving her, and in the final closeup Ford relishes the sensual pleasure the feat has provided.

The posthumous ascendancy of Mike has marked not only her rejection of Maria as mentor but also of her most important advice: "When you've done something unforgivable, you *forgive* yourself" (56)—Stoic-tinged advice familiar from other Mamet works, including *Edmond* and the interesting TV play *Bradford*. For her theft of the lighter seems to indicate that Ford has not forgiven herself, in spite of her protestation to Maria of the contrary. She is making her own punishment for her undetected murder; disgrace and exposure of the theft, or others like it, will inevitably follow.

Things Change presents a much more positive outcome of the "business" versus communion dialectic. It has close kinship with the "children's plays" *The Poet and the Rent* and *The Frog Prince*; and, of, course its co-author Shel Silverstein is a famous author of children's books. But, once again, Mamet's key themes and concerns are clearly present here. It is a reassuring comic fable in which an unlikely friendship thwarts the juggernaut of the Mafia. The odd couple—less odd than it would appear, however—consists of Gino (Don Ameche), an old-worldly Sicilian shoe-shiner and Jerry (Joe Mantegna), a low level mafioso hood "on probation." A Chicago "don" has bought the shoe-shiner to take the rap for a gang murder committed by a look-alike they want to stay free. The friendship is set in motion when Jerry decides, on his own initiative, and without telling the Mafia, to give Gino a weekend holiday in a posh Lake Tahoe resort before he must go to court the following Monday for sentencing. When they return, Jerry urges Gino to flee and renege on the deal, and indeed it transpires that the Mafia's plan is to have Gino murdered on his way to court.

So this "friendship," in the normal way of things, would not have been able to withstand the "business" forces of the mob, with its cynical opportunistic manipulation of one's "word" and the "deal," which the shoe-shiner takes literally and honorably and which to most of the Mob means nothing. Once again, as with Mamet's direction of *House of Games*, the compromised deadness of "business," and criminal or "professional" role-playing, is deliberately suggested in a robotic italicisation of lines, not only by the gangsters and their clones but also by the various cogs-in-the wheel of the luxury gambling hotel. And Mamet makes ironic and comic play with the way that the underlings accept, with no questions, the cryptic evasions of their superiors and the persuasive power of images of affluence—clothing, accessories, suite numbers—that carry their own unchallengeable authority. It is the hirelings' lack of information and their fear of asking for more that allows Jerry to carry out his weekend holiday with Gino at the Mafia's expense.

The strength of Jerry and Gino's relationship, in a short time, becomes considerable. They have shared ethnicity on their side—both are of Sicilian stock. But first the relationship is one of forced jailor-prisoner. Then Jerry rebels against the Mafia and sees himself as the older Gino's mentor to defy them and strike out as his own man. When Gino is deferential to the Mafia's possible wishes, Jerry says: "They? There *is* no "they." *I* am they. What do you want to do?" (15). At first, Jerry thinks thinks he is in "control" of Gino and preens in his own street-smarts in showing him the good life and wising him up about the workings of institutional—and individual—power and influence. But in reality he is being "taught" by Gino—by his sincerity, his courtliness, his moral sense, his drawing on Sicilian folk-wisdom that Jerry either doesn't know or has forgotten. Thus the relationship, by the end of the film, becomes one of peer communion in spite of their difference in age. But by itself, this relationship would hardly have been enough to defeat the "business" values of the Mafia.

What defeats the Mob and vindicates the redemptive power of Gino and Jerry's relationship is another "personal" relationship struck up by Gino and the Lake Tahoe Mafia kingpin Don Giuseppe Vincent (Robert Prosky). This overrides faceless organizational "business" power and replaces it with personalized exception. It is another relationship cemented by ethnicity—which in this work is a unifying force both in friendship and in Mafia solidarity, but by itself cannot guarantee loyalty and steadfastness.

This is epitomized in the important image of the old Sicilian coin given to Gino earlier by the Chicago don to cement the false deal ("The Sicilian people say . . . 'A big man knows the value of a small coin.' My friendship is a small coin, but it is all I have to offer you"[9]), which is passed on to Giuseppe in true rapport and with real heart. Giuseppe reciprocates by giving Gino a smaller coin still, a shiny modern quarter which can be used in a phone. ("This is not an old coin," he says. "It is a new coin. . . . But it, too, is a symbol. And should you ever need my friendship, you put this coin into a telephone. You call this number. Whatever you wish, if it is within the power of your friend, that wish shall be granted"[60–61].) Back in Chicago, Gino insists on staying to carry out the prison-sentence part of the bargain because "I give my word" (84). When Jerry realises the truth as the assassin is walking Gino to his death, Jerry gives Gino a reprieve by knocking the man out. But the fable-like *deus ex machina* is, indeed, the coin—for in the end, Gino uses it, and Don Giuseppe honors his word. The final sequences reveal that the would-be assassin has taken the rap for the original killing, that Gino is back working as a shoe-shiner, and that Jerry has joined him in his trade.

In *Things Change*, then, friendship is vindicated, and a valuable relationship endures. The phrase, "things change," has been used in various ironic contexts throughout the film: as a response to sudden good or bad turns of fortune, as when Gino wins, then loses $35,000 in a fixed gambling throw; as a philosophical response to the wearing out of shoes; brutally, as a cynical reason to justify breaking relationships or honorable promises. It is the stand-up comedian in Tahoe who first enunciates, in the ironic context of his tacky night-club act, the optimistic, fairy-tale-like premise that the action of the film finally demonstrates: "I saw a guy today down at the tables, shot thirty-five grand, one roll, craps out." He shrugs, says, 'Things change.' One thing that doesn't change is friendship" (41). Here, "business" pejoratives are vanquished through the ironic symbol of money. The "false" old coin has been exchanged for a "real" new coin, of no special market value, which nevertheless vindicates the miraculous powers of two friendships and an *honored* word—thus also vindicating Gino's "old-world" Sicilian values and setting the seal on an entertaining comic fable.

We're No Angels is also a comic fable, "suggested" by the 1955 film of the same name directed by Ranald MacDougall and starring Humphrey Bogart and Peter Ustinov and also by an earlier musical. But with the 1989 *We're No Angels* one has to make allowances for the considerable divergence between Mamet's wryly comic published screenplay, close in tone to *Things Change*, and the labored film realization by Neil Jordan. The film is set in 1935, so that the fable-like aspects of it can register more clearly to a modern audience. In this respect it is reminiscent of *The Water Engine*, but *We're No Angels* lacks the framing techniques to effectively foreground this historic distance.

Ned (Robert De Niro) and Jim (Sean Penn) are two convicts who are the forced accomplices of a killer making a jail break and end up just on the American side of the Canadian border—in an impoverished town grateful for any visitors because of its "miraculous" statue of a Virgin that "weeps." The fugitives are mistaken for two priests, celebrated authors of a book about miracles, who are part of a religious convocation in the town. The convocation will go on processional with the Weeping Virgin across the river border and back—and the monks will take along handicapped "afflicted" who hope to be cured. Ned and Jim go along with the misunderstanding, hoping that they can more easily cross the border undetected, for the psychopathic warden of the prison has arrived in town with a pack of vicious hound dogs. Ned is attracted to an unmarried mother Molly, who prostitutes herself to help with the cost of living and who has a deaf-mute daughter; and Jimmie finds inchoate rapport with a young priest who idolizes him for his supposed authorship. But then the killer is recaptured and blackmails Ned to get him across the border with them at any cost. During the processional, the killer is discovered and hold's Molly's daughter— Ned's "afflicted"—as hostage. In the fracas that follows, Ned and the girl end up in the river with the Madonna and nearly drown—but as a result of the shock she is "miraculously" cured of her handicap. At the end, Jim decides to stay in town and join the order, and Ned, Molly, and her daughter walk over to Canada together.

Again, communion—in the form of friendship and sexual attraction—triumph over the negativeness and self-interest of "business" and the constrictions of artificial order, whether they be the result of the criminal justice system or the discipline of Roman Catholicism. The diametrics of freedom and rigidity are encapsulated in oppositional imagery throughout: a priest at a last confession is kicked in the stomach; a *Bambi*-type deer in a pristine snowfall is run down by a car; a bullet slams into a missal book. The ideological extremes of the dogma of the Roman Church, on the one hand, and the criminal justice system, on the other, breed individuals who are maniacal and denatured and who function on an "eye for an eye, tooth for a tooth" system of quasi-Biblical, and utterly rigid, vengeance.

Opposing this rigidity are the principles of healthy compromise, belief, and instinct, which are seen as governing the development of positive human possibilities toward communion. As far as compromise is concerned, we find that the Church has learned the lesson of Elliott Ness—that means can be bent slightly if the right ends are achieved. For the "weeping Virgin" is an eye-con: Her tears are actually drops of rain coming in from a leaky roof. Father Levesque (Hoyt Axton), the head of the local order, confides to Ned that, though the weeping Virgin may be fake, he believes in the efficacy of the prayer that Her "authenticity" encourages in the faithful and in himself—and he says that She has never once let him down. Jim regards the importance of belief in a more populist and utilitarian way—if it gives you comfort, then it "isn't so bad." And instinct, rather than belief, prompts Ned to dive into the river to try to save the little girl, even though he can't swim; and instinct prompts him to grab both the girl and the outstretched hand of the Virgin under water to be floated, through Her, back to the surface and safety.

With the principles of compromise, belief, and instinct in operation, the major characters move away from the established and routine in human relationships to something fresher and more unexpected. At the outset, Jim and Ned are bonded not because of natural rapport but because they share the same jail cell and later are enforced "partners" in the jail break. They are denizens of a prison "Hell" characterised with hissing steam and rows of synchronized convicts digging copper, presided over by the Satanic, saliva-dribbling warden. But Ned and Jim are obviously already different in their interests: Ned has his eyes on the corporeal, and especially the voluptuous Harlow-look-alike pinned above his cot, whereas Jimmy, insofar as he is able, is asking spiritual questions such as what exists beyond the "bakery" (electric chair). The relationship of forced "partners" develops into that of "protégé-mentor" once more when Ned and Jim are on their own resources in the town. As Michael Wilmington pointed out in his review (*Los Angeles Times*, 15 December 1989, F 12), it is natural and credible that both men should be initially attracted to and feel comfortable with the monks—for both monks and convicts are isolated from the outside world. But each man then develops a new relationship with someone else, in consonance with his already established character traits—Jim with the priest and the church, in conformity with his desire to "do something" with his life and to wondrously take a dim-witted stab at the basic questions of existence and Ned in response to Molly's challenge that she needs a man and a husband and because she intrigues and attracts him. In the final frames, Jim voluntarily renounces his bond with Ned, so that Ned can go off with Molly, and so that he can go on asking his basic questions while feeling secure in the isolation from society and in the regular meals of the order and enjoying his rapport with the hero-worshipping young priest. In the final shot, Jim and his new friend enter the picturesque monastery with its large cross casting a kind of benediction on their bond. We are perhaps irreverently reminded a little of the loving relationship, in a different kind of incarceration, of Edmond and the Black Prisoner in *Edmond*.

The new work, *Homicide*, is still in production at the time of writing. Any comment on it now, therefore, must be both provisional and brief. It returns to the Chicago milieu of *The Untouchables*, and although the theme of "education" and the enlightenment of the hero is similar, the work is much darker. It also reprises the issue of ethnicity—the way that it can promote "teamwork" and a sense of solidarity, but also a xenophobia leading to a blinkered vision and destructive passions. The time period is now—and there is no mentor, no clear antagonist with the untrammelled evil of Al Capone, and many half-tones of light and darkness. This work, also, focusses less on the struggle between "business" and communion than it does on the questing character moving in a blighted landscape to a greater self-awareness. There is a close relationship in this respect to the earlier screenplay *The Verdict* and, among the plays, to *Edmond*.

All five of these works belong squarely within the corpus of Mamet's thematic and moral concerns as delineated in his major plays. They exemplify the battle of "business" versus the pull of communion and also the personal self-enlightenment of the individual passing through an extreme process of "departure, initiation and return," which may make communion possible in the future. Indeed, even in those films where the depredations of "business" are considerable, characters like Ford and Ness have achieved the liberation of having their façades and false masks stripped away and, thus, the wherewithal to begin to construct new realities for themselves. The same conclusion is reached, whether with positive or negative ramifications, at the conclusion of many of Mamet's plays, especially *Edmond, A Life in the Theatre, The Woods, Lakeboat, Reunion*, and *The Shawl*.

Works Cited

Campbell, Joseph. *The Hero with a Thousand Faces*. Bollingen Series, No. 17. Princeton, N.J.: Princeton University Press, 1949.

Carroll, Dennis. *David Mamet*. Macmillan Modern Dramatists. London: Macmillan, 1987.

Christiansen, Richard. "Designing Sets Well With Mamet," *Chicago Tribune*, 15 June 1979, Sec. 3, p. 10.

Mamet, David. *Five Television Plays*. New York: Grove Weidenfeld, 1990.

————. *House of Games*. A screenplay based on a story by David Mamet and Jonathan Katz. New York: Grove Press, 1987.

————. *We're No Angels*. A Screenplay. New York: Grove Weidenfeld, 1990.

————, screenwriter. *House of Games*. Dir. David Mamet. Orion, 1987.

————, screenwriter. *The Untouchables*. Dir. Brian De Palma. Paramount, 1987.

————, screenwriter. *We're No Angels*. Dir. Neil Jordan. Paramount, 1989.

————, and Shel Silverstein *Things Change*. A Screenplay. New York: Grove Press, 1988.

————, and Shel Silverstein, screenwriters. *Things Change*. Dir. David Mamet. Columbia, 1988.

Wilmington, Michael. "De Niro and Penn Try to Wing It in *We're No Angels*." *Los Angeles Times*, 15 December 1989, Sec. F, p. 12.

Note

All dates of plays and films given in the text are of first performance of the definitive version of the play and release date of the film.

Acknowledgment

I would like to thank David Mamet and his agent Howard Rosenstone of Rosenstone/Wender for letting me study the unpublished screenplays for *The Untouchables* and *Homicide*.

COMEDY AND HUMOR IN THE PLAYS OF DAVID MAMET

Christopher C. Hudgins

> And if I laugh at any mortal thing,
> 'Tis that I may not weep.
>
> Byron, *Don Juan*
> Canto 4, Stanza 4

As the film version of *The Untouchables* opens, the audience gets its first glimpse of Al Capone (Robert De Niro) as he's being shaved, surrounded by various stooges and members of the press. A reporter asks why he doesn't simply have himself appointed mayor of Chicago? Polite laughter. And De Niro's Capone then utters his first David Mamet lines with a grin: "Like a lot of things in life, we laugh because it's funny and we laugh because it's true" (De Palma).

Though Capone goes on to reject the reporter's idea because "I'm a businessman," in context the line accurately comments on David Mamet's use of humor throughout his canon. Capone answers the next reporter's question, denying that he uses violence "Because it's not good business." De Niro's delivery and the line's clear irony provoke laughter from the film audience. And then De Palma cuts to two mobsters shaking down the owner of a corner tavern. After the thugs have gone out the door, an adorable little girl tries to return their briefcase, which we know contains a bomb. We watch the bar explode.

The laughter at Capone, uneasy even at first, turns to horror—perhaps tinged with guilt for the complicity with Capone the first laughing response may imply. In a later scene, though, when Ness is despairing, a conversation with this same little girl's mother rejuvenates and inspires him to continue his crusade against Capone. Here, we laugh at something that is true *and* funny, and then we recognize a horrible reality behind that humor. But the recognition itself becomes rejuvenating, pointing toward moral action. There are multiple levels of irony involved in this complex use of humor, and perhaps the ultimate irony is that Ness must become just as violent as Capone and just as flippant about it in order to defeat him.

In much of Mamet's work for the theater, we are also induced to laugh at violence, sometimes overtly physical but more often subtle interpersonal or psychological violence of day-to-day behavior. Frequently, we are chilled by the subject of our laughter, and, I argue here, Mamet intends that complex process to be moral and redemptive.

Critics and reviewers comment repeatedly on Mamet's use of humor or on his use of the comic form, but there are few detailed analyses of either. Dennis Carroll understands "an ironic, comic dismay" to be at the center of much of Mamet's work and finds the 1983 Broadway performance of *American Buffalo* emphasizing "comic irony" (32, 33). Earlier, in 1977, Mel Gussow found Mamet's work characterized by "an irrepressible comic impulse" (B 1), and, more recently, Frank Rich found *Speed-the-Plow* in its 1988 production "By turns hilarious and chilling" (17). In her recent book on Mamet, Anne Dean writes: "Furthermore, Mamet's plays are extremely funny; even in their darkest moments, there is injected a flash of humor that tempers the tragedy" (222). And there the matter, after brief observation, usually drops.

One sympathizes with critics who do not pursue Mamet's use of comedy and/or humor very far, for it is a complex, vaguely dangerous topic. As Mamet points out in "A Playwright in Hollywood," the humor of a joke needs to be immediately obvious: "and if you have ever tried to explain why a joke you have just told actually *is* funny, you know what I'm talking about" (*WR* 76). Despite such risks, and recognizing that this essay is not going to be as funny as a Mamet play, I think that we need to analyze Mamet's use of humor and how that humor functions within the traditions of the comic form. For example, I'll concentrate on *American Buffalo* (1975), *Glengarry Glen Ross* (1983), and *Speed-the-Plow* (1988), for they reveal both a consistent pattern and a remarkable growth in the playwright I regard as American drama's most brilliant comic writer.

The sources and mechanisms of Mamet's humor are broad. The audience both laughs with characters who mean to be funny and laughs at the actions and dialogue of characters whose behavior, to them, is not funny at all. We sometimes do both at once. For example, the jokes in *Speed-the-Plow* are hilarious and frequent. As Bobby Gould and Charlie Fox contemplate the power, fame, and wealth that lie just around the corner of their incipient production of "a Douggie Brown film," Fox imagines one sycophant saying "I waxed Mr. Fox's car. He seemed pleased." Getting no response from Gould's temporary secretary, Karen, he goes a step further with another conjured line: "I blew his poodle, he gave me a smile" (34). Fox means to be funny, and he is. We laugh, but we also infer a number of ideas: that Fox is trying to impress Karen with his wit and with his potential wealth and power; that when no response is forthcoming he gets aggressive about it and tries to embarrass her with a flippant description of a rather remarkable bestiality; that sexuality to Fox is a tool of the trade; that profit is Hollywood's most important product, but that it's a means to the end of power; even that Fox is at least partially a victim of his culture in his greed and in his failure of imagination about what real success would mean in this arena. Nevertheless, despite all these potential inferences, we laugh at the joke, the line, more than at the man.

In other instances, we clearly laugh at the character. We laugh at Teach a lot in *American Buffalo*. When Bobby comes back to the "resale shop" with a bag of breakfast from the Riverside, including Don's plain yogurt, Teach tells Don, "You shouldn't eat that shit." The exchange is perfectly rendered, and it is also hilarious. "Why?" Don asks.

TEACH: It's just I have a feeling about health foods.
DON: It's not health foods, Teach. It's only yogurt.
TEACH: That's not health foods?
DON: No. They've had it forever.
TEACH: Yogurt?
DON: Yeah. They used to joke about it on "My Little Margie". . . .
TEACH: Yeah?
DON: Yeah.
TEACH: What the fuck. A little bit can't hurt you. (21)

Without going too far in an attempt to "explain the joke," I'll note that the sources of our amusement at Teach include his use of profanity, his basically uneducated patois, his ignorance of any food beyond the most basic, his suspicion of anything "new," the rhythms of the passage, particularly its use of repetition and parallel structure, and so on. And members of the audience may also infer much from their laughter at a character. We might note that Teach is generally wrong when he does try to teach; that he wants to teach so as to appear better than his "student"; that he doesn't really care about imparting truth or knowledge; and that, given a pervasive food subtext in the play, Teach is neither good "nourishment" for his companions nor himself. He doesn't know how to care for himself or others in the most basic way. In short, as Don comments later, he spews poison (101).

We need to understand two very basic attitudes Mamet exhibits toward his characters to grasp the "tone" of this humor, either as we laugh at a character's typical behavior or at his attempts to be amusing. In the first place, Mamet emphasizes repeatedly that he likes all of his characters. I think that emerges in the plays themselves, but we find convincing evidence in Mamet's hefty number of essays and interviews. In "A National Dream-Life," Mamet writes that "the protagonist represents ourselves" (*WR* 8), and he notes elsewhere that *all* the characters in *American Buffalo* were striving to be excellent men but that "the society hasn't offered them any context to be excellent in" (Bigsby 64). In another interview, Mamet comments that both writer and actors in this play were "not doing a play about other people. We were all doing a play about ourselves" (Bigsby, 84). And, again: "I don't write plays to dump on people. I write plays about people whom I love and am fascinated by" (Bigsby 111). Finally, Henry Schvey quotes Mamet as saying: "I always want everyone to be sympathetic to *all* the characters" (my italics, 92). In Mamet's world, then, laughing at *or* with a character should not negate the possibility of empathy or identification.

The second basic Mamet attitude that we need to grasp is that this playwright has always felt himself to be an outsider. His sympathies lie with the outsiders in his plays in their attempts to live *against* the world of the insider. The "exigent" would-be petty thieves of *American Buffalo*, the voracious salesmen of worthless land in *Glengarry Glen Ross*, the Hollywood types as they approach the "inner circle" of success, all are outsiders, and all evoke Mamet's sympathy and love, even as he condemns much of their behavior. What he admires is their vitality, their refusal to give up in the midst of their murky society, and that refusal is comic.

This outsider perspective emerges most strongly in "The Decoration of Jewish Houses," where Mamet writes that being "racially Jewish" means sharing "codes, language, and jokes and attitudes which make up the consolations of strangers in a strange land" (*SF* 8). That humor, Mamet emphasizes repeatedly, is self-deprecating—we laugh at ourselves with good humor directed at our own foibles. For example, in a wonderfully funny essay about his attending a Soldiers of Fortune convention in Las Vegas, Mamet describes his participating in a pugil stick fight and in target practice. The target practice description is typical: "I frightened the hell out of some tin cans at sixty or seventy yards, and then, content that those cans had been amply warned, we all rode back to Vegas" (Conventional [*SF*] 44).

That kind of laughing at oneself, and even at one's motives, is what Mamet requires of us as we first laugh at and then identify with his central figures, even the vicious ones. As outsider, the laughter at oneself is both defensive and healing. In "On Paul Ickovic's Photographs," Mamet begins: "I always felt that people look on me as an outcast—that the simplest request for a cup of coffee elicits a slight tightening around the eyes." He goes on to write: "I always felt like an outsider; and I am sure that the suspicion that I perceive is the suspicion that I provoke by my great longing to *belong*" (*WR* 73). On one level, most of us can identify with that blatantly honest admission of insecurity. Mamet adds that his version of living the life of the outsider is based on "observation," on "acute awareness," the typical habit of the Jew, he says, who lives with an "accepted vision of personal futility, and of the beauty of the world" (*WR* 74).

Mamet's sympathy for his outsider characters, then, is a celebratory observation as well as a cautious one, and that's how we should laugh at and with these Mamet characters, with a renewing sense of celebration. Among the great outsider-observer *characters* in dramatic literature is O'Neill's Larry Slade, but his laughter, we're told (repeatedly) is "sardonic," a laughter full of derision and scorn and skepticism. That humor is perhaps defensive, and perhaps reflects O'Neill's own; Mamet's humor is the opposite of sardonic. We laugh at his characters' behavior, which is our own, but we celebrate it, too, because of its uniqueness, its vitality, its comic refusal to surrender.

Mamet points out that his beloved Stanislavsky emphasized that the traditional purpose of drama is to celebrate the life of the human soul, and that some of the things we celebrate are funny, that some are shocking, and that some are sad (Schvey 91). Bigsby perceptively comments that Mamet manages to combine jeremiad with celebration (16). I'm reminded of Herbert Blau's marvelous *bon mot* that Beckett both lights a candle and curses the darkness (229). Mamet's curses are many, but even they are often funny, and his humor is potentially redemptive because when we laugh at his characters we can still see something in them to admire and coincidentally see in their foibles and ignoble behavior our own or our society's need for change.

Not far beneath the surface of much of Mamet's celebratory humor lie two very basic goals or wishes. In the first place, Mamet would like to live in a moral world, an ordered world, and to encourage the creation of such a world. As he points out, early on, "I'm . . . interested in what Tolstoy said—that we should treat human beings with love and respect and never hurt them (Wetzsteon 101). And, as he writes in "First Principles," we should adhere to principles which make our presentations honest, moral, and, coincidentally, moving, funny, and worth the time and money of the audience" (*WR* 25). That morality seems to be almost nostalgically connected to a near-classic sense of order. In "Observations of a Backstage Wife," Mamet writes that the "feeling of having *one's place* is a good feeling, and almost absent in our contemporary culture . . . we all long for order and dream of that imaginary society which would make us feel secure" (*WR* 151). And in attempting to achieve a moral order, ethical behavior, the theater and its humor, should "help teach that it is possible and *pleasant* to substitute action for inaction, courage for cowardice, humanity for selfishness." He adds, "In a morally bankrupt time, we can help to change that habit of coercive and frightened action and substitute for it the habit of trust, self-reliance, and co-operation" (First Principles [*WR*] 27).

The first subtext of Mamet's celebratory humor, the wish for a moral, ordered world, is closely connected to a second, that given a basically corrupt world what we all wish for most profoundly is love and a sense of belonging. In Mamet's world, no matter how corrupt or decadent the context, love *is* a moral or ethical choice. These ideas may appear to some sophisticates as banal, naive, embarrassingly soppy. I think Mamet perceptive when he observes: "As the Victorians assiduously expunged reference to sex, so we expunge direct reference to that which we desire most, which is love and a sense of belonging" (Some Thoughts [*WR*] 36). Much of our laughter during a Mamet play is aimed at people who destroy their possibilities for love or belonging. When we do see positive examples, our laughter either becomes very gentle or is not evoked at all.

The urge toward love and community in the face of a morally bankrupt world points toward a deeper level of Mamet's humor, an almost Yeatsian "gaiety" in the midst of tragedy. As he matures, Mamet is moving towards a more overtly religious vision, which I can best understand as a blend of Tolstoy, Shaw, and Martin Buber. As we shall see, in *Speed-the-Plow*, Mamet uses a complex humor, the fact that several characters laugh at some of these ideas (these "truths"?), to project them for the audience. In his essays, as usual, he is more overt. "A Plain Brown Wrapper" indicts the Reform Temple teaching of Mamet's youth, which implied that "metaphysics is just superstition— that there is no God" (*SF* 18). Despite this anti-theology, Mamet writes, "My coreligionists and I, eventually, sought out the God we had been denied" in various arenas, "all attempts to explain the relationship between the one and the all—between our powerlessness and the strength of the Universe" (19). After what has clearly been a long journey, Mamet writes, "I am proud of being a Jew, and I have a growing sense of the reality of God" (20).

I have no idea whether Mamet knows the Jewish existential theologian Martin Buber, but Buber's complex version of the "God is Love" idea in *I and Thou* certainly captures much of what Mamet has been writing about in recent years. As he commented in 1985, for example, in *The Shawl*, a play which details the relationship between a mystic and a female client, we move toward an ending that reveals the "hidden order of the world" (Freedman 64). In *Speed-the-Plow*, Mamet shows two characters who reject love, emblematically, and who poke fun at a script which is both central to the action of the play and whose "message," though we laugh at it, is quite serious. At the very least, the laughter centers our attention on "the relationship between the one and the all—between our powerlessness and the strength of the Universe." Here Mamet's humor is at its most beautifully apt, I think, and this play, like all great comedies, forces us to consider universal questions through its humorous depiction of our own manners. Again, as opposed to the essays' vision, the "morals" of a Mamet play come

not directly but as we laugh at truth, here a vision of a changing world
that reminds us of both Tolstoy and Shaw.

Several of our grand older writers on comedy shed a good deal of
light on Mamet's very traditional use of the form. In *The Life of the
Drama*, Eric Bentley, for example, writes that "Comedy is very often
about theft, exactly as tragedy is very often about murder . . . comedy
has fewer scenes of possession than of expropriation (or the plan to
expropriate). . . . In the comic world, if possession is the ultimate fact,
dispossession is the ultimate act" (305). The relevance of this
description of comedy's central emphasis to Mamet's world of would-be
thieves, of voracious real estate salesman, and absolutely rapacious
Hollywood businessmen is clear. Bentley goes on to write that greed is
central to comedy, often an offshoot of "falsehood and mendacity." But
he perceptively adds: "The other face of greed in comedy is tenacity, by
which men survive. It is hard to survive. . . . The comic sense tries to
cope with the daily, hourly, inescapable difficulty of being" (307).

Similarly, Robert Corrigan writes in his introduction to
Comedy: Meaning and Form: "The constant in comedy is the comic
view of life or the comic spirit: the sense that no matter how many
times man is knocked down he somehow manages to pull himself up
and keep on going. Thus, while tragedy is a celebration of man's
capacity to aspire and suffer, comedy celebrates his capacity to endure"
(3). It is this tenacity, this will toward survival, even venal survival,
that Mamet celebrates.

The term "comic irony" is the aesthetic key, I think, to Mamet's
work. That irony, of course, has to do with the relationship between the
audience and the play and the playwright beyond it. As Bentley
suggests: "In comedy, even if one cannot identify oneself with anybody
on stage, one has a hero to identify with nonetheless, the author. One is
proud to be lent the spectacles of Jonson or Molière. . . . Tragedy and
comedy are alike negative arts in that they characteristically reach
positive statement by inference from negative situations." He goes on
to note that "Finally, tragedy and comedy have the same heuristic
intent: self knowledge. What tragedy achieves in this line by its
incredibly direct renderings of sympathies and antipathies, comedy
achieves by indirection, duality, irony" (308–309).

Comic irony is a slippery term. As Wayne Booth points out in
A Rhetoric of Irony, "There is no doubt [that] explaining an irony is
usually even less successful than explaining an ordinary joke" (38). In

Booth's terms, Mamet practices a "covert," "stable," and "finite" irony. "Covert irony" is "intended to be reconstructed with meanings different from those on the surface" (6). Teach's speeches, for example, in *American Buffalo*, and Don's for that matter, about business are ironic; we must "reconstruct from them through a sophisticated process of inference" what Mamet believes or is expressing by indirection. "Stable ironies" are fixed "in the sense that once a reconstruction of meaning has been made, the reader is not then invited to undermine it with further demolition and reconstruction" (6). "Finite ironies" point toward "reconstructed meanings [that] are in some sense local, limited." This sort of irony "does not mock our efforts by making general claims about the ironic universe. . . . It does not say 'There is no truth' . . . or (in the sense of Edward Albee in *Tiny Alice*) 'We do not know anything'" (6).

Even covert, stable and finite irony "causes much trouble," writes Booth, essentially because we can miss the intended reconstruction, take the ironic statement for the author's true belief rather than his characters', and so on (171). In the works I've chosen as examples, I would argue both that we are intended to look down on the "wrong beliefs" and follies and sins, as Booth has it, of all of Mamet's characters at the same time as we are intended to sympathize with these figures and to recognize their sins and follies as much like our own— and often as rooted in the limited possibilities our culture affords us. Part of the "ironic indicator," here, that which points us toward ironic intent, is what Booth calls the conflict of "beliefs expressed and the beliefs we hold *and suspect the author of holding*" (73). The process works something like this in *Glengarry Glen Ross*, for example: the beliefs the salesmen express or act out are venal, greedy, immoral in that they sell nearly worthless land to gullible investors who cannot afford to squander their savings; the salesmen, taking advantage of such investors' dreams, can both make a living and feel powerful as they dupe their marks. We condemn that belief system and suspect that Mamet does, too. But we are caught up in the wonderful vitality of several of these salesmen, impressed by their talents and tenacity, by their struggle in this world, and by their spirit of community. Still, we laugh at them, at least until we recognize that their behavior, their bizarre self-interest, is quite like our own. And that recognition, being so unexpected, is the ultimate irony.

We know that some forms of irony are funny. Our most basic definition of Mamet's humor, that is, that we "laugh at truth" in Mamet's world, is deeply ironic. We're back to the idea of the simultaneous jeremiad and celebration. Irony still most basically entails a violation of expectations, and dramatic irony still most basically entails the audience knowing something that characters on stage do not. Both of these basic definitions "work" in a Mamet play, and work humorously, because of an *initial* feeling of *superiority* on the part of the audience.

Despite the frequency with which modern drama deals with what Mamet calls "the exigent," or with members of professions "other" than those of the typical playgoer, Mamet's works still violate basic audience expectations in numerous ways. We still don't "expect" plays to be about low-life junk dealers from the bowels of Chicago; we don't expect plays to be about sleazy real estate salesmen; we don't expect plays to be about Hollywood moguls who admit that they are whores only concerned with making a dollar. Despite our sophistication, our knowledge of plays from *The Lower Depths* to *The Ruling Class*, almost perversely, by now, we still expect that plays will concern middle class life, more or less mainstream manners. In Mamet's plays that basic irony is funny, for at first we look down on these characters as different than ourselves and find their manners amusing. That's true of the stumbling speeches of Bob and Don as *American Buffalo* opens, and of Teach's entrance with his "Fuck Ruthie" lines, and of the darker humor of the opening exchange in *Glengarry Glen Ross* between Levene and Williamson.

This laughter isn't very nice, may even be infantile, as Freud suggests. That feeling of superiority, and of consequent hilarity, is partially rooted in dramatic irony—that is, the audience's superiority to these characters entails knowing something they do not. Most basically, the audience recognizes that the author would disagree with *many* of the statements these characters make. When Don attempts to describe the American business ethic in praising language, we know that Mamet disagrees with that ethic even as he has Don espouse it so accurately. Don's language makes this a comic irony, but the basic situation is also comically ironic because of our inferring Mamet's position.[1]

Though Mamet's humor does often depend on the audience's initial feeling of superiority to these characters, it is not a vicious humor. As Bentley points out, there is a huge gap between wit and humor. Pirandello, he writes, in "Humor," clarifies this distinction "when he remarks that if you see an old woman with dyed hair and too much make-up, and she strikes you as ridiculous, you have only to go on thinking about her to find her sad. 'Humor' in writing is to include both these elements, where wit would rest content with the first" (312).

This humor-leading-to-sadness implies a kind of sympathy and a wish to see things change. It also suggests a type of forgiveness and a type of love. As Booth points out, "forgiveness is a central element in tragi-comedy, . . . an ultimate reaction to revenge" (329). We may immediately think of Teach in this context and his repeated, hopeful lines after his busting up Don's shop: "Are you mad at me?" (*Buffalo* 104). That is Teach's plea for love and community, even after such selfishly aggressive behavior, and Don grants him forgiveness, at least in part because he needs to forgive himself as well for his action toward Bobby. And Bobby forgives them both as he forgives himself and they him. It is an intensely ironic and intensely tender and gently humorous scene. Ironically, we're called upon to identify with these characters, to know ourselves and to forgive ourselves, I think, and to change.

Indicators of the intended ironic response abound in these three Mamet plays. For the reader, the initial ironic indicator in all three works are epigraphs. The one in *American Buffalo* is my favorite:

> Mine eyes have seen the glory of the coming of the Lord.
> He is peeling down the alley in a black and yellow Ford.

Certainly open to a variety of interpretations, the epigraph is comically ironic, for we don't expect that second line in conjunction with the opening from that old spiritual. For me, the irony points to the fact that in the culture we are about to see, the sacred, that which is of most importance, is earthy, that the lives we will see are different than our own, than what we expect, and that, though unusual, even mundane, these lives are holy. That interpretation emphasizes the first line's "Lord" and a comic understanding of why this driver seems so potent in this community. I think that it echoes some of Mamet's statements about the play, as well. Anne Dean, in her recent book, opens her discussion of *American Buffalo* with the epigram, too, but she sees it as evoking "a culture that has sacrificed spirituality to materialism" (85). She essentially emphasizes the second line and understands only criticism of this fast-driving Lord and his observer. Dean's emphasis misses the spirit of ironic celebration, even defiant celebration, implicit in both the epigraph and the play.

Like a good many of Mamet's plays, *American Buffalo* is about a triangle, here, the more or less competitive relationship among three men. In several of Mamet's essays, though, he makes clear that he sees such male "bonding" and communion as important and valuable. Teach, the most insecure and jealous of this lot, tries to oust Bobby both from Don's "job" and from his affections. On one level, Teach's maneuvering is apparently financial, just to make certain that Teach gets to do the "job." On another, Teach is desperate to have Don regard him as first in his affections, not Bobby, and so he undercuts Bob at every opportunity. That vicious behavior ranges from the lightly humorous to the horribly vengeful. Teach does succeed in getting Don to scrub Bobby from the roster, but Don recognizes that Teach is no more adequate for the job than Bobby and insists on calling in Fletch, the one man he really respects. Fletch never comes, despite Don's faith in him. He's been mugged by "some Mexicans" and is in the hospital. This element of the play has led several critics to observe an allusion to *Waiting for Godot*, but the humor is lighter than Beckett's, and Don is more clearly a positive figure than either of Beckett's two waiters.

Don has taken on Bobby as his responsibility, and Mamet admires that. In the midst of this scruffy environment, Don feels the love of a father for this boy, and that love is not undercut as it is so often in Beckett's work. As in all of Mamet's plays, though, love in *American Buffalo* is a complex mix of truly loving behavior and a wish to control others, to feel superiority or power. There's a soupçon of a wish to feel good about oneself, about one's generosity, here, too, and a wish to inspire loving behavior, gratitude toward oneself in the one so loved. In Mamet's world, there is also tremendously hostile behavior, which is often inspired by the same fear, the same need for security, that inspires love.

These potentially gloomy truths are presented in such a way that we laugh at them. That initial distance, that laughter, *can* lead to a questioning—something like "what's the implication of my laughter here?; why do I find myself sympathizing with the feelings of inferiority, of social anger these incompetent low-life characters project as they contemplate robbing someone who is probably much more like me than these figures?" In turn, that questioning can point toward both an intended emotional identification and toward the recognition of several themes. The laughter softens, and we can get the point. An audience, though, can also reject these characters and the play's themes as scandalous or hilariously empty, misinterpreting Mamet's ironic comedy.

Mamet sums up the play in an early interview with Ross Wetzsteon:

> What I was trying to say in *American Buffalo* is that once you step back from the moral responsibility you've undertaken, you're lost. We have to take responsibility. Theater is a place of recognition, it's an ethical experience, it's where we share ethical interchange. That's why Don's exclusion of Bob from the deal is so crucial. (101)

He goes on to emphasize his interest in Tolstoy, which we've previously noted: "we should treat human beings with love and respect and never hurt them. I hope that *American Buffalo* shows that by showing what happens when you fail to act that way."

Mamet emphasizes, then, that he intends his audience to learn something positive about ethical behavior by watching a negative example. He makes the ethical lesson more acceptable, and more entertaining, by making us laugh. The sources of this humor are myriad, and often entail that spirit of comic irony. A partial list would include malapropisms, elision of speech patterns, that is leaving out an expected word, cursing, contradictions or inconsistencies, linguistic rhythms, the humor of a general situation, and the stories or jokes of Mamet's characters. In one way or another, these instances of humor or laughter, always point toward an understanding of character or theme. That's the primary function of humor in Mamet's work. The most significant thematic area, as we've seen, from Mamet's perspective, has to do with love, community, belonging. Subtopics in most of his plays have to do with teaching, friendship, and business.

Examples of malapropisms abound. One of my favorites occurs early in Act I when Teach is trying to convince Don both not to use Bobby in the contemplated theft *and* that he admires Don's relationship with the kid. Loyalty to Bobby, he says, is admirable. "This is swell. It turns my heart the things you do for that kid" (34). If Teach spoke our kind of language, he'd have said "It touches my heart." "It turns my heart" is an ironic, comic blend of "It touches my heart" and "It turns my stomach." The misuse of the phrase is funny, but it also points toward the actual feeling that Teach has about this relationship, which upsets him for a variety of reasons. Clearly, he wants to exclude Bobby from the "business deal" for his own selfish interests. But Teach is really disturbed at the closeness of Don's and Bobby's relationship, to his own exclusion, to the point of jealousy. Thus, he undercuts his rival by criticizing Don for being "too loyal" to an inept kid and by referring to Bobby's drug use. That's dangerous territory, and Teach knows it. Don bristles: "You know the fucking kid's clean. He's trying hard, he's working hard, and you leave him alone" (35). Teach responds with sarcasm, but Don's objections gradually weaken. The seed for the betrayal has been planted.

Suddenly Teach picks up a strange object at the end of a rather long speech about not letting Bobby into the deal out of Bobby's own best interests (!). Don responds to Teach's question: "It's a thing they stick in dead pigs keep their legs apart all the blood runs out" (35). There's an example of elision—Don has omitted "to" and "so that," and the omission is both realistic and funny. The sudden incongruity, which I think of as humor of situation, labels Teach's and Don's behavior. The implement is threatening at some gut level, horribly graphic, brutal. "This is what they're doing to Bobby," is the emotional effect. That connection is underlined as Don, after a pause, returns to that topic—objecting "I set it up with him." But Don is already yielding as Bobby returns with the bag from the Riverside.

Our laughter at this ironic humor of situation, at malapropism and elision, at least in part, springs from that sense of superiority, which is also one reason that cursing in Mamet is so funny on one level. In his monumental *The Anatomy of Swearing*, Ashley Montagu recounts the wonderful story of Mark Twain's wife trying to show her profane husband what he sounded like by imitating him. Twain's response: "The words are there, my dear, but the music is wanting" (68).

There is plenty of music in Mamet's characters' cursing, which is quite realistic, but even so such cursing almost always provokes laughter in an audience. This particular "laughter at truth" points toward a number of ideas, as well. As *American Buffalo* opens, Don is rebuking Bobby for his failure to carry out his assignment to watch his "target," the man who bought the nickel. He emphasizes that he's not mad at Bobby, and he's clearly trying to teach him as best he can by using Fletch as a model. Swearing, particularly the use of obscenities, is a natural part of his patois, but at least a ripple of laughter occurs with the first obscenity: "Action talks and bullshit walks" (4) and continues with Don's praising Fletcher, who has "skill and talent and the balls to arrive at your own conclusions." That last phrase is funny because of its shaky grammar, but the rest of the laughter is coming because members of the audience still feel uncomfortable with swearing, particularly with the public use of the four-letter obscenities. When Teach enters, after "Good morning," his first lines are: "Fuckin' Ruthie, fuckin' Ruthie, fuckin' Ruthie, fuckin' Ruthie, fuckin' Ruthie." Don says "What?" And Teach repeats, "Fuckin' Ruthie . . ." Don says ". . . yeah?" (9), and Teach is off and running with his story. There's both a new vitality, and a more threatening tone, in Teach's swearing, and it's funny, too.

That this language is a part of these characters' natural, everyday speech may say something about the debasement of their culture, as some critics suggest, but that's certainly not the primary point. When Teach escalates the feeling behind the cursing, we laugh further, even as his hostility toward women comes bubbling up as rooted in Ruthie's having beaten him at poker the previous evening. We are further amused by Don's apparently not having heard him say "fuckin' Ruthie" five times and asking "what?" In context, Teach has simply misunderstood—Don wants to know why Teach is mad at Ruthie, as that ". . . yeah?" suggests. We laugh, anyway. Montagu points out that the middle class, the typical theater audience, uses blasphemies more than obscenities (87) and goes on to note that despite some loosening of attitudes toward sex, in some quarters four-letter words "are still generally considered vulgar, obscene and impure" (301). This is a vocabulary "that 'superior' people have never deigned to acknowledge, at least not until the second half of the twentieth century." He also notes that these words have the power "to amuse" (302–303).

In an earlier work on swearing, Julian Sharman comments that audiences, particularly unsophisticated ones, laugh at cursing (154). Of the more serious underbelly of such laughter, Sharman writes: "There are beings so dejected—so penurious—that their swearing constitutes their whole store of worldly opulence. They know it, too, in a fashion, although it has never been told them and they themselves are incapable of the telling" (151). Teach, Don, and Bobby don't quite fit in this class, but their swearing does provide them a kind of solace and a type of minor rebellion just a bit like Nora's in *A Doll's House*, and we find that amusing, too. We do see Teach calm down a bit after his "fuckin' Ruthie" outburst, but that swearing, here, also embodies a sense of belonging, of camaraderie. The unspoken logic: "we are all revolting against socially accepted behavior, and that makes us feel a type of communion, a belonging, an 'us against them.'" As Montagu argues: "Those who have been most frustrated in life can, by the magic omnipotence of words, achieve something of the power that in all other respects has been denied them" (333).

This combination of a symbolic, though fruitless victory over the oppressor and almost jolly claim of community with one's fellow oppressed is particularly obvious and particularly funny in Teach and Don's conversation about the girl friend or wife of their upper-middle-class coin-collecting target. Part of the humor depends on story telling. Don gradually spills out his yarn about his anger at the coin collector with wonderfully comic rhythms, often caused by interruptions of the straight narrative, and with some fine comic and musical swearing. Before he'll tell Teach the whole story, though, Don insists on making a call to the fence he's found. On the other end of the line, the fence is clearly putting down Don's numismatic ignorance. As he hangs up, Don mutters: "Fucking asshole." And Teach replies: "Guys like that I like to fuck their wives" (28). We laugh at the brazen audacity of Teach's line, especially, but we should recognize both the hostility of the "exigent" toward the more fortunate, *and* the vitality of the response, *and* the horrible aggression behind it all. It can be funny both because of our feeling of superiority *and* because the cursing *is* an escape valve. Teach is far too ineffectual and fearful of women, I think, either to be a rapist or a seducer. As Teach typically escalates Don's cursing, there does emerge, ironically, a sense of communion between the two. Basically, by elevating the cursing energy, Teach is backing up Don against the outside world.

The rhythms of the story and the context of the humor underscore the characters' ineffectiveness and their resentment of their social place, their envy and hatred for those above them. Don tells his story in short sentences and phrases, which Teach interrupts. An example:

DON:	So I'm about to go 'Two bits,' jerk that I am, but something tells me to shut up, so I go, 'You tell me.'
TEACH:	Always good business.
DON:	*Oh* yeah.
TEACH:	How wrong can you go?
DON:	That's what I mean, so then he thinks a minute, and he tells me he'll just *shop* a bit.
TEACH:	Uh-huh . . . (*Stares out of window.*)
DON:	An so he's *shopping* . . . What?
TEACH:	Some cops (29)

Both interruptions, Teach's line on business and his observation of the cruising cops, break the rhythm of the narrative and are funny—and point toward theme. The business line emphasizes the comic irony that business is the equivalent of theft; the obsession with the cruising police emphasizes that these characters do regard themselves as outsiders, worried about police activities to protect the "insiders," and that their behavior is ludicrous, certainly not that of hardened criminals—the mere discussion of the robbery makes them nervous, and that's funny too.

As the story continues, Don reveals the real source of his resentment, the motivation for his planning the theft. He's upset about the guy's attitude when he comes back looking for additional valuable coins: "He comes in here like I'm his fucking doorman . . . Doing me this favor by just coming in my shop" (31). Teach sympathizes, recognizes that Don's after revenge with the robbery, and then wants to know "Who's the chick?" (32). Don describes her riding a bicycle to hilarious effect: "The ass on this broad, un-be-fucking-lievable in these bicycling shorts sticking up in the air with these short handlebars." Teach chimes in: "(*Fuckin' fruits* . . .)."

The story of the girl is funny and serious in itself as well as in its interruption of the rhythm of Don's story line. Most audiences will at least chuckle at "un-be-fucking-lievable," an example of what Montagu calls "infixing" (315). But the humor rounds out our picture of the bicycling couple, the neighborhood, and the sources of resentment. The often-cited influence of Thorstein Veblen on Mamet is clear, the woman as one of the primary evidences or emblems of the man's success. The image here is of an urban area undergoing yuppification, and the resentment of the earlier denizens caught in the transition. The mere idea of the two on bicycles evokes that "(Fuckin' fruits . . .)" from Teach. And when Don describes the guy riding his bicycle to work, Teach snorts "With the three-piece suit, huh?" (32). As we laugh at the language, the rhythms of interruption, the cursing, we should also be able to understand the social situation, the resentment that leads to Don's and Teach's satisfaction with the mere idea of robbing this alien couple.

Reversals or contradictions and visual humor also account for some of our laughter. For example, Teach tells Don, early on, that he's sorry he mentioned Bobby's "skin-popping," but almost immediately reverses himself and then says he's glad he did say it (34–35). And Teach in his newspaper hat, looking in the mirror and worrying about looking like a sissy as he plans to protect himself from the rain is quietly hilarious and softens or balances the moving, emotional conclusion, preventing it from becoming too soppy or sentimental. As the play works toward its conclusion, though, the situation changes the way we laugh.

Teach is growing increasingly belligerent as Bobby bursts in with the story of Fletch in the hospital. In a frenzy, trying to keep Bob from talking with Don, he says: "You do not have to do anything, Bob. You do not have to do anything that we tell you that you have to do" (87). This ineptitude with language would have been funny in Act I, but here, given the betrayal, Bob's desperation, the mounting tension, the same linguistic patterns no longer amuse in the same way. There is some humor, but it's more grim, more tight-lipped. We experience a light comic irony, too, when Bobby finally reveals that he has lied in the first place, that he hasn't seen the mark go out at all. Bobby's report that the coin collector has gone out, we should recall, was what produced the idea of this evening's robbery in the first place. His confession leads to Teach's final violent eruption, his trashing of the shop, at which we definitely do not laugh. It's too brutal.

In short, all of the laughter, our ironic comic responses, point toward a number of inferences about this conclusion. Those inferences center on the loving relationships, here, the communal, but the thematic subcategories of teaching and business are there as well.

Bobby has told his lie because he's desperate to get back into Don's affection. The play has opened with Don giving Bobby a lecture about not fulfilling his assignment to watch the mark and about the virtues of business as opposed to friendship. Bobby has failed, again, in his eyes, when he gets the breakfast order confused. He's also earned Teach's ire by briefly talking with Ruthie at the Riverside. He's desperate to tell Don something to please him, then, and he does, by describing the guy's leaving (22). Don happily accepts that, even Bob's conclusion that he was wearing traveling clothes and was off to pick up his lady. If we're alert, we should know that Bobby is lying right off the bat—and that's comically ironic, particularly since it leads to Don's betrayal of Bobby to commit a burglary planned *because* of Bobby's lie.

That early lecture contains the initial "exposition" of theme, which we laugh at because Don's statements about business are inconsistent and contradictory. Several critics have analyzed these references to business and friendship and the image of the buffalo. I won't dwell on these areas except to note that even given his admitted anger at business, Mamet gets us to laugh at this stylized version of business as junk shop, at the value of the trinkets from "the thing," the Century of Progress Exposition held during the middle of the Depression, at the idea of business as theft. Don in his lecture to Bobby is sincerely trying to help Bobby learn how to live, but as he tells Bobby about Fletch, Bobby twice remarks that he thinks Fletch's business deal with Ruthie amounted to stealing. Don tries to point out the error of Bobby's thinking: "'Cause there's business and there's friendship, Bobby . . . and what you got to do is keep clear who your friends are, and who treated you like what. Or else the rest is garbage" (8).

We laugh at Don's rendition, but his basic message is true from Mamet's perspective. Don's next *action*, to send Bobby to the Riverside for some breakfast, begins the food subtext and does provide a "counter" for "who treated you like what." It's ironic, of course, that Don can't follow his own advice, his own wishes, even, and when he has agreed to betray Bobby, as Act I ends, his funny curtain line—"Fuckin' business"—is also deeply serious.

The play's violent conclusion still includes humor but on a much different level. Ironically, Teach has planted in Bobby's head the idea that Fletch is in "Masonic Hospital" during his rambling sarcasm about not believing Bobby's story about Fletch being mugged (88). When Don checks and finds that Fletch is not at Masonic, Teach is convinced that Bobby and Fletch have betrayed them. His temper erupts as Bobby begins to say once more that Ruthie and Gracie have told him about the incident (94). The level of violence reaches its most

210 Christopher C. Hudgins

frighteningly intense as Teach hits Bobby on the side of the head: "Grace and Ruthie up your ass, you shithead; you don't fuck with us, *I'll* kick your fucking head in (I don't give a shit . . .)" (94). Here, the situation makes this cursing distinctly unfunny. Donny implicitly joins in the violence, justifying himself by saying to Bobby "You brought it on yourself" (94). But as Don gradually returns to his best instincts, we begin to respond with humor again. Don is already upset that Bobby's ear is bleeding when the phone rings; Ruth tells them that Fletch really is in the hospital. We laugh at Teach, now, as he typically tries to avoid any blame, but Don is clearly going back over to Bob and recognizing his own flaws.

Bob now reveals that he's bought the new nickel for Donny (99), that it's not one that he and Fletch have stolen as Teach has suspected. *That*, in turn, emphasizes for Don the magnitude of his betrayal in the face of such love, ultimately leading to his recognition of Teach's perfidy and his attack on Teach. That, in turn, shows Bobby just how good a friend Don has been and will be again, despite this betrayal and leads to his confession. Just as Don hits Teach, Bob says "I eat shit" and gradually reveals his initial lie. And that, in turn, leads to Teach's trashing the shop with the pig sticker.

Once the violence is over, a very different tone settles over *American Buffalo*'s final moments. Gently humorous and loving would be my description. Don merely subdues Teach, calling him "Walt" for the first time in the play. He doesn't respond at all to Bobby's confession, yet. Teach blusters, but we're able to laugh at him again when he says "You don't know what I go through. I put my dick on the chopping block" (103). And we can feel a warmth even for this figure, in his need, when, after destroying the shop, he says to Don, "Are you mad at me?" Don doesn't respond at first, merely telling Teach to go get his car to take Bobby to the hospital, but he finally tells Teach, twice, that he's not mad. Teach makes that silly hat, his next-to-last line, "You should clean the place up" (106). Don simply says "yeah," and Teach says "Good."

Such evocations of the positive continue. Don tells Bob to get up, and he apologizes twice. Bob, in turn, says he fucked up, and Don assures him:

> DON: No. You did real good.
> BOB: No.
> DON: Yeah. You did real good.

> *Pause.*
> BOB: Thank you.
> DON: That's all right.
> *Pause.*
> BOB: I'm sorry, Donny.
> DON: That's all right. (106)

In the first place, the mutual forgiveness and recognition of fault, here, is wonderfully gentle. It reminds me very much of the tone of the ending of *Who's Afraid of Virginia Woolf?* In the second place, all those "goods" and "rights" suggest just how positive the ending is. It represents the re-establishment of a significant community, of a friendship, a traditional comic ending. "That's all right" as the play's final line is ironically comic and very serious—and in great contrast to the "Fucking business" line that concludes Act I. The humor, the mutually reinforcing moral choices of Don and Bobby, point toward this vision of community as very important. I think that Mamet's analysis of *American Buffalo* in the Schvey interview is quite convincing: "Don has yielded to temptation for material gain and that almost causes him to kill the thing he loves—and he recognizes his huge mistake at the end of the play." Mamet concludes that Don learns that *he* needs to learn a lesson about being an excellent man (94).

Various forms of humor, comic irony and the comic form, all point to an important truth at the core of *American Buffalo*. In the Schvey interview, Mamet says that he sees all of his works as optimistic, not cynical, about the possibilities of self-knowledge. That's true even of a work like *Glengarry Glen Ross*, where the humor is more brutal, at first, than in *American Buffalo*. In much the same manner as in *American Buffalo*, though, we initially laugh at these characters, then gradually learn to sympathize with them. In this play, we finally come to admire their skill, their vitality, in confronting their world, more so than in *American Buffalo*. This play, too, is more direct, less metaphoric, in its attack on American business. Its epigraph is "Always Be Closing," which, as anybody who has been involved in sales knows, *is* the key to success in this job and is also dehumanizing. The concentration on that bottom line, on "full-grossing" the customer, on *winning* the sales competition, on *beating* the customer into submission, produces both ulcers and hypocrisy about one's human relations. But still, these salesmen manage a kind of camaraderie that is important, even within a system that Mamet severely criticizes. As he writes in his essay, "In the Company of Men," "shooting, hunting, gambling, boxing, these activities *are* a form of love. And many times, . . . *beyond* the fierce competition, there was an atmosphere of being involved in a communal activity" (*SF* 88–89).

Mamet has written that *Glengarry Glen Ross* is "formally a gang comedy in the tradition of *The Front Page* or *Man in White*." He labels the first act an episodic detective drama and the second "A very traditional, formal last act of a comedy drama." And, he adds, "A gang comedy is a play about revealing the specific natures and the unifying natures of a bunch of people who happen to be involved in one enterprise" (Schvey 92).

The scenes in Act I provide broad exposition of this world from three different perspectives and provide exposition about the specific central event of Act II, the theft of the leads. Because of these early scenes, Mamet can use a comic dramatic irony to good effect in Act II, for the audience knows a good deal that not all the characters on stage know. Otherwise, the structures and sources of Mamet's humor and comic intentions are quite similar to those in *American Buffalo*. A good bit of the truth we laugh at is still contained in the resentment of these men against the outside world. For example, we learn about the lead system and the competition in scene 1 as Levene complains to Williamson, his office manager, and desperately tries to manipulate him, to sell himself, to *close*. In scene 2, as Moss complains to Aaronow about the lead system and the competition, on the one hand to keep their jobs, on the other to win that Cadillac, he is particularly harsh on Indians with names like Patel, who waste a salesman's time. He concludes that they like to talk to salesmen so that they can feel superior: "A supercilious race. What is this *look* on their face all the time? I don't know. (*Pause.*) I don't know. Their broads all look like they just got fucked with a dead *cat*" (12).

We laugh at this horribly racist and sexist line, partly out of our liberal superiority, laughing at the character. Simultaneously, though, we should recognize the complexity of Moss' frustration, that *he* feels inferior, that the only thing important to him in this job is the selling, and that these people, in his mind, get in the way of his livelihood. The reality of such a position, of the dehumanizing effects of *selling*, typically emerges in an at least semi-humorous speech:

MOSS: The whole fuckin' thing . . . The pressure's just
too great. You're ab . . . You're absolu . . . they're
too important. All of them. You go in the door. I
. . . "I got to *close* this fucker, or I don't eat
lunch," "or I don't win the *Cadillac.* . . ." (12)

The rhythm, the omissions, the profanity are funny. But
sympathy for the men and condemnation of the system should be
building, already, beneath the laughter.

In the third scene of the play, we watch Roma, the best of the
salesmen, engage in a monumental manipulation toward a sale of a
chance encounter at the Chinese restaurant. Pulling the mark in toward
intimacy, Roma *talks*—about great dumps, and a great piss, and a great
meal, and great fucks. The semi-monologue is hilarious, and leads to
Roma's best pitch, which would be paraphrased, in condensed form,
something like: "Value the moment, seize the day, because fear is
deadening, and you should act now, seize the opportunity, ignore the
risk, and *buy my land.*" Until that last line, I think Roma speaks for
Mamet. That's even more obvious in these lines: "What is our life?
(*Pause.*) It's looking forward or it's looking back. And that's our life.
That's *it.* Where is the moment? (*Pause.*) What is it that we're afraid
of? Loss. What else?" (28).

All of these attitudes, Roma goes on, spring from insecurity, and
greed and building a fortune is not the answer. The answer is: "I do
those things which seem correct to me today. I trust myself. And if
security concerns me, I do that which *today* I think will make me
secure. And every day I *do* that, when that day *arrives* that I need a
reserve a) odds are that I have it, and b) the true reserve that I have is the
strength that I have of *acting each day* without fear" (29).

As he buys the mark a drink and pulls out the brochures, we
certainly laugh at this manipulation. We also perhaps admire its energy
and bravado. But despite the goal of the conversation, the sale, there's a
strange sort of sincerity here, a heartfelt belief that comes through the
pitch. That truth beneath the humor echoes throughout the play. Strive
to act without fear, with courage. As Levene describes his great sale to
Roma, he emphasizes that he told Bruce and Harriet that they had to
seize their opportunity, that they'd "met possibility" and become scared,
that "'Now's the time,'" and they "wilted" and signed (47–48). As
Roma emphasizes, this sales technique is what Levene has taught him.
But the philosophy, the thematic statement echoes, as well. Once more,

that's an ironic thematic statement. We don't admire the goal, but we admire the vitality, the response to adversity, and, yes, even the strength of these manipulative men in this rotten business.

This comic subject reminds me again of Mamet's wonderful line that the theater should inspire "ethical behavior" and should reveal that "it is possible and pleasant to substitute action for inaction, courage for cowardice, humanity for selfishness" (First Principles [*WR*] 27). The play ironically places its most direct thematic statements in the mouths of these two salesmen, who both manage to act without fear, but who can't quite manage to substitute humanity for selfishness. Both Roma and Levene are certainly subject to fear, but they can also manage the courage to act "as if" they were not.

When Lingk shows up in the ransacked office to demand his contract be rescinded, Roma does have the reserve to stage a brilliant improvised deception with Levene hilariously and extemporaneously playing a wealthy satisfied investor. Roma has just praised Levene to the skies for his sale, and we watch a marvelous con proceed, which would have worked but for the equally comic revelation by Williamson that they've already cashed Lingk's check. Roma has almost had Lingk out the door to talk about his manhood at a bar (63), when Williamson, trying to help, spills the beans. As Lingk exits, his last line to the *clearly* dishonest Roma are: "Forgive me" (65). There's laughter, here, but it's become tight-lipped. Still, we admire Roma and Levene's act, and we're sympathetic as they curse Williamson and lambast him for not recognizing that you have to depend on your partner, that you have to learn that on the streets, doing the calls, that "you can't exist alone."

The cursing and the delivery are at least partly comic; the thematic statement about community is central. But as the play closes, the comic ironies mount in intensity. Williamson discovers that it is Levene who has stolen the leads because in the heat of his denunciation of Williamson, Levene says that Williamson had *made up* his story that Lingk's check has been cashed. The thief, having seen the contract on the desk, is the only one who could have known that. And, just as ironically, Levene tells Williamson that the theft, the *action*, taught him that he could still live vitally. He'd been contemplating suicide, but the theft "taught me something. What it taught me, that you've got to be *out* there. Big deal. So I wasn't cut out to be a thief. I was cut out to be a salesman. And now I'm back, and I got my balls back" (70). With that, Levene for the second time in the play launches into an attempt to sell himself, to convince Williamson to take cash or a percentage of Levene's sales to keep his mouth shut.

Williamson, though, just as ironically, knows that the sale to the Nyborgs on which Levene has built his confidence, probably won't hold because they've been known for years as "nuts" who "just like talking to salesmen" (71). With no hope of profit, Williamson prepares to turn in Levene. And with one more comic ironic twist, Roma comes up, full of admiration, to propose a partnership with Levene as "members of a dying breed" (72). Levene demurs as he goes in to talk with Detective Baylen, but Roma keeps right on selling the idea, keeps on closing, as Levene exits. He's planning to betray Levene, of course, and he summarizes the real deal for Williamson: "My stuff is mine, whatever *he* gets for himself, I'm taking half" (74).

Irony upon irony, then, concludes the play. Roma doesn't know that Levene has been caught, and we laugh at his ignorance. The bitter sweet quality of that laughter has two sources. In the first place, we have ironically wanted Roma's statement of admiration, his offer of partnership to be true—we've been closed. And in the second, we have come genuinely to admire Roma's dexterity, his talent, his fierce vitality or committedness to his calling, and we know that the calling itself is rotten at the core in what it does to both salesman and client. Perhaps, most complexly, we have wanted Levene to succeed, to be revitalized, and we've admired *his* friendship, as partner, for Roma.

Mamet, for some audience members, produces a sympathetic response to these men, which is comically ironic given the play's condemnation of what they do. The rather explicit statement of an existential theme, a call to action, out of their mouths, is ironic in that it's meant to be taken seriously, as its repetition and its demonstration in action suggest. And, finally, the betrayal, unlike the one in *American Buffalo*, doesn't result in a more profound reunion. Even the establishment of a new order, the proposed partnership of Roma and Levene, is undercut. The true comic insight or resolution, here, must reside in the audience's response, in its wearing of Mamet's spectacles. The ironic identification with these characters, though, can occur, and it should lead to a criticism of the system, of the culture, and a recognition of how to act morally, which can spring from our observation of these largely negative examples. Aaronow's last line in the play is "Oh, God, I hate this job." And Roma answers, almost simultaneously, "I'll be at the restaurant." And we know that he'll still be closing.

This betrayal without recognition or redemption on stage is similar to the general situation in *Speed-the-Plow*. There is no exact equivalent of the "theft" of the first two plays, but the emblematic Hollywood greed of Bobby Gould and Charlie Fox "robs" the American public at an epic level. Still, as in the other two plays, the system within which these two work comes in for more criticism than the men. Both Bobby and Charlie, though, are condemned for failing to recognize and respond to the need for love and for *choosing* a camaraderie based primarily on venality over the possibility of love and aesthetic potential. Though Bobby Gould is close to conversion, here, to love, he reneges and goes back to being an "old whore." The next time we see him, in *Bobby Gould in Hell*, he's been damned for much the same uncaring behavior. Implicit in this vision of *Speed-the-Plow* is that Karen is basically a positive figure, that the novel she supposedly loves has merit, and that Charlie's and Bobby's partnership at the end of the play is more like Levene's and Roma's than the generous restored friendship, beyond "Fucking business," at the end of *American Buffalo*.

These are not widely accepted interpretations of this play. Their accuracy, though, emerges both from Mamet's own comments in the essays and from our understanding of his use of humor and the comic form. Again, the first indicator of the intended comic ironic response is Mamet's epigraph, a rather long passage from Thackeray's *Pendennis*. The first cover of this novel boasted an allegorical portrait of "self and ambition and advancement" on one side and "Right and Love" on the other. The connection of the portrait and the general sense of the novel to this play is clear. Juliet MacMaster writes that the "question of how to love was central to the novel" and that the central conflict between "the starry eyed" and the "worldly wise" is left unresolved (60, 62, 70). Mamet sides with "love" over the "worldly wise" self and advancement, ironically with Karen, the loser, but he still recognizes something vital in Bobby Gould.

The more specific thrust of the Thackeray epigraph is to ask who "does his duty best: he who stands aloof from the struggle of life, calmly contemplating it, or he who descends to the ground and takes part in the contest?" After some comment on the "teacher . . . who . . .

cries out that . . . the works of the world are evil," and the mystic who flies from the world, the passage concludes:

> but the earth, where our feet are, is the work of the same Power as the immeasurable blue yonder, in which the future lies. . . . Who ordered sickness, ordered poverty, failure, success—to this man a foremost place, to the other a nameless struggle with the crowd—to that a shameful fall, or paralyzed limb or sudden accident—to each some work upon the ground he stands on, until he is laid beneath it.

Two points are extremely important, here. The passage alludes to some Power who created both the heavens and the earth and who orders human life. Ironically, this description sounds much the same as that Power which *The Bridge* describes. And secondly, despite the dark vision of the teacher and the mystic that the world is evil, that neither heaven nor earth can yield any "good," that Power has ordered "to each some work upon the ground he stands on, until he is laid beneath it." In the context of this play, that last sentence suggests that Mamet admires the comic struggle, in work, of even Bobby Gould, just as he has that of Roma and Levene and Don, Bobby and Teach. The epigraph, then, sounds one of Mamet's central themes, the (perhaps comic) nobility of the human struggle in spite of the certainty of death or decay. The seriousness of the epigraph ironically suggests that we should take the comic or caricatured vision of a similar Power in *The Bridge* very seriously.

The whole range of Mamet's humorous and comic talents are on display in *Speed-the-Plow* as it stingingly belittles the two male characters and their Hollywood business. That it is these men who belittle the novel suggests that they may be "unreliable" witnesses. The humor of the play, though, also includes the novel itself and its language, but, like several of Roma's statements, the novel's ideas are meant to be taken seriously. The novel's language, I think, is ridiculed because Mamet looks askance at works of art which are overtly didactic. In sum, we again laugh at truth, both in relation to what the novel says, how it says it, and how these male characters reject it as an image of truth which would not make a buck. Gould's rejection of that novel, to return to Mamet's central theme, is entwined with his rejection of love, always wrong in Mamet's world.

We've already glanced at the hilarious jokes and word play of the two men and suggested that the audience both laughs at the jokes themselves and at the men who tell them, inferring that their value system is impoverished, and so on. Bobby and Charlie, despite their relative success, still see themselves as outsiders. They've not yet arrived. The unseen Ross, on whom they wait, is one of the insiders, one of the truly wealthy and powerful, and they both aspire to his league. Mamet uses the phone to tremendous comic advantage in this context. In the first place, Bobby's conversations with his temporary secretary never work as he wishes. He can't even get a cup of coffee delivered to his office at first. And when his secretary does manage to raise Ross on the phone, Gould is invariably put off. These comic exchanges both amuse us and label Bobby as a vaguely ridiculous outsider. As Fox and Gould wait to meet their appointment with Ross, for example, Gould imagines that he'll simply say "One sentence. 'Doug Brown, Buddy Film,'" and that that will turn the trick. The phone rings: "Whoever it is, we'll be with Mr. Rrr . . . (*Pause.*) No problem whatsoever . . . you'll be *back* by then . . .? Absolutely so. Thank you. (*He hangs up. Pause . . .*)" (20).

This particular phone passage is very similar to the scene with Don on the phone with his fence. Gould's language is servile to Ross, in marked contrast to his tone with his secretary, whom he was beginning to abuse for putting anybody through so close to his appointment with Ross. His being taken aback is funny, on the one hand, and it empowers her on the other. As Ross cuts him off, Gould's "you'll be *back* by then . . .?" is also funny. That last italicized word emphasizes Bobby's continuing surprise that Ross can travel to New York and back so fast in the company's "Gulfstream." He's not there yet, and since he isn't, he's the sycophant now, not even having the nerve to mention that this sudden change of plans may damage the whole arrangement with Doug Brown. It is this insecurity, this lack of belonging, on one level, that makes Gould so desperate for both love (Karen's) and friendship (Charlie's).

Condemnation is the prevalent response to the play's humor at Hollywood's expense. Wealth itself and other results of success are comic targets. For example, Bobby is lavish in his praise of Charlie for having brought him the Doug Brown script rather than "crossing the street." Clearly, what Bobby *wants* to attribute to friendship is actually commerce. Charlie has always ridden on Bobby's coattails. Even when

Gould offers Fox the chance to pitch the script without him, Fox turns him down, simply because he needs Gould's connections and moxie. Further, neither can really envision the results of success. As they think about being rich, Gould comments: "Rich, are you kidding me? We're going to have to hire someone just to figure out the *things* we want to buy . . ." (23). The perks, the power and the broads, these are some of the empty goals of not only this particular American Dream, but, Mamet suggests, of that Dream in general.

Both Charlie and Bobby label themselves whores as they flirt with Karen. Fox suggests that Gould should decorate his office as a bordello and come to work in a soiled nightgown. Gould agrees without batting an eye: "after the Doug Brown thing, I come to work in that same nightgown, I say 'kiss the hem,' then every swinging dick in this man's studio will kiss the hem . . . . I'm a whore and I'm proud of it. But I'm a *secure* whore" (33).

Like the "thief" metaphor in *American Buffalo*, this is the central comic metaphor of the play. At the conclusion of *Speed-the-Plow*, Fox suggests that Gould has lost sight of what he *is*: "You're a chippy . . . you're a fuckin' bought-and-paid-for whore, and you think you're a ballerina cause you work with your legs? You're a whore" (94–95). The typical use of the image is reversed: these *men*, like most of us, will prostitute themselves, will violate their most private selves and precious dreams, to pursue an empty vision of success. And, on one level, that's because they see no other option.

Cursing, insults, and violence work in this play in much the same way they do in *American Buffalo*. At first we laugh at the language because it violates a middle class audience's expectations. We're still shocked, vaguely, at the idea that moguls talk like this, as witness this country's recent fascination and largely humorous response to Richard Nixon's language on those tapes. Here, though, our laugh of superiority largely grows out of a claim to moral superiority, I think, as opposed to the largely social superiority in *American Buffalo*. Gradually, as the humor of the situation decreases, as we build toward violence and serious issues of choice, this laughter at the cursing weakens or becomes more tight-lipped.

At the conclusion of that violent scene in Gould's office, Gould finally chooses Fox and his dream over Karen and hers; he sees Karen as failing him. Actually, I would argue, Mamet intends us to see Gould as failing. That understanding of comic ironic intent depends on our vision of the novel by that "sissy Eastern writer," *The Bridge.* Significantly, though not well known, Mamet has published a prose piece with the same title in *Granta.*[2] It's about a man who dreams of watching the nuclear holocaust from a bridge and wakes, gradually, to discover himself on the bridge of an aircraft carrier watching "Huge orange balls, evenly spaced" far in the distance (173). Again, then, with repeated lengthy and comic references to this novel, a parallel for his own short story, at the very least, Mamet is bringing to our attention some ideas of universal or metaphorical import. Several comments in his essays suggest that he agrees with the novel's ideas, even as he pokes fun at the style or presentation of the novel, the vehicle for those ideas, if you will. He certainly likes their tenor, nonetheless.

Most critics would differ, but Frank Rich commented that the "second script and the third character . . . push Mr. Mamet's drama and themes well beyond parochial show-biz satire." Rich goes on to note that "The more fun is poked at 'The Bridge' and its lofty warnings about the end of the world, the more it seems that a religious vision of salvation may be presenting itself to one of the hardened moguls, prompting him to change the world and maybe even to make better movies" (C 17).

Mamet's more direct statements in his essay, "Decay," are quite close to several ideas in *The Bridge.* Mamet writes that the highest purpose of the theater is "to bring to your fellows, through the medium of your understanding and skill, the possibility of communion with what is essential in us all: that we are born to die, that we strive and fail, that we live in ignorance of why we were placed here, and, that in the midst of this we need to love and be loved, but we are afraid" (*WR* 116–117). Theater should "address the question, How can I live in a world in which I am doomed to die?" (117).

Mamet's own answer, like Thackeray's, entails a struggle to recognize the reality of death and decay and a willingness, nonetheless, to fight against it, and to love, and hold firm to moral values. As he concludes for his audience of actors, "to quote Marcus Aurelius again: you receive a bad augury before a battle, *so what?* It's *still* your job to fight" (116). That *job*, à la Thackeray, in the theater, as in the movies, has to do with *refusing* that which is cheap and pandering.

In "Decay" Mamet also writes: "Our civilization is convulsed and dying, and it has not yet gotten the message. It is sinking but it has not sunk into complete barbarity, and I often think that nuclear war exists for no other reason than to spare us that indignity" (116). There is a glimmer of the novel's redemptive vision of radiation even in this 1986 address/essay: "There is a time to accumulate and there is a time to disperse, and the final disassembly is decay, which takes place so that new life may take place" (111). That's an old idea, one present in a good bit of American literature, too—Walt Whitman and Wallace Stevens come to mind—but in a nuclear age it's cast in a new form, both in Mamet's essay and in his theater. In *The Bridge*, Mamet creates a vehicle to confront his audience with "decay," with the "tenuousness of our social state," with the possibility of new purpose and order, and, in context, with a perspective on the world that makes both art and love all the more important—both of which Bobby Gould rejects.

In Act I, we do by and large laugh at the book, because we see it primarily through Bobby's and Charlie's eyes. Labeling it "not quite 'Art' and not quite 'Entertainment,'" Gould gripes to Charlie that he's "inherited a monster" for this courtesy read and proceeds to ridicule as he quotes (1, 2). When we see the book from Karen's perspective, it is no longer so funny—and the lines she quotes echo Mamet's ideas more clearly. The novel's central figure calls for courage and recognizes that "All fears are one fear. Just the fear of death" (63). And there is a healing subtext, that all radiation, "the planes, the television, clocks, all of it is *to the one end. To change us*—to, to *bring about a change*." Karen is paraphrasing and summarizing here, and she concludes "it comes from God" (64). Her interpretation is that the book says that Bobby was "put here to make stories people need to see. To make them less afraid. It says in *spite* of our transgressions—that we could do something. Which would bring us alive. So that we needn't feel ashamed. (*Pause.*) We needn't feel frightened" (79).

That certainly sounds very much like the voice of David Mamet in his essays. The audience at least puzzles over the book, but Gould, away from the studio, has been persuaded to make it and has been convinced that his "life is a sham" and that he should now "do something which is right" (90). After Fox has convinced him otherwise, back at the studio, and has won him over to his vision that Karen is simply "A Tight Pussy wrapped around Ambition" (103), who has taken him for a ride just to get ahead, Fox reads one last line from the book as he kicks Karen out: "The earth burned. But the last man had a vision. . . ." Again, though the language is overblown, the idea of the line is a fine testimony to just the sort of courage and nobility in the face of death or decay which Mamet advocates so eloquently in his own essays and celebrates in his plays.

Part of this understanding of *The Bridge* as both comic object and serious thematic comment or catalyst, depends on a vision of Karen as largely sincere in her affection, both for the book and for Bobby Gould. William A. Henry, III, cites director Gregory Mosher as saying that "The audience is meant to go out asking: Is she an angel? Is she a whore?" (99). In Act I, she's neither; she's a conventional comic stereotype, the dumb, inept, attractive secretary with whom the men toy. Karen's apparent naivete may well be a pose, as may her initial questions as the men strut their stuff for her. Still, three times she asks why the movie business is "garbage," as the men claim. Finally she gets this answer:

> FOX: Why? Why should nickels be bigger than dimes? That's the way it is.
>
> GOULD: It's a business, with its own unchanging rules. Isn't that right, Charlie? (77)

Naive or not, it is Karen who centers our attention on the need and possibility of change. Again, when Karen comes back in after failing to get Bobby's luncheon reservation, Bobby is trying to interest her by boasting of his success with the Doug Brown film. Her response: "Is it a good film?" (53). And Bobby proceeds to summarize the "commodity" system of film production for her. But Karen continues to question, comically to point us toward a truth, and ironically begins her conversion of Bobby. What if there were something good in the book by the sissy Eastern aesthete, is the essence of her question. And Bobby at least jokingly recognizes or admits the error of his ways: "Hey, I prayed to be pure. . . . I did, I said God give me the job as Head of Production. Give me a platform to be "good," and I'll be good. They gave me the job. I'm here one day, and *look* at me: A Big Fat Whore" (57).

Admittedly, this is part of his seduction attempt on one level, but there is also something very real about Bobby's potential for Goodness, here. Whether she is sincere or not, Karen again comically centers our attention on one of Mamet's central themes when she says "I would think that if you could keep your values straight, if you had *principles* to *refer* to, then . . . " (58)—her implication being that one could then make correct decisions. Gould agrees, again partly for the seduction and partly because he is genuinely drawn to her. That leads to his idea of her reading the book and making her report that evening at his home, a traditionally comic set up.

Act II begins, though, with Karen's quoting and summarizing the novel: "He puts his hand on the child's chest, and he says 'heal,' as if he felt he had the power to heal him, he calls on God. . . . the thing which he lacked, he says, was *courage*" (63). The text is funny; the idea is serious. And the passage glosses what's going on in this scene, for, though Karen *is* "promoting" Bobby, she's also trying to heal him, and herself, through love. Ironically and comically, both are trying to seduce the other on a variety of levels, both have ulterior motives, and both could triumph over those motives. There are some great comic bits, here, because of the duality of the action. Karen says "You *know* what I want to do" in response to Bobby's offer to help her (69). Thinking sex, he's taken aback and then comically surprised at her conclusion: "I want to work on the film." But that's not sheer venality, as is emphasized by his own comic mistake of thinking she means the prison film. Her insistence on working with *The Bridge*—"I'd do anything"—is both comically sexual *and* underlines her true feeling for the work she praises. Gould, of course, at this point still resists the film.

His conversion to the film takes place off stage. That conversion is, at least in part, due to his developing love for Karen and his need for her love, not just the casual seduction. Gould's first lines in Act III are "I'm not going to do the film." He's referring to the Doug Brown vehicle and responding to Charlie's long speech, which begins the Act. The gist of Charlie's lines is that he's been up all night worrying about credits, shares of profits, and "Am I worthy to be rich?" This speech is in such marked contrast to Karen's language and ideas at the end of Act II as to make it appear even more venal and shallow than usual. As such, it indirectly comments on the value of Karen's ideas, despite their comic expression. When Charlie finally understands that Gould is not kidding, he asks for reasons. And Gould tells him "I was up all night thinking." But Gould wasn't thinking about money. He was thinking about "why I was called to my new job." And he's decided to make *The Bridge* because "I believe in the ideas that are contained in the book" (88–89).

But back in the studio, in his long-time milieu, Bobby's conversion is not temptation proof. We should recognize, though, that

his "reconversion" to *Fox's* gospel is wrong, that the system is being
indicted both for its destruction of love and art. Fox takes the role of
Teach, here, in a number of ways. His "test" for Karen is a simple one.
Fox asks her "If he had said 'No,' would you have gone to bed with
him?" (102). Karen at first refuses to answer, and then Gould
paraphrases the question himself.

Karen answers the question truthfully, and that "No" distresses
Bobby so horribly that he finally rejects her. The climax of this scene,
Bobby's decision, is sudden and subtle in the text. Karen says, "Bob,
we have a meeting" (105). That does it. Coming from Karen's mouth,
ironically, the logic Bobby always accepts from Fox hits him hard. His
conclusion is that the film is *all* that Karen is interested in. Fox says,
"I rest my case," and Gould goes off to change his shirt for his and
Fox's meeting with Ross, chillingly dismissing her: "We're rather busy
now. You'll excuse me. Mr. Fox will show you out."

By now, we are no longer laughing. A serious loss has occurred.
Fox has won. Bobby has reverted, and he's done so out of fear, the fear
that she has indeed "loved" him only for what he could do for her. But
Karen's wish for herself and for Bobby Gould is that they produce the
good ideas they have found in *The Bridge*, not the *garbage* Doug Brown
film, which she has rejected. Charlie's friendship, on the other hand, is
almost totally shallow, venal, and hopeless of change.

The concluding pages blend comedy and a tremendous sadness.
Karen is sincere in her conclusion "I don't belong here" (106). That
suggests a recognition of the triumph of the venal in this social
structure, and the defeat of the comic emblem of art and of love in the
face of fear and decay. Bobby and Charlie do belong here, and they
continue to struggle in this incredibly warped system, where it's an
anomaly to produce a film based on ideas one believes. As Fox and
Gould head up for their long-awaited meeting with Ross, Bobby is
already nostalgic for Karen: "She told me I was a good man." Fox tells
him that such "grace" is not for him. And we're sorry that Gould's
choice has been the wrong one.

Still, the play's final lines ironically echo the Thackeray
epigraph:

> FOX: . . . Bob? After everything is said and done.
>   What are we put on earth to do?
> GOULD: We're here to make a movie.
> FOX: Whose name goes above the title?

GOULD: Fox and Gould.
FOX: Then how bad can life be? (108)

The play's final question is for the audience. And its answer, I think, is that making a movie, "some work upon the ground" is good in itself. But the question also comically suggests that that "truth" of Fox and Gould, of the American dream in general, could be much better, could change, could include the kind of love that Karen and the novel offer in the face of decay.

The last lines of Mamet's own prose piece, "The Bridge," describe his narrator watching "Huge orange balls, evenly spaced. He knew that they were protective devices and were linked together—though he could not see the links" (173). The narrator has faith that there is a pattern, an order, in the universe, even though he cannot see it or understand it. The conclusion of the prose piece clearly echoes the last lines of the novel quoted in *Speed-the-Plow*, the reference to the last man's vision in the face of nuclear destruction.

Mamet's comedy and his use of humor are both ironic and complex. We return to an order, of sorts, at the end of a Mamet play, though we often laugh at that order as wrong-headed. But there is always a vision of needed change implied by Mamet's ironic humor, coupled with a tremendous love for his characters and for humankind in general. Henry, in his review of *Speed-the-Plow*, writes that the title "appears to derive from a blessing in medieval verse and song, "God speed your plough." He goes on to note that according to Ron Silver, "it means, approximately: 'Do your work and God will help you.'" That title, too, as Mosher points out, also "has to do with turning fresh earth—and of course there is a sexual pun" (98). The title is typical of Mamet's comedy and humor in general. It reverberates; it's thematic, entertaining, and funny. In this instance, finally, it's both a prayer and an indirect statement of faith in both the divine and the human. Mamet's comedy and humor are "moralistic," but it is a subtle, ambiguous moralism, not overtly didactic. That we laugh, with him, at his characters, and at ourselves, is a huge part of our enjoyment in response to a Mamet play, and that laughter points toward the celebration of life at the core of all of Mamet's work. That this most talented of contemporary American playwrights is comically evoking a religious vision I find wonderfully ironic. In another of Mr. Booth's felicitous phrases, David Mamet is definitely among the company we can keep with deep, even ethical, pleasure.

Notes

1. Hans Robert Jauss' work on a "receptional aesthetic" elucidates this pattern, but space prohibits developing this idea. See my essay, "Intended Audience Response, *The Homecoming*, and the 'Ironic Mode of Identification'" in *Harold Pinter: Critical Approaches*, ed. Steven H. Gale (Rutherford, N.J.: Fairleigh Dickinson University Press, 1986), pp. 102–117, for a discussion of this aesthetic. After defining his fifth category of audience response, "the ironic mode of identification," Jauss argues that an audience denied normative identification can respond to negative examples either with laughter and derision or with "norm breaking intensity," as intended—that is with a positive revolt from behavior newly recognized as negative but commonplace. See Hans Robert Jauss, "Literary History as a Challenge to Literary Theory," trans. Elizabeth Benzinger, *New Literary History*, 2 (1970–71): 7–37; more specifically relevant, Jauss, "Levels of Identification of Hero and Audience," trans. Benjamin and Helga Bennett, *New Literary History*, 5 (1973–74): 313, 314, 316. For an interesting alternative perspective, see Richard M. Coe, "Beyond Absurdity: Albee's Awareness of Audience in *Tiny Alice*," *Modern Drama*, 18 (1975): 371, where he argues that the ordinary theatergoer cannot identify with "grotesque characters."

2. Many thanks to a gracious and thoughtful Leslie Kane, both for passing along information from Ruby Cohn on the *Granta* prose piece and for providing me with a copy of the unpublished script of *Bobby Gould in Hell*.

Works Cited

Bentley, Eric. *The Life of the Drama.* New York: Atheneum, 1964.

Bigsby, C. W. E. *David Mamet.* Contemporary Writers, ed. Malcolm Bradbury and Christopher Bigsby. London: Methuen, 1985.

Blau, Herbert. *The Impossible Theater: A Manifesto.* New York: Collier, 1965.

Booth, Wayne C. *A Rhetoric of Irony.* Chicago: University of Chicago, 1974.

Carroll, Dennis. *David Mamet.* New York: St. Martin's, 1987.

Corrigan, Robert W. "Comedy and the Comic Spirit." Introduction to *Comedy: Meaning and Form.* Ed. Robert W. Corrigan. San Francisco: Chandler, 1965.

Dean, Anne. *David Mamet: Language as Dramatic Action.* Rutherford, N.J.: Fairleigh Dickinson University, 1990.

De Palma, Brian. *The Untouchables.* With Kevin Costner, Sean Connery, Robert De Niro. Script by David Mamet. Paramount, 1987.

Freedman, Samuel G. "The Gritty Eloquence of David Mamet." *New York Times Magazine* 21 April 1985, pp. 32–64.

Gussow, Mel. "The Daring Vision of Four New Playwrights." *New York Times,* 13 Feb. 1977, Sec. B: 1, 9, 13, 14.

Henry, William A., III. "Madonna Comes to Broadway." *Time,* 16 May 1988, pp. 98–99.

McMaster, Juliet. *Thackeray: The Major Novels.* Toronto: Univ. of Tornoto, 1976.

Mamet, David. *American Buffalo.* New York: Grove, 1977.

———. "The Bridge." *Granta* 16 (Summer 1985): 168–173.

———. "Conventional Warfare." In *Some Freaks.* New York: Viking, 1989, pp. 1–6.

———. "Decay: Some Thoughts for Actors, Theodore Spencer Memorial Lecture, Harvard, Feb. 10, 1986." In *Writing in Restaurants.* New York: Viking, 1986, pp. 110–117.

———. "The Decoration of Jewish Houses." In *Some Freaks*, pp. 7–14.

———. "First Principles." In *Writing in Restaurants*, pp. 24–27.

———. *Glengarry Glen Ross.* New York: Grove, 1982.

———. "In the Company of Men." In *Some Freaks*, pp. 85–91.

———. "A National Dream Life." In *Writing in Restaurants*, pp. 8–11.

———. "Observations of a Backstage Wife." In *Writing in Restaurants*, pp. 142–60.

———. "On Paul Ickovic's Photographs." In *Writing in Restaurants*, pp. 73–74.

———. "A Plain Brown Wrapper." In *Some Freaks*, pp. 15–20.

———. "A Playwright in Hollywood." In *Writing in Restaurants*, pp. 75–79.

———. *Some Freaks.* New York: Viking, 1989.

———. "Some Thoughts on Writing in Restaurants." In *Writing in Restaurants*, pp. 34–38.

———. *Speed-the-Plow.* New York: Grove, 1985.

———. *Writing in Restaurants.* New York: Viking, 1986.

Montagu, Ashley. *The Anatomy of Swearing.* New York: Macmillan, 1967.

Rich, Frank. "Mamet's Dark View of Hollywood As a Heaven for the Virtueless." *New York Times*, 4 May 1988: Sec. C. p. 17.

Schvey, Henry I. "The Plays of David Mamet: Games of Manipulation and Power." *New Theatre Quarterly* 13 (1988): 77–89.

Sharman, Julian. *A Cursory History of Swearing.* Rpt. from the 1884 original. New York: Burt Franklin, 1968.

Wetzsteon, Ross. "Theatre Journal—David Mamet: Remember That Name." *Village Voice*, 5 July 1976: pp. 101, 103, 104.

INTERVIEW WITH GREGORY MOSHER

Leslie Kane

Gregory Mosher began his career in Chicago in 1974 as director of the Goodman Theatre's Stage 2. During his eleven years at the Goodman, where he served as its Artistic Director from 1978–1985, Mosher directed or produced more than eighty plays, half of which were world or American premieres, including works by Edward Albee, David Rabe, John Guare, Michael Weller, Tennessee Williams, and David Mamet, with whom he has enjoyed a significant and mutually rewarding relationship.

Respected for his seamless staging, dynamic directions, spare, stylized productions and commitment to a writer's theatre, Mosher has directed most of the premieres of Mamet's plays including *American Buffalo, A Life in the Theatre, Edmond,* for which he won an Obie, the Pulitzer-Prize-winning *Glengarry Glen Ross* (American premiere), *Speed-the-Plow,* and most recently, *Bobby Gould in Hell,* affording Mamet a security few playwrights enjoy.

The interview with Gregory Mosher took place on May 16, 1990, in Mosher's office at Lincoln Center, where since 1986 he has served as its Director. Mosher is a warm, soft-spoken, self-effacing man whose admiration for David Mamet is immediately apparent. While our conversation focused on their association of fifteen years, it was continually punctuated by Mosher's extensive knowledge of contemporary theatre and by his reminiscences and humor.

Kane: You originally went to the Goodman in 1974 as director of its Second Stage. How did you meet and begin working with David Mamet?

Mosher: It was just a fluke. I came to Chicago to work with a guy named Bill Woodman, who I had known from Juilliard, and David brought his theater company back to Chicago, where he grew up, from Goddard, where he was going to school, and started the St. Nicholas Theatre Company. And we were just, you know. . . . I was twenty-five and he was twenty-six, and we were trying to get on with our careers, and we bumped into each other. It was not an arranged marriage.

Kane: I didn't think it was an arranged marriage, but it was fortuitous, certainly.

Mosher: It was amazingly fortuitous for me, certainly.

Kane: When you were appointed Artistic Director of the Goodman in 1974, you appointed David Mamet Associate Director. What did you think that David Mamet would add to the Goodman?

Mosher: Well, I thought he would add two things. Well, many things: one, his just great taste about what is a good play and what isn't a good play. And I'm still learning that. When you're a young director and producer, you make a lot of mistakes. You fall for things all the time. You fall in love with a bad play. So, David was there to kind of catch me. Sometimes he would say, "I think this is a bad play," and I would say, "I think you're wrong." And almost invariably he turned out to be right. The play was just not seaworthy, and it would sink somewhere about the third week of rehearsal. He was there as a general aesthetic conscience and to remind one why one was doing this, which was not to earn the love and admiration of the subscribers. It was not to get good reviews. It was to pursue this abstract thing of artistic expression. He was also there as a signal to the Chicago community that this was going to be a writer's theater, a Chicago theater, and a contemporary theater, and that any museum aspects that were left over at the Goodman would be eliminated. Not from Bill Woodman, because I really want to emphasize that Bill was the first guy in decades to do premieres, to bring Edward Bond and Brian Friel into the theater. Bill also started using the Chicago acting community extensively, so that what I did was an extension of what he did. But David was really the fulfillment of that whole idea.

Kane: What is it about the Chicago-trained actor, or actors who were working in Chicago, that made you want to work with them then and also continue in many cases to work with them now?

Mosher: Well, they're just good. I mean there was an unspoken assumption that New York actors were better than Chicago actors. It was classic. American actors feel that about English actors; so do a lot of American producers. When I first went to Chicago, I felt that I didn't understand the city. I would look at the Organic Theatre, and I would say that this doesn't look like the theater, because it certainly didn't look like what I had seen on Broadway, or even off-Broadway. New York theater's main influences are the English and the Actor's Studio, home of the Method. Chicago is another point on the compass. Ultimately, if you take the best of these schools, they're going to be just fine with each other. If you put Laurence Olivier and Marlon Brando and Joe Mantegna on stage together, they would immediately have—with a good director—a unified production. Once you're not talking about geniuses, it's a little harder to make it combine. I like Chicago acting because it's simple and emotional without being indulgent. It's never about wearing emotion on your sleeve. It's about getting on with the play. And a lot of that comes from Second City sketches. What I love about it is that it leaves so much to the audience's imagination. The point is not that we do a play on a bare stage. The point is that the audience fills it in. They actually do the work.

Kane: Typically a Gregory Mosher production is expressionistically stripped, except, for example, a few artifacts of acting in *A Life in the Theatre* or a few cups in *Glengarry*. How do you account for the more realistic, cluttered stage in *American Buffalo,* which was your first production?

Mosher: Well, I never thought of *American Buffalo* as being realistic. I think the set budget for *American Buffalo* was $100; and furthermore, it was done in a rehearsal room at the Ruth Page Auditorium, which we were using for the Goodman Mainstage shows. So, in the day we would rehearse the Mainstage shows and at night we would perform the second stage shows. And, so not only did it have to cost no money, it had to be able to be stripped every day. There were all these chairs at the Ruth Page Auditorium, which used to be a Moose Lodge, and so I thought, we'll build the set out of chairs—hundreds of metal chairs—and that will be the back wall. So it was probably, in fact, the most abstract set that Michael Merritt and I ever created together. I have the drawing here somewhere which shows the chairs sort of hanging in the air, hanging in a sort of terrific pattern. So, that was that. We didn't give it a lot of thought at the time, but I knew very specifically that it shouldn't be realistic, and that it shouldn't look like a set that you'd have in a television show. I did do a realistic set in New York when the play opened at St. Clement's (which was the first New York production in 1976), that had actual walls and a real doorway, and I thought that it was horrible, really, really bad. It hurt the play terribly.

Kane: Several playwrights, August Wilson, Sam Shepard, and Harold Pinter, have worked with the same director or the same theatre. Do you and Mamet have an "honor system" whereby he offers you everything he writes and you choose to direct everything that he offers you?

Mosher: No. David has never been under any obligation. He may have felt one internally, but I have never tried to impose that feeling on him. I used to be hurt when he wanted his plays done somewhere else, or when he wanted somebody else to direct them, or even when he wanted to direct them himself. But that was when I was young and vulnerable. I've never *not* wanted to do a play David wrote. Actually, that's not true. I turned down *The Water Engine*, which he showed me right after *American Buffalo*. I didn't quite get it when I read it, and it was stupid of me.

Kane: I saw it at the Public Theatre when it was directed by Steven Schacter.

Mosher: Well, when Steve did it in Chicago with Bill Macy, that was the show. It was truly weird, a brilliant and astounding fable, and it was more of a satire in New York, somehow. Same director, same intention, but a different audience, different leading actor, different expectations. David's always been seen as a comic writer in New York, which of course he is—one of the great writers of comedy ever in the American theater. But, in Chicago, we don't think of him as a comic writer, in particular. We know he's a funny writer, but we always understand that his purpose is serious, and in New York it's taken ten years now really to understand the essential seriousness of these plays.

Kane: Can I ask you a troubling question regarding *Lone Canoe?* Were you able to foresee that *Lone Canoe* was going to be a disaster?

Mosher: No. David and I were very much influenced by Bruno Bettelheim's *The Uses of Enchantment*, which was published about a year before we did *Lone Canoe*. David had just begun to achieve real national recognition in theatre circles as the genius he is. His life was changing, and so rather than write another play like *American Buffalo*— you know, three tough guys talking dirty—he wanted to write a fable. And it turned out that the fable that he wanted to write was about the price of fame. So we said, "we'll do a story that six-year-olds can understand and will love." You can't take a six-year-old to *American Buffalo*; I suppose you could now, but you couldn't then. So, we did it. We had this set that was inspired by Vakhtangov, a great Russian director and protégé of Stanislavsky's. Between the fable and the Vakhtangov set design, we got to opening night, and we had four hundred critics—two hundred critics and their guests—in a seven-hundred seat theatre and it was impossible. And a sort of riot broke out. All during previews some people liked the play and some people didn't like the play, but in general it mystified everyone and it delighted a lot of people. But after opening night, it was just wild. People wrote that we had disgraced Chicago in the eyes of the nation.

Kane: Because it was a quasi-musical and it was so different from the rest of the work Mamet had done?

Mosher: Well, people said "thee" and "thou;" and that side of David is just as important as the motherfucker side of David—the two strains in him. So, that's the story of *Lone Canoe*. It became an easy joke, because there were people who were jealous of David. There were people who didn't take David seriously, because he was from Chicago. There were people *in* Chicago who didn't take him seriously, because he was from Chicago—people who thought that both of us were arrogant punks and thank God we had gotten our come-uppance. But, they were basically second-rate people. Fuck 'em. What was alarming about *Lone Canoe* was not that it failed, because we both had a lot of failure in our lives, but that we were expected to join in on the joke. For years people would come up at board meetings or public gatherings and kind of give you an elbow in the ribs and say, "Hey, I saw a play the other day that was almost as bad as *Lone Canoe*." And all you could think was, "Well, you're an insensitive boor, aren't you?" So that was that.

Kane: Mamet's favorite production is your *Edmond* production at the Goodman in 1981. What was it about that production that you think impressed him so much?

Mosher: Well, it was just great acting from eleven actors playing twenty-five parts—and a stunning performance from Colin Stinton. And, I think he hadn't seen it along the way. He was in New York through rehearsals, and rather than watching us struggle and get scenes wrong ten times before we got them right, by the time he saw it, it was really working. So, instead of trial and error cul-de-sac failed rehearsals that are just part of the rehearsal process, chasing down blind alleys for four hours, it was, "Wow, look at what you did with my play." It's wonderful, I'm sure, when you are a writer and you come in and say, "*that's* what I meant; that's good." But, it's a great, great play. It's easy to say that plays are ahead of their time, but that truly was way ahead of its time.

Kane: I've yet to see a production, but it's incredibly powerful to read.

Mosher: Stunningly powerful, and now it makes complete sense. It is a play about Bensonhurst and about exploding hatred. He just got there first, and people thought he had lost his mind and was exaggerating horribly. But, of course, what playwrights do is to imagine the future, somehow. I think the hard part about being a writer, and all the really good writers that I know have this, is not the ability to write it down. What they all have is the ability to *see* the culture and *see* things that are right in front of your nose, but that nobody else has noticed. That's the tricky part. And that's what was great about O'Neill. O'Neill couldn't write a line of dialogue if you put a gun to his head, but he sure looked out at America, and he said at the turn of the century, "We blew it. It doesn't work. The American Dream failed. It's a tragedy, America." A few years after the presidency of Teddy Roosevelt, and what was about to become the "American Century," here was a guy saying, "No, no, no. I don't care how optimistic you guys are. I don't care what kind of empire you think the United States is going to create. I don't care that the United States's entry into World War I made victory possible. It doesn't matter. I look at this country and I see tragedy." So anyway, David has that, or O'Neill has David's gift, or vice versa, and it's what Miller has or Guare or Richard Nelson or Albee has. And anyone that I particularly admire, like Wally Shawn. As David says in *The Shawl*, "to be clairvoyant is simply to see clearly." It's not about reading the future. It's about just seeing clearly, unimpeded by this barrage of opinion that comes at you every day. Being able to see through it.

Kane: Yet, so much of what works in *The Shawl* is mystification.

Mosher: Yes, of course. A play only works when there is a great deal of paradox and ambiguity. The minute you can say who the good guy is in *Speed-the-Plow*, the minute you can say whether Edmond is a good guy or not, there's no play there. You can say who the protagonist is; that's quite clear. But, is he a good man? Well, why do the play if the answer to that is obvious in the first minute? Does he want to be a good man? Yeah, I think every one of David's protagonists wants to be a good man. They're just faced with impossible choices. The choice of the protagonist in *Speed-the-Plow* is: am I faithful to my best friend or am I faithful to myself?

Kane: Faithfulness to best friend is a theme that may be traced from Mamet's earliest plays to his most recent screenplays.

Mosher: Yeah, loyalty is tremendously important. I mean, there are *great* speeches about loyalty in *American Buffalo*.

Kane: Is this a result of the relationship that you have had with him— or that he has with the actors—or do you think that it is a personal value?

Mosher: I think the idea of loyalty is absolutely important to him personally. He is the most loyal person I have ever met. I'm sure that he would literally die for you, and he inspires that feeling in other people. He's loyal about little things; he's loyal about huge things. It's just very important to him. So, when you have a conflicting loyalty, when the loyalty to your best friend—whoever that best friend is, your pal or your spouse—it doesn't matter; it's just a metaphor for the play. That's about as high as it gets. The only thing that could possibly transcend that would be being loyal to yourself or being loyal to God, which is the same thing. And that's the dilemma. There is no right answer for Bobby Gould. That's what makes *Speed-the-Plow* a good play.

Kane: To a varying degree all of Mamet's plays introduce a schism between what a character says and what he does. Mamet scripts are notable for their paucity of stage instructions. How do you implement and emphasize this schism, particularly in the lyrical plays?

Mosher: That's very simple. We'll just take a couple of random words. They're not from a David Mamet play, although they could come from *Sexual Perversity*. "Hi, come here often?" "Only when my husband and I are visiting our in-laws." Now, those are the two lines of dialogue. They would seem to be about social habits or travel plans, or something. That's what the text is about. We're both laughing because it is so obviously a pick-up line and a rebuff to a pick-up line. So, what you stage is the pick-up, not the travel inquiry. You can't stage the text; you can only stage the action. You can stage his trying to pick the woman up; you can stage her rebuffing him. And you can stage it with enormous subtlety and sophistication. The pick-up line can be sophisticated or crude, and the rebuff can be sophisticated or crude, regardless of the text. She can pour a drink down the front of his pants and say the line sweetly. That's what the rehearsal is: always to find the action underneath. Now, this is not exactly the same thing as the subtext. Subtext usually refers to what people are feeling: I'm excited, I'm horny, I'm sad, I'm lonely. Do you understand what I mean? Directing is the process of deciding, according to what you think the playwright's intentions are, what the series of actions are in the course of the play.

Kane: Joe Mantegna has said about David Mamet that "he knows what he wants and knows where he is going." Does that make your job as director more difficult?

Mosher: Oh no, that makes it easier. What he means by that is that he knows what the guy wants. *What* the guy wants, that's what the action is. It's really hard in *Speed-the-Plow*, because what the guy wants is to do the right thing. Now, the audience has to decide at the end of the play whether he did the right thing. We go to *Glengarry*, and it's easier. What the guy wants to do is sell real estate.

Kane: He doesn't want to save his neck?

Mosher: In *Glengarry*? No, the guy's harder than that. It's just that he's—I don't know what the phrase is that we used because that was seven years ago—but they all had a phrase. That play was about a bunch of people; each one of them was just maximizing their power. A crucial line in the play was the customer saying, "I don't have the power." So, it was about who's got the power and who can get the most power. When I first staged the play, I thought I had staged it quite well. We were opening in Chicago, the reviews were great, the audience was loving it. But, David was very unhappy with the production, and I didn't know why. And he didn't know why. Then he wrote me a long letter, and he said, "look, this is not a play about love. *American Buffalo* is a play about love; *A Life in the Theatre* is a play about love. This is a play about power. This is a play about guys, who when one guy is down, the other guy doesn't extend a hand to help him back up. This is a play where the guy who's up then kicks the other guy in the balls to make sure that he stays down. That's not what's happening on stage, and you have to find a way to make it happen." That was easy. Once I knew what aspect of his intentions were not being served by the production, it was simple. Six hours of rehearsal. But, sometimes you don't know what it is that you've missed in the production.

Kane: Is his collaboration generally in the form of a letter?

Mosher: That was unusual. We were in different cities, and I think it may have been easier for him to organize a very complicated series of thoughts on the page, rather than over the telephone, which is what it would have been. He's always felt free—I've always tried to encourage him to feel free—to say whatever he wants about the production. He knows that ultimately he has the final say on what the actors say, and I have have the ultimate say on how they say it, or any other aspect of the production. But, it's so collegial now that it's hard to know where one of us stops and the other starts. I don't mean to imply that I have anything to do with the text, because I have absolutely zero skill in that regard, but I frequently turn rehearsals over to him now. I don't need to be running rehearsals in order to feel in charge of the production. And it's easier than my translating what he says. You know, there are very carefully created, and usually carefully observed, conventions in the theater. The playwright does not speak to the actors. It's just not done. Nobody speaks to the actors except the director. And, so if the playwright has a comment, he says it to the director, and the director says it. Now, this, of course, is always whispered or said in private in another room. So, for years, Dave said, "Greg, can I talk to you. . . ." So, finally I said, "Just say it. If I disagree, I'll tell you." I'm not worried about the disagreement. That's the nice thing about working with him. And then if it's Mantegna, or Macy, or Stinton, then it's like family; we have spent literally thousands of hours together in rehearsal rooms and bars.

Kane: That was one of my questions regarding your working with Joe Mantegna, W. H. Macy and J. J. Johnston in numerous productions. How do you achieve unity of language in a production with a Ron Silver or a Treat Williams, who is not familiar with "Mamet language," as you call it?

Mosher: They just come to it. I mean there's no overt attempt to teach them. It becomes magnetic north, and people are just drawn to it. But, then you don't have Ron in the show or Treat in the show unless you think he's sympathetic to it. It's not like there's some dogma or some technique, really. When you're dealing with actors as good as those two guys are, you don't worry about it. It's not acting class. It's not my job to teach Treat or Ron or anybody else that accomplished how to act or to give them another way of doing it. It's simply my job to make sure that David's intentions are fulfilled. We'll all get there together. Everyone wants to cooperate. If somebody doesn't want to cooperate, well, he should go be in another production.

Kane: You have said a number of times that it is the role of the director, designer and actor to serve the intentions of the playwright. Do you then cede artistic decisions and authority to the playwright in terms of casting or design?

Mosher: It depends from playwright to playwright. If we're talking about David, not only do I want his intentions to be served, I usually also want him to be happy, because he doesn't do these things to get rich. Having pleasure in the work is very important for all of us. I don't mean that you're not exasperated and frustrated and depressed during the process of creating something. That happens, but there is also enormous pleasure in that process and the results of it. So, it's not ceding authority, but I do confer with him a lot, yes. It's so understood that we'll do that.

Kane: When you left the Goodman to become Director of Lincoln Center in 1985, your first production was a Mamet double-bill, *Prairie du Chien* and *The Shawl*. It received a somewhat chilly reception. Were you surprised, given your success at the Goodman?

Mosher: No. It got a chilly reception from people who have traditionally given chilly receptions to David's plays. The Pacino version of *American Buffalo* did very well, but it didn't get a good *Times* notice; *Glengarry* was panned by *The New York Times*. People forget that, but it was only the Pulitzer Prize that allowed that play to run. But, otherwise it got good reviews. Joe Mantegna was ignored in *The New York Times* review, a performance for which he won the Tony. So no, I don't expect critics to like the plays. I knew that it was important that we were starting here. The theatre had been dark for five years. I thought, well, who do you go with if it's opening? If you're managing the Mets and it's the first day of the season, you go with (Dwight) Gooden. You put the guy on the mound. You got Kareem (Abdul Jabbar), you play Kareem. He's your guy. So, when I came here, I knew it was going to be David's theatre as much as it was mine. The plays were beautiful and wonderful and magical. They were thrilling. The first words of this theatre when it reopened were spoken by a man called the Storyteller (well, the actual first words were spoken by Bill Macy—"cut," he said in a game of cards), and then the character named the Storyteller began, and he told a story. Then, in the second play, Mike Nussbaum played a man who has magical power, like Prospero. What do you do with a strange kind of power? Do you make money with it, do you exploit it, do you abuse it, do you cheat, do you magnify it? So, this clairvoyant's assistant is consistently saying, "Let's go out and make some money," and the guy's saying, "No, I have to respect this power, which I don't even understand, although it's inside me." So, it's a metaphor for reopening the theater. It was a metaphor for artistic creation. The plays were modest; by that I mean that they weren't billion dollar productions. They were beautifully acted and beautifully designed. They were a great signal. It was totally unimportant to me how they were received. If I were going to get fired after one show, I'd rather be fired after doing one of David's plays, than after doing a play of William Shakespeare's or Eugene O'Neill's.

Kane: Many critics have said that Mamet's recent plays, particularly *Speed-the-Plow,* are more cynical than his previous work. I find a contradiction between Mamet's apparent quest for ethnic identity and spirituality expressed in recent essays and criticism about Mamet's growing cynicism. Would you comment?

Mosher: Well, I think that David is an extremely spiritual person, who's very plugged in to the day-to-day world. He understands scoundrels. But, he's not being a satirist when he writes about God or characters looking for God. In *Speed-the-Plow* Karen says to Bobby Gould, "You prayed to be pure." He says, "I was kidding." She says, "No you weren't; I looked in your heart." Of course he prayed to be pure. I don't want to speak for David, and you can't reduce the plays to one message, but one of the things that characterizes David—what makes David David—are his contradictions. He is many times the most courtly, gentlemanly guy you could imagine; other times he's terrifying. You see raw strength coming out of him. It's not that one of them is him, and the other is an act or a mask. They are both him. A guy who's at home reading Aristotle is no more or less the guy in his backyard shooting tin cans, or taking his daughter on a vacation. They're all Dave. And yet, certain things unite the plays, thematically, of course. One of these things is trying to do good in a bad world. You see it in *The Untouchables.* We've got gangsters, and we've got a hero who says, "We have become what we beheld."

Kane: *Bobby Gould in Hell*, like so many other Mamet stage and screenplays, situates two con men center stage. How do you make each of these productions unique?

Mosher: Oh, David did that. I don't have to do it. It never occurs to me about how to make this production different from the last one. I swear to God. Sometimes you're in the middle of something and think, "Oh shit, that's just like the last time," but that's just technical. That's like adjusting your tie in the morning or adjusting your shoelaces. It's not about anything important. Those are tiny, tiny details that you've repeated. No, it never occurs to me how to make the productions different, because the plays are different. I can see you don't believe me, but it's true.

Kane: I believe you, but I think that you're also self-effacing. I think you're giving credit to Mamet where there may, in fact, be much more input from you than you are acknowledging.

Mosher: No. I've got to say that it seemed absolutely obvious to me that the only way to do *Bobby Gould in Hell* was in an English drawing room.

Kane: Which is wonderful, considering that *Edmond,* Mamet's other portrait of Hell, was set in New York City.

Mosher: I don't know why it was clear to me that *Bobby Gould in Hell* should be set in a drawing room. All it says is "The Devil's Office." That's the only stage direction. It could have been a high tech office. I can tell you all the reasons that it's not a high tech office, but they have to do with me, not with David. They have to do with my understanding of what David's intention was in the play, which is not to satirize yuppies. The minute you put the guy in a Rolex, the minute the guy looks like the guy on Wall Street, then the audience thinks they know what the play is about before they watched the play. You put it in a drawing room, the audience, I hope their response is "Hmmmm." The moment when they figure out that Bill Macy—this man in fishing drag—is the Devil, it's just a great moment. They all figure it out at slightly different times in the first thirty seconds of the play, and it was infinitely more satisfying to me than one big laugh when they figured out that it was the Devil. I like that. I like playing *up* to the audience. I like treating the audience as smart, because then they'll act smart.

Kane: Well, wasn't your intention at the Goodman—and I presume at Lincoln Center, as well—to challenge the audience? Do you think that the audience can be challenged to improve society or do you simply want to challenge their moral values?

Mosher: I don't want to challenge the audience. First of all, it's not my job to do anything except stage the play. But I don't think David wants to challenge the audience any more than James Joyce or William Shakespeare wanted to challenge the audience. I think these people just have something they need to express the way you or I need to scratch when it itches. That's what they *do*. Some peculiar combination of DNA and their childhood made them need to express themselves. Call it God who gave them this talent. Now, if they alter this God-given ability to push a paint brush around, or to write dialogue, or to take photographs, you know, well then, great. That's another step up. If they have a unique take on the world, that's another step up. I think it's all afterwards when you're in the interview that somebody says, "Did you want to challenge the audience?" and you say, "Well, yes," and then they say, "David Mamet, famous for wanting to challenge. . . ." You know what I mean?

Kane: I was responding to your previous comment that if you force the audience to think, then they will act smart.

Mosher: Yes, but you don't have to force them, just as you don't have to force somebody to appreciate a good meal. You just serve the good meal.

Kane: Although you have produced Arthur Miller, Edward Albee, David Rabe, and Michael Weller, you have realized what appears to be a mutually rewarding relationship with David Mamet for fifteen years. What can we expect in the future?

Mosher: Well, the BBC production of David's adaptation of *Uncle Vanya*. And when he writes another play. And we're trying to make a movie of *Edmond*, so if there are any film producers reading this book, please give us money.

Kane: I was not aware that you were involved in his film career.

Mosher: Well, I'm not, up to now. We're trying to make a movie of *Edmond*, which I think will obviously make a great, great movie. David tends to talk to me about the film scripts, anyway, and never talk about the plays. Suddenly, a play arrives in the mail or I get a phone call from David: "You're going to get a play tomorrow." I say, "when were you writing a play?" and he says, "I've been kind of working on it." And there is this complete ready-to-go play.

Kane: Didn't *A Life in the Theatre*, which is dedicated to you, arrive as a welcome surprise in this manner when you were at the Goodman?

Mosher: Right. I think that the play is dedicated to me because it's the only one in which I was involved in the structure. *A Life in the Theatre* was set all over town. It was set in a Chinese restaurant, and in a gym, and in an office, and in another restaurant, and backstage—in all these places. I sort of had the idea that you could set it all in a theater. You didn't have to go to a Chinese restaurant; you could eat Chinese take-out. It was fun. You always long for the old days. There was Nussbaum, and Mantegna, and me, and Dave, and the great Tommy Biscotto, a stage manager we all loved in Chicago who died of AIDS—the first guy I knew who died of AIDS, before AIDS was AIDS. And, there we were at The Ruth Page Auditorium. Five feet of snow in Chicago, forty below, and we're the only people out on the streets. No buses. No taxis. No subways. We were rehearsing this play that we loved and going out into the night through these snowdrifts. That, to me, is happiness.

Kane: And yet, you all began to move in different directions. In fact, Mamet has suggested that it would be unnatural—indeed, unhealthy—if you all didn't begin to develop independently and move away from connections of your youth. I was wondering if that is why you assumed the position of Director at Lincoln Center?

Mosher: Well, I had been at the Goodman for eleven years. Enough was enough. I'm from the East, so to me this was just coming home.

Kane: But, it was also quite a challenge to take on Lincoln Center. It's had an uneven history.

Mosher: I didn't want this particular job. I knew it was time to leave Chicago. I didn't want this job, especially, but John Lindsay was very persuasive, and I was a great admirer of John. And ultimately, it was one of those things you had to do, because the rest of your life you would have wondered what would have happened if you didn't do it.

Kane: I thought that there may have been an affiliation with Juilliard that you wanted to resume.

Mosher: No. It's never been a fortuitous relationship. I don't know what the future will bring.

Kane: It does seem, however, that David Mamet has been extraordinarily prolific and promises to continue to be so.

Mosher: One of the things that separates the men from the boys here is, can you *keep* writing. There are a lot of one play playwrights or two play playwrights. There are *very* few writers who keep writing.

Kane: In the American theater, Arthur Miller and Tennessee Williams immediately come to mind.

Mosher: Sure, but one of the reasons we say Arthur and Tennessee is that they kept writing unlike—who's a great one-play playwright?— Tad Mosel. Who's another one-play playwright? Funny, I can't think of one right now.

Kane: I can't think of too many, not ones that I teach or ones that you have staged.

Mosher: That's the point. Ibsen wrote thirty-eight plays; Shakespeare wrote thirty-seven plays; Molière wrote God knows how many plays. It's fun for David. I think he loves being in the rehearsal room; he loves actors. It's showbizzy to say that, but he does. Actors delight him, I think, the way they delight Hamlet.

Kane: Because of his personal frustration in acting or because he takes pleasure in providing the material?

Mosher: Everything. If David were here, he'd say, "I like it because they still smoke." It's family; it's joking. The level of joking among people, that sort of gang, those of us who all knew each other before anybody was famous, before Joey was famous, before David was famous. I can't tell you how funny rehearsal is, and the level of abuse that goes on. It's a real privilege that you feel doing it. As a kid, my fantasy was never to win Tony awards. It was to have a family of colleagues. That's the great thing. It's not about anything else, really. It's just about that: to still be doing it, to still have it make you laugh.

INTERVIEW WITH JOE MANTEGNA

Leslie Kane

Trained for the stage at the Goodman School of Drama in 1967–68, Joe Mantegna made his professional stage debut in 1969 at the Shubert Theatre in Chicago as Berger in *Hair*. A member of the Organic Theatre in Chicago for five years, Mantegna's early stage appearances include Judas in *Godspell*, Decker in *Bleacher Bums* (which he co-wrote), and *Huckleberry Finn*. Mantegna first appeared in a Mamet production in 1977 as John in *A Life in the Theatre*. His principal stage roles include Ricky Roma in *Glengarry Glen Ross* (1984) and Bobby Gould in *Speed-the-Plow* (1988).

Launching a film career in 1985 in *Compromising Positions*, Mantegna appeared in *The Money Pit* (1986), *Offbeat* (1986), and *Suspect* (1988), and starred in *House of Games* (1987) and *Things Change* (1988), both of which Mamet wrote and directed. In 1990, Mantegna appeared in *Godfather III*, *Queen's Logic*, and *Alice*.

Mamet's latest movie, *Homicide*, which features Mantegna in a principal role, will be released in 1991.

Mantegna's awards include a Joseph Jefferson Award, New York Dramatist Guild Award for *Bleacher Bums* (1979); an Emmy for a PBS production of *Bleacher Bums* (1980); Antoinette Perry Award, Drama Desk, Joseph Jefferson Award, and Tony for Best Supporting Actor for *Glengarry Glen Ross* (1984); Best Actor Award for *Things Change* (1989), Venice Film Festival.

This interview was conducted on October 10, 1990, on the set of *Homicide*. Mantegna, who has enjoyed a close personal and professional relationship with David Mamet since 1974, spoke about his various roles and about his relationship with Mamet—as playwright, film director and friend—with great sensitivity and humor.

Kane: The Organic Theatre in Chicago, where you launched your professional career, has been described as anarchic in spirit, improvisational in method, carefully rehearsed, and totally daring. In terms of physical energy Gregory Mosher has observed: "The Organic made the Steppenwolf look like a 'ladies tea party.'" Would you comment?

Mantegna: Well, it certainly was a product of the sixties. Stuart Gordon, who was the Artistic Director and the founder, pretty much symbolized that company. He was—and still is—one of the most imaginative, talented people I have ever worked for. He's basically a hippy from the sixties who never really grew up. And we were just a reflection of that. I think he had a very good knack of getting together talented people and letting us kind of run rampant with our own ideas. The one thing I think that was valuable about being with that group is that we created just about all of our own work. In other words, we didn't usually rely on existing plays or scripts. We would create our own plays, some original, some based on novels. We felt we were doing something exciting at the time, but it kind of happened in a way that in the back of your head you always hoped it would. Our heroes, people like the Living Theatre and Open Theatre, a lot of the groups from the fifties and early sixties, were based in New York and elsewhere. And I think history is proving that a lot of the so-called Chicago companies, like the Organic, Steppenwolf, and others, have gone on to at least make some sort of mark in this business. I felt it was a very valuable five years spent for me in terms of helping me get to where I am now.

Kane: It certainly seems so. Stuart Gordon has said of Chicago: "Chicago has a very low bullshit tolerance." Do you think the low bullshit tolerance accounts for David Mamet's early successes?

Mantegna: Well, I think it probably, perhaps in a way, helped shape David in his writing and his attitude about this business as much as it's done mine and all of us from there. I think I know what Stuart means by that, and I tend to probably agree with that in the sense that Chicago is unique. It's a unique place. It's not just geographically the center of the country; in a lot of ways it's the center of this country. The business we're in, this sort of entertainment business, if you want to call it that—the theater, the film, television business—it's not an industry in Chicago as it is in the East Coast and the West Coast. And I really sense that difference, especially having lived in all three areas. So, in other words, to get respect, to progress forward in our business in Chicago, you have to do it *in spite of* everything, not because of everything as it is in the other coasts, where they cater to you more and there's more media attention. We used to joke about it. You could be the most successful thing going in Chicago for ten years and still be nobody and nobody knows who you are.

Kane: Gregory Mosher echoed your exact sentiments when I asked him about *Lone Canoe*. He said *Lone Canoe* was not the disaster that critics thought it was, but they were willing to crucify Mamet despite previous successes.

Mantegna: No, it sure wasn't. It was just typical. Shows would be very successful in Chicago and run sometimes a year, a year and a half, then go on to New York. It's not just that they would get slammed, but some of the critiques would be vicious: "Well, this thing ran a year in Chicago, so what do you expect? Mayor Daly's run there twenty-two years, so what else is new?" So, it was almost like there was a backlash against it; we were the farm guys coming in to try to succeed in the big city. But, something happened right around the middle eighties. Then, all of a sudden, it seemed that if you were from Chicago, you could do no wrong. It went from one extreme to another; neither is correct. It was just that the conditions were right there during that period of time to nurture interest in this business, and I think part of the reason was that Chicago has a low bullshit tolerance, so you work a little harder because it's not easy. The only way to exist is by success. At the Organic it seemed like our most successful shows were shows that we did *after* we had run out of money, when our budget was down to nothing, because we knew our back was against the wall. Almost subconsciously, it stirs the creative spirit.

Kane: While you were at the Organic, David Mamet offered you roles in *American Buffalo* and *Sexual Perversity in Chicago* and you turned him down.

Mantegna: Well, that's not entirely true. He didn't offer me a role in *American Buffalo* only because at that time there was no production of *American Buffalo* that coincided with me doing it. What happened is that I did do the initial reading for it. I remember I was working at the Organic in *Huckleberry Finn*, and he came by the theater because he was a friend and a fan of the theater's. He asked if two other actors in the show and I would mind reading this new script he had written. So, it was after our performance that night that we all sat around—actor Jack Wallace, Brian Hickey, and myself—and we read *American Buffalo*. I read the Teach role. It was the first time, I imagine, that David had heard it being read by actors, and it was for his benefit so that he could figure out how he wanted to change it. And then we thought, *this* is interesting. We debated the ending among other things. Then, he subsequently went on and did a production of it later, but it never got to a stage where I was asked to be involved, because, I think, I was doing something else at the time. But it is true with *Sexual Perversity* that he did come to me with Stuart Gordon, because they did it first at the Organic, and they asked if I would play the role of Bernie. This was 1973 or 1974 and those were tough times. We were making twenty-five bucks a week sometimes. So, I elected to drop out of the next Organic show, because I just needed to make some money, and I got a job as an understudy in *Lenny*. They were paying me infinitely more just to understudy a lead in *Lenny* than I would have earned in the next Organic show. So, while I liked David's script very much, economically I couldn't do it and thought not much of it. I'd take a pass and they understood. But, looking back on it, it's one of the few regrets I have in this business that I didn't do that, because it would have just been nice to have done that original production of it. And you learn something from that, too, because I think I did learn that ultimately, unless it's dire need, artistic decisions can't be ruled by economics in this business. I've tried to live more by that. I think that was one example of how, ultimately, it comes back to haunt you a little bit because, in retrospect I probably could've gotten by without the extra fifty or a hundred bucks, if need be. But, it would have been nice to have done that production as part of my whole career.

Kane: Gregory Mosher said the same thing to me about *Water Engine*. When it was first offered to him, he didn't understand it and passed. And now, he looks back on it and says, "of course."

Mantegna: That's okay. I regret it, but I don't anguish over it because you do what you do. The decision seemed the right one at the time. But, I'm glad it worked out later.

Kane: In *A Life in the Theatre* you play a young actor, John, whose confidence and arrogance grows with his career. How would you compare John to Bobby Gould in *Speed-the-Plow*?

Mantegna: I never did. We're talking over ten years in between the two roles. But, as I think about it, there's something somewhat valid there. I think a lot of what drove John is similar to what drove Bobby Gould. Bobby Gould is also a reflection of David's writing and how it has gotten thicker as he has grown in the past ten years, in the sense that there's more to Bobby Gould. In other words, *A Life in the Theatre* is a wonderful play, and there's a lot of insight into these two characters just from what they say, and David's a master of not giving you a lot of back story. In other words, what you see is what you get. You invent for yourself who these people are. That's his real talent there. He doesn't waste hours of explanation like, "When I was this boy . . . blah, blah, blah." But what I think has happened, as in the case of *Speed-the-Plow*, there seems to be more subtext behind the words. This is especially true for the character Bobby Gould. Maybe, it's not even inherent in the script; maybe it's more inherent in me.

Kane: After *A Life in the Theatre*, you moved to Los Angeles, and the next time you collaborated with David Mamet was in *The Disappearance of the Jews*. Wasn't it shortly thereafter that you were offered the role of Ricky Roma?

Mantegna: Yes.

Kane: Was that as a result of your performance in *The Disappearance of the Jews*?

Mantegna: I don't think so. I don't think one really had anything to do with the other, just as I don't think my doing *Disappearance of the Jews* was based on what I had necessarily done before with David. I mean, we started our relationship during those early years at the Organic when we first met. Our relationship hasn't changed from that first day to today. There was a certain kind of mutual admiration we had for each other, and then a friendship developed. No doubt that everything we've done together is another brick in the wall—one more thing that bonds us together, builds a history between us. But, I don't necessarily have the feeling that one thing immediately before the other necessarily leads to the other because it happened so casually. I can't remember exactly how it happened. The show may not even have been up yet—we may have just been in rehearsal for *Disappearance of the Jews*—when I think David said something to me like, "You know, I've got this new play I'm thinking of doing next year. I think you'd be interested." It was casual, and before you know it, you get a script in the mail and there it is and then you read it and it happens. More than once I've accepted working for David without ever seeing any script, without knowing what it was about. He'd just basically call and say, "Hey, I've got this play or I've got this movie." And I'd say, "Yeah, great, call me when it's done."

Kane: In *Glengarry Glen Ross*, *House of Games*, *Speed-the-Plow*, and *Things Change*, you make split second switches from oily deviousness to foul-mouthed indignation; from virtuoso speeches to carefully wrought repetitions without punctuation. Colin Booth, who has appeared in British productions of Mamet's plays, has suggested that finding the right way to say something in a Mamet play is like a treasure hunt for the actor. Do you agree?

Mantegna: Yeah, I do. I think that's a pretty correct statement. As I said, the great thing about David is the way he can say so much with so little. When I start working with David, it's difficult for me to read scripts sometimes for a long while, because everything else seems so over-written. It's like, why is this guy spending a page to say this when I've just worked with a guy who can say the same thing in two sentences? And the flip side of that is having that ability to say so much in a concise way necessitates you being able to really be on the money in translating that amount of dialogue correctly. There are certainly other writers who have that capability, such as Shakespeare and Pinter. As much is said between the lines as with the lines.

Kane: I'm thinking particularly of a scene in *Things Change* where you're trying to get the car started to get away from the mansion and you're repeating "okay." Every "okay" has a slightly different nuance.

Mantegna: Well, that's the thing. I mean, that's the thing one has to be on the lookout for. In other words, you can't treat David's work cavalierly. You can't treat his work casually. I have directed a few things in workshops. People come to me, especially when they want to do something of David's and often ask me to direct things for them, and if they are people I know, and if I have the time, I'll do it. And one danger I see actors always fall into, because of David's use of the vocabulary, especially as contemporary as it can be, is to take that erroneously as a license: "Well, he's just talking, we'll just ad-lib this a little bit or we'll change this." They think because it sounds like "street" or natural speech that therefore it's acceptable to expand upon it. And that's the greatest danger of his work. That's the one thing you must not *ever* do, because he has painstakingly created his dialogue so specifically to get whatever impact he expects to get out of it. I'm not saying that it's always written in stone—there's no room for debate about it—because every day he and I will talk perhaps about little things about it. But ninety-nine out of one hundred times I've done everything he's written as written and just tried to make those lines work, even if it's something as simple as "okay, okay, okay." It's my job to make that work. I've worked with other writers who would basically say, "I don't care what you say. Put it in your own words if you like." But, no, with David's words, that's part of the joy of working for him, working with him. I can't say enough about how each year that I know him my admiration for him as a writer, as well as other things, just grows. Because I find that, for me as an actor, that's the most important thing. Just like for a carpenter, without his tools he's nothing. So as an actor, as we say in the theatre, "if it's not on the page it's not on the stage." So, if the writing is not there, I'm on my own. I might as well be an improv actor, which I'm really not.

Kane: Mamet has called *Glengarry* a gang comedy about men, work and unbridled competition. In other words, "Hooray for me and fuck you." As an actor, how do you convey that?

Mantegna: Well, it was a great joy to convey it, I can tell you that! I think that the big secret to *Glengarry* for me, the big turning point for me—when I say turning point, there comes that moment when you go from perhaps total or partial confusion to "A-ha! I think I have it." Whether or not you do, at least you think you do. And for me it was falling in love with the character as opposed to looking at him from the outside saying, "Oh God, look at this guy. This guy's really despicable. I wouldn't want to meet this guy" or "I'm glad I'm not this guy," that kind of thing. Going from there to, "Well, wait a minute. *I am this guy*. Gee, I don't think I necessarily think I'm this kind of bad person." In other words, all these attributes that perhaps to somebody else were sleazy or despicable, to me were all attributes. They were confidence, they were power, they were respect, they were compassion, caring. All of a sudden, I saw all these great qualities in Ricky Roma. All of a sudden I fell in love with all these . . . this was the American Dream. These were the ultimate capitalists, and that's what we are, that's what this country is. And I felt what was great about the play is what David was saying, "Fuck it, I'm not apologizing for it." In too many plays guys are bemoaning, "Gee, I hate to do this to you," but David is saying, "Fuck it, no, what do you mean we hate to do it to you? We love to do it to you, but we don't even think we're doing it to you. We're doing it for ourselves and hopefully we're doing it for you, too. If it comes off that we're doing it to you, well that's your problem." In the case of that play, we did a great deal of research which was very helpful.

Kane: I understand you were given tips on selling from IBM salesmen.

Mantegna: Oh, we had everything from IBM salesmen to Fuller Brush ladies. And the one thing we learned is that the greatest salesmen, the ones who are really the greatest, are not your crooks—are not your sleazy, you know, the classic stereotype used-car salesman who's trying to sell you a lemon. The *best* salesmen are the guys who totally, fervently, one hundred percent believe in what they're doing and what they're selling and really believe that your life would be better if you buy this item from them. Whether it's swamp land in Florida, or wherever it is, if you really believe that you would be better off buying this thing, then sometimes it's a matter of not even the object. One of the sales maxims is "sell the sizzle, not the steak." In other words, it's not even important what the thing is; it's why are you buying it? That's why to me *Glengarry* became, as some people said, *The Death of a Salesman* of the nineties or eighties. In a way it's true, but in the other way—the way it's very different, is that Willy Loman probably should never have been a salesman, whereas Ricky Roma was born to be a salesman. This was the ultimate salesman play, I think.

Kane: But isn't that what you do as an actor: you're selling a character?

Mantegna: Yes, absolutely. That's what made it so enjoyable to play that character for as long as I did. In retrospect, it's certainly one of the top two or three characters I've ever played in my life, because it was a constant affirmation of that. What a sense of power that gave me every night to just go out there and to be able to say: "I'm the best at what I do here and I'll sell you the Brooklyn Bridge if I have to. I have that power to do this." There was a lot of positive mental attitude there, you know. I used to go to Reverend Ike's sermons years ago, because I always thought he had a pretty good rap, where his whole thing was believe in yourself. You know, get up in the morning, look in the mirror and say, "I'm rich and elegant." That's what that play, at least for that character, is about.

Kane: Referring to Ricky Roma in *Glengarry* and the con man, Mike, in *House of Games*, Mamet has suggested "the same thing that makes a good con man makes a good salesman—the ability to suspend feelings of humanity." Do you think you suspend feelings of humanity in these roles? A few minutes ago you spoke about having compassion, as well as power.

Mantegna: Yes. I wouldn't quite put it that way, because I think you never completely suspend humanity. Hitler suspended humanity in the sense that you take people and you pop them in ovens; that's a total suspension of humanity. But, you take a character like Ricky Roma, as I said, whereas I don't doubt that his main drive and his pursuit of success is for himself, what also helps make him successful is that he's doing what he actually thinks is beneficial for another person. In other words, there's an imbalance there: it's 99% me, 1% you. But I think it's wrong to play any aspect of "I'm gonna get you," or "you don't exist for me, you're a dog, you're nothing: all you exist is for fodder for my mill." I don't think that's true. I think there's a genuine compassion there. It's misdirected, maybe, because as a character I'm seeking that point of compassion to further my own gains, but there's a genuine concern for helping you.

Kane: So, you're trying to help Lingk, for example, with his wife? You genuinely feel that you're doing a good thing?

Mantegna: I do genuinely feel that I'm doing a good thing. Absolutely. Of course, I want to be handsomely rewarded for that by selling the land, but let's face it, that moment exists in the play where I pretty much strip the whole thing away and I stop talking about real estate. I'm basically talking to the guy about his life. Like, wait a minute, let's talk about you being a man here for a second. Let's forget about real estate; let's talk about you, buddy. Let's talk about your problem. And even though, in that sense, Ricky Roma's doing this perhaps for an ulterior motive, the beauty of it is that he's genuinely getting at a real problem here and maybe this guy will learn something from it. Everybody wins. It becomes an everybody wins situation. I get the money; maybe this guy is able to deal with his life a little better. *House of Games*, I think, is probably less so, moving more toward a guy who, if you're going to talk about suspension of humanity, there may be a greater degree of it there. But yet, even there, it's said in the play, what did you expect? She came to him, she wanted information, she wanted to learn about the world of the con man. How better to show her than to put her knee deep into it and actually become part of it? We both got what we wanted out of this situation.

Kane: In an early scene in *House of Games*, you and Margaret are sitting at the bar. She is prying you for information and quite clearly wants to be drawn into the con.

Mantegna: Yeah. And at the very end I tell her all that, before I get shot. I basically tell her, what did you expect? You asked me what I do for a living. So, in other words, I never really deceived her. In fact, I constantly kept dropping hints along the way saying, "Hey, this is what I do." In fact, the first time we meet we almost pull it off.

Kane: Is it intentional that you don't pull it off? Is that an arrangement?

Mantegna: I don't know. I think that's up to the individual. I've thought that myself. In other words, how intentional was all that? I don't know. It's kind of a puzzle, isn't it? I think it's even a question at the end if Mike is dead, as far as that goes. Who knows? It was his gun. It could have been an elaborately planned con. I don't know. In playing it, I always played it for the moment. If it's real for the moment, it will work for everything else. That's another great thing about David's works; they're so well constructed. You don't have to worry about dropping little clues or hints that will help the audience figure this out later. No, you just play the moment as real as you can. If it's all been constructed well, it will all come out in the end.

Kane: After *Glengarry*, you appeared in Mamet's *House of Games* and *Speed-the-Plow*. In both, you literally and figuratively screw the women characters. Mamet has been criticized for his portrayal of women and I wondered if you would comment on it?

Mantegna: Yeah, my only comment on that, I think, would be that Tennessee Williams sometimes has been criticized for his male characters. I don't know if it's David's responsibility, or anybody's responsibility, to be across the board balanced in everything they do. I think it's fairly plain to see that, if you look at David's body of work, his strongest characters seem to be men. Most of the plays have only men in them. But they're some of the greatest male roles ever written. So, the point I'm trying to make is that maybe if I were an actress I could be critical about it and say, "Gee, I wish this guy could . . . blah blah blah." But I don't think it's necessarily a requirement there. In other words, I can't climb into David's head and say, I wonder what's going on in there, what's his feeling about women? That's not my job. My job is to take what he's written and say, okay, now how do I make this work for you? I never, in any of those instances, felt that this is either not appropriate or something that was out of the ordinary or something not necessary. It's all just another aspect of that particular piece, you know, that play, that film. And, so you just make that work. But you take a movie like *House of Games*, I mean the movie's about her. Here's a case where, I felt, he really took the challenge. He probably felt, "Hey, I'm tired of people always telling me I never write for the women; here the central character will be this woman."

Kane: In *Things Change*, Don Ameche tells a wonderful story about "the ant and the grasshopper." Would you characterize Mamet's characters as either ants or grasshoppers?

Mantegna: Yeah, I'd characterize Mamet's characters as grasshoppers.

Kane: All of them?

Mantegna: Well, all the ones I play.

Kane: All the ones you play! Because that was my other question— whether you were worried about being typecast as a Mamet sleaze? But, essentially, as you were saying before, you don't view it as being sleazy.

Mantegna: No, not at all. And I shouldn't even say that they're all grasshoppers, because I don't think Jerry in *Things Change* is. I think that's Jerry's problem. When people have asked me, "Well, in *House of Games* and *Things Change* what's the difference between the two guys you play?" I have said, "Well, I think of it this way: in *House of Games*, Mike Mancuso is this character however you perceive him, that's who he is, and in *Things Change*, Jerry DeStephano *thinks* he's Mike Mancuso." And that's the difference. The point is that one guy *is* this character and the other guy *thinks* he is that character, but he's not. The reason Jerry winds up shining shoes is that's probably really what he should have been doing from the beginning. In other words, it's that whole Peter Principle. He should have never been a gangster in the first place; he's not suited for that job. As far as my concern about being typecast, as long as the roles that David, or others, create for me are great roles, I would never for an instant worry about being typecast. I think you only get typecast if you're stuck doing bad stuff consistently of a certain genre. Is De Niro worried about being typecast as a gangster? He's done pretty well.

Kane: You have been quoted as saying that, "Mamet tells people he writes with me in mind, which I guess means I'm the guy." Are you Mamet's on-screen voice?

Mantegna: You know, you'd have to ask him that. And, I've never even really said that. People will tell me, "It's been said that he writes for you," and my response to that always is, "Well, I guess I'm the guy in the sense that if I'm given the role, then I play that role." But I've never, ever gone on record as saying David Mamet writes for me, because there's never been an instance where David's said that to me. People make that conclusion, and that conclusion may be true, but there's been no reason for me to say, "Hey, Dave, did you write this for me?" What do I care? When I mean I'm "the guy," I mean as long as I've been the guy who gets that phone call that says I want you to play this part, that's what counts. And where the muses came from that stirred David to create this character, I don't care. I'm not looking that horse in the mouth, if you know what I mean. It's flattering to think that you have—that anyone would have—some sort of impact on the creative juices of a person with that kind of talent.

Kane: Mamet's new movie, *Homicide*, originally scheduled to be shot in Chicago, has been delayed and recently begun filming in Baltimore. Was the delay due to your unavailability?

Mantegna: No, not at all, not at all. It's true that this movie has been delayed. We had talked about doing it as early as two years ago, but no, that was never the reason. It was always reasons beyond my control. In other words, I never knew what it was. I mean, every single time that they thought it was going to happen, I was ready to take that portion of time to do it. When it looked like there were going to be conflicts sometimes, we always prefaced it with, "Well, okay, but I've got this thing coming up. Can we push it two weeks here or one week there?" That was never a problem. There were always other reasons. I mean, David has been through a lot both professionally and personally this last couple of years, and I tend to think a combination of all those things were reasons for it. But, it never really concerned me much because everything I've done for him, you know, they happen when they happen. Things usually aren't written in stone—it's part of the casualness that we like to work in. If you were able to be on this movie for this whole time, or if you could compare it to another film, you'd realize that it's all so relaxed. We all look forward to working together because the atmosphere is so great. It's low pressure. He's the sweetest guy in the world to work for because there's a lot of joking around on the set. I mean, he prints takes of screw-ups so we can show them at the end of the day. Or he'll purposely do "stuff," especially if it's someone's first scene in a film, either a new actor or an old friend. David will tell me, "Now, put the funny nose on." I mean, we don't take it all that seriously. We take it as seriously as we need to, but what I'm saying is some people take this business—please, they think we're curing cancer or something. We're still just making a movie.

Kane: Gregory Mosher has told me that he's never not wanted to do a Mamet play. Do you share this view?

Mantegna: No, not totally. I don't feel I'm obligated to do everything David offers me. I've obviously proved that. I was also offered *Lakeboat* when it was done at the Goodman back in 1980–81, and I turned that down because, at the time, I had just moved to California, and it was not right for me to pick up and leave and go back to Chicago during that period because I was just starting to get some headway. I think it's a reciprocal thing. He's not obligated to come to me to act in his work, and I'm sure he understands that I'm not always obligated to do everything that he may offer me. But, I'd like to think that it'll always work out. Let's face it, I haven't turned him down lately; let's put it that way!

Kane: For good reason I would think, particularly if this role in *Homicide* is as rich and complex as you suggest.

Mantegna: Yeah, that's what I mean. If it's there, it's there. How fortunate for me that a guy who I am so fond of, and so dedicated to, is so talented, because it would be a real drag to always have to say, "Sure, I'll do it," and think, "Oh God, what am I doing?" It's like Shakespeare. Again, I use a Shakespeare example. I've used this before, but people say, "Gee, don't you think it's, you know—do you worry about doing so much stuff for him?" And I say, "Yeah, right." It'd be like I was in the 1600s and Shakespeare said, "Now, look, you've played Lear and you've played Shylock, I've got this other role,

Hamlet." "Oh, I don't know, Bill; I better pass on this one. Give somebody else a shot." Give me a break. As long as the stuff's there, I'm going to do it.

Kane: Mamet has said that despite differences in your ethnic backgrounds and education, you are both "Chicagoans from the old neighborhood," even though they are different neighborhoods. What does he mean when he says, "Joe and I are very much alike"?

Mantegna: Well, exactly that. We are eighteen days apart in age, first of all. I was born on the thirteenth and he was born on the thirtieth of the *same* year. So, he grew up in Chicago; I grew up in Chicago. Sometimes I think about that. I think, isn't it kind of funny and strange that in 1947, in November, these two kids were born within eighteen days of each other and grew up with totally separate lives, one on the South Side of Chicago and one on the North Side of Chicago, and probably had very similar life experiences based on, if nothing else, geography. And, so right there you have a certain kind of thing happening that had nothing to do with our relationship later on but adds to it. Because, in other words, sometimes when people hear us talk, I've been told that it sounds like one guy talking, because we talk in almost a vernacular; we understand each other. We can talk in code, almost. It's not code. It's just two guys who are forty-three years old from Chicago talking to each other. Do you know what I mean? It cuts through a lot of that bullshit. Let's face it, if David was British and I was American, there's a whole sort of background that—not that we'd have to overcome—but that we wouldn't share in common. But, boy, he and I share so much even just subconsciously, because we can talk about kinds of people or places or things that one can only share with somebody who's from your hometown. Let's face it, that helps. Again, what a break for me.

Kane: I understand that he has nine new projects that he is working on.

Mantegna: What's so great about this guy, is that he puts it on the line every year, every day. There are some guys who build careers on one thing. David's pumping it out, so it's like full speed ahead, here I go. Here's my play, here's my screenplay, here's these concepts for TV shows, here's my essays. It's like, you know, whether you like it or not, it's out there. That takes guts, too, I think. It's easy to sit back, you know, and think, I've won a Pulitzer Prize. It's like, let's wait a few years before I write another one. No, he whips them out. Success scares a lot of writers. And I totally understand it, because I see it in other actors. I see it in other people, too. In other words, they had a certain degree of talent and all of a sudden they really hit it—bang! And hit a big one. Then from that moment on they never, ever even get close to that thing. And part of it, I sense, is almost like a fear—they almost didn't even believe they'd get to make it that big, and when they did, subconsciously, they think they'll never do it again, so they don't. Confidence is not one of the things David lacks. People ask me, "Has he changed much since you first met him? Has success changed him much?" And my feeling always was, success caught up with David; he didn't catch up with it. I think he knew from day one, "I can do this, I know I can do this." He hasn't changed a bit. If anything, he's more relaxed now, because it's like, "Whew! It's about time." And I think that's great, that kind of confidence is great. Again, it's that fine line in playing his characters. Someone can call that cockiness, or you look at it from the other side of the street, it's confidence.

Kane: Like Ricky Roma?

Mantegna: Exactly. Someone would say, "Boy, that's bold of you to think that." It's not bold. It's confident to think that. It just depends how you look at it.

Kane: I have recently read about a notorious Passover Seder attended by the cast of *Speed-the-Plow* and David Mamet where references to "let's play hide the salami" merged with "let's hide the Afikomen" and appeared the next night as part of a new line in *Speed-the-Plow*. Can you add to this?

Mantegna: Well, we were just kind of joking around having a good time at the Seder. Ron Silver started to explain to all the non-Jews who were there what each of the aspects of the evening were, and when he got to the part of "hide the Afikomen," somebody said something, and I think David then made the comment, "Yeah, Joe, in your neighborhood you used to play that too, didn't you, but you called it something else!" And then it just became like a little joke on that and sure enough the next day here was this line. You could almost hear the wheels whirring in David's head as it happened at the table, and the next day here comes this line that actually incorporated both those things, because now he was taking this phrase, and in a way using it as a reference to the sexual joke we had made about hide the salami. So, again, it's just another instance of, here's this guy with this ear that can just out of the air pick up a phrase and then incorporate it into the piece.

Kane: Several of Mamet's plays and films pit one character against another, raising the issues of isolation, vulnerability, and survival of the individual at the expense of the community. Yet, themes of loyalty and community—especially extended families of men—would appear central to Mamet's theater and film. Having worked with him for thirteen years, are these the two sides of David Mamet: on the one side, individual survival and on the other, fierce loyalty?

Mantegna: The sense that I have is that it's always the individual against society.

Kane: It comes back to, "If I can exploit you, I will?"

Mantegna: Well, not so much that, but I think it maybe comes down to we're all in this *alone* as opposed to that old saying, "we're all in this together." In other words, what's first and foremost in importance is that you have to do what's right for you.

Kane: Ethics be damned?

Mantegna: Well, not necessarily ethics be damned, but maybe someone's ethics be damned. Everybody operates on a different rule of ethics. I think a lot of these guys play very close to the rules, but they play according to a different set of rules. You know, at the end of *House of Games* Mike Mancuso says, "I never killed anybody, I never shot anybody." She shoots him. Who has overstepped the bounds of ethics?

Kane: Who's the criminal?

Mantegna: Who's the criminal here? Exactly. Ricky Roma in *Glengarry Glen Ross*, he's doing what he does—he sells real estate. He's trying to help this man. He believes it, and in some ways I think it's true. The self seems to be of real importance here, but there's always this sort of camaraderie in Mamet's plays, *Buffalo*, *Sexual Perversity*, and the relationship with Jerry and Gino in *Things Change*.

Kane: In *Some Freaks*, Mamet has written eloquently about the company of men.

Mantegna: David writes what he loves: men playing poker, living in this world of danger and guns, smoking, and rough talk. He loves it. He's not a voyeur; he's a participant, as Hemingway was.

Kane: That's an interesting analogy, because so many have likened the two.

Mantegna: Well, I think that's the reason, because they were as much characters themselves as the characters they created. But, you read *In Cold Blood*, and you look at Truman Capote and there's a real dichotomy there.

Kane: Mamet seems to have maintained a personal and professional "family" with Robert Prosky, Mike Nussbaum, J. J. Johnston, W. H. Macy, Michael Merritt, Gregory Mosher, and you for more than fifteen years. Aside from issues of personal loyalty, which are crucial to Mamet, what are the advantages or disadvantages of working with the same group of Chicago-trained performing artists, many of whom I know are involved with this *Homicide* project?

Mantegna: Well, first of all, it's not all as it appears. Take Prosky. He only met Bob during *Glengarry*. Bob was about the only one in that cast that was from the outside. But, then David started a relationship with him. And, also, the point about being a Chicago-trained actor. I don't know if that's even a proper phrase for it; it's just the guys he grew up with and the actors he knows.

Kane: And trusts?

Mantegna: Yeah, but I don't know if it's so much their training. It's just the fact that they are basically his friends. Why not surround yourself with the people you know? There certainly are advantages to it, for the same reason that we worked on our company system in Chicago with the Organic Theatre. It cuts through a lot of the red tape. You spend less time acquainting yourself to each other than you do the work. The acquaintance period is over; you already have that. You don't have to go home and get to know your family every day. You can get down to business. A lot of people work that way. Woody Allen works that way, as does Coppola. Most of the guys that work consistently do that anyway, you tend to find out. But people surround themselves with people they're familiar with who get the job done. I think it helps all of us. It's good for David, good for us.

Kane: Gene Siskel has suggested that you and Mamet are showing signs of becoming the best actor/director team since Robert De Niro and Martin Scorcese. I've learned that Mamet does not intend to direct his new screenplay, *Hoffa*. Do you expect to be offered a role?

Mantegna: Very often when David writes things, he does suggest me for roles and tells me that. He even said in *Hoffa* that there is this one role he thought I'd be very good for, and then he kind of drops my name each time. But, while I think working for David obviously has done incredible things for me in terms of my career, outside of the work I do for David, I probably have less chance to do David's work—scripts that David himself has written but that he doesn't direct—with other directors than an average actor. And understandably so, because I think there might be a stigma attached to directors who do pieces written by David of using me, because then there may be a misinterpretation on the part of the public or the press that whenever you do something written by David, you can cover yourself by using Joe. And I almost could understand that, because I don't know if I would use me if I was directing something of David's, because then I think the director needs to be able to say, "Look, I love the script, but I'll cast it my own way. I'll use my own voices for these characters." I don't really hold much hope of recreating Ricky Roma because I know David's not going to direct it. He sold the rights. When I auditioned for *The Untouchables*, as a joke, and this is the honest to God's truth, because David had recommended me for Capone, I walked into the room, I looked at Brian De Palma (I had met Brian a few other times), and I said, "Brian, I'm not going to waste your time. You know and I know that you're going to have De Niro gain fifty pounds and play this part." We all "Ha Ha Ha" laughed and that was six months before they cast the movie. So, all I'm saying is no, I don't expect it and I totally understand it.

Kane: This morning you mentioned to me that David Mamet was working on what he considered to be a trilogy that would include *Disappearance of the Jews* and two other plays. Certain critics have referred to *American Buffalo, Glengarry Glen Ross*, and *Speed-the-Plow* as a business trilogy. I've never seen Mamet refer to them in that way. I wondered if you thought that was an accurate description or if you thought he intended to write it as a trilogy?

Mantegna: No, I don't think he intended to write it that way. I think American business, in all of its aspects, is a real driving force for him. I think he's really motivated by it and intrigued by it, whether it be the business of show business or real estate or the Mafia, or whatever. I think it's a theme that he likes to dwell on, but I don't think he goes into it with the intent of, "I have this whole thing thought out and it's this trilogy or whatever it is." It's just that thematically they're all similar.

Kane: You recently directed an updated version of *The Bleacher Bums* for the twentieth anniversary of the Organic. Is this the beginning of a career in directing?

Mantegna: Well, I like it. I like directing theater. As of right now, I have no desire to direct film. I feel comfortable directing theater, I mean, that's my background. Just like in anything, I think I'm old enough to be able to say I think, hopefully with some degree of truth. I know what I can do and what I can't do. I won't say that I have the exact same confidence as a director as I do as an actor, because I haven't done it as much, but I have that kind of confidence. I don't feel that I'm out my league or I'm doing something that I can't do. Film directing I do. I think it takes a real unique personality, and once again I think it's a testament of David, that he really jumped right into that and learned as many of the aspects as he could and is doing a tremendous job of it, something that is extremely stressful and complicated and takes many different demands than theatre directing. It's a whole different ballgame.

So, while I can see doing more theater directing, I don't see film directing right over the horizon.

Kane: Mamet has just published a book on film directing, referring to himself as a man who has had a car accident and survived to describe how to drive safely. Was *House of Games* "a car accident," and do you detect a difference in Mamet's confidence level in directing *Homicide?*

Mantegna: Well, what's funny is, I don't think it's changed at all from the first one. In other words, to anybody from the outside looking in, he's not acting any differently or doing anything differently than he did on *House of Games*. I think internally David probably has a lot more peace and is a lot more at ease. I never sensed for a minute from the first day I worked on *House of Games* with him that this wasn't a guy who had been directing twenty years. He exuded that kind of confidence—I'm not saying he didn't make mistakes or didn't often refer to someone else or try to learn something—but he never hesitated for a moment or reached that point where he said, "I can't do it. I can't handle it." I've even read myself where he's talked about the night before shooting when he threw up and was nervous and sick, but he never ever let that out. But, that's David and if you know David well, you just know that's him. It's like, "Okay. Full speed ahead. Here I go! Here I come!" But, I think it's just great that he has those two films behind him, and after this one he'll have a third. It's just going to make him better and better. Because he's tough. He'll take whatever knocks that they dish out, and he'll just push on as he always does and he can back it up. Because I have no doubt that he'll be as successful a film director as he's been a writer.

BIBLIOGRAPHY

Primary Sources

PLAYS

American Buffalo. New York: Grove, 1977.
American Buffalo, Sexual Perversity in Chicago, and The Duck Variations: Three Plays. London: Methuen, 1978.
Bobby Gould in Hell. New York: French, 1991.
Camel. Unpublished. 1968.
A Collection of Dramatic Sketches and Monologues. New York: French, 1985. Includes *Two Conversations, The Power Outage, The Dog, Film Crew, Four A.M., Food, Pint's a Pound The World Around, Deer Dogs, Columbus Avenue, Two Scenes, Conversations with the Spirit World, Maple Sugaring, Morris and Joe, Steve McQueen, Yes, Downing, In the Mall, Yes But So What, Cross Patch,* and *Goldberg Street.*
Dark Pony. New York: Grove, 1979. In *Reunion and Dark Pony: Two Plays.*
The Disappearance of the Jews. New York: French, 1982. In *Three Jewish Plays.*
The Duck Variations. New York: French, 1977. In *Sexual Perversity in Chicago and The Duck Variations: Two Plays.* New York: Grove, 1978.
Edmond. New York: Grove, 1983; London: Methuen, 1986. In *The Woods, Lakeboat, Edmond: Three Plays.*
The Frog Prince. New York: French, 1983; New York: Vincent and Fitzgerald, 1984. In *Three Children's Plays.*
Glengarry Glen Ross. New York: Grove, 1984; London: Methuen, 1984.
Goldberg Street: Short Plays and Monologues. New York: Grove, 1985. Includes *Goldberg Street, Cross Patch, The Spanish Prisoner, Two Conversations, Two Scenes, Yes But So What, Vermont Sketches, The Dog, Film Crew, Four A.M., The Power Outage, Food, Columbus Avenue, Steve McQueen, Yes, The Blue Hour: City Sketches, A Sermon, Shoeshine, Litko: A Dramatic Monologue, In Old Vermont,*

and *All Men Are Whores: An Inquiry.* Title play in *Three Jewish Plays*; in *A Collection of Dramatic Sketches.*

Joseph Dintenfass. Unpublished. 1984.

Lakeboat. New York: Grove, 1981. In *The Woods, Lakeboat, Edmond: Three Plays.*

A Life in the Theatre. New York: French, 1977; New York: Grove, 1978.

Lone Canoe, or The Explorer. Unpublished.

Mackinac. Unpublished. 1972.

Marranos. Unpublished. 1972–73.

Mr. Happiness. New York: Grove, 1978. In *The Water Engine and Mr. Happiness: Two Plays.*

Old Neighborhood: Jolly, "D," The Disappearance of the Jews. New York: Grove: 1991.

The Poet and the Rent: A Play for Kids from Seven to 8:15. New York: French, 1981. In *Three Children's Plays.*

The Power Outage. New York Times, 6 August 1977, sec. L, p. 7. In *Goldberg Street: Short Plays and Monologues.*

Prairie du Chien. New York: Grove, 1985. In *The Shawl and Prairie du Chien: Two Plays.*

Reunion and Dark Pony: Two Plays. New York: Grove, 1979.

The Revenge of the Space Pandas, or Binky Rudich and the Two-Speed Clock. Chicago: Dramatic Publishing, 1978. In *Three Children's Plays.*

The Sanctity of Marriage. New York: French, 1982.

Sexual Perversity in Chicago. New York: French, 1977. And *The Duck Variations.* New York: Grove, 1978.

The Shawl and Prairie du Chien: Two Plays. New York: Grove, 1985.

Short Plays and Monologues. New York: Dramatists Play Service, 1981. Includes *The Blue Hour: City Sketches, Prairie du Chien, A Sermon, Shoeshine, Litko: A Dramatic Monologue, In Old Vermont,* and *All Men Are Whores: An Inquiry.*

Speed-the-Plow. New York: Grove-Weidenfeld, 1988.

Squirrels. New York: French, 1982.

Three Children's Plays. New York: Grove, 1986. Includes *The Poet and the Rent, The Frog Prince,* and *The Revenge of the Space Pandas, or Binky Rudich and the Two-Speed Clock.*

Three Jewish Plays. New York: French, 1987. Includes *The Disappearance of the Jews, Goldberg Street,* and *The Luftmensch.*

The Water Engine: An American Fable and Mr. Happiness: Two Plays. New York: Grove, 1978.

The Woods. New York: Grove, 1979. In *The Woods, Lakeboat, Edmond: Three Plays.* New York: Grove, 1987.

ADAPTATIONS

The Cherry Orchard. Adaptation of Chekhov's play. Literal trans. Peter Nelles. New York: Grove, 1987.

Red River. Translated and adapted by David Mamet from Pierre Laville's play *Le Fleuve rouge.* Unpublished. 1983.

Three Sisters. Adaptation of Chekhov's play. New York: Grove, 1991.

Uncle Vanya. Adaptation of Chekhov's play. Literal trans. Vlada Chernomordik. New York: Grove, 1988.

Vint. Adapted by Mamet from Avrahm Yarmolinsky's translation of Chekhov's story. In *Orchards.* New York: Broadway Play Publishing, 1987, pp. 15–24.

SCREENPLAYS

Ace in the Hole. Paramount, completed 1990.

Deerslayer. Paramount, completed 1990.

High and Low. Universal, completed 1990.

Hoffa. Twentieth Century Fox, completed 1990.

Homicide. Directed by David Mamet. With Joe Mantegna and W. H. Macy. Producers Ed Pressman and Michael Hausman. Shot in Baltimore, Fall 1990. Cinehaus/Bison Films.

House of Games. Based on a story by David Mamet and Jonathan Katz. Directed by David Mamet. With Joe Mantegna and Lindsay Crouse. Orion, 1987. (New York, Grove, 1987).

Malcolm X. Warner Brothers. Not released.

The Postman Always Rings Twice. Directed by Bob Rafelson. With Jack Nicholson and Jessica Lange. Paramount, 1981.

Things Change. Written with Shel Silverstein. Directed by David Mamet. With Joe Mantegna and Don Ameche. Columbia, 1988.

The Untouchables. Directed by Brian De Palma. With Kevin Costner, Sean Connery, and Robert De Niro. Paramount, 1985.

The Verdict. Screenplay by David Mamet and Sidney Lumet. Directed by Sidney Lumet. With Paul Newman. Columbia, 1982.

We're No Angels. Directed by Neil Jordon. With Robert De Niro and Sean Penn. Paramount, 1989. (New York: Grove-Weidenfeld, 1990).

SELECTED OTHER WORKS

"The Bridge." *Granta* 16 (Summer 1985): 167–173. A prose piece.

"Conventional Warfare." *Esquire*, 5 March 1985, pp. 110–114. In *Some Freaks*.

"First Principles." *Theater* 12 (Summer–Fall 1981): 50–52. In *Writing in Restaurants*.

Five Television Plays. New York: Grove, 1990.

The Hero Pony. New York: Grove, 1990. Collection of poems.

On Directing Film. New York: Viking, 1991.

"One April, 1988." *The Paris Review* 30 (Summer 1988): 197. Poem.

The Owl. (With Lindsay Crouse.) New York: Kipling, 1987. Children's book.

"A Playwright Learns from Film." *New York Times*, 20 July 1980, Sec. B, p. 6.

Some Freaks. New York: Viking, 1989. Essays and addresses.

"Truck Factory." *Chicago Tribune*, 10 December 1989, magazine *Voices*, pp. 11–12.

"Wabash Avenue." *Chicago Tribune*, 7 October 1990, magazine *Voices*, pp. 34–35.

Warm and Cold. (With drawings by Donald Sultan.) New York: Fawbush/Solo, 1985. Poem.

Writing in Restaurants. New York: Viking, 1986. Essays.

Secondary Sources, Annotated

BIBLIOGRAPHIES

Carroll, Dennis. *David Mamet*. New York: St. Martin's, 1987. pp. 162–165.

   Primary and secondary sources including archival collections and videocassettes in the TOFT (Theatre on Film and Tape). Production history, pp. 1–17.

Davis, J. Madison, and John Coleman. "David Mamet: A Classified Bibliography." *Studies in American Drama, 1945–Present*, 1 (1986): 83–101.

   Primary and secondary. Listing over 400 items, Davis's and Coleman's is the most exhaustive recording of publications by and about Mamet through late 1985. A valuable starting point for Mamet research.

King, Kimball. *Ten Modern American Playwrights: An Annotated Bibliography.* New York: Garland, 1982. pp. 179–186.

Primary and secondary. Selected seminal listings.

Schlueter, June. "David Mamet." In *Contemporary Bibliographical Series: American Dramatists.* Ed. Matthew C. Roudané. Detroit: Gale Research, 1989, pp. 141–169.

Primary and annotated secondary. Production history. Substantial list of interviews through 1987. Schlueter's review of critical reception to Mamet productions is excellent.

Trigg, Joycelyn. "David Mamet." In *American Playwrights Since 1945: A Guide to Scholarship, Criticism, and Performance.* Ed. Philip C. Kolin. New York: Greenwood, 1989, pp. 259–288.

Primary and annotated secondary. Production history of premiere productions from 1972 to 1988 includes critical reception. Extensive summaries of critical studies, Mamet's impact and influences, critical assessments of individual plays, significant awards, and suggestions for further research. An indispensable tool.

INTERVIEWS

Harriott, Esther. "Interview with David Mamet." In *American Voices: Five Contemporary Playwrights in Essays and Interviews.* Jefferson, N.C.: McFarland, 1988, pp. 77–97.

This interview, conducted in London in 1984, covers all the usual questions about background, work, response to criticism, and impact of the Pulitzer Prize. Mamet's answers reveal some interesting opinions on women playwrights, his relationship with the National Theatre, the absence of stage instructions in his plays ("a good play should be able to be done on the radio" [89]), and the relationship of Aristotelian theory to his work. One of the most interesting exchanges concerns the nature of Mamet's language, which Harriott terms "inarticulate." Mamet takes strong exception to the use of the word: "You understand exactly what the character is saying. . . . You can't have a drama with inarticulate people in it" (81).

Nuwer, Hank. "A Life in the Theatre: David Mamet." *Rendezvous: Journal of Arts & Letters,* 2 (1) (Fall 1985): 1–7.

This post-Pulitzer interview, conducted in Chicago, has brief but generally worthwhile answers by Mamet, focusing primarily on the usual: work habits, intentions, attitudes. Mamet says theatre is the *"most* essential aspect of modern life" (3) in that it can return spirituality to our lives. He speaks briefly on his long-time admiration for hustlers, a midwestern influence, cultivating an audience, and his willingness to do late rewrites during rehearsals.

Roudané, Matthew C. "An Interview with David Mamet." *Studies in American Drama, 1945–Present* 1 (1986): 73–81.

Conducted in December 1984, Roudané's is a scholarly interview that addresses the issues of Mamet's thematic concerns, his dramatic form, his artistic response to a hostile universe, and focusing on cultural and spiritual dimensions of the American Dream myth. Mamet's responses are especially thoughtful on the structural distinction between *Glengarry Glen Ross* and *American Buffalo* and the reactions of the audience that they engender, on the nature of his language which he terms poetic, and on the storytelling dimensions of playwriting that he views as a mark of maturity.

Savran, David. "David Mamet." In *In Their Own Words*. New York: Theatre Communications Group, 1988, pp. 132–144.

Savran's introduction locates in Mamet "a society in its death throes," with the focus on estrangement "a schism between character and action" (133). The interview (an expanded version of one published in *American Theatre*) was conducted with Mamet in New York City in 1987 and is one of the best available. Savran's questions are pointed and mostly scholarly, Mamet's responses lengthy and philosophical. Mamet comments on playwrights (Beckett, Pinter, Williams, Miller, Brecht), his own methods, and the current state of American theatre. He reiterates his theatrical production values ("honesty, simplicity and directness" [139]) and restates that theater should deal with what "can't be dealt with rationally" and how this idea separates him from Miller, Fugard, or Wally Shawn's confrontational methods. Mamet dismisses critics and quite seriously offers possibilities (such as war and plague) from among "the many alternatives for decay and dissolution" inevitable for society. A lot of people, says Mamet, are "kind of looking forward to it" (141). He foresees a time of social unheaval, with writers once again put "in jail for what they write" (144) and propounds with stoic resignation a bleak but fascinating view of the coming end.

Schvey, Henry I. "Celebrating the Capacity for Self-Knowledge." *New Theatre Quarterly* 4(13) (Feb. 1988): 89–96.

Organized under subheadings such a "Against the Non-verbal Theatre" ("All of us read Artaud, we're very influenced by Artuad, but finally it does not work" [90]), "Dramatic Diversity in Chicago" and "'Glengarry' as Gang Comedy." Schvey's interview is easy to search and especially useful. "Drama," says Mamet, "is about conflicting impulses of the individual" (92). Characters are created by fragments of that individual. He discusses self-revelation in an Aristotelian context, *American Buffalo* as classical tragedy, *Edmond* as morality play, and defends *The Woods* against its detractors. Under "Cinema and Theatre," Mamet explains that films give him a wider channel for his productivity and that the perfect movie, as opposed to theater, "would have absolutely no dialogue in it" (95). In the final section, "Problems of Directing," Mamet advices directors of his plays to "keep it simple: that's the beginning and the end of it" (96). Schvey is an intelligent questioner; Mamet's responses are serious and well-considered.

RECENT (1988–1990) AND SEMINAL CRITICISM

Allen, Jennifer. "David Mamet's Hard Sell." *New York,* 9 Apr. 1984, pp. 38–41.

A behind-the-scenes look at the genesis of *Glengarry Glen Ross* and the excitement surrounding its initial Broadway run. Following mixed reviews for his past several plays and considerable time devoted to film work, the new play was important to Mamet's reputation as playwright. Allen interviews Mamet in a restaurant four days before the play's opening and offers a vivid account of the energy and anticipation at the time. She reviews Mamet's biographical and theatrical history and his philosophy of teaching ("I'm a pedagogue by nature" [40]).

Almansi, Guido. "David Mamet, a Virtuoso of Invective." In *Critical Angles: European Views of Contemporary American Literature.* Ed. Marc Chénetier. Carbondale: Southern Illinois University Press, 1986, pp. 191–207.

This overview of work from *Lakeboat* to *Glengarry Glen Ross* argues that Mamet is a "poet and critic, chronicler and parodist, of the stage party," (191) whose best work excludes and precludes women. Moreover, the playwright's ear is "especially attuned to the sounds, rhythms, cadences, allusions, contradictions . . . and exclamations" between two pals who as "working or drinking mates" (193) or colleagues or rivals focus their complaints on women. Almansi doubts whether one can—or should—admire Mamet's characters, but he is convinced one should admire the playwright's ability to create music out of obscenity.

Ansen, David. "An Offer You Can't Refuse." *Newsweek*, 31 Oct. 1988, p . 72.

Ansen considers *Things Change* a logical progression from *House of Games*, with Mamet revelling in "rediscovered storytelling, the old-fashioned art of spinning and twisting a tale." He finds the "ritualistic" dialogue and "theatrical" staging appropriate to the film's "fablelike nature" and praises the performances of Mantegna and Ameche.

Barbera, Jack V. "Ethical Perversity in America: Some Observations on David Mamet's *American Buffalo*." *Modern Drama* 24:3 (Sept. 1981): 270–275.

Despite its allusions to Chicago, Barbera contends that the focus of *American Buffalo* is an urban American subculture whose language is characterized by street vulgarity and elliptical expression. Arguing that "part of Mamet's intent in *American Buffalo* is to expose the shoddiness of the American business ethic" (273), Barbera correlates ethical perversity at both ends of the urban spectrum—a philosophical position inspired by Thorstein Veblen, whose influence on Mamet has been noted by the playwright in numerous interviews—with Teach's "ideas of emulation" and "snob appeal of what is obsolete" (274) (the attractiveness of rare coins and World's Fair memorabilia). Satirizing Teacher's definition of free enterprise Mamet, in Barbera's view, "*has* written a play of intellectual content" (275).

Bigsby, C. W. E. "David Mamet." In *A Critical Introduction to Twentieth-Century American Drama: Beyond Broadway*. Cambridge: Cambridge University Press, 1985, 251–290.

Volume three of Bigsby's superb series on American drama devotes a chapter solely to Mamet. Bigsby's work is mandatory reading for anyone interested in Mamet scholarship. This forty page analysis places the playwright in the limelight left vacant by Albee's decline in influence. Bigsby says that like Albee, Mamet "is concerned with language as poetry" and "is a poet of loss" (252). He compares *The Duck Variations* to Albee's *The Zoo Story* and discusses critics who mistook *American Buffalo* as poorly plotted naturalism. He looks at Mamet's dialogue, his place as a realist, and likens Mamet's relationships to Pinter's as "a struggle for dominance" (267). Bigsby proceeds to account for all the major plays through *Glengarry Glen Ross*, with the most attention given *Sexual Perversity in Chicago*, *A Life in the Theatre*, *The Water Engine*, and *The Woods* (which reads, he says, like a parody of Albee). Like Beckett, Mamet is "concerned with dramatising a largely plotless world in which nuance and gesture become of central significance," and like Pinter deconstructs his "ostensibly realist environment" (287).

————. *David Mamet*. London: Methuen, 1985.

Bigsby's was the first book-length consideration of Mamet and is fine work. He expands comments offered in his earlier chapter and includes excerpts from interviews with the author. This is seminal work and resists summary. Twelve plays are examined at length, with full chapters given to *American Buffalo*, *Edmond*, and *Glengarry Glen Ross*. He defines Mamet as "a moralist lamenting the collapse of public forum and private purpose, exposing a spiritually dessicated world in which the cadences of despair predominate," with the occasional relationship an echo of our lost "state of grace" (15). Mamet exposes our myths of "masculine self-sufficiency . . . in a world that has lost its epic dimensions" (16). Bigsby's conclusion deals briefly with *The Shawl*, in which he sees the need for faith stressed among typically hopeless characters. The book's final pages create an intriguing profile of Mamet as man and as playwright, based on interview, observation, and plays. Bigsby feels that theater is not merely Mamet's art "but also his subject" (136), the plays constituting a series of studies on characters alienated from both a past and a shared present, yet retaining an imperfect trace of "a surviving will toward harmony" (130).

Blumberg, Marcia. "Eloquent Stammering in the Fog: O'Neill's Heritage in Mamet." In *Perspectives on O'Neill: New Essays*. Ed. Shyamal Bagchee. Victoria: University of Victoria, 1988, pp. 97–111.

Blumberg perceives in Mamet "the failure of the American Dream and the concomitant moral and spiritual bankruptcy of American society at large"; moreover, Mamet is building "on O'Neillian foundations" (97). She compares the urban dramas of *American Buffalo*, *Glengarry Glen Ross*, and *Edmond* with *The Iceman Cometh*, regarding "variations in leitmotif, tone and emphasis, while their use of language exposes the differing zeitgeist" (97). Although the playwrights share a musical use of language, Mamet strips O'Neill's basics to a minimalism of "one-upmanship, aggressiveness, self-interest and repressed tensions," (101) nowhere offering the support Hope's Bar extends its patrons. According to Blumberg, Mamet's characters have dissolved social contracts; past and future give way to the needs of the present, whereas O'Neill's characters look at the present only through "a fog of alcohol-induced pipe dreams"

(107). An interesting study, although the uneven comparison of three plays to one seems to imply Mamet's subordinate position to O'Neill.

Brustein, Robert. "Show and Tell." *New Republic*, 7 May 1984, pp. 27–29.

Brustein offers an excellent comparison between the Dustin Hoffman revival of Miller's *Death of A Salesman* and *Glengarry Glen Ross*, which ran concurrently on Broadway. He argues that Mamet "fashions powerful epiphanies . . . out of dramatizing what the salesmen sell" (28) and laments this lack of knowledge in Miller's play. Brustein gently criticizes Miller's "social realist melodrama," (27) at the same time remaining nostalgically respectful; he praises Mamet for his play's lack of polemic yet its potent assault on the American livelihood of selling, which in *Glengarry Glen Ross* assumes "the magnitude of a quest for the Holy Grail" (28). He recognizes Roma and his associates as greedy con men, yet notes their energy, camaraderie, and even backstreet heroism. Brustein is primarily concerned with Mamet's play, which he considers a masterpiece transcending its realism, returning a "tragic joy to the theater" (29) comparable to the understanding of O'Neill's last plays.

———. "The Last Refuge of Scoundrels." *New Republic*, 6 June 1988, pp. 29–31.

Another valuable review by Brustein, this one focusing on *Speed-the-Plow*. He associates the play with *American Buffalo* and *Glengarry Glen Ross* as presenting loyalty and male friendship as the last values in a deeply corrupted society. Brustein considers *Speed-the-Plow* Mamet's funniest play, also "the airiest . . . since the characters are playing for relatively low stakes" (29). He notes Bobby Gould's conversion between acts is "in Chekhovian fashion" and senses an almost Hemingwayesque admiration for "people who perform their tasks with wit and grace," regardless how vacuous the job. Brustein feels, interestingly, that the casting of Madonna created "an almost Pirandellian effect," with the play's theme of art's vulnerability to commercial concerns "being realized behind the scenes" (30).

Bruster, Douglas. "David Mamet and Ben Jonson: City Comedy Past and Present." *Modern Drama* 33(3)(Sept. 1990): 333–346.

Bruster discusses similarities between the work of two dramatists separated by four hundred years, namely, the satire of venality and its embodiment in character, explosive language distinguished by the rhetorical mode epanalepsis (repitition of the same word or clause), city dramas, parodic trinity, dependence of business upon theatrical methodology and dramatic illusion, and creeping cynicism and pessimism. Arguing persuasively and citing examples from Mamet and Jonson, Bruster contends that parallels "owe their existence to similarities in ideological convictions and the historical position of their respective societies" (345).

Canby, Vincent. "Mamet Makes a Debut with House of Games." *New York Times*, 11 Oct. 1987, p. 94.

Canby sees the early poker scene in *House of Games* as symbolic of Mamet the filmmaker, who is sometimes "bluffing outrageously." He comments that the Seattle locale is "ambiguous, mysteriously dislocated. . . . Anycity, U.S.A." Mamet's style is "deliberately artificial" and the monotonous delivery of lines presents words "as if they were italicized." Canby thinks the artifice mostly successful, although sometimes one senses the controlling intelligence just off screen.

Carroll, Dennis. *David Mamet*. Houndmills, England: Macmillan, 1987.

Carroll's book on Mamet divides plays along thematic lines, its chapters dealing with business, sex, learning, and communion. Mamet's variety of styles (ranging from an Apollonian impulse toward poise, control, and ascension, and Dionysian plays of compulsion and destruction [4]), has rendered him elusive to critical pidgeonholing. Carroll warns that tracing a chronological "development" can be deceptive and prefers the thematic focus. He sees in Mamet "Brechtian, dialectical implications. . . . Many of the plays posit a societal malaise that no changed political system could alleviate" (19). Carrol's discussion of the plays is excellent, as is his chapter "The Plays in the Theatre," which considers the special problems of reading Mamet's plays—which can appear skimpy and ambiguous in print—and the imperative for directors of clear and simple production values. Carroll discusses the choice of a realistic or metaphoric set, determination of the crucial subtext, and the demands Mamet places on actors. "Mamet in Context" deals with translations, short plays, and plays for children, and compares Mamet to several contemporaries, especially Shepard and Rabe. Carroll defines Mamet's unique importance, aside from his dialogue, as an "unsentimental sense of personal and social morality, his wry but sharp sense of dialectic, and the vigour of his characters' intent" (155).

Christiansen, Richard. "The Young Lion of Chicago Theater." *Chicago Tribune Magazine* 11 July 1982, p. 9+.

This detailed and nostalgic account of Mamet's long association with Chicago begins with the first productions of *The Duck Variations* in

1972. Christiansen reviews Mamet's early life: lean times, support of Stuart Gordon and the Organic Theater, formation of Mamet's St. Nicholas Company. Christiansen speaks with many of those involved at the time as he traces Mamet's ascent to national prominence in a series of successes dealing with "the failure to connect with and care for other human beings" (12). By the time the St. Nicholas Theater—a frantically renovated garage and print shop—opened with *American Buffalo*, Mamet's increasing popularity in New York was already causing his divided time between the two cities. Mamet then became associate director, under Mosher, of Chicago's Goodman Theatre, where *Lone Canoe* was produced, his first critical failure, which Christiansen contends "brought the Mamet cycle in Chicago theater to an end. . . . It finished the string of premieres of ascending importance that his work had enjoyed in Chicago" (14). The author reminisces, with Mamet, on the "magic" of Chicago theater in the mid-1970s, wondering if anything as good will come again for the city or the playwright.

————. "David Mamet." *Contemporary Dramatists*. Ed. D. L. Kirkpatrick. 4th ed. Chicago: St. James, 1988, pp. 338–340.

This overview discusses Mamet's consistent success with idiomatic dialogue but "wildly variable results" (339) as a prosaic, poetic language. For example, he contrasts the laughable *Lone Canoe* with the brilliance of *Edmond*. Mamet's major theme, says Christiansen, remains individual relationships, the crucial "bond of friendship, family, and love" (340) his characters cling to.

————. "The 'Plow' Boy." *Chicago Tribune*, 9 Feb. 1989, sec. 13, pp. 18–20.

Supported by quotations from Mamet, Christiansen discusses *Speed-the-Plow* as apocalyptic, stoic, and polemical. Mamet adds interesting comments on the play's origins, the difficulty of deciding on an appropriate title, New York theater, writing, his loneliness on the set of *Things Change*, and with seriousness on our society's imminent collapse: "It's all going to come down" (18). Christiansen sees *Speed-the-Plow* as exemplar of this "world built on greed and cynicism wasting its opportunities for doing good" (18).

————. "'Vanya' Revisited." *Chicago Tribune*, 29 Apr. 1990, sec. 13, p. 12.

A brief article of interest due to Mamet's thoughts on Chekhov. Mamet worked from a word-by-word translation of *Uncle Vanya* and discusses the difficulties and challenge of faithful adaptation. "You've got to paraphrase a little," he says, while remembering the rhythm of the line is part of its meaning. Mamet's fascination with Chekhov reveals an obvious relevance to his own plays: "It's the absolute end of an era, when the dreams of the play's characters have come to naught." Michael Maggio, director of Mamet's version of *Uncle Vanya* for Chicago's Goodman Theatre, admires the sparse modernity, yet the poetry and appropriateness, of Mamet's adaptation. "David's is the only one that distills the language so perfectly, and so beautifully."

Daily, Bob. "Mamet on the Make." *Chicago*, May 1988, p. 104+.

This lengthy feature, reported from the Chicago set of Things Change, is the finest yet on Mamet as film director. Directing is "more fun than writing plays," says Mamet. "You get to play dollhouse every day" (105). Daily adds that the job gives Mamet the control, authority, and celebrity he relishes. He interviews both Mamet's father and sister and argues that Mamet's coterie of actors and workers, his "Old Cronies," constitute a surrogate family to replace a "separated" childhood home. Concerning directing, producer Michael Hausman speaks of Mamet's good instincts and his ability with people. Mamet discusses a director's need to be a "bit of a generalist" and the necessity of working within a small budget, which not only frees one from studio pressures but forces one "to think about what you really need" (137). Joe Mantegna comments concerning his own quintessentially Mametic characteristics: "I was that city rat that David maybe was looking for" (139); he likens Mamet to Hemingway in confidence. Daily extends the comparison, noting Mamet's thematic concern with "the male tribe" and his athletic competitiveness. The obligatory review of Mamet's Chicago heritage is unusually interesting and fresh.

Dean, Anne. *David Mamet: Language as Dramatic Action*. Rutherford: Fairleigh Dickinson University Press, 1990.

As its title suggests, Dean's recent text on Mamet is concerned with what the playwright himself has maintained, that language not only describes but prescribes one's actions. Her selection of plays is limited, but each is given a full chapter's consideration: *Sexual Perversity in Chicago, American Buffalo, A Life in the Theatre, Edmond, Glengarry Glen Ross*. The strength of Dean's study—a revised doctoral dissertation—is her linguistic deconstruction of Mamet's "very original use of free verse" (222) in individual exchanges, rather than analyses of entire plays. One of Mamet's greatest achievements, offers Dean, is "his ability to suggest what lies just beneath the surface . . . communication frequently has less to do with actual language than with the silent empathy that exists between speakers" (25). She proceeds, often perceptively, to locate an "almost Chekhovian subtext" (26) in a wealth of examples. The introduction includes a discussion of some of Mamet's screenplays—*House of Games* and *The Postman Always Rings Twice*—and credits *The Verdict* as having had a great impact on the composition of *Edmond*. Mamet's language reflects both "the inner pressures of his characters and the confusion of the urban environment" (31).

Demastes, William W. "David Mamet's Dis-Integrating Drama." In *Beyond Naturalism: A New Realism in American Theatre*. Westport: Greenwood, 1988, pp. 67–94.

Demastes considers Mamet as one of the "new realists" and notes how a focus on language rather than action to reveal character shifts traditional Aristotelian philosophy. Mamet's world is not strictly naturalistic, but a somehow "truer" representation; nor does Mamet's message include a naturalistic inevitability. He has moved away from the social commentaries of O'Neill or Miller toward "a more fundamental ontological concern" (70). In this context of naturalism Demastes discusses several plays and considers the many critics who have praised the playwright's "realism." To what extent, for example, are *Reunion* and *The Woods* realistic, to what extent distilled poetry? The longest discussions are reserved for *American Buffalo* and *Glengarry Glen Ross*, both of which "deal with the business ethic and the interrelatedness of language and action" (86) in a seemingly realistic setting. Dialogue that seems to communicate but does not is comparable to a social fabric intact only on the surface.

Denby, David. "What's in a Game." *New York*, 19 Oct. 1987, pp. 101–102.

In an intelligent but critical review of *House of Games*, Denby believes the inherent joy of con games slightly at odds with the seriousness of the film's tone. Mamet's lack of interest in women continues in the androgynous Margaret Ford; to Denby, she's a perfect victim, "a patsy." The huckster is more intriguing, a "philosophical nihilist" whose truths work only toward deception. Mamet's "more entertaining, plainer version" of Pinter's style celebrates the "con man's warrior pride" (101) through his nerve, intelligence, and ability. Denby is put off by Mamet's flat, stylistic direction, which drains the film of much of the excitement it should have.

————. "Small Change." *New York*, 7 Nov. 1988, p. 102.

Denby criticizes *Things Change* as too thin and stodgy for effective farce. Mamet toys with ritualized Mafia ceremony, a world where Gino's silence can be mistaken "as the reticence of power. . . . In a formal, impenetrable society, a man who says nothing can never be found out." He accuses Mamet of sentimentality and contends that without "nastiness and cynicism" the writer has little left.

Ditsky, John. "'He Lets You See the Thought There': The Theatre of David Mamet." *Kansas Quarterly* 12(4) (Fall 1980): 25–34.

A worthwhile and detailed examination of Mamet's early plays, placing Mamet in an American theatre that expresses itself through inarticulateness. Ditsky defines Mamet's language as "Chicagoan-Pinteresque" (33).

Eder, Richard. "David Mamet's New Realism." *New York Times Magazine*, 12 Mar. 1978, pp. 40–47.

Eder's early profile sees Mamet as necessarily moving away from the absurdists' deadend proclamation of meaninglessness, in "the direction of celebrating life" (40). It had been barely two years since Mamet's plays first appeared in New York; Eder discusses the already established Mamet voice, the desperate energy of the dialogue, a distorted world of lessons "learned wrong because of the unreasonable ferocity" (42). He criticizes a tendency to use few characters and looks briefly at several plays, concluding with *The Water Engine*, which had opened in New York days earlier. Eder seems to feel that beneath Mamet's linguistic complexities a simpler story is told, one of characters stuggling "from their isolation toward each other" (42).

Feingold, Michael. "The Way We Are." *Village Voice*, 9 Nov. 1982, pp. 81–82.

Feingold offers an unusually thoughtful interpretation of *Edmond*. He feels it is Mamet's "strongest and deepest play to date" and praises the range and importance of its social criticisms. The protagonist is "Everyman, American style, and an avatar for the author's rage" (81). Feingold recognizes the complexity of addressing a sickness that is both spiritual and social; the play's main difficulty is attempting to view Edmond as both "a saphead and a myth-figure," the necessity to both destroy and praise him. This discrepency of intention accounts for the awkward veering of Mamet's dialogue from street-wise middle scenes to an overblown and abstract finale, which jars the ear "so harshly it almost seems to be deliberate" (81). Mamet, the author contends, shares Edmond's dilemma while searching for ways to rise above it, giving the play both its problems and its weight. The "inflated language . . . odd mysticism . . . [and] brutish action" (81) all remind Feingold of Strindberg. *Edmond* is not a solution but a statement of a problem; he commends Mamet's courage to "cross-breed his art with life" (82).

Freedman, Samuel G. "The Gritty Eloquence of David Mamet." *New York Times Magazine,* 21 Apr. 1985, p. 32+.

This article focuses on biography and legacy with Freedman placing Mamet firmly in the tradition of Chicago writers. Referring to Saul Bellow's Augie March, James T. Farrell's Studs Lonigan, and Hemingway's Nick Adams, Freedman sees the legacy of vigor and corruption in *Glengarry Glen Ross*'s salesmen and in Mamet's writing. Mamet's characterizing concern with legacy as dramatized in *A Life in the Theatre, The Shawl, Squirrels, Goldberg Street,* and *The Disappearance of the Jews* may be traced to "the instability he felt in his own upbringing" (42). Referring specifically to Mamet's Jewish parents, their rejection of ethnic identity, the undercurrent of hostility between Mamet and his father, and the trauma of divorce, Freedman contends that any number of student-teacher dynamics may be viewed as "a search for a father figure" (46). While Mamet is certainly more than the sum of his experiences, argues Freedman, his idiosyncratic lifestyle, fierce loyalty, recurrent thematic and metaphoric use of confidence games, fractured families, and hostile language can be explained in part by personal experience.

Gale, Steven H. "David Mamet: The Plays, 1972–1980." In *Essays in Contemporary American Drama.* Eds. Hedwig Bock and Albert Wertheim. Munich: Max Hueber Verlag, 1981, pp. 207–223.

The strength of Gale's essentially uncritical essay lies in its examination of Mamet's episodic structure in *Duck Variations* (14 scenes), *Reunion* (14 scenes), *A Life in the Theatre* (26 scenes), and *The Woods* (3 scenes). Repeatedly drawing parallels between Mamet and Pinter, Gale suggests that Mamet's accomplishment and promise lie in his ability to write characters who are believable and human and his ability to focus on interpersonal relationships. His summary of *A Life in the Theatre,* with its teacher-student motif, is especially useful, as is his negative evaluation of *The Water Engine,* which he linguistically and thematically compares to other Mamet plays.

Gussow, Mel. "Mamet's Hollywood Is a School for Scoundrels." *New York Times,* 15 May 1988, Sec. 2, p. H5+.

Gussow feels that *Speed-the-Plow*'s indictment of Hollywood contrasts with Mamet's affection for acting (*A Life in the Theatre*) and his admiration for radio (*The Water Engine*). *Speed-the-Plow* belongs not with these "romances of a kind," but in the harsher, more sinister business vein of *American Buffalo* and *Glengarry Glen Ross*, where loyalty is overcome by self-interest. In *The Bridge* passages Gussow senses no satire; thus he decides Mamet "is equally cynical about those who want to save our lives and those who want to wreck our lives" (5). The Karen role recalls other Mamet heroines with "an other-worldliness" (55); Madonna's "ingenue" is drawn into a con game (this time of Hollywood) in a way reminiscent of *House of Games* and *The Shawl*.

Harriott, Esther. "David Mamet: Comedies of Bad Manners." In *American Voices: Five Contemporary Playwrights in Essays and Interviews.* Jefferson, N.C.: McFarland, 1988, pp. 59–76.

Harriott's essay is thoughtful and intelligent, but she is committed to proving her thesis that Mamet may be reduced to one central theme: comedies of bad manners. While she dismisses *Edmond* as a "flawed and awkward" play whose "story is primitive, serving primarily as the occasion for an hallucinatory projection of scenes of urban terror," (73) and views *The Woods* as a play of sexual alienation with little of *Sexual Perversity in Chicago*'s "quirky ribaldry" (70), she likewise takes issue with critics who view Mamet's plays, especially *The Water Engine*, as other than "an agreeable little spoof" (69). The essay's strength lies in an extended analysis of *Lakeboat*, Mamet's early play which rarely receives attention. In Harriott's view it is one of his best, "announcing all of his characteristics at their strongest: his unerring ear for the American vernacular . . . minimal structure of conversation . . . striking aural impact . . . abundant use of obscenities, and the energy of the writing" (63). She contends Mamet is "a serious writer with a comic voice" whose concern with sound and comic routine energizes *The Duck Variations* and *Sexual Perversity in Chicago*; when he abandons that voice "he is only solemn" (72).

Henry, William A. III. "Madonna Comes to Broadway." *Time*, 16 May 1988, pp. 98–99.

Ostensibly a behind-the-scenes look at the casting of Madonna in *Speed-the-Plow*, the backstage attention offered the play itself is enlightening. Director Gregory Mosher says that Madonna brought to the role of Karen "a backbone of steel." Mosher continues: "The audience is meant to go out asking one another: 'Is she an angel? Is she a whore?'" (99). Henry praises the play's performances and the expected Mametic energy, but is bothered by Bobby Gould's largely off-stage conversion and the ambiguity over whether *The Bridge* "is brilliance or bilge," which should determine the impact of the play's conclusion. He wonders whether *Speed-*

the-Plow is "an outcry against Hollywood or a cynical apologia" (99) by a writer increasingly involved with film.

————. "Having a Hell of a Time." *Time* 18 Dec. 1989, p. 78.

This review of *Bobby Gould in Hell* contends that the play's subject is simply "how to live morally in this world rather than the next. . . ." Mamet is fascinated, says Henry, with the dynamic of why people prefer to make excuses rather than to live better.

Herman, William. "Theatrical Diversity in Chicago: David Mamet." In *Understanding Contemporary American Drama.* Columbia: University of South Carolina Press, 1987, pp. 125–160.

Chapter four of Herman's general overview is a long analysis of Mamet. The text is a competent introduction to the customary critical interpretations of Mamet's major plays. Herman begins with several pages of biography and Mamet's conception of theater. "Nearly all of Mamet's plays," posits Herman, "hinge on the opposition of two individuals" (126). He follows with lengthy comments on *Sexual Perversity in Chicago* (Mamet's "contemporary Restoration comedy" [132]), *The Duck Variations, American Buffalo, A Life in the Theatre,* and *Glengarry Glen Ross,* concluding with a brief section on "Other Works."

Hodgson, Moira. "Theater." *The Nation,* 18 June 1988, pp. 874–875.

Hodgson applies the tired epithet of Mamet as "a poor-man's Pinter" (875). She agrees that *Speed-the-Plow*'s central theme is loyalty, but her primary concern seems to be the weakness of the role of Karen, a typical Mamet female. Rather than full characters, she argues, Mamet's women "always seem to function more as plot elements, as sources of complication" (875).

Jacobs, Dorothy H. "Working Worlds in David Mamet's Dramas." *Midwestern Miscellany* 14 (1986): 47–57.

Jacobs' article suggests that "Mamet's unique contribution to American theatre [is] the dramatization of men at work" (47). Writing variously on working conditions on a lakeboat (*Lakeboat*), in theater (*A Life in the Theatre*), in a real estate office (*Glengarry Glen Ross*), or in a restaurant (*Reunion*), Mamet contrasts ideological promises with economic reality. Jacobs compares the work environment in Mamet with that dramatized in plays of Brecht, Odets, Miller, O'Neill, and Hecht.

"Conditions of work, economic demands, tangibility of the product, all figure in Mamet's scrutiny of the writer as craftsman" (51).

Kael, Pauline. "The Current Cinema." *New Yorker*, 14 Nov. 1988, pp. 127–129.

Kael recognizes *Things Change* as an attempted fable, and she is reminded of several previous "fairy tale" films, from Frank Capra's 1933 *Lady for a Day* to Hal Ashby and Jerzy Kosinki's *Being There*. However, Kael is more concerned with how Mamet "cons the audience" by bringing them into "a hip complicity with him" (128) concerning the actors' games and the corrupt way of the world. She contends that the consciously flat performances and Mamet's minimalism are a strategy (as in *House of Games*) to suggest "a knowingness, a disdain for elaboration or development. . . . People can feel one up on the action . . ." (128). The secret of *Things Change* is Mamet's "yearning for a day when men kept their word," (129) but he isn't able to deliver a satisfying or authentic resolution.

Kane, Leslie. "Time Passages." *The Pinter Review*. Annual (1990): 30–49.

Building upon David Mamet's acknowledgement that "Pinter was probably most influential when I was young and malleable," Kane traces the thematic and structural influence of early Pinter plays on early Mamet plays. Paralleling Pinter, observes Kane, past events in such plays as *Sexual Perversity in Chicago, Reunion*, and *American Buffalo* "are reported but uncorroborated, past betrayals are paradigmatic, characters are unreliable, chronology is disrupted, narrations are typically erotic and/or fantastic, minutiae are explored in depth" (34). However, this insightful essay considerably furthers our understanding of the function and pervasiveness of narrative in Mamet's later work through close textual scrutiny of *Prairie du Chien, The Disappearance of the Jews, Glengarry Glen Ross*, and *Speed-the-Plow*. Convincingly, Kane argues that the continuing "influence of Pinter on Mamet's dramaturgy" is more subtly realized through Mamet's brilliant fusion of betrayals of confidence, conscience, and cultural history and "elaborate narratives that enhance, recover, and protect self-image" (43).

Kauffmann, Stanley. "Tangled Web." *New Republic*, 16 Nov. 1987, pp. 22–23.

Deceit, says Kauffmann, is the central theme in all Mamet's work and "is to Mamet what sexuality is to Pinter . . . the secret animal within us" (22). *House of Games* presents a surface world with a second code of honor concurrently beneath, and beyond it all is "an even deeper deception: the illusion of control." From the opening shot onward, Kauffmann sees the film not as realistic, but an abstract "series of artifices" (22) comparable to the con men who inhabit it, in contrast to the presumably stable world of institutional psychology. He considers the "emblematic" use of intensified dialogue and the appropriateness of Joe Mantegna and Lindsay Crouse in the lead roles. The entire film is a stylized ballet "danced before realistic settings" (23).

————. "One Weekend." *New Republic*, 7 Nov. 1988, pp. 26–27.

In *Things Change*, Kauffmann again perceives Mamet's theme as deception, but with plot contrivances and cleverness replacing *House of Games'* evocation. He questions the plausibility of the story and compares it unfavorably to the earlier film. The screenplay is peculiar for Mamet in that it has no underlying themes, and Kauffmann is critical of the casting of both Mantegna and Don Ameche. Curiously opposed to some reviews of *House of Games*, Kauffmann here praises Mamet as director, citing Mamet the writer as a liability.

Kelly, Kevin. "Good Mamet, Passable Madonna." *Boston Globe*, 4 May 1988, pp. 77+.

Kelly recalls the audience's anticipation before the Broadway opening of *Speed-the-Plow*. The casting of Madonna made the evening "one of those peculiar blends of art and entertainment—the very issue in the center of its dramaturgy" (79). The play recalls *Glengarry Glen Ross* in that Mamet makes no moral judgments of his characters. Kelly believes that the motivations behind either film the play proposes, the impulses toward either commerce or art, are both equally and purely selfish. "One may seem pecuniary, the other profound. In the scheme of things, does that make any difference?" (79).

Kerr, Walter. "Verbal Witchcraft Produces Magical Responses Out Front." *New York Times*, 12 June 1988, Sec. 2, p. 5+.

Kerr addresses the revitalized, almost magical use of language in several recent productions, his first and lengthiest comments devoted to *Speed-the-Plow*. He has determined three levels of "verbal witchcraft" operating: between characters, by the playwright, and as "cabalistic sounds . . . producing magical responses" (5) in the audience. *Speed-the-Plow* is "*about* self-consciousness in the presence of language" (22). For Kerr, Madonna's Karen emerges as the priestess of this linguistic cult; she respects words and finds in them an awesome power.

Kohn, Alfie. "Therapy Gone Awry." *Psychology Today*, Apr. 1988, pp. 64–65.

Kohn is concerned with the largely unsympathetic portrayal of psychologists in film; therapists are usually either parodied or harshly censured. Kohn is impressed, however, with *House of Games*, "a view of psychotherapy gone awry" which demands attention. The film's cold and distant Dr. Margaret Ford, for whom patients "are case studies, not people," (64) actually "sinks below the level of the confidence man." The "kicker," for Kohn, is that the therapist forgives herself for something which should be unforgiveable. Mamet's psychotherapy takes place in a moral vacuum, hence its danger. Kohn sees in Mamet's "value-free therapy" (65) a serious indictment of much of today's clinical practice.

Kolin, Philip C. "Mitch and Murray in David Mamet's *Glengarry Glen Ross*." *Notes on Contemporary Literature*, 18(2) (Mar. 1988): 3–5.

Kolin posits that the ominous hidden real estate bosses in *Glengarry Glen Ross* represent the "new robber barons" (4) of capitalism, doling out false hope from a distance and epitomizing the sharp division between friendly cooperation and competitive self-interest.

Kramer, Mimi. "Double or Nothing." *New Yorker*, 25 December 1989, pp. 77–80.

Kramer considers at length the recent "Oh Hell" double bill of Mamet's *Bobby Gould in Hell* and Shel Silverstein's *The Devil and Billy Markham*. She theorizes that here the two authors seem to have reversed their likely roles in collaboration on *Things Change*. Mamet's play is the whimsical of the two, noticeably lacking in obscenity and set in the sedate Hell of a men's club. It is to this male purgatory that Bobby Gould, protagonist of *Speed-the-Plow*, is summoned along with a woman he mistreated. "Mamet's Hell," says Kramer, "is a place of moral inversion: the Devil is a kind of Fisher King" and Gould the "archetypal Mamet hero" (78), charming, competent, honest about his dishonesty, an "Everycad" defending himself against Mamet's "Shavian morality" (80). Kramer praises Mosher's direction, the recasting of Gould with a perplexed Treat Williams, and offers insight on the styles of acting that Mamet fosters. *Speed-the-Plow*, she says, lacked a confrontation between the two persons struggling for Gould's soul; *Bobby Gould in Hell* is like the proper last act of that play, a fiery, symbolic battleground which simultaneously gives "the bitch her due" and is "a misogynist's nightmare" (80). Mamet shows a new facility in handling endings.

Kroll, Jack. "The Profane Poetry of David Mamet." *Newsweek*, 19 Oct. 1987, p. 85.

Kroll's concise article discusses the ease of Mamet's transition from acclaimed playwright to filmmaker. Kroll peeks behind the camera of *Things Change*, quickly reviews *House of Games*, and includes comments from both Mamet and Lindsay Crouse. Mamet recalls the violently negative reactions by Hollywood to much of his early screenwriting and his breakthrough when producer Michael Hausman took a chance on letting him direct *House of Games*. Mamet adds that his generation has "always wanted to move between theater and movies. That's the dream" (85).

—————. "The Terrors of Tinseltown." *Newsweek*, 16 May 1988, pp. 82–83.

In another succinct commentary, Kroll reviews *Speed-the-Plow* and calls Mamet our "master of language of moral epilepsy" (82). In a world that is little more than a marketplace for hustlers, he likens *Speed-the-Plow*, "on its deepest level," (82) to the Hollywood pathology of Nathanael West's *Day of the Locust* and F. Scott Fitzgerald's *The Last Tycoon*. Kroll finds the play scathingly funny, the performances (including Madonna's) excellent, and praises Mamet's "artist's intelligence" at juxtaposing comic, superficial characters against the "Big Questions" (83) posed by *The Bridge*.

Lahr, John. "Winners and Losers." *New Society*, 29 Sept. 1983, pp. 476–477.

Lahr's superb review of *Glengarry Glen Ross* places the play in a distinctly American landscape of panic, fear, and humiliation caused by capitalist propaganda. Also drawing from *American Buffalo* and comments by Mamet, Lahr presents a dichotomous society where the presence of "winners" necessarily implies an abundance of "losers." He holds that competition prevents characters from "seeing themselves as part of an exploited class, but only as unlucky individuals" (477); megalomania is mistaken for drive. Mamet adds that "America has always been enslaved by the myth of the happy capitalist" (477). This concise, insightful essay is more general interpretation than close textual scrutiny and partly explains the success of Mamet in Britain despite the playwright's use of American idiom.

Lieberson, Jonathan. "The Prophet of Broadway." *New York Review*, 21 July 1988, pp. 3–6.

Although primarily a review of *Speed-the-Plow*, this article also recaps Mamet's career and offers a brief critical overview of his accomplishments. He is disappointed with *Speed-the-Plow*, a work he finds "at moments startling to watch yet morally unchallenging, even insipid" (3).

He quotes at length from the play, much of which he considers implausible, and compares these more articulate, less menacing characters to earlier roles in *American Buffalo*, *Lakeboat*, and *Sexual Perversity in Chicago*. Lieberson feels that Mamet struggles too hard for laughs in *Speed-the-Plow*, which is akin to "vaudeville" or "Miami Jewish comics" (4). Lieberson believes Mamet a moralist, but finds the message in *Writing in Restaurants* paradoxical and unclear. For Lieberson, the plays remain "snapshots of hell animated by rough humor" (6) and morally unengaging. His attempt to reconcile *Speed-the-Plow* with Mamet's essays is subjective but interesting.

London, Todd. "Chicago Impromptu." *American Theatre*, July/August 1990, p. 14+.

London has written one of the most useful and comprehensive analyses of the development of Chicago theatre and Mamet's connection to it. He cites the groundbreaking innovations of Viola Spolin, Sheldon Patinkin, and Paul Sills, whose Playwrights Theatre Club inspired the Compass Players (1955), the nation's first improvisational theater. London discusses the impact of the Compass, whose heirs included David Shepard's St. Louis Compass and Chicago's influential Second City. At Hull House, Robert Sickinger not only introduced Chicago premieres of Beckett, Camus, Pinter, and Albee but made professionals out of community theatre people such as Mike Nussbaum and David Mamet, Chicago's first playwright. Sickinger's legacy was passed, as was Second City's, to Stuart Gordon, who in addition to founding the anarchic Organic Theater influenced the establishment of the Off-Loop Theatre movement. Summarizing Mamet's involvement at the Goodman Theater, his collaboration with Gregory Mosher, and his impact in Chicago theatre, London contends that Mamet introduced a new level of professionalism, "reinvented midwestern machismo" (63), and opened the way for second generation playwrights. Quoting Mosher English concludes, Mamet "'is the lynchpin . . . the apex of it all'" (63).

Lundin, Edward. "Mamet and Mystery." *Publications of the Mississippi Philological Association*, 1988, pp. 106–114.

To find support for a broad, often vague definition of "mystery," Lundin looks primarily at the endings of three plays: *American Buffalo*, *Edmond*, and *Glengarry Glen Ross*. He deals with "mystery of characters," which involves characters failing to "achieve what they desire" (106); and the "mystery of dramatic action" in Mamet's endings, with the final mystery the audience's: "How, then, shall we live?" (107) "Mystery" extends to Mamet's language, as in *American Buffalo*, where dialogue is "both realistic and opaque," with "a lack of connection between emotion and its referent" (108). With little action and many events taking place off stage, these plays must be interpreted "contingent upon the unknown—i.e., mystery" (109). In most of his plays Mamet places the "burden of resolution" (113) on us. The article is not without its merits but limited by the catch-all use of its central phrase.

Nightingale, Benedict. "Is Mamet the Bard of Modern Immorality?" *New York Times*, 1 Apr. 1984, Sec. H, p. 5+.

In this insightful review, Nightingale holds that *Glengarry Glen Ross*'s sales competition is comparable to a perfect Skinnerian box for the human rat. The salesmen have been tantalized and threatened until they become liars and cheats. The extended logic of business is crime. The play is "a braggadocio show of power by men who know their true powerlessness" (5) and finally victimize themselves as much as others. Mamet, says Nightingale, writes about his "shark-pack" with either sympathy or a kind of admiration, according to strength. Gone is the self-justification necessary to characters (*American Buffalo*); the working day is now simply "a macho adventure" (23).

O'Brien, Tom. "Obsession & Memory." *Commonweal*, 4 Dec. 1987, pp. 703–704.

O'Brien sees in Mamet's "obsessed" fascination with hucksters a metaphor of the writer's "constant play with illusion and reality" (704). He finds *House of Games*' ending enigmatic, perhaps an expression of feminine anger slightly out of place.

Oliver, Edith. "Mamet at the Movies." *New Yorker*, 16 May 1988, p. 95.

To Oliver, *Speed-the-Plow* is "vintage Mamet, passionate and witty and terribly funny," bringing to life the playwright's world of corruption.

Peereboom, J. J. "Mamet from Afar." In *New Essays on American Drama*. Eds. Gilbert Debusscher and Henry I. Schvey. Amsterdam: Rodopi Editions, 1989, pp. 189–199.

Peereboom suggests that a lack of European productions of Mamet have forced potential audiences to become readers instead, and this may account for plays being criticized as static and language oriented. Perhaps, he grants, a play like *The Woods* performs better than it reads. Mamet's characters are most persuasive not when they show their own complexity, but "when their statements are designed to challenge the world and make room for them to act" (191). Peereboom is enthusiastic about the rapid energy of *Sexual Perversity in Chicago* and *American Buffalo*, but discusses flaws in *Glengarry Glen Ross* and *Edmond*, both "only partly representative of the author's talent" (195). Briefly considered are *Reunion, The Duck Variations*, and *A Life in the Theatre*. Peereboom contends we should discard Mamet as a critic of "contemporary culture or society," (196) and what we are left with are individuals responsible for themselves. He sees a movement in Mamet's work from the "sitting and talking" (197) early plays to a more active involvement and wonders whether these roads may somehow merge.

Polsky, Ned. *Hustlers, Beats and Others.* 1967. Chicago: University of Chicago Press, 1985.

"This book is about the sociology of deviance" (xi). Particularly invaluable to understanding Mamet's use of con men is Polsky's insightful examination of the hustler's methods of deception, specifically the short con. Outlining the hustler's cardinal rule—never show your real speed—Polsky examines the pool hustler as con man; the victim, or prospective victim; the hustler's orientation to him. He considers the hustler's specialties and modus operandi, his use of monickers (nicknames), his view of hustling as a long-standing craft tradition, and his argot.

Rich, Frank. "Mamet's Dark View of Hollywood as a Heaven for the Virtueless." *New York Times,* 4 May 1988, p. C17.

Rich argues that *Speed-the-Plow* "may be the most cynical and exciting yet" of the literary tradition of Hollywood exposés. The play is a culminaton of Mamet's talents, focusing on the "tribal hustlers" found in much of his other work, and continues to chart Mamet's progress as an inventive storyteller. *Speed-the-Plow's* "violent catharsis" reminds Rich of *American Buffalo*, while mystical quotes from *The Bridge* recall *The Water Engine's* haunting chain letter. The complexities of the Karen/Gould relationship suggest "that religion might be the last refuge of whores." Rich believes Mamet has written a Hollywood play ironically and purposely *un*cinematic (two sets, three characters).

―――. "Mamet's Tasteful Hell for a Movie Mogul." *New York Times,* 4 Dec. 1989, Sec. B, p. 1.

This review of *Bobby Gould in Hell* discusses women as a recent and problematizing addition to Mamet's plays; in this latest effort they are cause of "a masculine bafflement as timeless as the Old Testament. . . ."

However, Rich says Mamet is not a misogynist, that his women "are more
the Other than the Enemy." Mosher's direction make this Mametic "two con
men at center stage" look and sound fresh.

Roudané, Matthew C. "Public Issues, Private Tensions: David Mamet's
    Glengarry Glen Ross." *South Carolina Review*, 19(1) (Fall 1986):
    35–47.

Roudané discusses the tension between private and public interests
in Mamet's work, where the intrusion of "public issues, often in the form of
business transactions, permeate the individual's private world" (35). He
compares this to Alexis de Tocqueville's *Democracy*, which concerns itself
with locating and reconciling a private morality with commercial society,
and also notes the influence of Veblen's *The Theory of the Leisure Class*.
Roudané says Mamet dramatizes issues where public and private "become
entangled, canceling any authentic human response" (37). He discusses in
Tocquevillian terms characters' collapse into private interests and the "nonrealistic," poetic quality of a language striving for survival and redemption.
Glengarry Glen Ross and *American Buffalo* share belief in an "a priori . . .
unencumbered freedom of the individual" (43) and subordination of public
relations to business concerns. Central in Mamet, says Roudané, is "the
entropic influence of a business-as-sacrament world on the personal spirit"
(46).

Schlueter, June and Elizabeth Forsyth. "America as Junkshop: The Business
    Ethic in David Mamet's *American Buffalo.*" *Modern Drama*, 26(4)
    (Dec. 1983): 492–500.

In this perceptive analysis of *American Buffalo*, Schlueter and
Forsyth underscore the centrality of the buffalo nickel as not only the
object "upon which the plot depends" (492) but also as the symbol of
money that is "the mainstay of the American business world" (493).
Focusing on both the setting of the junkshop and the linguistic and
metaphoric patterns, Schlueter and Forsyth suggest that "the rhetoric of
business affords the would-be criminals" confidence to carry out the theft,
but does not "disguise personal desperation" (497) when the quest for cash
devalues human and metaphoric junk. Teach, whose confused notions of
ethics, loyalty, and morality are directed linked to "the American myth of
opportunity," (494) explosively assaults both Bob and the junkshop when
the chance for financial gain proves elusive.

Simon, John. "Word Power." *New York,* 16 May 1988, p. 106.

Simon writes of the inextricable connection between power and language in Mamet's work, "more than a metaphor yet not quite a causal relationship, which gives a Mamet play its dreamlike quality." He wonders, however, whether this is all beginning to wear thin in *Speed-the-Plow.* The minimal plot reduces to variations on one "basic bitter joke" and depends too heavily on the skills of its actors.

Storey, Robert. "The Making of David Mamet." *Hollins Critic,* 16(4) (Oct. 1979): 1–11.

This special issue devoted to Mamet remains an important piece of early criticism. Storey defines Mamet's America as a fulfillment of Gertrude Stein's definition: greedy, surfeited with action, perhaps over-complicated. He discusses a verbal dalliance so prescriptive of character "it is often fruitless to analyze their 'psychology'" (3); the Pinter influence; Mamet's "mocking simplicity" (4). Storey insightfully, if generally, looks at *The Duck Variations, Sexual Perversity in Chicago, American Buffalo* (a Brechtian analysis of business), *The Water Engine,* and briefly *A Life in the Theatre* and *The Woods.* "Mamet's characters," says Storey, "*are* their language; they exist insofar as . . . their language allows them to exist," (3) but this language can also alienate and provide "meretricious patterns" (11) for remaking lives. A lengthy, accessible, and still necessary essay.

Travers, Pete. "Holiday Hits and Misses." *Rolling Stone,* 11 Jan. 1990, p. 30.

In a capsule review of *We're No Angels,* Travers finds Mamet's "theme of redemption . . . sweet but slight." He wonders whether the screenplay may be a Mamet joke, the prison buddy film satirized in *Speed-the-Plow.*

Vallely, Jean. "David Mamet Makes a Play for Hollywood." *Rolling Stone,* 3 Apr. 1980, pp. 44–46.

Vallely's article deals with Mamet's first screenplay, *The Postman Always Rings Twice.* Mamet is quoted on the difficulty of adapting Cain and, most importantly, on the differences between film and theater and the advantages and disadvantages of each. While the stage is more immediate and open to improvisation, film is to Mamet "a symbolic medium" (46) based on narrative and the suspenseful release of information.

Veblen, Thorstein. *The Theory of the Leisure Class*. 1899. New York: Penguin, 1953.

Veblen's first and most influential book has had a tremendous impact on Mamet and his beliefs. Veblen argues that the leisure class, exempt from labor, sets standards to which every other class must attain. Veblen's most famous term, "conspicuous consumption," indicates a system of spending for no purpose other than prestige, where wealth is equated with success. Mamet, in interview with Matthew Roudané, attributes to Veblen the idea that "sharp practice inevitably shades over into fraud . . . [and] fair play becomes an outdated concept" (74). Several critics have cited the impact of Veblen's theories on such plays as *American Buffalo* and *Glengarry Glen Ross*.

Whitaker, Thomas R. "'Wham, Bam, Thank You Sam': The Presence of Beckett." In *Beckett at 80/ Beckett in Context*. Ed. Enoch Brater. New York: Oxford University Press, 1986, pp. 208–229.

Whitaker's essay addresses itself to the indebtedness of Stoppard, Pinter, Fugard, Soyinka, Mamet, and Shepard to Beckett. Referring specifically to *The Duck Variations, American Buffalo*, and *Edmond*, Whitaker argues that Mamet has given American expression to the presence-in-absense or intimacy-in-isolation dominating Beckett's work. Whitaker illuminates the relationship between dialogues of Didi, Gogo, Pozzo and Lucky, and Hamm and Clov, to those of Don, Teach and Bob, George and Emil, and their more distant and aggressive cousins in *Glengarry Glen Ross* and *Edmond*. Inarticulate mumblings, banality, aggression, evasion, and desperate vacuity inform Beckett's legacy in Mamet.

INDEX